The Philosophy of Change

The Philosophy of Change

Comparative Insights on the *Yijing*

CHUNG-YING CHENG

SUNY PRESS

Cover: *Nine Peaks after Snowfall*, Huang Gongwang (1269–1354), ink on silk, hanging scroll, Palace Museum, Beijing; and "Square-Circle Diagram of Sixty-four Hexagrams," attributed to Fu Xi, which offers two different orderings of the sixty-four hexagrams.

Published by State University of New York Press, Albany

© 2023 State University of New York

All rights reserved

Printed in the United States of America

No part of this book may be used or reproduced in any manner whatsoever without written permission. No part of this book may be stored in a retrieval system or transmitted in any form or by any means including electronic, electrostatic, magnetic tape, mechanical, photocopying, recording, or otherwise without the prior permission in writing of the publisher.

For information, contact State University of New York Press, Albany, NY
www.sunypress.edu

Library of Congress Cataloging-in-Publication Data

Name: Cheng, Chung-ying, author.
Title: The philosophy of change : comparative insights on the *Yijing* / Chung-ying Cheng.
Description: Albany : State University of New York Press, [2023] | Includes bibliographical references and index.
Identifiers: ISBN 9781438494050 (hardcover : alk. paper) | ISBN 9781438494074 (ebook) | ISBN 9781438494067 (pbk. : alk. paper)
Further information is available at the Library of Congress.

10 9 8 7 6 5 4 3 2 1

Dedicated to my wife, Dr. Linyu Gu

Contents

Preface ix

Introduction: Comparative Insights and the Philosophy of the *Yijing* 1

Chapter 1 On the Origins of Chinese Philosophy: Three Aspects of Origins 11

Chapter 2 Classical Chinese Views of Reality and Divinity 61

Chapter 3 The Trinity of Cosmology, Ecology, and Ethics in the Confucian Personhood 85

Chapter 4 Toward an Integrative Pluralism of Religions: Embodying Yijing, Whitehead, and Cobb 105

Chapter 5 On Neville's Understanding of Chinese Philosophy: The Ontology of *Wu* (无), the Cosmology of *Yi* (易), and the Normalogy of *Li* (理) 141

Chapter 6 Time in Chinese Philosophy 165

Chapter 7 On the Hierarchical Theory of Time with Reference to Chinese Philosophy of *Dao* (道) and *Qi* (气) 207

Chapter 8 Leibniz's Notion of a Universal Characteristic and Symbolic Realism in the *Yijing* 231

Appendix: Greek and Chinese Views on Time and the Timeless   261

Notes   267

Selected Bibliography   281

Index   291

Glossary Index   299

Preface

Comparative Insights and the Philosophy of the *Yijing*

This book serves as a second and complementary volume to my previous publication: *The Primary Way: Philosophy of the Yijing*. In that book I laid out a comprehensive and systematic philosophy based on the symbolism and text of the classical document and its traditional commentaries. The present volume advances my study of the Yijing into analysis of its philosophy in comparison and contrast to modern Western philosophies. In this volume, I focus on critically comparing and contrasting philosophies of science, religion, and metaphysics in Leibniz, Whitehead, Neville, and Cobb, along with classical Chinese views on reality, divinity, knowledge, and morality. This volume of eight chapters begins and ends with questions related to the character of Chinese metaphysical traditions that contrast with the mainline metaphysical traditions found in Western Europe and North America. It is argued throughout this volume of essays that the philosophical underpinnings of mainline accounts of basic concepts in Chinese culture are ultimately rooted in key claims found within the Yijing 易經 and its standard commentaries, the Yizhuan 易傳.

To advance this project in critical comparative/contrastive philosophy, I begin by laying the groundwork. The opening chapter of this volume thus presents an extensive historical and anthropological survey of the origins and early developments of Chinese philosophy. I develop this survey alongside of a comparative study classical Greek metaphysics. Indeed, this comparative approach is pervasive from beginning to end of the current volume. And I again return to the Greeks in the later chapters where I have occasion to develop a comprehensive philosophy of time. The inquiry advances in chapter 2 into a more intensive investigation into the question of reality and divinity in the commentaries of the *Yijing*, Lao-Zhuang Daoism, and the *Zhongyong*. Together these preliminary chapters provide an extensive and intensive introduction to context and concepts of Chinese philosophies.

Building on the groundwork laid out in chapters 1 and 2, chapter 3 demonstrates the applicability of *Yijing* philosophy to contemporary discussions in philosophy of ecology and environmental ethics. Here, again, in the domain of ecology and environmental ethics I focus our discussion on a comparative analysis of *Yijing* and Whitehead-based theories of persons and the world. Continuing the discussion, I then turn in chapter 4 to integrate critically analyze and synthesize theories and methods of science, philosophy, and religions. In this chapter, I again explore the issues at hand from the respective perspectives of the *Yijing* and Whitehead-based systems. I further move the borders of the discussion here to critically engage with contemporary theologies and metaphysics of John Cobb and Robert Neville, respectively. Between the arguments laid out in chapters 3, 4, and 5, I go beyond bounds of my first volume and now bring the philosophy of the *Yijing* fully into the domain of contemporary philosophies of ecology, environmental ethics, and religion.

A comparative/contrastive study of the Yijing persistently forces me to clarify fundamental concepts of change and time. Thus, chapters 6 and 7 propose a systematic theory of time based on an extensive study of Western and Chinese philosophical paradigms of time. I seek to elucidate different concepts of time. Nonetheless, the analysis of time herein is not only clarificatory. A novel, synthetic philosophy of time, reality, and creativity emerges through the hermeneutic engagement between these different paradigms of time.

I finally close this philosophical discussion with a chapter dedicated to Leibniz's substantial study of the Yijing. Here my discussion demonstrates again how the Yijing can and has contributed to modernity, but it moreover shows how the *Yijing* stands unique in its worldview apart from Leibniz's modern concepts of theology and science. Indeed, as stated at the outset, the extensive and intensive analyses of the *Yijing* in this volume demonstrate the continued relevance and creativity of this classic work to contribute novel insight into contemporary discourses on metaphysics, epistemology, ethics, and philosophy of religion.

In preparing this volume, I have received various encouragements from discussions with various colleagues who are interested in my work. I wish to thank them all; I also hope that the publication of this book would provide some satisfaction to them as it would to me. I do wish to say a word of special thanks to my former student Dr. Nicholas Brasovan who has helped me to copyedit my whole manuscript and who finally has helped me to revise my original twelve chapters into the present more compact eight chapters. Finally, I wish to thank my editor at SUNY Press, James Peltz, who had great patience in waiting for the readiness of my manuscript.

Introduction

It is often asked what Chinese metaphysics is in Chinese philosophy. To answer this question, one has to beware of the Greek connotations of the term *metaphysics*. The Greek idea is that there is a world of study beyond physics. Perhaps the Chinese philosophical distinction in the *Great Appendix* (系辞, *Xici*) of the *Yijing* (易经) between what is below form (形而下) and what is the above form (形而上) could reflect the Greek idea of metaphysics versus physics. However, this reflection cannot be taken too seriously or too exactly. The relationship between the metaphysical and the physical in the Greek tradition assumes an ontological difference and duality, whereas the Chinese distinction between above form, which is called the *dao* (道, the way), and below form, which is called the *qi* (气, the vital force), does not necessarily imply dualism or separation. On the contrary, the distinction in the Chinese traditions suggests mutual identity and interpenetration.

However, we can still talk about Chinese metaphysics in both Greek and Chinese senses because we can recognize a world of being and reality that is not a matter of change and transformation and a world of changing reality and changing appearance that is not a matter of being and reality. This is the philosophy that the *Yijing* presents to our understanding. Thus, it is interesting and important to see how metaphysical views in the Western tradition could contrast with the Chinese metaphysical view of the *Yijing*.

The differences between the two suggest profound understanding on the part of both traditions regarding life and cultural experiences. Philosophically, it can be said that the Greek sees ontology as prior to or independent of cosmology, whereas the Chinese sees ontology as inseparable and inherent in cosmology. In this light, the Western philosophy tradition as derived from the Greek, and also perhaps the Jewish culture, can be said to seek permanent being as reality and truth on the one hand. The Chinese philosophy, on the other hand, takes change and transformation as ultimate reality and truth. This of course bespeaks of the uniqueness and essential importance of *Yijing* and its philosophy.

Given the above understanding, it is clearly important to explore how Chinese philosophy gives rises to the philosophy of *Yijing* and how its onto-cosmology (the unity of being and change) differentiate from the ontological characteristics of the Western philosophical thinking. This also means the Western approach would form a strong background against which *Yijing* philosophy stands out and presents a new perspective of understanding ultimate reality. For this purpose, I have collected eight essays of my comparative studies between some Western approaches and the *Yijing* approach or the general Chinese philosophical approach. I have concluded that the *Yijing* onto-cosmology would often provide a better solution to ontological issues in philosophy because it can be seen as being closer to what we really experience as reality. In the following I summarize each essay in order.

In chapter 1, I investigate the question of origins of Chinese philosophy and suggest that Chinese philosophy begins with observation and reflection of birth, change, formation, and transformation of things in the universe; and that leads to development of a cosmology of change with a system of symbols that have been used for divination. I mentioned three factors to do with the beginning of a philosophy tradition. Each represents recognition of unity of actual being and the becoming of the being, and the importance of non-being of what has become from being. We see early Chinese texts indicate an intrinsic reverence for heaven and ancestral spirits that provide the source of meaning for ethical, social, and political life of the Chinese people. These involve ideas of *li* (礼, propriety), *shen* (神, spirit), *de* (德, virtue), and *shangdi* (上帝 the Lord/source on high), which on analysis arises from non-being to being in the becoming of human being. Second, there are reflections on the dialectical and bipolar onto-cosmological elements in reality that provide the backbone for a methodology implicitly guiding and conditioning the way of perception and thinking in Chinese philosophy. These are seen, for example, in the accounts of the relationship between yin and yang. Finally, there is also a timely awakening to potentiality and creativity of the human subject, which provides the basis for a cosmic naturalism and an intrinsic humanism, whether collective or individual, and whether political or moral.

As a result of the political breakup of the central kingdom of the Zhou (周), there arose the humanism (in the form of Confucianism) and naturalism (in the form of Daoism) that could be said to issue from the philosophy of change that was formed at the beginning of Zhou. After a philosophy of Yi (阴阳家), Confucianism (儒家, *rujia*), and Daoism (道家, *daojia*), subsequently, several other important schools arise in the Chunqiu period (春秋时代), including Moism (墨家, *mojia*), Legalism (法家, *fajia*), and Logicism (名家, *mingjia*).

The second chapter concerns the question of reality and divinity in Chinese philosophy. Reality and divinity are first addressed in the *Yizhuan* 易传, which is the commentary to the divinatory text of the *Yijing*. There onto-cosmology is discussed in terms of *taiji* 太极 and dao 道. The appearance/reality distinction is denied in this text, because *taiji* is presented as a source that is not a changeless being behind the myriad events. Instead, it is the totality, or organic unity, of changes that continuously unfold in the world. In this sense, changes and the constant and continuous regeneration of things in reality are what reality is made of. The dao is how things come into being and how they grow and develop in a process of time.

Yijing metaphysics is reconsidered as cosmogony and cosmography, and *yin-yang* theory is expanded to explain a field of multi-interactive harmony. Consequently, the *Yizhuan*'s view on reality argues for reality as a recursive but limitless regenerativity, not like a circle, but like a spiral.

On this basis a critical comparison of Daoist and *Yizhuan* notions of Dao is presented. Daoistic understanding of this key concept includes 1. Dao is essentially immanent, even though displaying facets of transcendence-within-immanence; 2. Dao is equated with *wu* 无 and *xu* 虚 ("non-being" and "void," respectively); that is, it is indescribable and non-substantial. On this point, Dao incorporates being and non-being (有 *you* and 无 *wu*); 3. The first principle of the dao is reversion and return (反 *fan* and 复 *fu*); 4. People can embody the dao. On the basis of these four points, it is indicated how the Daoist philosophy of *wu* contrasts with the *Yizhuan* critical realism, which emphasizes the importance of both *wu* and *you* and their interaction in the form of the *yin-yang*. Besides, whereas Daoism tends to deemphasize the role of humans in creative reality, *Yizhuan* underscores the creativity of cultivation in human action and knowledge. It is further pointed out that the onto-cosmology of the Dao is different from the theo-ontological metaphysics that is promoted within mainline philosophical and religious accounts in Western philosophy contexts.

Chapter 3 raises three questions. First, is there a different formulation or understanding of humanism that might moderate its human-centeredness? Second, are there criteria according to which things in nature and in the human world can be equally and properly treated, based on considerations of the world of nature and humanity together rather than merely on considerations of a single human being or on the human world alone? Finally, if any such criteria exist, how might a human apply such criteria so that he or she might act morally within the world of nature and develop an ethical attitude or habit that would preserve such criteria?

In response to these three questions, two types of humanism are distinguished. One is "exclusive humanism," which exalts the human species, placing it in a position of domination over the universe, and another is "inclusive humanism," which stresses coordination between powers of nature and humanity. Confucianism is a form of "inclusive humanism." Even though the *Analects* (论语 *Lunyu*) appears to consist primarily of virtue ethics and its political application, one cannot ignore the broad underlying onto-cosmological discourse of the *Zhouyi* 周易, *Yizhuan* 易传, *Mencius* (孟子 *Mengzi*), and *Zhongyong* 中庸 that gives vitality and spirit to the values and ideals of classical Confucianism.

This view of Confucianism can be seen in the quintessential triadic interactions of heaven, humans, and earth, the foundation of ethical principles. In light of this, human beings can carry out their activities in a way similar to the onto-cosmological activities of heaven and earth. In this way, an ecological ethics can be constructed. This is done not through striving to dominate or exploit one's environment, but through recognizing the interrelations of all elements of the cosmos. This chapter closes with the account of the distinctions in the approach to environment and nature found in mainline Confucian and Daoist traditions, on the one hand, and between contemporary Confucian and modern technological discourses, on the other.

Chapter 4 addresses the issue of Integrative Pluralism of Religions, which embodies *Yijing*, Whitehead, and Cobb. First of all, three forms of religious pluralism are distinguished. The first form is differential pluralism, which recognizes the difference between all existing religions or even future religions. The second form is complementary pluralism (attributed to Cobb and Griffin), which sees all existing religions or future religions as complementary forms of religious practice or believing. The third form, then, is integrative pluralism, which is intent on showing that all religions are to be regarded as integral parts of a holistic developmental process of humanity and its understanding of the world. This integrative form of pluralism is important because it would provide a philosophical basis for harmonizing different religious worldviews while also offering an open and creative vision for relating their differences to a creative whole for mutual learning and growth. The third option is advanced to avoid relativism while preserving uniqueness, for the other two forms seem to be confronted with the problem of relativism.

The primary model of integrative pluralism comes by way of Whitehead's philosophy of process and creativity, and the *Yijing*'s onto-cosmological framework of the great ultimate (太极 *taiji*), the principle of creativity (生生 *shengsheng*), *dao* (道 the way), *yi* (易 change), and the opposite of feminine and masculine (阴阳 *yin-yang*).

With this model, Whitehead's notion of God is onto-hermeneutically reinterpreted in terms of *taiji* and *yin-yang*. Indeed, this discussion as a whole draws heavily upon metaphysical onto-cosmology and creativity as a justification and source for onto-hermeneutic reinterpretation of religious thought into novel terms, which are extended, enriched, reevaluated, and expanded outside of their original, intra-systemic, contextual meanings.

In the history of Chinese thought, many models can be found for integrative religious pluralism. Even Confucius himself advocates a principle of "harmony and difference at the same time." It can be therefore claimed that genuine harmony requires a creative unity to bind all different parts into oneness. Then we have to say that each part would have to contribute to the maintaining of the central harmony as its universal principle and value. In this case, one can have both plurality and unity, existing in the form of unity in plurality and plurality in unity.

This notion of the harmony of complementary differences further leads into the idea of ontological interdependence, found in both Whitehead's ontological principle of relativity and *Yijing*'s system of hexagrams as displayed in their interconnectivity. A distinction is then made between an ontologically creative (non-personal) god and an ethical (personal) god. It is maintained that all religions share in the ideals of a primordial creator or onto-creativity, but they differ in their depictions of salvation and ethical ideals attributed to a personal god. As a consequence, there is a means for interrelating religions on a common onto-cosmological ground, while yet recognizing its ethical plurality.

In chapter 5, I am especially concerned with Robert Neville's understanding of Chinese philosophy. There are three areas of his contributions: the area of ontological creativity, the area of systematic creativity, and the area of creativity in the cultivation of the human person and human society. The way Neville develops his philosophy is perhaps best understood in light of an underlying system of the *Yijing*. To support this claim, five points are made. First of all, Neville's concern with the argument of *creatio ex nihilo* is implicitly presented in the *Zhouyi* 周易, where the "Active Originator" (乾元 *Qianyuan*) is the beginner, creator, and ruler of the ten thousand things. Second, we must see the symbolism of *Qian* (乾, active and strong) and *Kun* (坤, receptive and soft) as limiting archetypal symbols abstracted from all creative relationships and thus applicable to all creative relationships. Next, the primary cosmology of the *yi* (易, transformative) as explained in terms of the great ultimate is no doubt a demonstration of the process of cosmological differentiation and the ramification with its implicit order derived from the ontological creativity. Subsequently, in the *Yizhuan* one can see a framework of thinking that integrates reality and values in a single onto-cosmology of creativity. Finally, the *Yizhuan* philosophy of change could also be understood as a "theorizing of theories," as Neville describes it.

On the basis of these insights, a thoroughgoing comparison of Confucian and Christian traditions is presented, highlighting the normative and regulative roles that propriety expresses as experienced through ritual practices.

In chapter 6, I come to deal the concept of *shi* (time) in Chinese philosophy. Because change and transformation always involve a process of becoming in time, it is important to recognize time as a basic cornerstone of onto-cosmology of the *Yijing* in particular and in Chinese philosophy in general. I began with alternative accounts of time as it is worked out in three phases of cultural development in the European West. In Greek philosophy, time has been concocted as appearance but not as reality. The truth and the real have been construed in terms of the timeless or eternal; truth has been particularly conceived as being time-transcendent since its emergence in Platonic philosophy in the fifth century BCE. With Aristotle, time was given a further teleological dimension. This "transcendent-teleological theory of time" was played out through the Medieval Age and eventually came to culminate in the European enlightenment from which two divergent notions of time arose: the objective scientific theory a la Newton and the Kantian transcendental philosophy of time as a necessary form of intuition of mind. This comprises the second phase of Western philosophy with regard to time.

Within Heidegger's writings one finds a third phase of Western philosophy. According to Heidegger, time is neither a transcendental condition, nor an objective entity, nor a natural state of motion or movement of objects, but instead a sense of care and anxiety with regard to the pure possibilities of human existence. Heidegger's account, however, with its emphasis on the human existence, is still essentially subjectivistic.

Against this philosophical background, it is proposed that we move toward an account of the intersubjectivity and interobjectivity of time, not just the subjectivity of time or just the objectivity of time, no matter how sophisticated each may appear. The total integration of time in terms of human existence and in terms of an enlarged unity of man and the world would be the next important task for our enterprise of understanding time. This is where *Yi*-philosophy comes in as totalistic and configurational theory of time as change. Change is the unifying thread or core concept throughout this discussion. *Taiji* and *dao*, for example, are explained as two sides of change. Moreover, time is here equated with change, and itself is explained in terms of *taiji* and dao. It is recognized that people participate in change, being affected by it as well as initiating it, and thus it is argued that people similarly participate in time. With regard to human activity, time is considered as timeliness (*shizhong* 时中 or simply as *shi* 时 in the sense of timing), or timely activity, which is a characteristic of *ren* (仁, benevolence), and so is an aspect of moral activity in Confucianism.

In chapter 7, we are confronting the "Hierarchical Theory of Time with Reference to the Chinese Philosophy of *Dao* and *Qi* (气, vital force)." It is argued that time must be times or concrete processes and events whose beginnings and endings must be concretized, where each beginning can be further considered an ending and vice versa. Furthermore, an event or a process constitutes a whole and is based on a whole entity or a nexus of related entities. Time is necessarily embodied in a structured and many-leveled hierarchy of motions and changes, which are reflected in the integration and disintegration of the individual whole and related things.

Consequently, this chapter argues for a "hierarchical theory of time," which is a comprehensive notion of time in general conceived as composed of sequential stages or levels, nested in concrete occurrences of events. This theory is based on the onto-cosmological principles and considerations of harmony and change, as well as the creative interaction of opposites and polarities. Apart from explicit references to the *Yijing*, various relevant concepts of *dao*, *qi*, and *yin-yang* can be drawn from Daoist and Neo-Confucian sources.

The last chapter analyzes Leibniz's notion of a universal characteristic and symbolic realism in the *Yijing*. Leibniz has argued for improvements of science based on reason, which means that we can reason to truths by way of using a good system of symbols, which he calls characteristic symbols (CS). An essential requirement for such symbols is that they correspond to precise concepts that allow demonstration and demonstrative certainty. His study of mathematical analysis enabled him to believe in a universal calculus or general analysis of human ideas, which is to be founded on two principles: the principle of contradiction and the principle of sufficient reason. However, I propose to have two kinds of systems of characteristic symbols: one is used for inferential and analytical purposes, the other for interpretative and decision-making purposes. The former would provide a system of preestablished principles or axioms of consistency, whereas the latter would suggest or invite us to recognize a system of post-established norms or actions of harmonization. We can therefore move from a universe defined by a closely set rationality to a universe opened up by a dialectical rationality, which is adaptive to an ever-developing universe. We can even come to a better appreciation of onto-cosmology, like the one proposed in the Neo-Confucian Zhou Dunyi's 周敦颐 *Taiji Tushuo* (太极图说 Explanations of the Diagram of the Great Ultimate). This becomes particularly attractive once we take into account both the strength and limitations of Leibniz's metaphysics of God and the contingent truths in his Monadology.

Apart from the chapters, this book also includes an appendix that considers some important ways related to the main themes of this book as introduced above. In the appendix I provide a short but significant comparison between Greek and Chinese philosophical views of time and timeless. In the Greek view, time is represented as images and appearances as distinguishable from the timeless as forms and numbers in a transcendent relationship between the two (the timeless transcending time). In the Chinese view on the contrary, time has no such transcendence. Time is exemplified in the notions of change and transformation in terms of *dao* 道 and *qi* 气. If one can speak of transcendence of time at all, it is only to mean to identify oneself with the source of change or the power of change. This notion is then extended and expanded to explain the notions of immortality in Daoism and Confucianism.

In conclusion, this book has introduced many important issues and concepts that I believe are worth being elaborated so that it may continue to deepen our understanding of Chinese and Western traditions of metaphysics. Theoretically speaking, this comparative study would conduce to an important recognition of the distinction between a theory of being namely ontology and a theory of being-becoming namely onto-cosmology, the former belonging to the Western and the latter belonging to the Chinese. The future is to see how ontology and onto-cosmology can be integrated such that being must always involve becoming and thus ontology has to be understood in contexts of cosmology. Finally, the studies in this book presuppose an understanding of the philosophy of the *Yijing* as initially presented in my first book, titled *The Primary Way: Philosophy of Yijing*.

1

On the Origins of Chinese Philosophy

Three Aspects of Origins

In this opening chapter, we rehearse the origins of Chinese philosophy. To speak of the origins of Chinese philosophy, we need to take into consideration how origins of any philosophy are to be decided. There are three such considerations. First, insofar as philosophy is a conscious effort to formulate views and values as expressions of fundamental beliefs of a people, philosophy cannot be separate from the cultural background and cultural tradition of a people. By "culture" we mean "a cluster of beliefs and behavior patterns involving specifically among other things expressive activities of language, art, literature, philosophy, the use of tools, craftsmanship, and religion." In this sense, philosophy serves an expressive function of its underlying culture par excellence. Thus, one may have to trace a philosophy to the beginning of a culture and find its determinants in the cultural experiences, activities, and proclivities of a people. In other words, one must find the general characteristics of the philosophy in the cultural experiences and tendencies of a people.

There is no complete axiomatization of a culture and hence no complete axiomatic formulation of the philosophy of a people. This is not only because we cannot completely articulate a culture and its potential in a closed system of principles, but also because philosophy exists primarily as a form of creative exploration into life and reality, even though it draws its lifeblood from a cultural fountainhead. Hence, to identify the origins of a philosophy, one needs to look to the specific core of a culture that sustains the philosophical need and ignites the philosophical fire. We can generally identify this core of a culture in terms of the ideals and goals of life that are worthy of pursuit and that can be used as standards of value judgments for the large portion of the society. One may even suggest that philosophy is developed primarily to conceptualize the ideal aspirations of a people at a certain stage or under certain specific circumstances of the cultural development of a people. Actually, the common ideals and values would be considered forming the core or coming from the core of the cultural experiences of a people.

Philosophy as an ongoing general activity must be seen as evolving and emerging from a practical activity of life that is centered on solving problems of correct knowledge, genuine understanding, and fair appraisal of matters important to life, whether individual or social. On a social level, problems of resource distribution, power organization, and regulation of interpersonal behaviors are inevitably essential and vital concerns of a people. Hence, ways of thinking and understanding are essential and vital to any philosophical inquiry, which serves to search for and suggests problems as well as critical solutions and attitudes toward those problems. Consequently, a second consideration pertaining to the beginning of a philosophy lies in an inquiry into the essential ways of thinking about life and reality in the full spectrum of human activities and experiences. This can be done either by looking into various activities of a people over a period, as suggested by Michel Foucault's archeological approach to knowledge, or by looking for an originative system of thinking that both conscientiously reflects and normatively guides the process of thinking of a people.

The third consideration pertaining to the beginning of a philosophy concerns the theoretical constructions resulting as a product of philosophical thinking or cultural activities of a people. Philosophy in this context does not exist as the cultural pre-understanding of a people or as a hidden form of thinking guiding the problem-solving and evaluating mind of a people. It becomes instead a clearly stated or articulated idea or system of ideas in the form of explicit language. The philosophical idea may be simply stated or may be developed as a system of discourse-forming general propositions. In either way it addresses some fundamental issues or ideals of life as well as some basic views of reality. Life and reality have come to be fully encountered as basic problems, and all other problems are to be related and reduced to them. Hereby the subject of philosophical thinking also stands out as a specific historical person and thus acts as a human being who philosophizes and hence as a *philosopher*. Still, one must investigate a historically given view on life and reality as the beginning of a conscious philosophy. The criterion for such a philosophizing activity is rationality in the form of propositional language or discourse. But one has to understand and thus interpret the language and discourse as an assertion and expression of philosophical thinking in maturity.

In the above I have identified three considerations regarding the origins of a philosophy: origins as historicity and cultural experience, and origins as hidden methodology and underlying view of reality and life, and finally origins as conscious assertions of ideas and ideals. When we use the term "origins" we have in mind a multidimensional view of origins that must be pluralistically conceived. In fact, in order to effectively understand origins of a philosophy or a philosophical tradition, we have to face the following questions: What are the fundamental concepts or categories of that philosophical tradition? In which theoretical contexts are they asserted or presented? What is the underlying view of reality that leads to or is presupposed in the philosophical understanding or assertion? What is the guiding methodology or way of thinking for the philosophical idea or ideas? Finally, what kind of cultural experiences or ideals define or give rise to this way of thinking or this way of forming a view? These questions define our three senses of "origins" in a reverse order, namely historicity, practicality, and theoreticity. The three senses of "origins" form a unity in that each requires the other two in making the notion of origins interesting and relevant. To speak of origins only in one sense, one will not be able to answer all questions of origins. These senses of "origins" could apply to the problem of origins of any philosophy as a human activity, insofar as this activity cannot be reduced to a single act or view but must assume many dimensions that are essential to the rich meaning of "origins."

Historicity and cultural experience provide the context for the emergence of methodology and cosmology, which in turn provide the context for the emergence of the language and construction of a philosophy. To go back to our point about the relation of one dimension of origins to another dimension of origins, this relation is to be aptly described as that of partial determination and partial creativity, which implies partial indetermination and partial non-creativity. This means that philosophy as it arises from a cultural experience and its primary methodological/metaphysical self-reflection can assume many forms and can take many routes of development. This is how philosophy has been developed. And there is always the prospect of creative development of philosophy—particularly if we realize that philosophy is itself an exploration into the creativity of universe, creativity of life and creativity of mind in response to the creativity of universe. This also underlines the fact that philosophy is an unending pursuit requiring a universe of infinite possibilities. Because there is no conceivable ending to a creative universe and a creative mind, that arises from the creative universe, there is always enough indeterminacy and thus creativity inherent in any given formulation of a philosophy.

Another relevant point to be made in this connection is that philosophy can have an impact on the social and cultural development of a people. Whereas philosophy arises from a cultural tradition, it also gives rise to new forms and new directions of cultural activities of a people. It is in this sense that philosophy is the best index or indication of the cultural state of a people and thus forms an organic unity with the ongoing development or growth of a culture. Philosophy may be thus regarded as a self-refining, self-critiquing, and even self-fulfilling process of a cultural tradition, albeit combined with creativity drawn from the individual or collective mind of a people.

Three Strains of Thinking in the Origins of Chinese Philosophy

Based on the preceding discussion, we can now identify three strains of thinking in the primary cultural experience of the Chinese people: these three strains of thinking serve as beginnings of Chinese philosophy. These three strains of thinking present the fundamental orientations and directions of Chinese philosophy as well as set the stages for Chinese philosophy. They are inherent in the primary cultural experience of the Chinese and form the earliest core of Chinese cultural and intellectual life. But they themselves are interrelated in terms of succeeding stages of ontogenesis and inter-animation. In other words, one stage of thinking gives rise to another without canceling out the first stage. Hence, each later stage is founded on an earlier stage, and one should consider a later stage as arising from the context of earlier stage or stages.

What then are the three strains of thinking in early Chinese culture, which constitute a paradigmatic model for origination and inspiration of Chinese philosophy? They are (1) an intrinsic reverence for heaven and ancestral spirits that provides the source of meaning for ethical, social, and political life of the Chinese people; (2) a dialectical bipolar onto-cosmological reflection that provides the backbone of a methodology implicitly guiding and conditioning the way of perception and thinking in Chinese philosophy; and (3) a timely awakening to potentiality and creativity of the human subject, which provides the basis for a cosmic naturalism and an intrinsic humanism, whether collective or individual, and whether political or moral, in the formation of early schools of Chinese philosophy. In the following, I discuss these beginnings of Chinese philosophy and their interrelations in the given order.

Initial Trust and Primal Order: Ancestral Spirits and the Mandate of Heaven

According to recent archaeological findings, the ancient Chinese had settled at a period earlier than Neolithic time (circa 5000 BCE) in both the Northeastern and Northwestern parts of China, centering their tribal community life in ancestral gods (ancestral spirits) and natural gods (natural spirits).[1] In this period known as Yangshao Culture/Dawenkou Culture/Liangzhu Culture/Hongshan Culture/Hemudu Culture, objects of a sacramental nature and sites of worship (temples) and burials consistent with the practice of ancestral worship are found as a common feature. One may regard this time as marking the specific era in the pre-history of China, aptly called the period of Jade, which lasted at least another two millennia.

Since the time of Longshan Culture (2600–2100 BCE), the period reputed to be reigns of the sage-kings Yao and Shun, Chinese culture centering on sacrifices to natural and ancestral spirits had spread further south including Henan, Shandong, and Hubei, and a natural process of integration of scattered communities had taken momentum in the eve of formation of a unified political state, the Xia.[2]

Two observations can be made concerning the formation of the early Chinese culture as described above. First, it leaves no doubt that the practice of *li* (ritual/rite) found its beginning in the ancestral worship as early as the period of Jade. In fact, the word *li* bears a component precisely indicating the offering of patterned jade for sacrificial ritual. Though no philosophical discussion has taken place regarding how the practice of *li* has been initiated, the sacrificial practice dated back to the period of Jade gives us an insight into how *li* arose in connection with the ancestral worship and worship of natural spirits. There is no doubt that clans and tribal communities based on family lineage had been firmly established by as early as 2500 BCE within the period of Jade. A family system possibly affords the benefits of care and security yielded by family. Moreover, it ensures a sense of stability, order, peace, and solidarity provided by the family conceived as rooted in the same ancestral spirits. It is through the recognition and reverence of the ancestral spirits that the unknown in the past becomes familiar and the fear toward the unknown in the past is overcome. This is metaphysically equivalent to finding stability and security in the consanguinity of blood and continuity of time.³

A third important element relevant for the establishment of the *li* in the ancestral worship is the experience of an order of the higher and lower, the senior and the junior. To be higher and senior, however, is not to say that the higher and the senior should merely dominate the lower and the junior. On the contrary, the higher and the senior should protect the lower and the junior, whereas the lower and the junior should respect the higher and the senior for the benefit of maintaining a holistic totality of order in which the higher and the lower, the senior and the junior, will have their respective places and roles. With regard to this holistic totality, all individual parties are mutually dependent and complementary to one another. Beside, the higher and the senior basically correspond to the earlier and the later, and therefore in the course of time the lower and the junior can in turn become the higher and the senior, just as the latter had been the lower and the senior in the past.

In this deep experience of ancestral temporality, one can detect elements of totality, mutual placement, mutual support, interdependence, and a natural process of transformation and return. This in fact suggests the initial and inceptive experience of the *dao*, that leads to the formation of the philosophy of the *yi* (易 change and transformation) and the philosophy of reverence (*jing* [敬] and piety. The key point for this experience is the experience of time in the act of reverence for the ancestral spirits as related to us. This experience can also be titled reverence for existence in the passage of time. "Reverence" (*jing* 敬) in this context is an intentional/existential state of piety, solemnity, and carefulness of a person toward a situation being conceived or experienced to be an ideal object of emulation and identification. What needs to be stressed in this experience of *jing* is that even though there is a distance between the higher and lower, there is also at the same time closeness and attraction between the ideal and the actual. In the experience of reverence, one reveals one's subjective existence by facing the limitedness of oneself on the one hand and the consequent acknowledgement of an ideal being beyond oneself on the other. It is in both limiting and stretching of oneself that the essential meaning of the *li* is formed.

Concerning the reverence for the natural spirits, the ancient Chinese, like any other ancient people, wondered about natural events and phenomena in their environment and were in a situation to respond to, explain, and understand them. But instead of developing a full-scale mythology or organized primitive religion, their response to natural processes of nature is a matter of accepting the natural world without excessive mythological impersonations. There is a general awareness of life: nature as a whole is seen to be full of life. In fact, both heaven and earth for a long time have been regarded as implicit principles of potential vitality and life-giving powers. There is a general tendency to attribute magical power (*mo* 魔) and personality to natural objects such as mountains and rivers, but this is because they appear to have life and to have the power to provide life. If a power is found to destroy life without giving life or bringing order to life, it is to be eliminated from being considered a spirit (*shen* 神) via a more powerful human intervention. The myth of Hou Yi's shooting the harmful extra nine suns is a telling point. We might suggest that in the life-world of the ancient Chinese what is important is life in the totality of nature, and an entity is nothing to be worthy of reverence if it does not benefit life and specifically human life as a whole.

In fact, the term "*shen*" suggests the power of extending or stretching life. Without this power of extending or stretching life, a spirit cannot be an object of reverence given the above sense of reverence. The term "*gui* 鬼" is also used to denote a spirit linked to the past. Like *shen*, it is to be revered as being capable of benign and beneficial influence on life in general. The difference between *shen* and *gui* is that the former is spirit considered generally without reference to a past existing history, whereas the latter is referred to in light of a past existing history; that is, the *gui* has its trace in past and came as a trace from the past. When the ancestral spirits are considered *shen* and not as merely *gui*, the emphasis and focus are placed on their life-preserving and life-protecting power.

To go back to the ancestral worship, it is not only that the *li* (礼 propriety) was first introduced as a rule-governing proper attitude and proper behavior of making sacrifice to the ancient spirits, but also that the notion of *shen* was clearly conceived by way of the experience of the presence of a benign power of life-protection and life-preservation. It is also to be noted that, when the family relationship extends by way of marriage and rise of new generations, the common source of the family becomes the revered centering origin of all the life in the family. In this sense, the common source, which is worthy of reverence, is the supreme divinity *shangdi* (上帝 Lord on the High). As we see in the ensuing discussion of chapter 2 of this work, the term *di* 帝 also bears the sense of "Source," which bears important significance for classical Chinese views of reality and divinity. Here, we continue with an anthropological investigation of the concept. This notion of "*shangdi*" is known to the Xia and Yin peoples. In fact, we have good reasons to believe that it is through the fusion of the communities of different peoples under the reigns of Xia and Yin that the supreme divinity of *shangdi* was born. Now if we consider all lives in nature, then there should be a common source of life and thus a common source of all things in the world. If we try to reach for an ultimate common source for all natural lives in the form of natural spirits, then we can see how the notion of heaven (*tian* 天) as life-generating and life-preserving power is formed. This notion of *tian* took shape relatively late, and it did not become well established until the beginning of the Zhou in the twelfth century BCE.

Since the Zhou people had integrated all other peoples within an even larger scope than their predecessors, Xia and Yin, the notion of "*tian*" as a comprehensive notion absorbs as well as replaces the notion of *shangdi*. Together with this, of course, the *li* system also became more complete and more comprehensive regarding a proper placement and ordering of all things in the life-world of the Zhou people. This system of *li* of course is superimposed by the *li* to heaven. The symbolic meaning of this development is that the Chinese people had become more unified and more integrated to the extent that a comprehensive unification and integration of the social life and political life had taken place. We may now conclude that there exists an intrinsic organic interrelation between the rise of beliefs in *shangdi* and *tian*, the institutionalization of *li* as a system of social orderings and the formation of a unified social-political economy based on agriculture.

The spirit of this development is the sense of non-separation between individual man and his family, his community, his state, and nature at large. There is a deeply rooted sense of affective accord and consanguine harmony among all these entities, and this is expressed by the notion of *jing*: the sincere attitude in acknowledging the differences of things and their positions in a totality of reality that bring out their differences and at the same time preserve their equally genuine identities. It is in this sense that the fundamental values of comprehensive harmony (*he* 和) and comprehensive transformation (*hua* 化) in Chinese culture have come into being, even though they may not have become fully articulated until seventh century BCE. Given this background of *jing* (reverence) for understanding *li* (propriety), it is clear that *li* does not simply mark out a principle of difference and discrimination but also implicates a principle of totality and comprehension that procreates and preserves the difference. But above all *li* implies an existential communicability and required mutual acknowledgement between two different entities in a framework of totality. It is on this basis that the Chinese mode of thinking and the Chinese notion of humanity are to be systematically developed.

As a partial explanation of the rise of *li* together with its inner dimension of *jing* in the sense we have described, we may point to the influence of the concrete time and concrete space, namely the geological and climatological environment, in which the ancient Chinese had found themselves. In this temperate space-time zone, there are seasonable changes and blending of mountains and rivers in the fold of heaven and earth that impressed the ancient Chinese as always generating varieties of life and forming an inseparable unity. If we compare this environment with those in which the ancient Greek, the ancient Hebrew, and the ancient Indian respectively found themselves, we cannot but see that each culture reflects as well as embodies some dominating qualities of its large environment. These qualities bespeak not only the economical, political, and social institutions of each people, but also their primary living style, their way of thinking, and their mode of idealization. There is no doubt that their basic orientations in life and their ultimate values for life, whether individual or collective, are also affected by the overall respective influences from their environments.[4]

Of course, it is to be remarked that human factors also form an integral portion of the environment. The sense of cohesion and harmony prevails when there is no essential need or stress for competition, conquest or conflict in history. The Chinese people as a whole have experienced a sense of centrality and totality and thus seem to have strived for more integration and cohesion in history than any other people. This no doubt contributed to the philosophical awareness of harmony as an underlying strain of both cosmos and society in the sphere of Chinese culture.

In connection with the notion of heaven, the notion of the "mandate of heaven (*tianming* 天命)" arose as a consequence of the defeat of the Shang by Zhou. As heaven assumed the central and overarching position of power, all major changes such as the changeover of political authority were held to have been derived from the influence and determination of will of the heaven, hence the notion of the "*tianming*." The appearance of the "mandate of heaven" underlies both the universalization and the centralization of the power of a supreme being, because the notion of "*ming*" was basically a matter of originating and commanding action via one's free will and free choice. In fact, the term "*ling* (令 command)," a cognate of "*ming*" (命), was very much used in the oracle inscriptions (*buci* 卜辭). In this sense of "*ling*," all natural events are conceived as results of the *ling* of the *shangdi* or *tian*. Whereas *ling* expresses the will and command in a gesture, *ming* (命) indicates specifically the verbalization of the *ling*.

In the fall of the Dynasty of Yin, the Zhou founders read the message that the *ming* of *shangdi* is not fixed and instead will change according to the virtues (*de* 德) of the rulers in holding their power of reign over the people. It was clear to the Zhou rulers that it was the support of the people that was crucial for the defeat of the Yin and the rise of the Zhou. Therefore, at the time when the mandate of heaven was conceived to be the basis of political change, an awakening to the importance of winning the support of the people was also taking place. This awakening led to the reflection on the doings, abilities, and intentions of the rulers. This is the origin of the notion of "*de*" or virtue. *De* is the power of securing the following of the people, and nothing will secure the following of the people except one's ability and intention to protect the people by a ruler's restraining and controlling his desires and arbitrariness. That "*de*" becomes eventually a moral notion governing individual development and self-cultivation as well as social acceptance and approval is no doubt based on this historical reflection on power change and is intimately linked to the notion of the *tianming*.

The more the inconstancy of the *tianming* is experienced, through the failures of a ruler's lack of *de*, the more urgent the importance of cultivating oneself becomes. In this process, the authority of heaven would become diminished and a moral humanism will take its place even to the point that the mandate of heaven is to be internalized and identified with the nature (namely the capacity and potentiality of *de* in a person), as in the *Zhongyong* (中庸). This is evidently one source of Confucianism. It needs not be pointed out that there is a slow change of the meaning of the notion of *ming* as well. As the mandate of heaven is conceived to cause life and determine status of life, what life is and what status and fortunes life receives are therefore regarded as a matter of *tianming*. But under the circumstances when people lose sight of heaven because of the felt weakening of the power of heaven, the *ming* naturally becomes an autonomous power conceived to be responsible for the what and how of life, hence arising the notion of *ming* as fate or "already determined." It even goes one step further: the *ming* as the determining power not only becomes transformed into a determined state but also becomes a predetermined state, as testified by popular beliefs. It is against this transformed notion of *ming* in popular beliefs, which may exist even in Confucian thinking, that Mozi directs his critique at the end of fifth century.

Emergence of Integrative Wisdom: Dialectics and Cosmology in Union

In separating reality from appearance, objectivity from subjectivity, the ancient Greeks sought the immutable and unmoved as the essence of the real and the objective. In contrast, the ancient Chinese from the very beginning recognized and accepted change and transformation as irreducible attributes of the world, including both things and human selves.[5] In fact, when we now look at the main differences between Western philosophy and Chinese philosophy, we must point to this fundamental divergence. The Chinese stress and grasp the changing, the becoming, time, and temporality, they not only distinguish their metaphysics of reality and nature from the main trend of Western philosophical traditions, but also set them apart from the orientations of Indian philosophy.

For the Chinese philosophers, the experiences of changes in the world, in the seasons, and in one's life are not a reason for getting away from changes, nor are they reasons for denying the ultimate realness of the world. On the contrary, these experiences lend insight to the Chinese thinker into the true nature of things and human self: there is creativity for development, transformation, interaction, and integration in nature and in human self. This also suggests to him the organic wholeness of the world in which the changing and the unchanging, the objective and the subjective, merge and form a continuum because of the pervasiveness of change. To the ancient Chinese, this way of understanding reality is naturally simple and authentic as self-evidenced by the experiences of changes alone.

It is in the tradition of the *Zhouyi* (周易) that the experiences of changes in nature by the ancient Chinese became consciously organized and articulated into a system of thinking about and describing reality. As nature is seen as dynamically moving and changing, the dialectical way of thinking as embodying natural forces of changing can be said to truly capture the nature of reality. It is in this sense that focusing on changes gives us the simplest and most direct way of understanding reality: it is to "map" reality of changes as changes of reality without mediation and without distortion. In this direct and simple way of thinking, one may see that reality of changes becomes self-reflexively conscious of itself by way of incorporating the self-conscious mind into the world of changes. This is the philosophical way to understand the meaning of "*jianyi* 简易" when the term was used to convey the meaning of changes in the term "*yi*." But then it is through the way or method of "*jianyi*" (direct presentation of changes) that reality of changes becomes represented, which reveals itself to include changes (*bianyi* 变易), constancies (*buyi* 不易), and combinations of changes and constancies.

The influence of the *Zhouyi* as a way of thinking in Chinese philosophy cannot be understated. Not only has it introduced a method of organizing thoughts about any matter of importance, but it has also served as a way of revealing or discovering features of reality. More important than this, the *Zhouyi* has provided a way of achieving balance, centrality, harmony, and comprehension, as well as transformative development and return of things man has confronted. The reason why it has this capacity is that it is itself a revelation of reality as reality is and becomes, and yet it is expressed in the symbolic form of the simplest processes and states of the change-reality. It thus is capable of revealing the open structure or trace of a transforming reality as well as applying to any single aspect or item of reality experienced by man.

Because of the intended completeness of the *Zhouyi* understanding of reality, it finally provides a way of understanding, controlling, and deciding about the future yet unknown to human beings. In this latter function, the *Zhouyi* serves to integrate the present, past, and future of time into a whole in which human beings can play an active role and make a positive contribution. In the following, I elaborate on important aspects of the *Zhouyi* as a way of thinking and the impacts it has made on Chinese philosophy.

The *Zhouyi* has focused on the totality of reality and thus has developed a complete system of reality. The completeness starts from the basic observation of complementary opposites or polarities as defining a whole. The simplest complementary opposites are *yin* (shady) and *yang* (bright) on sides of mountains and banks of rivers. The *yin* signifies absence of light, whereas the *yang* signifies presence of light. *Yin* and *yang* make a difference to things, as things can be regarded as *yin* or *yang* according to the lack or presence of illumination of light. As it is natural to see light as energy, motion, and penetrating power, the *yang* acquires characteristics suggestive of creating life and sustaining reality. On the opposite side, the *yin* is naturally associated with characteristics suggestive of concealment, passivity, receptivity, and comprehension. What is important to note is that if change is possible at all as it is, the simplest way to experience or closely monitor change as real is to see it as going from the stable, the hidden, and the possible to the dynamic, the disclosed, and the actual, and vice versa. In this simple process, you experience the basic unit of *yin-yang* transformation, which defines a unity and a totality. In it one also sees the complementarity of opposites and the potentiality of progressive return and reversion. Of course, the *yin-yang* relationship of contrast, interdependence, and unity can be realized in an apparently non-transformative spatial context: there is the soft and there is the firm existing side by side. But then insofar as there is a unity and whole to contain and present this contrast, this contrast is a harmony and balance that provide a richer experience of changes.

What is important in understanding the totality and unity of *yin-yang* is that the *yin* and *yang* have to be recognized as opposite qualities in the primary context of the dark and the bright, which when seen as absence and presence of light suggest the absence and presence of being, respectively, and thus nonbeing and being. The *Daodejing* is the first philosophical text to disclose this and refers to this with the claim: "The being and nonbeing mutually generate each other." The text also refers to the latter relationship as "The high and the low mutually lean on each other."

How does one see the *yin* and *yang* as a universal feature for all unities of things? This may require one to see the wholeness and hence the unity of things in the first place. Not only can *yin* and *yang* not be separated from each other, but they also must not be separated from a totality of things to be seen. The seeing of the totality of things is a phenomenal understanding that sometimes depends on the intuitive, comprehensive, and detail-discerning opening-up of the mind of the person. In the *Xici*, the description of the inventive activities of the sage-king Fu Xi gives us a retrospective insight into his formation of the initial symbolic system of the *yi*, the eight trigrams (*bagua* 八卦). Fu Xi has to look up to the heavens and inquires into the earth; he has to look carefully on things far from him and does the same on things close to him, namely his own person. It is through a scrupulous and meticulous observation and inquiry that he has come to the configuration of the *bagua* system, which signifies a totality of things—namely the large nature—and which presents the phenomenally most outstanding constituent forces and processes of nature to be understood as a set of *yin-yang* relationships.

It is not again until in the *Xici* that this *bagua* system is seen as arising from a process of onto-cosmological thinking: the original ultimate unity called *taiji* (太极) gives rise to the norm-setting *yin-yang*, which in turn gives rise to four natural forms, which in their turn again generates the *bagua*. This is no doubt a later articulation of the dialectical thinking underlying the understanding of the totality and dynamics of nature. This dialectical thinking leads on the one hand to the formation of an onto-cosmology of fundamental forces and principles referred to as *qian* (乾)/*kun* (坤)/*kan* (坎)/*li* (离)/*dui* (兑)/*gen* (艮)/*xun* (巽)/*zhen* (震), and on the other hand to the formation of a realistic cosmology of natural forms and events referred as *heaven/earth/water/fire/lake/hill/wind/thunder*. What this development suggests is that the dialectical way of thinking in the *Zhouyi* requires a process of comprehensive observation and inquiry, analysis and synthesis or integration. The integrative aspect of this way of thinking is twofold: it integrates all elements of observation into a structure of relationships, and it allows the relationships to be an open system so that it can extend to other things not yet specifically covered. This latter point pertains to the symbolic nature of the structure and the ability of interpretation in the dialectical thinking.

In this process one sees not only the openness of the system, but also that *yin-yang* exists as a pervasive feature of reality on many levels of complexity and relative to many dimensions of structure from many points of view for many different purposes if we allow the subjective and evaluative capacity of mind to play a role. This also suggests that the onto-cosmological reality generated by the *Zhouyi* thinking is an open world of infinite possibilities in which new relationships can be discovered and realized. There is no end to differentiation and integration as there is no end to a process of continuous observation and inquiry, analysis, synthesis, and interpretation.

It is by way of this potentiality of the *Zhouyi* that the *Zhouyi* has influenced the development of Chinese philosophy in both its form and its substance, pertaining to both the way of thinking in the *Zhouyi* and the creative onto-cosmology generated by this method of thinking. I have specifically pinpointed the *Zhouyi* way of thinking and organization as "comprehensive observation," which consists of macro-observation of large features of the nature as well as micro-observation of minute features of the nature. In regard to the latter, the *Zhouyi* sees that things and events have beginnings in a stage of smallest and almost imperceptible movements of forces. To see the large trends of things, one has to perceive the smallest beginnings and makes changes accordingly relative to a purpose. This view not only underlines the importance of micro-observation but also underlines the importance of participatory agency for a human subject.

The *Zhouyi* has focused on harmony as the inceptive state for creativity (*sheng*) and on harmonization as the natural end state of reality in a process of change and transformation. To explain the variety of things and vitality of myriad life-forms in nature on the basis of the simplest unity of *yin-yang*, creativity has to be assumed. In fact, by creativity, it is meant a natural differentiation from the original unity of reality and the development of life and life-activity in nature, which culminates in the formation of human beings as a species. The original unity of reality is called the "*taiji*" (the great ultimate) in the *Xici* commentary on the underlying cosmology of the *Zhouyi*.

Cosmologically, one can say that the *taiji* has *yin-yang* activated in the sense of initiating the reality of the world in terms of activity and transformation. When this activity and transformation continue, the maintenance of creativity of reality amidst change and transformation requires *yin-yang* complementarity, not just their opposition. When this occurs, this is harmony. But this may not happen at any time in the process of creative change and differentiation of things, because there could be opposition without complementarity at any stage in the process of change. Yet the initial creative impulse of the unity of reality is for continuous continuation of the creative, and hence the creation of reality for creativity. In this sense the process of change is therefore a process of harmonization related to an ideal state of harmony as the end state that of course is another inception for creativity. The *Zhouyi* has implicitly assumed this onto-cosmological point of view when it sees the combination of water and fire as a harmony and called it "completion" (*jiji* 既济), which from a reverse point of view becomes "incompletion" (*weiji* 未济), the starting point for creative transformation toward harmony.

This cosmological point of view enables us to see the world as ceaseless activity toward realization of harmony and at the same time as harmony on some level readied for further creative development. In this understanding, the world is given a meaning in terms of which man not only justifies his position in the world but also sees a role in furthering the harmonization of the world and elevating the world to a higher level of creativity. It is in this sense that harmony becomes a central value for both cosmological and anthropological activities. It is also in this sense that human beings are considered capable of participating in the cosmological/cosmogonic activities of reality. Man can be said to embody the nature of the ultimate reality that is essentially the inceptive unity of reality for creative change. This also leads to the later Confucian view that the nature (*xing* 性) of man is what heaven has endowed him with (*ming* 命). In substance, this means that man is endowed with the nature of ultimate reality of by heaven and thus is capable of creative advance and participating in the cosmological process of creativity. For the Confucian it is important for the human being to make this a moral self-understanding and a moral duty.

Given consciousness of human heart-mind, it is consistent also to assume that any inceptive state of existence is a basis for creativity that leads to harmony or a state requiring harmony. Heart-mind activity specifically can be said to demonstrate this view, because any such activity changes a state of existence as well as a view of reality. This point is actually made later on in the Confucian philosophy of the *Zhongyong*. In light of this point, the inceptive state of harmony of mind is called "centrality (*zhong* 中)," rather than "harmony (*he* 和)," whereas the end state is called harmony. But it is worth pointing out that as heart-mind is founded on the same onto-cosmological principle of the *taiji* or unity of the *yin-yang*, and is thus cosmo-spiritually identical, the centrality (*zhong*) as the original state of heart-mind is also a harmony, that harbors creativity as its nature. It is not a state of void or inactivity of emptiness as sometimes is assumed. The difference between centrality and harmony is a not a matter of substance, but a matter of differentiation and integration of feelings in response to the impact and activation of things from outside the heart-mind. This is no doubt a form of participating in the changes of the world, as this leads to a repositioning and transformation of the human self in the world.

Given the above understanding of the onto-cosmological philosophy of the *Zhouyi* and its implications for understanding human existence and human heart-mind or nature, we are in a position to see how this philosophy can turn out to be practical in guiding man's decisions and actions. One of the most important practical tasks for human decisions and actions is to know and master the future. But the problem is that as the future is not yet formed, how could we ever hope to know it? The insight of the *Zhouyi* is that we may configure the future in terms of the onto-cosmological model of understanding based on the totality of *yin-yang* and its creative tendency toward harmonization and harmony. Another factor that should not be lost sight of is the ability of human participation in the cosmological process and thus the ability of the human being for defining and shaping the onto-cosmological order.

Keeping this in mind, we are able to understand how the *Zhouyi* can be seen as a book of divination or perhaps even could be first formulated explicitly as a book of divination. It is important to see divination (*bu* 卜 and 筮 *shi*) as a practical art of knowing and mastering future to be practiced on occasions of momentous importance. But then the knowing and mastering must be correctly understood, as just suggested. If we do not have a clear understanding of the onto-cosmological insights of the *Zhouyi*, if we do not see the working of such an onto-cosmology behind the form of divinatory practice, and if we do not consider the whole system of forms (*gua*) as presenting or hiding such an onto-cosmological way of thinking, we are not in a position to understand the working of the divination, not to say the inner logic of divination.

Given proper understanding of the dialectics and onto-cosmology of the *Zhouyi*, we can now recognize several relevant philosophical aspects of divination that reflect some dominating features of Chinese philosophy in general. First, divination provides a linking point of the onto-cosmological thinking with the spiritual thinking in the ancient Chinese tradition. As there are natural spirits in the world and as there is the supreme authority of heaven as an overseeing spirit, the future could be incorporated as part of the totality of the world and human existence; thus, the future and present can be integrated as a whole. In this regard, to divine is to consult the natural spirits and heaven for knowledge and control over happenings in the future, particularly concerning matters of importance to life and state.[6]

Second, in divination the future is projected into the present on the basis of the cosmology of the *Zhouyi*. In this event, the whole system of the *gua* must be presupposed as a background body of judgments to be drawn out for consultation concerning the future. Although it is not clear how early the system of the *gua* had been formed, it can be safely assumed on the basis of historical and archeological evidence that the set of the sixty-four *gua* in the *Zhouyi* were formed in the beginning of the Zhou. Earlier systems of the sixty-four *gua* may have existed, but it also can be imagined that the system of sixty-four *gua* arises from accumulation of inspired judgments of divination. In this sense divination may exist as a simple appeal to the natural spirits on each occasion of divination, and it is through a long process of experiment and trial, fitting-out and collation, comparing and verification, that a systematization of the *gua* and their judgments are finally settled. But this again must assume that an onto-cosmological model of understanding the world and self had emerged at the same time, because without this there is neither basis nor standard to make the collation and fitting of the *gua* with experiences.

It is thus reasonable to assume that the systematization of the *gua* was accomplished in the time of King Wen of Zhou. By that time the belief in heaven as a dominating and unifying spirit in the world had emerged; accordingly, divination would have then been an implicit appeal to heaven rather than to any other spirit. The unity of spiritual reality and the unity of political reality go hand in hand, and these in turn are accompanied by the systematization and ordering of the *gua*, thus the appearance of the *Zhouyi*, which hides a cosmological philosophy of reality and a dialectical way of thinking under the disguise of divinatory practice.

It is necessary to point out that in actual divination, the future is configured on the basis of the existing onto-cosmology and is interpreted in light of the dialectical and onto-cosmological meanings of the underlying philosophy. This means that the future is structured in accordance with the principle of creative transformation and that human participation is required for determining the outcome of the transformation. There is not a single trace of fatalism or determinism. The divination provides an opportunity for the individual to participate in the developing of the world as well as that of his future. The divination thus provides a way of integrating the future and the past of an individual in the present, and thus calls for the creativity of the individual for self-realization in the divinatory situation. One may even simply regard divination as a practical way of participation of the self in the transformation of the world. In this regard we can easily notice that divination is an integral part of the dialectical way of thinking in the *Zhouyi*. This leads directly to the unity of theory and practice or knowledge and action, which, in light of our understanding of the *Zhouyi* tradition, is evidently profoundly onto-cosmological in nature.

A final point about the divinatory nature of the *Zhouyi* is that divination is not a forecasting action but a decision-making process calling for will of power, courage, wisdom, patience, and cosmological insight of the individual involved. Hence we may see the divinatory practice of the *Zhouyi* as providing a process of self-control and self-cultivation and thus a morality of self-understanding and self-transformation that became further stressed in the forthcoming Confucian thinking.

In the above we have seen how the *Zhouyi* could be understood as a way of dialectical thinking and as a cosmological modeling at the same time. As such, we also see how the *Zhouyi* has wielded influences in the development of Chinese philosophy, because, as we shall see, all major classical schools of Chinese philosophy can be related to it, and their way of thinking at large can be traced to it. This is not to reduce all Chinese philosophy to the philosophy of *Zhouyi*, but to show how *Zhouyi* can be regarded as an originating point and matrix of Chinese philosophy, especially if we take philosophy as a cosmos-thinking enterprise. Again, this is not to analogize early Chinese philosophy to the early Greek philosophy, because there is an essential difference between the two: *Zhouyi* is both cosmological-dialectical and practical-participatory, whereas the early Greek cosmology remains only cosmological-dialectical. In this comparison, one sees that Chinese philosophy actually starts as a combination of intellectual and practical interests.

On the level of practicality, there is a common ground between *Zhouyi* and *Liji* (礼记), which describes the origins of the *li* as we have discussed in the first section. Both are to guide human life for harmony and unity, as harmony and unity are experienced in life in its primary stage. But the origin of the *li* is from the sources of feelings representing the affective aspect of human life, whereas the origin of understanding (*ming*) is in the domain of intellectual observation and reflection as well as in the domain of hermeneutical interpretation. The former gives rise to a moral and religious order and thus an enrichment and growth of society and state, whereas the latter gives rise to an intellectual and rational order and thus presents an onto-cosmological understanding and thinking in the individual human self. In a certain sense, the dialectical way of thinking of the *Zhouyi* becomes self-fulfilling, for between *li* and *ming* there are opposition and complementarity, and thus there is harmony from the beginning to end. This harmony is the basis for the inspiring development of the Classical Schools of Chinese Philosophy in the so-called "axial age" beginning with eighth century BCE. (Recall, the *Yi* began as a way of thinking as early as before the Xia Dynasty in the sixteenth century BCE.)

Creative Integration: Humanistic Awakening and Naturalistic Understanding

In the above we have presented and analyzed the indigenous beginnings of ancient Chinese culture in terms of two main traditions that are rooted in the basic human experiences of life and nature undistorted and uninterrupted by any major human trauma. These two traditions are the tradition of the *li* (礼 propriety) and the tradition of *zhi* (智 wisdom). The former is affective in nature and represents the natural human feelings toward vicissitudes of life, whereas the latter is cognitive in nature and represents human knowledge of changes in nature. The development of the former culminates in the institution of *li* and the formation of belief in *tian* and *tianming*, whereas the development of the latter culminates in the construction of the symbolic system of the *Yijing* in which the onto-cosmology of nature and its dialectics dominate.

We may now see the birth of Chinese philosophy as resulting from a creative integration of the affective tradition of *li* and the intellectual tradition of *zhi* in the form of a response to the social-economic changes and the consequent disintegration of the Eastern Zhou. The birth of Chinese philosophy in actuality takes the form of the emergence of humanism and naturalism in the period of eighth to fifth century BCE (770–476 BCE, historically referred as the period of *Chunqiu* or Spring and Autumn), which leads to the rise of Confucianism and Daoism in the personages of Confucius and Laozi. But then the crucial questions emerge. How did the affective tradition and the cognitive tradition merge to give rise to humanism and naturalism? On what condition or conditions or against what kind of background did this merge occur? What kind of transformation has taken place? When we have answered these questions, we have answered the question of how Chinese philosophy began. In this sense the origins of Chinese philosophy are to be seen in both the shaping of the cultural forces leading to the formation of the classical schools of Chinese philosophy and the actual formation of the classical schools of Chinese philosophy.

Although it is not the place to reflect on the causes of the disintegration of the Zhou political order in the late seventh century BCE, it is relevant to point out that the well-ordered Zhou political and social structures in institutionalized *li* had been outgrown by economic, demographic, social, and political changes of the time onward from eighth century BCE. The existing order simply could not cope with the conflicts and contradictions between central authority and local feudal powers, between competing feudal lords, between political titleholders and newly arising groups of economic influences. There are both natural and human factors contributing to this large-scale change. Population growth demanding better organization of productivity is a natural factor. But a dominating source of change certainly came from the very socioeconomic and political structures of the Zhou: on the one hand, the peace and stability of the system produced potentiality for substantial change and a need for substantial change; on the other, the political form of the system was neither open nor flexible enough to accommodate this substantial change.[7] Thus one may say that the disintegration of the Zhou ensued from the rise of the new economic and political powers, and it was not simply the demise of the past and the tradition. This explains why the *Chunqiu* period is politically chaotic but economically, socially, and culturally very lively. It was a period awakened to a need for a new political order based on its social and economic development and hence a period in search of a new political order that would be commensurate with the economic and social vitalities of the time.

This understanding enables us to see how various schools of philosophy arose and had early beginnings in the period of *Chunqiu* and continued to develop and blossom in the succeeding period of *Zhanguo* or Warring States (475–221 BCE) before China was unified under the reign of Qin. Each school began with a conscious awakening to the need for a new world-order and continued with engagement in a theoretical or practical search for such an order. Each school therefore could be regarded as a response to the fading and breakup of the Zhou system of *li* by way of a new vision of the larger world, a new vision of a more reflective humanity, and a new interpretation or new definition of the past and tradition. It is in this light that each later school developed its own outlook of the world, nature, man, and their relationships—some conservative, some liberal, some more or less transcendent, some more or less immanent. But they all centered on the place of man in a new world-order. Humanism and naturalism are two main trends that arose to function as fountainheads for all major schools of philosophy in the classical China of the *Chunqiu* and *Zhanguo* periods.

It is in this light that we can see that the conservative humanism of Confucius and the liberal naturalism of Laozi may still share something in common, namely, the cosmic understanding based on the *yi*-oriented way of thinking in the *Zhouyi*, because the latter serves to liberate the human thinking from the tradition of the personalized *tian*. They differ in regard to their attitudes toward preserving or casting off the tradition of the *li*. Even though Confucius is generally regarded as conservative in his ethical and political thinking, he nevertheless shows innovation by giving new meanings to old terms such as *junzi*, *li*, *ren*, and so forth. Still, Confucius was not quite in step with the vital forces of economy, society, and politics at his time, and this explains why his philosophy was not accepted or even appreciated by influential people of his time. His philosophy would not find a home until a social and political order had already been established as such—as in the second century BCE. Similarly, the above view explains why it was the Legalist philosophy that captured the attention of the political ruler of the time because it revealed the vitality of forces working toward the formation of a new political, economic, and social order.

How did humanism and naturalism arise under the above circumstances? If we take humanism as the awakening to the importance and centrality of human beings in acquisition of knowledge, definition of reality, and construction of values, then any breakdown of an old world-order implies and presupposes the self-awakening of humanity in terms of its creativity and its importance. Hence, with the disintegration of the Zhou *li*, it is natural to see the stirrings of humanistic spirit at various levels. In the first place, natural spirits had lost their appeal, and intellectual people came to see that it was human beings, not spirits, who determined or affected the rise or decline of social and individual life. In the *Zuozhuan* (左传) there are many passages indicating the value priority of people over spirits; thus, one Ji Liang says that "People are the concern of spirits; hence, sage-kings take care of people first and then devote time to spirits" (*Zuozhuan*, Huan Gong sixth year). There is also one historiographer, Yin, who comments on his ruler's superstition on spirits: "If a nation is to prosper, the ruler is to listen to people; if a nation is to fall, he is to listen to spirits" (*Zuozhuan*, Zhuang Gong thirty-second year). In connection with this denial of the importance of spirits, there is the reinforcement of belief in the self-cultivation and self-responsibility for human action and hence the disclaiming of relevance of a pre-determining fate. Hence even regarding the use of divination, what is revealed is seen in a human context and evaluated in light of abilities and virtues of a person. It is not seen as the working of the *tianming* or spirits or fate. Divination only provides an occasion for configuring and organizing background knowledge for one's judgment on human actions. Thus, considerations of human factors always weigh heavily in one's judgment. One Zhou official, in answering a query about an unusual natural event of the falling of a meteorite, asserts, "Fortune or misfortune are determined by the human person" (*Zuozhuan*, Xi Gong sixteenth year). This indicates a vague recognition of the powers of human self-determination. We see a similar recognition in the "Hong Fan" (洪范) chapter of the *Shangshu* (尚书): "If you have great doubt, consult your mind, consult your assistants, consult your subjects, and consult divination by oracle bones and milfoil stalks." A ruler has to use his intelligence and wisdom to make decisions, and is not expected to exclusively depend on divination for decision-making.

One important feature of the humanistic awakening in the Spring-Autumn period is that human agency is fundamentally located either in the collective of people or in the single person of a ruler. It is recognized that people in a state, not spirits, or even *tianming*, make a difference to the state and that the ruler must have virtues in order to govern well a state. We may thus see this humanistic awakening as consisting in the discovery of human autonomy and human self-importance in the caring and control of people by the ruler, who should rely on his own abilities and virtues in making the caring and control of people possible. In a sense, it is a political humanism or a collective humanism, a humanism that distances itself from the belief in *tianming* and focuses on the human agency of government in the exemplary and caring functions of a ruler. However, it is this political humanism that provides a basis for developing a universal individual-centered moral humanistic philosophy of Confucius.

The core of naturalistic understanding is the recognition of importance and centrality of natural factors for explanation of things in the world. In regard to the rise of naturalism, perhaps the most noteworthy fact is the widespread recognition of nature and the world as resultant states and activities of fundamental forces identified as metal, wood, water, fire, and earth. This is the five-power (*wuxing*) theory of nature that started in the early beginning of Zhou. Again in the "Hong Fan" chapter of the *Shangshu*, the five powers are described in terms of their respective natural qualities: water has the quality of flowing down, fire the quality of flaming up, wood the quality of growing bent or straight, metal the quality of alternation, and earth the quality of being farmable. Although this way of describing the five powers is not purely naturalistic, it has specified certain capacities or potentialities of the five powers and hence five types of natural processes in relation to human actions in an objectively experienced way. This suggests that the five powers are recognized in the contexts of the interaction between nature and man, where nature is cultivated or husbanded toward maintaining human life. We may regard this as a naturalistic-pragmatic conceptualization of nature. But the development of the five powers theory is such that identifying qualities or relations of the five powers have expanded by association or correlation with other concrete things in nature or human experiences. That this is possible is due to certain objective similarities of qualities present in things in the world or certain similarities of response-feelings on the part of human subjects. From a transcendental deductive point of view, human mind seems to have the capacity of identifying the natural processes or human experiences and their relationships in a coherent and yet applicable way. But from a metaphysical point of view, the associative-correlative way of thinking in five powers represents a pervading unity and mutuality of order in the world, which perhaps can be best expressed by Alfred North Whitehead's notion of "unity of feeling."

In fact, with this "unity of feeling" to be objectively as well as subjectively understood, the five powers become natural symbols referring to some underlying real processes and forces in nature that bind to human experiences in a vast network of interweaving relationships. This is a process that we may use the Whiteheadian term "symbolic reference" to designate. Given this understanding, the naturalism in the *Chunqiu* period is one of organicism—not that of mechanism as modern science would have it. In fact, when we take into consideration the generative-destructive order and relations among the five powers, we can see these as natural organic processes taking place under appropriate conditions. There is no absolute causality in these, nor is there a linear functional variability among them. The world is conceived in a circle of mutual circulation and mutual give-and-take, and hence the generation and destruction among the five powers indicate a dynamical structure of harmonization and thus reflect a state of nature in organic interdependence and harmonious balance.

This naturalism of five powers is easily linked to the philosophy of change, namely the *Yijing* tradition. On the one hand, the *yin-yang* distinction is enriched by the five powers in terms of their mutual support and mutual balance; on the other, the five powers theory is enriched by the organic structure of interdependence in the eight trigrams. In fact, we can see that the so called post-heaven (*houtian* 后天) diagram of the trigrams reflects, or perhaps is suggested by, the generative/destructive order in the theory of the five powers. Apart from the distinction between the image-oriented representation of the eight trigrams and the stuff-oriented representation of the five powers, these two theories could naturally merge to form an onto-cosmology of nature and world. Indeed, an onto-cosmology of *yin*, *yang*, and five powers was systematized in the work of Dong Zhongshu (董仲舒) of the second century BCE. This would be the acme of the organic naturalism beginning with the *Chunqiu* period and dating in its turn to the very beginning of the *Yijing* and the five powers theory in the "Hong Fan" chapter of the *Shangshu*.

In this period, a vivid picture of the nature in terms of the activities of *qi* is formed. In the first place, there is the conception of *yin* and *yang* as two *qi* based on observation of the upward movement of growth as *yang* and the downward movement of decline as *yin*. As early as the period of King Yu in Zhou, Pei Yangfu explains the earthquake as a state of "the *yang* crouching cannot get out and the *yin* suppressing cannot evaporate" (*Guoyu*, *Zhouyu* first part). There are also the so-called *liuqi* (six vapors) referring to the natural events of darkening (*yin*), brightening (*yang*), wind, rain, night, and day, which are said to give rise to five tastes and five colors and five sounds.[8] A medical doctor named He used this theory to explain various diseases in terms of various excesses of these *qi*, which indicates the beginning of a medical philosophy on the basis of naturalistic understanding to be completed in the later *Huangdi Neijing* of the Zhanguo period. From many instances like this, we can see how the organic naturalistic beliefs have developed and been applied in understanding both natural and human phenomena or incidents, which would otherwise be interpreted in terms of spirits and fate or the mandate of heaven.

This is indeed a rich tradition that is developed very early and developed very well with good results. What is important to note is that this organic, naturalistic understanding is a result of the "organic and pragmatic attitude" developed from desire to see meaning and relevance of nature for human affairs. But resulting from this attitude is a methodology of "comprehensive observation" (*guan*), which leads to detailed and ordered descriptions of natural events and human experiences in correlation. This perhaps explains the very beginning of the *Yijing*. But as the development of the *Yijing* shows, there comes from this a consciousness of the self-sufficiency of explanation of things and events in naturalistic terms without resorting to spirits or heaven. This naturally contributes to the general gradual replacement of the conception of *tian* (the heaven) by the conception of *dao* (the way) as the ultimate source and ground of explanation of things and happenings in nature and man. Thus, as early as seventh century BCE, Zi Chan had remarked that "The way of heaven is far and the way of man is near" (*Zuozhuan*, Zhao Gong eighteenth year). Combining this organic naturalistic understanding and the pragmatic collective humanistic spirit, a life philosophy of "rectifying one's virtues (*zhengde* 正德), developing utilities (*liyong* 利用) and improving life (*housheng* 厚生)" had been suggested (*Zuozhuan*, Wen Gong seventh year), which harkens back to the early period of the agricultural political culture of the Xia.

In the above we have delineated the two main trends of thinking arising from the historical development of early Chinese culture, which I characterized as the tradition of *li* and the tradition of *zhi*. The tradition of *li* is inner-oriented and society-centered and opens an order of social interdependencies and human inter-subjectivity, a life-world of human values and *telos*, which culminates in the belief and awareness of the heaven and its mandate. On the other hand, the tradition of *zhi* is outer-oriented and nature-centered and opens an order of natural forces and event inter-objectivity. This is also a life-world on a different level, which presents the large world of things from a comprehensive natural point of view detached from human interest as embodied in the *Yijing* organization of the eight trigrams. These two traditions are not really separate or separable, for they together arose from the cultural experience and consciousness of a totality of ordered beings in which human beings form an integral part. Combined, the two traditions thus constitute a totality of inherent balance and harmony to be developed in philosophy as methodology or as ontology when circumstances create appropriate occasions for such development. In this sense, the breakdown of the *Zhouli* is crucial for the philosophical awakening in the classical Chinese philosophy, for it has released the potential for development by weakening the holding and restraining powers of the political and social institutions in the *Zhouli*. This new development is creative and integrative in the sense that the inner resources of *li* and the outer resources of *zhi* can be combined to give rise to new forms of thinking that could be centered in different directions. In the case of political humanism, it is clear that the belief in *tianming* is lost and a new confidence and awareness of human autonomy and self-responsibility set in. Philosophically, this indicates a replacement of the mandate of heaven by the mandate of people: the term was not used by the Confucians until Mencius in his quotation of the *Shangshu*, "A state cannot rely on spirits or the heaven for its existence, but has to survive and thrive on the basis of the support of the people inspired and encouraged by the virtues and wisdom of the ruler." This is indeed an awakening of the human spirit in a collective sense. To enhance the understanding of human existence and its value in terms of this understanding becomes the central task of Confucius and his school. It is to be pointed out that it requires a human ability to see and recognize the moral autonomy of the state independently of the tradition and thus represents an outer-oriented mentality revealed in the *zhi* tradition. In fact, we may even say that it is the development of the *zhi* tradition that makes the humanistic awakening possible and in actuality causes it and strengthens it as well. Thus we can say that the rise of political humanism shows how the two traditions come to a merging and how this merging takes place via the interaction between the two traditions.

In the similar way in which the tradition of *zhi* prompts the tradition of *li* to develop into the political humanism, the tradition of *li* has stimulated the tradition of *zhi* into the development of the organic naturalism. The natural world is given an organic coherence by the internal sense of linkage and relevance informed by the world of *li* and social intersubjectivety. Particularly, when the spell of heaven is removed, the world of nature is revealed as nature qua nature and thus seen as having its own autonomy. This natural autonomy eventually leads to the conception of the *dao* as the ultimate originating source and the sustaining process of things in the world. It is in the *dao* that the spell of heaven has been transformed. But, as in the case of political humanism, the human being is not separate from the world, so that the human being as part of the world is not separate from the *dao*, and the natural forces and processes are regarded similarly as parts of the *dao*. When society is seen as incapable of fulfilling the aspirations of human mind, the return to the *dao* by transcending the social and political becomes the natural consequence of the organic naturalism that is of course the Daoist creed. At this point it is clear that organic naturalism is also a result of the creative integration of the two ancient traditions biased toward nature, instead of man, as in the case of political humanism.

An illuminating case of the creative integration of the two traditions is found in Zi Dashu's reinterpretation of *li* in terms of imitation of nature. Zi Dashu quoted Zi Chan as saying: "*Li* is the canon of heaven, the norm of earth, and the principle which people follow in their action" and then suggested that all the rules of *li* that govern human relationships and behaviors are introduced to match, symbolize, follow, and accord with natural events, natural phenomena, natural processes, and thus to control or balance and edify human emotions and actions and consequently to harmonize with nature of heaven and earth, and to endure (*Zuozhuan*, Zhao Gong twenty-fifth year). This view leads to the reformulation of *li* as embodying and reflecting patterns (*li*) of nature or heaven and earth in the *Liji* and *Guanzi* ("Neiye" chapter).

Axial Thinkers and Formation of Philosophical Schools

In general, we may regard the development of Chinese philosophy in the classical period from 475 to 221 BCE as a creative process in which the two ancient traditions of culture came to interplay in response to the social and political changes of the time. The above-mentioned political humanism and organic naturalism are the natural consequences of this creative process. But they are not philosophical schools; rather, they are the dominating trends that lead to the formation of the philosophical schools. They provide the atmosphere, the incentives, and the cues for the coming period of philosophical blossoming, the blossoming of "a hundred flowers" and the flourishing of "a hundred schools." In a sense, all the philosophical schools are critical responses to the breakdown of the political and social system of the time by drawing inspirations from the resources of political humanism and organic naturalism. This of course does not mean that all philosophical schools are variations of political humanism or organic naturalism or their combinations.

In fact, while we may see political humanism and organic naturalism as two proto-typical positions as well exemplified and further developed by Confucianism and Daoism, they may not exhaust all the possible developments of philosophical positions. We may see them as ways of thinking in which man and nature are made the centers of thinking, and political order and natural harmony are made the goals of human striving. That these ways of thinking may be adopted does not guarantee that they may not produce philosophical positions that modified or even deviated from these positions. In fact, while these two positions may serve as starting points of thinking, they may transform into something quite different and even straightforwardly opposite. This is allowed by the dialectics of the *Yijing* onto-cosmological way of thinking that underlies the organic naturalistic position. Furthermore, the most important factor that could determine the formation of a philosophical position is the experience and insight a thinker has in regard to the impacting problems of political reality. This must be granted: the political reality of disintegration of the *li* order of Zhou and the consequent struggle and competition for political control toward stability is a deep and profound experience no thinker can ignore or can lay aside, even though all thinkers may have resorted to different ways of expression with different focuses.

Mencius expressed the central problem of the time to be political and social stability (*ding*). His perception and insight into this problem are that the world will be "stabilized by being unified" (*ding yu yi*). Hence the central problem of the time is how the world is to be unified. This is the same goal as well illustrated by the Zhou order of *li*. If one wants to enjoy the stability and order as in the Zhou, one has to face the problem of unifying different states in that time. This seems to be the underlying wish and assumption of all the philosophical schools, for all their thinkers are confronted with this problem as a pressing life-issue. This problem becomes growingly acute and pressing as time goes by. Thus, by the time of the fourth century BCE, the focus of political and philosophical thinking had become very much centered on the task of unification as an ideal state of social well-being. This is how Legalism arises and gradually assumes a dominating role in approaching the problem of unification.

Legalism developed from combining and comparing various earlier schools of philosophy such as Confucianism, Mohism, and Daoism. It absorbed different ideas from these various schools. From Confucianism, it adopted centering on controlling the masses by authority and the doctrine of evil nature of man (Xunzi). From Moism, it adopted the principle of equality and utilitarianism. From Daoism, it took up the principle of non-action (*wuwei* 无为). Yet the most important factor determining the orientation and substance of the Legalist thinking is the consideration of the urgent need for a centralized and unified government. Hence the Legalist position becomes realistic, utilitarian, non-humanistic, and perhaps even non-naturalistic. Yet one still can see how it is related to the two main resources of cultural consciousness.

Legalism is not the only school that evolved into something new from the past. Mohism in the earlier time had learned a good deal from Confucianism, but it had become a new type of social and political philosophy that in one sense is ultra-conservative because of the Mohist belief in the *tianzhi* (will of heaven) and yet in another sense is very much forward-looking and realistic, which is partly compatible with both the humanistic outlook and the organic-naturalistic way of thinking and partly not so compatible.

Apart from the four major schools mentioned above, the Chinese classical period also saw the emergence of the Name School (*Mingjia* 名家), the *Yinyang Wuxing* (阴阳五行) School, the Military Strategy School (*Bingjia* 兵家), the Agronomy School (*Nongjia* 农家), and the Diplomatic School (*Zonghengjia* 纵横家), which constitute, together with Daoism, Confucianism, Mohism, and Legalism, the nine schools of thought in the classical period. The Military Strategy School and the Diplomatic School are realist and applied schools of practical thought. Even though there are theoretical components of these schools, these schools consist in applying fundamental principles of the *Yijing* to practical matters for the purpose of finding a solution to a realistic issue or problem. The Agronomy School represents a political and social philosophy that dates to the ancient practice of non-separation of labors. It is motivated as a solution to the problem of how to reconstruct or construct a political form of governmental control. This leaves the *Yinyang Wuxing* School and the Name School to be explained.

It is clear that the *Yinyang Wuxing* School as headed by Zou Yan is a natural product of interest in applying the empirical theory of five powers and the cosmic philosophy of the *yinyang* developed by the *Yijing*. It is basically a cosmological theory and a philosophy of history, which is quite compatible with political humanism and organic naturalism, and may be actually encouraged by ideas and views of political humanism and organic naturalism.

As for the Name School (mingjia 名家), it may be said that the school originates from the issue on the relation of name (*ming*) to actuality (*shi*). This issue becomes a central problem for philosophical schools because this problem is closely related to the problem of reconstructing name and/or actuality to accommodate the disintegrated Zhou order of *li*, which originally embodied the unity and correspondence of *ming* with *shi*. It is also clear that the Name School, as represented by Gongsun Long, does not face up to the challenges of political humanism and organic naturalism, but can be seen as a direct or indirect response to the disintegration of the social and political reality of the time.

We may now organize these philosophical schools in terms of their positions and views in relation to solutions of problems bearing upon society and government. In the first place, it needs to be pointed out that for each philosophical school, we must pay attention to the founding person who has presented insightful views on human nature, human destiny, history, society, government, and the world. Hidden in these views we can also glimpse into his understanding and experience of the material, personal, social, and political reality of his time. Although there is some intimate relation between his self-reflection, convictions, aspirations, and evaluations on the real world of his time and the theoretical thoughts of his philosophy, this relation creating a unity of his thoughts and the whole person, there is no clear causal link of the thinker's social, political, or even economic situation with his self-understanding and theoretical thinking. As a thinker, he should reflect the whole age and whole world in which he finds himself, and at the same time he should also think and speak for the whole age and the whole world to which he belongs. In such thinking and speaking, he presents the underlying humanity in the universal forms of ideas and principles, which go beyond his age and his world and yet mold and shape his age and the world or the age and the world to come.

In fact, we must see that in their times and relative to their backgrounds, all these founding thinkers became what they are, whether Daoist, Confucian, Mohist, or Legalist, and had specially lent themselves to such molding and shaping efficacies, because they were "reality in making," be it social, political, or spiritual. There is a special fluidity and a special transformability that allow different approaches to thinking through the problems and issues presented by the time and the world. These are the age and the world as we have mentioned in which there were the disintegration of the form and the emancipation of energy at the same time. These are the age and the world that have presented a point of epochal inflection that could go down the drains or might reach to the skies. Which thought or idea or view comes to catch on as the most possible and most needed depends upon the time and the world as well as the nature of human thinking.

In historical retrospection, both the classical age and the classical thinker in that age who played the founding role for a school of philosophy warranted the special distinction of standing out for trans-valuation of values and reconstruction of tradition or for creation of new standards and new paradigms. Karl Jaspers called the age of this type the "axial age" for mankind. In the same vein, we may call the thinker of that age the "axial thinker." We may thus see that all the philosophers, especially the noted and influential ones, in this classical period of Chinese history are the "axial thinkers," who have responded critically to their age and the world of their time, and who have developed directions and visions on a trans-valuation of values for the whole humanity. They did this based on what I have described as the creative integration of the *li* and *zhi* traditions. What is creative in their insights and convictions is derived from their existential involvement with the world and humanity. They are critically responding to a pervasive crisis of the social, political, and human disintegration, opening up to all possibilities that call for evaluation and transformation of reality.

Whether an "axial thinker" must reflect a social class or a social background in a causal manner is not to be absolutely determined. There is neither reason nor conclusive evidence to believe that an "axial thinker" is confined to the interests and feelings of the social class to which he belongs. He is a member of the world, a member of a whole society, a member of a social class, a resident of a special locality, and an individual person at the same time. To call him an "axial thinker" is to underscore the fact that he thinks for the world, a whole society, a social class, a special locality, and himself at the same time. We need not see the philosopher as being merely engaged in the ideological struggle for his class in the social and political reality of this time. We must see particularity in universality and vice versa; otherwise we could not understand the nature of "axial thinking" and the nature of an "axial thinker." In other words, we do not have to subscribe to the Marxist interpretation of the philosophical thinking in the Chinese classical period. But, on the other hand, there is no harm in acknowledging the existential links of theoretical views and insights of the philosophical schools with the axial thinker's self-understanding and evaluation of his age and the world as well as the social and political reality of his age in voicing his views and insights as critical responses to the social and political reality of his age. For the social and political reality did provide an occasion and incentive for his theoretical views and insights with a hidden dimension of self-understanding and evaluation of his age.

Another characteristic of the "axial thinker" is that the axial thinker is able to exercise influence on his generation and the succeeding generations in a natural and spontaneous way. There is no political maneuvering of his thinking for influence, because it is not ideology, nor is it created as ideology. It is a creation on the social and cultural level, not on the political level. The philosophical influence it captures comes out through social and cultural channels such as teaching, lecturing, and conversation or dialogue in a basically academic or intellectual environment. It is in this natural and open communication with society and culture and even humanity at large that a seminal philosophical idea may capture the feeling and provoke the thinking in others, particularly the young generation, and hence a philosophical school would be formed as a natural consequence. In fact, when we speak of the philosophical school (*jia* 家) in the Chinese classical period, we are only able to do so in a retrospective way. For the "axial thinker" did not normally perceive himself as forming a school, particularly at the early stage of the formation of the school. In fact, it is by the time of Mencius, and even by the still later time of Xunzi and Zhuangzi, that we come to see the term "*jia*" being used. There is no reference to the "*jia*" in the time of Laozi and Confucius. The conclusion to be drawn from this observation is that Chinese philosophical schools are formed from the natural spreading of ideas that reflects both the social and cultural trends of the time and the appeal of the ideal and ideas of the "axial thinkers" as founders of the schools.

Given the above understanding of the "axial thinking" and the formation of philosophical schools in the Late Chunqiu to Warring States period, we may now see how major Chinese philosophers as "axial thinkers" came into being and how their philosophies as "axial thinking" are developed as critical responses to the social and political reality of their times on the one hand, and as disclosures of human values based on underlying human potentialities on the other. We may in fact distinguish three types of critical responses among these philosophers, each of which represents an attitude of critique and valuation of the confronted or given social and political reality of the time as well as an effort toward replacement or reform of such reality. We may indeed also regard each type as indicating a historical stage of the evolution of the social and political reality of the time and thus representing a typical critical response to that historical stage of the period.

The first type of the critical response is to abandon the social and political reality of the time and thus in this sense to transcend the social and political reality in a quest for something totally remote or absolutely utopian. This also implies a thorough critique and rejection of the status quo, whether political, social, or cultural, from a point of view that makes this critique and rejection meaningful, not only possible. This means that this rejection and abandoning are those of the social and political reality per se and in so doing presupposing or revealing a deeper reality, the reality of nature or the *dao* (the way). One may also say that the social and political crisis of the period has prompted the philosopher's insight into reality on the level of nature and thus leads to a radical criticism of culture, knowledge, humanity, and society of the time. This is the position of Daoism as initiated and represented by the *Daodejing* of Laozi in the sixth century BCE.

In the *Daodejing*, there are two main themes: first, the deconstruction and critique of human knowledge and cultural artificiality and their consequential desire-ridden struggles; second, the disclosure or presentation of an onto-cosmological point of view that shows the selfless, desireless, speechless, ceaseless creativity of life and truth. The former theme leads to the idealization of a government of non-interference, no-government, or non-action. The latter theme leads to a full-scale philosophy or metaphysics of *dao*. In the long run, the *dao*-metaphysics has had profound impact and influence. It set the stage for the development of a more systematic thought about reality at large and in the ultimate, which gives new meaning to life and death and transforms philosophies such as Buddhism and Neo-Confucianism. Of course, the philosophy of the *dao* does not arise in arbitrariness. It arises as a continuous expansion and elaboration of the organic naturalism we mentioned above. It is in the *dao* concept that all things in the world become thoroughly integrated.

It is clear that all things can be understood as coordinated and interacting in a certain way. Like a multiple body problem in modern physics, the problem of coordinating all things in the world requires a force and a process far greater than any known single principle to be observed among things. Yet the insight into the *dao* is to see both the totality of things in coordination as well as the coordination of all things and anything. The coordinating force is conceived in terms of polarities of the *yin* and *yang* and the transformation of polarities in things. As a whole, the process of the *dao* exhibits dialectical interaction, reversion, regeneration, and boundless harmonization and balance. However, to see all these and to grasp their meanings and usefulness requires insight into the invisible hidden sides of things, their inceptive movements as well as their infinite involvements with one another. It is to see things of being (*you*) as being of things that is generated from the void (*wu*) or the nonbeing without forms or substances, for the *dao* as the coordination of things and as source of movements of things cannot be said to be being in any substantial sense. Thus, in general, Laozi proclaims: "The *dao* which can be spoken is not the constant *dao*; the name which can be named is not the constant name" (*Daodejing*, chapter 1). Speaking and naming change the nature of things, and there is a stage where there is no name and no speaking and hence no-thing. It is important to note that the *dao* of Laozi has finally replaced the notion of heaven (*tian*) as the ultimate reality for philosophy and to a large extent for common society. The process of depersonalization of the *tian* in the organic naturalism has reached its height in the philosophy of the *dao*. From this it is also noted that the *dao*-metaphysics continues the tradition of, and is nurtured by, the philosophy of the *Yijing* and in its turn enriches and nourishes the philosophy of the *Yijing*.

Because the philosophy of the *dao* in Laozi is deconstructive in regard to the social and political reality of the time, it can be plausibly said to be the earlier or first response to the disintegration and collapse of the *li* order of the Zhou. The despair and the distrust in the social and political bespeak a stage in which the crisis of a collapse of the long-term and whole fabric of stability has caused in a trusting and sensitive mind. In this sense we may place Laozi as the first "axial thinker" of the period. The project of Laozi's "axial thinking" can be said to be deconstructive, hermitic, and transcendental. His critical response to the social and political can be likewise labeled. Zhuangzi follows Laozi in suit (as Zhuangzi himself acknowledges). But Zhuangzi takes a more sophisticated attitude toward the social and political world. He can accept the reality at its face value but relativizes it to the world of the *dao* and thus enjoys his roaming and wandering into it without attachment and anxiety. He is even able to discover infinitely many relativist worlds in the world of the *dao* and thus reaches a spiritual freedom that has no counterpart in the realist world of society and politics.

Now we come to the second type of critical response to the social and political reality of the time. This is the Confucian response of *reconstruction*. Instead of deconstructing, abandoning, or rejecting the social and political reality, Confucius, based on his cultural experience and historical reflection, comes to see redeeming values of the tradition of *li*. Even though the Zhou *li* of the past cannot be fully restored, for Confucius it is important to develop and cultivate the spirit of *li* for setting the society and politics into a correct form and channel. Confucius also discovers the existence and power of *ren*, namely, a power of moral transformation of the human individual in his relation and transaction with other men. The Confucian faith is that, if each individual is able to develop this *ren* quality, he is able to restore and reformulate *li* on a social and cultural level and therefore to reconstruct the world of human harmony and human values in which each has a place of worth and an environment for self-realization and self-fulfillment.

What is *ren* 仁 in the Confucian philosophy? *Ren* is the defining quality of humanity that has the power of expanding humanity from the center of an individual to a community of well-ordered human relationships and harmonious fellowship, in which each individual will be better developed and each life better fulfilled. Being anguished by the collapse of the social order of *li*, Confucius searched for a foundation and a source of the *li* that he felt was needed for reestablishment of the *li* and reconstruction of the integrity of the society and government. He had found *ren* in the sensibility, feeling, and power of human care for others as well as for the total benefit of the society. He appropriated this concept from the affective tradition of political humanism in which the ruler is to act benevolently toward his people so that his rule can be justified and safeguarded. But, by contrast with the political humanist attitude, Confucius transformed this political *ren* into a moral and human *ren*.

There are three points to be made about this transformation. First, the compassion and benevolence toward people as a whole is now enlarged to include feeling and action toward individual persons in society and thus is not confined to the performance of the ruler alone. Second, it is not the ruler alone who is capable of practicing *ren* or should practice *ren*. All human persons are capable of practicing *ren* and should practice *ren* in order to be more human and more humanized. This means that humanity and goodness of an individual is invested in the common good and goodness or well-being of the society and other persons. *Ren* therefore enables an individual to be a ruler of his own and a moral ruler in setting examples and standards of good and right. Third, *ren* is seen to be the internal power of a human person that can be exercised at will and that requires constant care and attention to grow into a perfection that pertains to the growth of the human person. In this way a new concept of human person is introduced; namely, a human person is capable of moral and spiritual growth or perfectibility apart from his physical growth. Whereas there is a limitation of the physical growth of a person, there is no limitation of his moral or spiritual growth that has its symptomatic approach to the ideal person called the sage (*shengren* 圣人).

What matters most for a person is his continuous and never-to-be-forgotten effort to achieve *ren* in his life, and in doing so he is called the "morally ruling person" (*junzi*).⁹ On the other hand, if a person fails to pay attention to the cultivation of *ren*, the quality or power in him that makes him care for society or community of people, and if instead he only cares for his immediate personal profits and material well-being, he is called the "small person" (*xiaoren* 小人).

It is Confucius's insightful discovery that all human persons have *ren* 仁. It is no less an important discovery that *ren* 仁 is the basis and the foundation for *li* 礼. Confucius had not discussed how *li* reveals *ren*. But he nevertheless came to see that *ren* is a road toward practice of *li*. In this sense of *li*, *li* is not necessarily any given set of prescribed rules or institutions of social order, it is the morally and culturally needed or required norm and decorum for harmonization of human relationships in society as well as the social order embodied in proper institutions. *Li* as such enables human persons to avoid uncivilized fights and conflicts and provides nourishment and moral space for moral and spiritual growth of each person. It is in this sense that Confucius speaks of *ren* as "overcoming the self and practicing the *li*." To overcome the self is to discipline and control the self lest it acts on self-interest alone or acts on personal desires in matters of social relationships. This requires the person to always reduce self-interests for the benefit of others and the society. Thus one will be able to care for others and do things benevolent to others. This means leaving space for and giving respect to others. Allowing space and giving respect to others precisely constitute the spirit of *li*.

To find the proper rule or proper form of this *li*-spirit requires understanding history, culture, convention, and custom and thus requires respecting historicity and culture at large. But in this sense of establishing the *li*, not only will the tradition and history have restored their importance and their places in society, but the creativity and wisdom of the individual will also come to play a useful role. This is how a *li* can be restored and reconstructed or even revised, modified, or added for the benefit and consequently for the goodness and well-being of society.

There are other meanings of *ren* that make *ren* the foremost and constant virtue to be cultivated, not only for an unmediated bearing on human actions but also for mediated relevance to all social, moral, and political norms. In other words, although *ren* is manifested in loving all human persons (*airen* 爱人) and doing things for the benefit of others and not doing things that would hurt others, the intended effect of *ren* in terms of social harmony and preservation of culture is preserved or made possible via other virtues such as *li* 礼, *yi* 义, *zhong* 忠, and *xiao* 孝, et cetera. In this sense, *ren* should be the source and basis for other virtues and should be also the completion and perfection of all virtues. In analyzing the relation of *ren* to *li*, we have seen that *ren* provides the impetus for *li* reform in that *ren* would create and found new *li*. It is in the same vein that *ren* can be said to create and found other virtues insofar as it is the ultimate source and ultimate justification of other virtues. We may regard *ren* as the formless and most centralized or most internalized virtue that always requires expression and exteriorization by way of other virtues, or, to put it the other way, the articulation of *ren* in any form calls forth consideration of or creation of another virtue. Thus, for externalized form of an action we have *li*. But before one sets on an outer form of action, one has to determine the right or proper way of acting toward a person, even though one has the motive and objective in benefiting the person and/or the society. The right and proper way of action calls for a close analysis, knowledge, and understanding of the circumstances and action, as well as the person to which the action is directed. It calls for an objective assessment of the situation as well as a volitional commitment to one's judgment so that one's action will be consistent with the total understanding and perception of the total order of things. This is then the spirit of *yi* as a virtue in the sense of rightness or propriety on the objective side and justice and righteousness on the subjective side. In this sense *yi* substantiates *li* and manifests *ren*.

Relative to *li* (practicing), *yi* is the essence of *li*-action, just as relative to *yi*, *li* is the realization of *yi*-perception/thought. But relative to *ren*, *yi* is the objectification of *ren*, just as relative to *yi*, *ren* is the motivating force of *yi*. One thus sees the graduated relation toward outer expression in *ren* > *yi* > *li* and gradated relation toward internalization in *li* < *yi* < *ren*. Because *li* is ultimately rooted in *ren*, an accepted or received *li* can be seen to point to a judgment of propriety or properness in *yi* as mediation. *Yi* is the mediation between *li* and *ren* just as *li* is the consummation of *ren* and *yi*, and *ren* is the motivation and integration of *li* and *yi*. These relations form a mutually enriching and complementary circularity and trinity among the three virtues once they are formed and demarcated in relation to one another, even though we have to also recognize at the same time the originative unity of the three in *ren*.

In understanding this, two further remarks can be made. First, in distinguishing between *li* and *yi*, one need also to point out that whereas *li* is role and status oriented in light of societal order, *yi* is reason and thinking oriented in light of a reflection on the meaning of the social structure or social order by a person. Second, *ren* can be seen to be the core and the beginning for *li* and *yi* and by the same token for all other virtues, and thus can be seen as the defining nature of a human person. It is through Mencius that this defining of nature of a human person is expressed in direct intuition and experience of fundamental moral feelings, whereas this defining is seen in the *Zhongyong* as metaphysically derived and based on the original or originating creativity of the ultimate reality called heaven to be titled the "mandate of heaven." In any case, *ren* eventually becomes the ultimate potential and sustaining nature of a human person. It is by way of this retracing that one can see how *ren* can be metaphysically or onto-cosmologically conceived as the onto-cosmic nature of the *dao* of heaven and thus the principle and way of life-creativity.

Second, as *ren* can be seen as a process of concretely realizing and expanding the nature of a person in external and actual form and substance, *ren* is conceived as ultimately articulated in the concrete personal form of the sage (*shengren*). In this sense *ren* is the most concrete and most perfect "form" of all virtues and thus the final embodiment and integration of all virtues.

Without too much detail, one can see how *zhi* (intelligence and wisdom) and *xin* (integrity and faithfulness) become the other two vital Confucian virtues in the Confucian system of personal, social, and cosmic ethics. In order to make correct judgment about action toward *yi* and *li*, one needs *zhi* to work with. *Zhi* is the resource and thinking power for correctly determining values of things and for correctly seeing truth of affairs. It can be seen thus as the first and primary power of objectification in distinction from the primary power of subjectification in *ren* even though *ren* is still the rooting nature of a person. Thus we can see the placement of *zhi* as an intermediary between *ren* and *yi*.

Finally, *xin* is the self-reflection of self-sufficiency of *ren* as a virtue ultimately rooted in nature of man and the heaven. It is the faith bridging the subjective and the objective that makes judgment and knowledge, decision-making and action possible. It is thus the very initiating state as well as the final state of existence for all virtues as actualities. In fact, it is the sustaining base for realization of all virtues, which is inherently embodied or present in all virtues. It is specifically an integral part of *ren* that entitles *ren* to social self-justification and social self-expression. Hence *xin* can be called the hidden virtue-making virtue that expresses itself in any action of nature of man and in any accomplishment of a virtue in a society. In this way we can regard *xin* as another name for initiation and integration of virtues as realization of a social order.

Confucius had paid attention to *zhi* and *xin* but not at a great length, yet the importance of these concepts and their final incorporation into the core system of the Confucian ethics via later Confucians' thinking leave no doubt for us to say that they deserve mention in the ontogenetic analysis of the Confucian philosophy.[10] We have gone to great length in describing the Confucian position in terms of the Confucian ethics. The significance of this effort is to accentuate the social and political orientation of the Confucian position in contrast to the Daoist. Unlike Laozi, Confucius did not wish to give up or bypass society and government as a way toward solving the social and political problem for the time being or once and for all. Although not denying the relevance of the natural and the transcendent, he sees the necessary redeeming value of a social and political system for fulfilling and realizing the value of a human person. In fact, he sees society and government as necessary instruments for such realization. But unlike the political humanist, Confucius wants to base the social and political on the moral perfection or moral cultivation towards perfection of individual persons. In doing so, he would give society and government a human and moral foundation and motivation. And in so doing he is also able to retrieve *li* from the past for the use of the present as well as to deliver *li* from a foundational source of the humanity of individual persons. This last point serves to mark out Confucius as a philosopher who is engaged in the enterprise of *reconstructing* the social and the political on the basis of the human and the moral.

There are two senses of this *reconstruction*. First, he wishes to reconstruct the *li* of the social and political from the humanity of *ren*. Second, he wishes to *reconstruct* the *li* of the social and political from the existing culture and history, in combination with the creative force of *ren* of the individual. In both of these senses Confucius vindicated himself as a *reconstructionist* or *retrievalist* in his approach to the problem of his times. His philosophy is both an answer to the urgent issue of his times and an answer to the perennial problem of relating the individual to the society and government on the one hand and to the culture and tradition or history on the other.

Because his reconstructionist or reformist position links the past with the present, the concrete mundane with the principled thinking, Confucius is seen as a conservative from the progressive-minded and only-forward-looking philosophers such as the Legalist, but as a utopian enthusiast from an anarchist transcendentalist position such as the Daoist. In reality, the Confucian position has its traditional elements and its innovative force. But given the pressing tendency and need of the time, he was not ready to fully meet the needs of the time and thus ended with disappointment and frustration over his failures to attract political implementation. But he had succeeded to awaken and inspire posterity to the way of the mean and the way of harmonizing and integration of stability and creativity, the form and content for a full realization of humanity on both a social and a human level.

After Confucius, Mencius developed the philosophy of *yi* and the philosophy of nature of humanity to a full extent. He stressed the inner creative force of nature of humanity (*xing*), which is equivalent to *ren* in a broad sense. But in doing so he stressed the inner point of view at the expense of the outer point of view represented by Confucius's consideration of learning (*xue*) and *li*. It is not until Xunzi that elements such as learning and *li* are paid close attention to and become largely emphasized. Xunzi developed a full philosophy of social and political institution founded on his full philosophy of *xue* (learning) and *li*. In constructing his philosophy, he also came to see the importance of *zhi* and rationality of mind. Thus we can regard Xunzi as a *rationalist humanist* in distinction from Mencius as an *idealist humanist*. It is quite possible that in stressing the social elements of conditioning, Xunzi may fail to give proper account of the creative force of the nature of man and thus opens the way toward the full *constructionist* view of human nature and human society in the Legalist philosophy.

Before we confront the Legalist view, we should also note that the post-Confucius work *Liji* endeavors to develop a full theory of society and political reconstruction on the basis of self-cultivation (via the chapter titled *Daxue*) and to explore the metaphysical foundation of human nature and its onto-cosmological source and expression (via the chapter titled *Zhongyong*), perhaps in conjunction with the writings of the *Commentaries* on the *Yijing*. The significances of such efforts will not be tackled here. This is merely to indicate how the Confucian reconstructionist position had initiated and inspired a large school of philosophical and cultural thinking whose impact and influence are beyond Confucius's own generation.

Next to Confucianism, we may mention Mohism as representing a variation of the reconstructionist point of view. Mozi had learned Confucianism in his early years, but seeing the ineptitude and self-complacency of many Confucians in his time, he formulated his own social philosophy of universal love (*jianai*) and mutual benefit, and his political philosophy of heavenly will (*tianzhi*) and willful conformity in his zest to reform and save the society. He was not only a thinker but also a person of action, for he tried to implement what he believed and thus started the Mohist community, which was economically self-sufficient, craftsmanship-oriented, and militarily prepared for just wars.

The utilitarian, practical attitude combined with a rational mentality, geared for persuasion and defensive argumentation, had eventually transformed the Mohists into Neo-Mohists, who became the forerunners of logic and science in early China. The reason why we characterize Mozi as reconstructionist is that Mozi had redeemed the ancient belief in *tianming* and stressed the importance of society and government, but introduced new methods of thinking and judgment for reconstructing the presently disintegrated society.

We now come to the *constructionist* position of Legalism. By constructionism I mean the efforts to conscientiously construct laws, methods, skills, and conditions for the ordering of society and rule of people after a thorough critique and rejection of relevancies of history and culture. To construct requires systematic rationality on the one hand and will to power on the other. Both presuppose a clear determination regarding the objectives of state and society. In the classical period of Chinese history, the rise of the Legalist constructionism was not accidental. It begins with Shang Yang's doctrine of rule by *fa* (law). *Fa* is not law legislated by people or people's representatives in modern democracies. It consists of commands and regulations that dictate what is to be done and what is not to be done in the interests of the objectives of the state and the ruler. Hence *fa* is basically commanding and regulatory and pertains to matters of punishment and awards. In an extended sense, *fa* includes institutions that organize resources and people for the strengthening and enrichment of the state and the ruler. Hence farming and warring become the two major areas covered by *fa*.

In short, the essence of *fa* is found in the central control of people and society by the state or the ruler in terms of organization, regulations, rules of action, and means of punishment and awards. It is based on the social psychology of conditioning and egoistic ethics of self-interest and fear. *Fa* is *efficacious* insofar as it is under the control of the state and the state has the power to enforce the *fa*. Thus it is through the rule by *fa* that an objective of state can be efficiently attained. We may call this constructive attitude in society and politics "political realism," which is a flat denial of humanism, whether political or moral.

The doctrine of *fa* proved successful in the state of Qin and in other states. By the time of Han Fei, it was widely perceived that *fa* is the most powerful tool for achieving a state goal, and the use of *fa* had created a powerful machine of control in the state of Qin. In response to the need of time, it was clear that the old *li* has disintegrated so much so that there was no way to make it back, certainly not by the reconstructive programs of education and moral cultivation of the Confucian school, nor by the altruist and chivalrous efforts of the community-oriented Mohists. What was needed was a powerful state to have the authority and means to implement a social order that guarantees stability and peaceful living. It is apparent that in envisioning the need of unification of the whole China and the means for unification by *fa*, the Legalist had realistically responded to the issue of the time. It is the reason why Han Fei had attracted the attention of the First Emperor of Qin. In saying this, we may see Legalism as the product of the most realistic historical forces of the time, while it denies the relevance of a history of past for the use of the present. In stating the historical development of rule by *fa*, I wish to point to the historical trend and the background for the dialectical formation of schools from Laozi to Han Fei.

Apart from promotion of *fa*, the Legalist had seen the importance of *shu* (skills of control and management) and *shi* (position and situation) for exercising efficient control of ministers and subjects in attaining the state objectives. Shen Buhai stresses the importance of *shu* primarily for the ruler's discriminating between goodness and badness, that is, the ability or inability of his ministers. Shen Dao, on the other hand, points to the importance of position a ruling person occupies. A position commands a certain power of coercion and persuasion. But the power of coercion and persuasion comes from other factors such as titles and trust and influences one may hold with regard to certain people or to people in general. All these pertain to the idea of *shi*, a power position whether one recognizes it or not. But both Shen Bu Hai and Shen Dao are also strongly for rule by *fa*. It is evident that for them *fa* is primary. *Shu* and *shi* are vital elements needed for the successful rule by *fa* because they pertain to the effective control by *fa*. In Han Fei, *fa* is primary, but one needs *shi* to enact the *fa* and implement *fa*, or make *fa* a tool of rule. How to apply *fa* in a given situation for a certain goal is a matter of *shu*. In this fashion the three are unified for establishing the Legalist philosophy of control and leadership, which for Han Fei and other Legalists should suffice to reach the realist goals and change the present order of society under the pressure of present order of things.

There are certain things needed to be said about Legalism. First, all the Legalists reject institutions of the past and appeal to new ways of governing and control. Specifically, they reject the Confucian ethics of befriending relatives and respecting the highly placed. This means that they rejected the *li* that is based on human emotion. *Fa* is based on utility and rationality that has no consideration of emotion and human relations. This is the constructive side of this arrangement. Second, Legalists look to the future and explain the past history in terms of evolution. In this sense, history, tradition, and culture would play little role in the construction of the social and political reality. Third, Han Fei has insights into the nature of man in that man is basically for himself (*ziwei*) and thus can be motivated and molded by consideration of self-interest, fear, and desire under conditions of *fa*. This is a behaviorist approach to human nature that is not considered either good or bad in any metaphysical sense. Fourth, given the constructive view of history and society, Han Fei criticized other schools, specifically Confucianism and Mohism, as "foolish and false learning" and as "useless disputes." His principle of criticism was to scrutinize many facts in order to see whether names match them. It was apparent to him that the social and political reality of his time did not match nor warrant either the Confucian program or the Mohist program of reconstruction. Tradition, no matter how we reconstruct it, would not generate the needed power or drive for social progress and political control.

Although Han Fei had developed a highly constructive view of society and government, he was not a positivist and remained interested in the nature of the world. In fact, his philosophy included an important proportion of metaphysics and dialectics. Perhaps, under the indirect influence of the *Yijing* and the direct influence of Laozi, Han Fei had come to develop a dialectics on three levels.

On the first level, the level of nature, there are co-existing polarities such as large and small, square and circle, et cetera, which Han Fei calls "pattern" (*li*). They are opposites that form a unity or continuum to which individual things belong and in terms of which individual things find their natural positions. But no thing is determined on a fixed point, and everything will change according to dialectical laws of transformation from opposite to opposite under relevant conditions. This implies that it is in the nature of things to change, and change takes place when things have reached their utmost development or when other external conditions for change obtain. This point is no clearer than on the level of human existence.

On the human level, it is clear that there is no absolute perfection, for every person has his limitations and weaknesses. Han Fei says, "There is a point where wisdom cannot help; there is a point where force cannot raise, and there is a point where the strong cannot win" ("*Guanxing*" chapter). It is also evident that opposites will naturally transform toward each other. For Han Fei, the Laozi saying "Misfortune is where good fortune resides and good fortune is where misfortune is hidden" means that unless one is in control of oneself and watches oneself carefully, the transformation will take place because the conditions for transformation will naturally obtain. Human persons are easily prone to go to extremes. When this happens, weaknesses ingress into their situations. This is the principle of "things will reverse when developed to extremes."

On the third level, the level of prudence and wisdom, a person should be aware of the dialectical principles of transformation from opposite to opposite, and make efforts to apply them to one's actions and to human affairs in general. This means that a person should come to know the specific conditions of transformation for each human action and human affair, and in doing so come to follow the *dao* and obey the objective order of things (*li*).[11] Han Fei stressed the importance of planning and design for the purpose of control in light of knowledge of things and their potentiality for change. This utilitarian and constructivist attitude toward control marks out his difference from the Daoist position on spontaneity and natural conformity.

Han Fei had basically followed Laozi in accepting the metaphysics of the *dao*. It is natural to understand why Han Fei the great Legalist comes to absorb Daoism into his philosophy. Not only did he need a justification for his philosophy of *fa*, but he also needed an ultimate principle for the practical application of *fa*. *Dao* as source of everything with its dialectical principles of transformation serves this purpose. The grounding of *fa* on the *dao* and the grounding of application of *fa* on the *dao* are absolutely and logically required. In fact, the idea of "doing everything by doing nothing" (*wuwei er wubuwei*) gives rise to the ideal of an invisible ruler in perfect and absolute control without making any effort. Yet, as natural as this ideal seems to be, it cannot be really attained, because a ruler, unlike the *dao*, is not totally free from his desires and feelings, and thus cannot achieve the state of non-action either in formation of *fa* or in application of his *fa* by means of *shu* or *shi*. In this sense, the Legalist attitude contradicts the Daoist position. It is to be noted that Han Fei, unlike Laozi, stressed the contrariness of some opposites that requires a solution in terms of struggle and overcoming. Whichever among the two will succeed is to be seen in time. But in Han Fei's effort in reinterpreting Laozi one sees Han Fei's wish to resolve this contradiction to his advantage.

It is interesting however to see how Han Fei has strived to absorb the Daoist metaphysics and its *deconstructive* wisdom into his *constructive* philosophy of social and political control. For this purpose he introduces the notion of objective principle of things in their natural and specific contexts, namely the notion of *li* (pattern, order, reason). Although the term "*li*" had been used earlier in Shang Yang's writings, it is Han Fei who raises *li* to the level of metaphysical understanding. For him, *li* is the pattern whereby a thing becomes a thing ("*Jie Lao*" chapter in *Han*

Feizi). The ten thousand things all have their different *li* simply because they are different things. What is then the relation between the *dao* and the *li*? The answer is that *dao* is the totality and receptacle of *li* to which *li* belongs and on which *li* depends (ibid.). Whereas *li* is more or less fixed, though changing according to change of things, *dao* is always changing in time and in fact should form the motive force for the change of things. Thus *dao* and *li* are related in terms of patterns emerging from changing things, for particularity rises and resides in universality.

With this understanding of *li*, Han Fei comes to found his philosophy of social and political control on the methodology of "understand/embody the *dao*" (*didao*), "follow the *li*" (*luli*), "deepen one's wisdom" (*zhishen*), "reach for a strategy or plan" (*jide*), and finally "become capable of controlling all things" (*neng you wanwu*). If one is able to control everything, he will win out against his enemies ("*Jie Lao*" chapter in *Han Feizi*). The highest goal of Han Fei in constructive philosophy is to use constructively the *dao* for the purpose of implementing *fa* toward successful control.

It is interesting to note that Legalism as the last major response to the reality of the time shows a return to Daoism, albeit a return for the incorporation of Daoism for political use. This shows a defeat of the original purpose of deconstruction, emancipation, and abandonment in Daoism. The deconstructive has been constructed or in a sense reconstructed, but not in the Confucian sense of appropriating the tradition of *li*. This suggests a practical ending of the classical period of the philosophical thinking as a critical response to the world of the time. In this ending, culture and history are suspended or *aufheben* in the interests of realist social and political construction. Philosophy becomes a matter of casting social and political policies.

The state of Qin succeeded in unification of China in 221 BCE and had answered the urgent issue of the time. But time would not stop for this: when this purpose was served, an opposite movement was to begin. What is suppressed for the supreme political construction now comes back to play its proper role, for there are far more abundant forces of change and needs in social and individual entities that are beyond the scope of the Legalist constructionism. Hence, the Legalist construction finally exhausted its span of time and a new age of deconstruction and reconstruction set in. This is the coming back of the *dao* and the *li* as well as the setting of the stage for the grand reconstructive enterprise of Han Confucianism.

Concluding Remarks

In the above we have analyzed and discussed the rise of Daoism, Confucianism, Mohism, and Legalism as four major schools of philosophy arising from the matrix of the early Zhou culture consisting of the tradition of *li* and the tradition of *zhi* as well as from a critical response to this cultural matrix. Different times and different social and political awareness differentiate these positions, and yet there is nevertheless abundance of innovative creativity. There is also inner logic in this web of schools that follows and embodies the dialectical principles of transformation. The whole story of origination suggests the creative development of a cultural *taiji* into opposite and complementary forms of difference. But in a historical course of development, these complementary forms also appear to be contradictory and competitive. Which form will dominate at which time and under what conditions is for the creativity in history to determine. What is clear is that there is no historical determinism of everything, but rather that there are always co-determining forces that include human participation and human self-determination. In this sense, the origins of Chinese philosophy consist of creative efforts to reach totality, stability, balance, and harmony in an ever-fluid context of social, political, moral, and historical developments. There are many other schools that we did not discuss. But it suffices to say that they all fall under the same spell of historical and political co-determination. Even the School of Names (*Ming Jia*) cannot be understood without this backdrop. This means that in Chinese philosophy there is the uncut umbilicus from which all philosophical ideas and categories derive their nourishment and to which there is always a dynamical feedback, which would change the settings and foci of the philosophical thinking. The deconstructive, the reconstructive, and the constructive attitudes respectively represented by Daoism, Confucianism (and Mohism), and Legalism can be said to capture the three modes or moods of the philosophical mentality: *to transcend, to integrate, and to construct* with regard to history, culture, society, and politics. It may be noted that transcendence in Chinese Daoism did not reach an extreme limit, namely to totally cut away and to identify a transcendent "something" such as in Christianity or to point to a transcendent "no-thing" such as in Buddhism. But this is precisely the characteristic wisdom of Chinese philosophy: to reach to the center and respond to infinite possibilities. In a sense, not only are the three modes dominating points on a circle, they are also interacting and mixing. Yet they are capable of forming a permanent dynamical harmony and unity in a theoretical perspective.

It is from this source, a higher level of consciousness and achievement than the pre-Daoist and Pre-Confucian Zhou culture, that all later philosophical inspirations and influences of power came and thrived. This same source, moreover, enacted the transformation of incoming philosophies such as Buddhism and led to new forms of presentation and articulation in response to outside stimulations. It is in this light that not only Chinese Buddhism and Neo-Confucianism are to be understood, but even modern and contemporary Chinese philosophy to the present date such as Marxism and Maoism. In this sense, to explore origins of Chinese philosophy makes it possible to illuminate and unravel the philosophical understanding of Chinese philosophy, past and present.

2

Classical Chinese Views of Reality and Divinity

Introductory Remarks

Reality and divinity are fundamental issues for any philosophical tradition because they embody fundamental human concerns for the human person. In fact, we cannot deny that the question of divinity arises as we ask how we could justify our lives, settle our feelings, and decide on our actions. For this reason we can hardly touch on any philosophical problem without raising questions of reality or questions of human origin and human destiny. Thus, in a certain sense, all philosophical questions are disguised questions of reality, human destiny, or perfect existence. In dealing with the Confucian tradition, there is no exception. One may say that the whole development of the Confucian philosophy is premised on a fundamental understanding of the human being as a paradigm of reality and potential divinity. The crucial thing about this development is to realize the truth of being of the human person and to fulfill this truth by continuous practice of self-cultivation. Now from the vantage point of our time, as we look back to the very beginning of Confucianism, and also look over the variegated evolution of the Confucian philosophy, we cannot but think of the problems of reality and divinity as the constant motivating power for both its beginning and its evolution.

In this chapter I begin with the very beginning, namely, with an introduction to the *Yijing* (易经) view of reality as embodied or developed in the *Yizhuan* (易传). Then I discuss the Daoist view of reality—not only with an interest in an exposition of Daoism, but also with an interest in its role in shaping and contributing to the formation of the Neo-Confucian spirit. Then I elaborate on the Chinese sense and explication of *shen* (神), spirit or divinity, and introduce the *Zhongyong* (中庸) notion of *cheng* as its pristine source.

The *Yizhuan* Theory of Reality

In the *Xici* (系辞) *Commentary* of the *Zhouyi* (周易) we witness the emergence of the two basic concepts that characterize the ultimate reality experienced by the human person. These two basic concepts are that of the "great ultimate" (*taiji* 太极) and that of "the way" (*dao* 道). Both concepts are derived from human experience of the formations and transformations of things in nature, which are referred to as *bianyi* (变易) or *bianhua* (变化 change). In a sense, the concepts of "great ultimate" and "the way" represent a general characterization of and a deeper insight into the general nature of change. In the first place it is said, "Thus the change has its Great Ultimate from which Two Norms (*liangyi* 两仪) are generated. The Two Norms generate Four Forms (*sixiang* 四象). Four Forms generate Eight Trigrams (*bagua* 八卦)" (*Xici Shang* 11). We know that the sixty-four hexagrams are then generated from the doubling of the Eight Trigrams. This process of generation is remarkable in establishing a cosmological picture of the rise and development of reality as a world of things as well as in providing a cosmographical way of thinking to be symbolized in the systemic structures of trigrams and hexagrams. This process of generation we may also call the *dao*. The sustaining source of this process of generation is called the *taiji*. The *dao* is *taiji* in its process aspect, whereas the *taiji* is the *dao* under its origination aspect. Together they refer to the same thing, namely, the totality of reality, creativity, change, and transformation.

We may call this cosmogonic and cosmographical way of thinking and description of reality and world the "*onto-cosmology* of the *taiji* and the *dao*." The "onto-" part of the term "onto-cosmology" suggests the meaning of the *taiji*, and the "cosmology" part of the term suggests the meaning of the *dao*. Because it is this theory of the *taiji* and the *dao* that forms the backbone and mainstream of the metaphysical thinking in the 3,200-year history of Chinese philosophy, we should regard it as the fundamental theory of reality in Chinese philosophy. Confucius in his late age had studied and commented the Book of Changes, which, since then, has been regarded as one of the Confucian classics, even the leading one. No doubt, there exist elements of Confucian reflections in the *onto-cosmological* commentaries called the *Yizhuan* (commentaries on the *Zhouyi*, developed in the fifth to third centuries BCE), but these could be seen as basically implicit in the contexts of the underlying philosophy or view of reality in the original *Zhouyi* texts and symbolism. This means that the *onto-cosmology* of the *taiji* and the *dao* is not just Confucian but also an articulation of the ancient way of thinking, observation, and interpretation of reality in China. However, in order to distinguish it from the later Daoist approach to reality in the Daoist School of Laozi (around the middle of the sixth century BCE—exact dates are uncertain) and Zhuangzi (c. 370–300 BCE) and its elaboration of the philosophy of the *dao*, we may refer to it as the "*Yizhuan* theory of reality," because this theory is suggested and implicitly formulated in the *Yizhuan*, particularly in the *Tuan* and *Xici* portions of the commentaries.

In order to understand the *Yizhuan* theory of reality as the fundamental Chinese theory of reality, we should in fact take note of the following six characterizations of the metaphysical way of thinking with regard to our experience of change:

1. *Reality as inexhaustible origination.* We can trace the beginning of the presentation and development of the world reality to the beginning of a root source. This root source, called "the great ultimate" (*taiji*), is the absolute beginning of all things, but it is also the sustaining base for all things even at present because all changes of the world are based on it and contained in it. In this sense, the *taiji* is in fact the primordial and inexhaustible source of the creative and transformative force of all changes, which is conveyed by the notion of "creativity of creativity" or "generation of generation" (*shengsheng*) in the *Xici*. In this sense reality is not something stationary or static underneath a world of fleeting phenomena, nor is it a world of forms or ideas reflected in a world of imitations or veiled by a screen of illusions or delusions. Furthermore, it is not something accessible only by abstraction of human thinking or revelation of a transcendent God, as in Christian theology. Reality is concrete, vivid, and holistic not only in the sense

that all things are interrelated with a whole as originally defined by the oneness of the *taiji*, but also in the sense that changes and non-changes underlying the changes are organically part and parcel of the same thing. On this account there cannot be strict demarcation or bifurcation between appearance and reality. In this sense, reality is made of changes and the constant and continuous regeneration of things. Any scheme to divide or stratify reality will only serve a limited purpose and will be rendered inept by confrontation with reality. This means that all theories of reality bear with reality the nature of change and must be subject to the continuous challenges of an ever-developing and becoming process of formation and transformation. Therefore, we may understand the *taiji* as not just primary origination but constant or ceaseless origination. In a Whiteheadian spirit, we may say that the world is in the making and is constantly and forever in the making.

2. *Reality as polar-generative process.* When the *taiji* gives rise to things in the world, it does so by bringing in a whole of polarities, the positive and the negative, or the *yang* (the brightening/the moving/the firm) and the *yin* (the darkening/the restive/the soft), respectively. These polarities are sub-contraries that exist simultaneously and are conspicuous on a specific level. They are also simultaneously contraries that are hidden on more concrete levels of things. In this latter sense, they are identifiable with the *taiji* because the *taiji* as the source of all changes is always hidden under all things. The generation of new things occurs on the basis of the coexistence and interaction between polarities. Unlike Whitehead's postulation of the rise of novelty from pure ideas, novelties in this model derive from internal dynamics of the becoming of world, from which a division into the *yin* and the *yang* and a combination of the *yin* and the *yang* are the basic ways to give rise to new things. The novelty of things is inherent in the very source of the world itself, and it is also inherent in the creative potential of a thing, which requires the interaction of forces.

3. *Reality as multi-interactive harmony.* An individual thing or an individual class of things always has two sides: the *yin*, which pertains to its stationary state of existence and its receptivity to the outside world (it is its given nature), and the *yang*, which pertains to its dynamical state of developing its propensities in its interaction with the outside world. As the *yin-yang* polarities are definitive of individual things or individual classes of things, it is in the nature of the thing itself that it must interact with the outside world. It is in this process of interaction that a thing fulfills its potentialities of nature and runs its course of bounded existence. It is in maintaining itself as a given nature that we can speak of the "centrality" of a thing, and in properly taking and giving with other things we can speak of "harmony" between or among things. There could be non-centrality and disharmony in the formation and transformation of things, which would be a problem and a crisis for its identity and its survival in the world of reality as things. Hence, we have the natural dispositions of a thing to maintain its own centrality and to reach harmony with other things. But in the case of human persons, these two aspects of existence must be cultivated in order to enhance and realize the fulfillment of the human propensity and potentiality.

It is said, "One *yin* and one *yang* is thus called the *dao*. To follow it is goodness and to complete it is nature" (*Xici Shang* 5). How do we understand this in reference to individual things? The *dao* is how things come into being and how they grow and develop in a process of time. The process of one *yin* and one *yang* is made of the alternation, conjunction, and mutual interaction of the positive and negative forces, as well as the positive and negative activities of the individual things that result in the formation and transformation of things.

4. *Reality as virtual hierarchization.* The world is made of many levels, each of which is a combination of the *yin* and the *yang* forces or activities of things. For the *taiji* and the *dao* model of cosmogony and cosmography (and hence onto-cosmology), there are genuine general features of the

yin and the *yang*, which are understood as rest/motion, darkness/brightness or invisibility/visibility and softness/firmness, closedness/openness, retrospective-propensity/prospective-propensities, and other such properties. Although these properties are basically described in phenomenal and experiential terms of human persons, there is no reason why they could not be described in a logical and scientific language of abstract and primary properties. Perhaps one could identify the *yin* and the *yang* elements or processes in the genetic code and the theory of supplementary particles, as many people have done. Similarly, there is no reason why values, emotions, and intentions could not also be described in the language of *yin* and *yang*. In this light, *yin* and *yang* should be regarded as neutral and variant operators, which act to generate relationships and changes. The important point to remember is that as there are levels of simplicity and complexity of structures and activities in a scheme of things in being and becoming, so there are levels of *yin* and *yang* in the world of reality. On the highest and most general level, there is the great ultimate (*taiji*). On the second level there are the *yin* and the *yang*. On the third level there are Four Forms. On the fourth level there are Eight Trigrams. This can go on forever and without limit. But individual things must be seen on an individual level of the *yin* and the *yang*, which represent a complex hierarchy of levels of *yin* and *yang* as well as a complex world of *yin-yang* interactions. This means that the individual thing or person is only understood and acting in a context of a field and a web of forces: in this context one is still capable of making a creative impact on and a contribution to the formation and transformation of the world.

5. *Reality as recursive (like a spiral rather than a circle) but limitless regeneration.* Although the commentaries of the *Zhouyi* do not mention the recursive and regenerative nature of *yi* (change), the presentation of nature in eight trigrams and of the world in sixty-four hexagrams in the original symbolism dating back to 1200 BCE and appended

judgments of divination, clearly suggest that nature is a process of both collective and distributive balance. The symbolism and judgments suggest that nature, moreover, functions as a process of return and reversion, as observed in the rotation of seasons and celestial cycles. The interesting thing to note is that once we can represent the world in a collectively inclusive and individually exclusive enumeration of stages or facets, these stages and facets will have to recur as patterns or forms of understanding, or existential characterizations on a special level. We can limit our understanding and characterization to a special level or in a particular domain and then work out or design some definitive categorical system of description or projection. That is why we could use the eight trigrams and sixty-four hexagrams at the same time, because they belong to different levels of relevance and meaningful description. What is implied in this description of reality is that reality is both limited and limitless: it is limited on a specific level of description that serves a human purpose, and it is limitless because any specific level of description could only serve a purpose in a limited way, as it can be transcended or abandoned for a higher or more specific level of description. We may say that there are virtually unlimited numbers of levels of description, just as theoretically there could be an unlimited number of systems of scientific knowledge in the progression of scientific inquiry. On each level of description there is the recursion of the finite categorized reality. This is so because it is in the nature of change that the world of reality has to be regeneratively represented. This may be called regenerative recursion. It is this regenerative recursion that gives stability to the process and may be called structure of the process.

In the *taiji* and the *dao* model of reality, what is shown in the symbolism of the *yi* is a regenerative recursion by reversion; namely, the stage of the *yin* has to revert to a stage of the *yang* in order to realize creative change, and vice versa. It is in the process of time that the *yin* and the *yang* are interacting by alternating. Because of this, one could expect that reaching the limit of the worst would mean a return to a better condition. Although in practice it is difficult to know whether one has reached the worst, or how long the getting better would last, from the perspective of the *Zhouyi*, it is nevertheless possible to conceive of reality as an alternation between good and bad on the same level as a natural process of change.

6. *Reality as organismic totality*. From the above description, the world of reality in the model of the *taiji* and the *dao* is totalistic in the sense that all things are included and there is nothing beyond it. It is said that "the *Book of the Changes* is extensive and all-comprehensive. It contains the way of heaven, the way of man and the way of earth" (*Xici Xia* 10). For the early Chinese, the world of reality was confined to heaven, earth, and ten thousand things among which the human person stands out as the most intelligent and the one capable of forming a tri-partnership with heaven and earth. Everything in this reality comes from the *taiji* and follows or embodies the *dao*. Hence, there could not be anything outside this world of reality with the *taiji* and the *dao*. This implies that there is no transcendent being outside this world, and in fact nothing is to be conceived beyond the world of the *taiji* and the *dao*.

When we come to Laozi, we find that even when the notion of emptiness or void (*wu* 无) is introduced, what the term *wu* stands for is part and parcel of the universe of the *dao*. The *dao* in Laozi is simply enriched by something called the void or non-being (*wu*). Similarly, when Zhou Dunyi (周敦颐) (1017–1073) speaks of the ultimateless (*wuji* 无极) giving rise to the great ultimate, he is simply extending the *dao* to cover both void and non-void. There is no break between the void and the non-void, and hence one does not have a transcendent nothingness or emptiness apart from reality. In this non-transcendence we do not speak merely of immanence but also of totality. Immanence refers to values and powers inherent in the things themselves, but totality refers to all the interrelated parts of all things in reality. The reason why things belong or hang together is that in the ultimate reality all things are not simply contained but rather are all interrelated or even interpenetrating. The organismic nature of the totality dictates that not only can there not be any object "outside," but all things exist together by way of mutual support or even mutual grounding. This is how immanence of heaven in the nature of humanity leads to an interminable exchange between, as well as a unity of, humanity and heaven.

The Daoist Theory of Reality

Although the *Yizhuan* has developed the fundamental metaphysics of the *taiji* and the *dao* in Chinese philosophy, which inspires or perhaps grounds the Confucian view on the moral propensity of humans, it is in Laozi's *Daodejing* (*Classic of* Dao *and* De) that we find a better thematic theory of the *dao*. It might be said that a fuller but a more distinctive theory of reality was formulated in the *Daodejing*. We may call it the "Daoist theory of reality." It has been frequently argued that it is the Daoist theory of reality of the fourth century BCE that has influenced the *Yizhuan* theory of reality of the third century BCE. It is even suggested that the "*Yizhuan* theory of reality" is basically Daoist.[1] But this would seem to not be the case: the reason being that there exists a tight consistency and coherence of ideas in the *Yizhuan*'s notion of reality and creativity in reference to presuppositions that could be easily seen in the ancient texts of the *Zhouyi* and the even older practice of divination. On examining the basic methodology of thinking and the empirical beginning of the *Zhouyi*, I have pointed out that it is in the presupposed view and way of thinking in the *Zhouyi* symbolism and judgments that both the idea of the *taiji* as a root-source of creative change and the notion of the *dao* as a polar-generative process of totalization were developed.[2] It is interesting to note that both of these ideas are also present in the *Daodejing* text as well as in the *Yizhuan*.

A better suggestion would be that both the *Daodejing* and the *Yizhuan* share the influence of the *Zhouyi* and that they develop as a result of this influence and an effort to understand the presupposed meaning of the *Zhouyi* symbolic texts. Hence, there is no denying that there are shared grounds of *onto-cosmology* (as formulated in the above six characterizations) between the two. But there should also be no denying that there is a difference between the Daoist approach to reality based on the presuppositions of *Zhouyi* and the Confucian approach to reality based on a creative understanding of Zhouyi. The high consistency of the Zhouyi and Yizhuan theory of reality reflects a Confucian emphasis on the moral and social relevance and importance of our understanding of reality. Understanding reality is essential for a moral person to become genuinely moral, for morality consists in practicing the comprehensive care for life in society and politics as derived from the way of heaven, as is understood in the Yizhuan theory of reality. Insofar as the book of the Zhouyi is infused with the spirit of pragmatism, a concern with rectitude, and an ethics of action, it is clear that the Yizhuan theory of reality is a continuation of the Zhouyi philosophy, which is further cultivated in the later stage of Confucius's life as a classical *ru* (cultured and learned) thinker who could also have embraced the Zhou values in terms of their cultural and moral humanism.[3]

On the other hand, the *Daodejing* text, though to a great extent exhibiting the underlying spirit of the *Zhouyi*'s understanding of reality as a process of change, reversion, and return, has its distinctive features. These features can be perhaps interpreted as a creative response to, and a serious-minded critique of, its own times. For this reason, the Daoist approach to reality must be treated independently as a new development of the theory of reality in Chinese philosophy.

There are four major distinctive features of the Daoist theory of reality that can be regarded as differentiating it from the *Yizhuan* theory of reality. In the first place, the *Daodejing* introduced a unique notion of the *dao*: the *dao* that is not embodied or conveyed by language. The first sentences of the *Daodejing* say, "The *dao* can be spoken, but it is not the constant *dao*. The name can be named, but it is not the constant name" (chapter 1). What, then, is the *dao*? It is apparently the power or force underlying all changes and transformations of things in the world. The key here is that even though each thing has its way of change, all things share a common moving or motivating force for change. They also share in being in a common time and in a common space with one another. This oneness is further experienced in interrelatedness among all things in the world. But this power of change and this oneness are not separate from each other, nor are they separate from the world or each individual thing of the world. It is difficult to express this beings-wide all-encompassing oneness, comprehensiveness, and moving motivating power. When we choose the word "*dao*" to indicate or refer to this power, we cannot identify it with any of the things in the world because it is not one of the things our language describes. It is more or less like an inaccessible object such as the moon, to which we may point with the finger. Hence the *dao* is to be experienced, reflected upon, and intended in our speech, but it cannot be identified. Yet this is not to say that the *dao* is nonexistent—although it is invisible, inaudible, and intangible—nor is it to say that its existence is non-efficacious, although it is non-substantial. On the contrary, the *dao* is full of power and functions in all natural activities of things in the world. Specifically, one can even see that the *dao* is a power giving rise to all things without owning them, sustaining all things without dominating them, enabling things to act on their own without claiming its own work (*Daodejing*, chapters 10, 34, 51).

The *dao*, which we may call the "creative spirit of the world," therefore is real and profound and can be considered the absolute beginning and primordial source of all things. In this sense the *dao* can be said to exist before heaven and earth and to be the forerunner of all things and the mother of all lives. It is also the naturally-of-its-accord spontaneity of things. Hence Laozi says, "While man follows earth, earth follows heaven. Heaven has to follow the *dao*, and the *dao* would act of its own accord" (*Daodejing*, chapter 25).

With all this said, the important thing to keep in mind is that although the *dao* is not the same as anything in the world, it is not separate from the world, nor does it transcend the world. Moreover, although as the source of change and the basis of being for all things, it is not to be conceived as God in whatever sense a Western religion or theology may attribute to God. It is rather the very nature of things when they are considered as an interrelated whole and as a unity of multiplicity of being that exhibits its creativity and novelty through multifarious change and abundance of life. One sees in the *dao* a dialectical unity of transcendence and immanence, namely, the transcendence of immanence and the immanence of transcendence in the relationship of nature and individual lives in nature. This understanding becomes even more intensified in the works of Zhuangzi, which stress the *dao* as self-transformation (*ziran*) of things and the interpenetrating power of oneness (*daotong weiyi* 道通为一).

We now come to the second feature of the Daoist theory of reality. Because the *dao* is indescribable and non-substantial, it is conceived of as "void" or "empty" (*wu, xu* 虛). It is said that "*Dao* is void and its function is infinite" (*Daodejing*, chapter 4). This voidness of the *dao* is also directly referred to as non-being (*wu*) by Laozi when he says, "*Wu* is to name the beginning of heaven and earth, and *you* (being) is to name the mother of ten thousand things" (chapter 1). In fact, in order to appreciate how *wu* is a process of being's emergence from non-being, one might also see how *wu* is a process of non-being's emergence from being. To become non-being is to void existence of all determinate characteristics and to go back to a state when all determinations of characteristics are in the offing. Things come into being, in other words, from a nebulous and indeterminate state of non-being in which non-being could even be understood as indeterminacy of being. There are many passages, in fact, that would lead one to this view, for example, *Daodejing* chapters 14 and 21. In this sense, *wu* could be regarded as one aspect of the *dao*, the other aspect of which is simply *you*. *Wu* is no-thing or having no-things (*wuwu* 无物), and *you* is having-things (*youwu* 有物). As *dao* is a power creative of all things as well as the process of creative production, it has both the activity of *wu* and the activity of *you*, just as all things have both the *yin* (emptying) and *yang* (substantiating) functions. It is through the interaction of these two functions and their conjunction that things become what they are and reach a state of harmony. It is said, "all ten thousand things are holding *yin* in their back and embracing *yang* [in the front], and in an intimate and strong mixing [*chong* 冲] of the two vital forces [*qi*] a harmony results" (*Daodejing*, chapter 42). It is also in this sense that Laozi speaks of the "mutual generation of *you* and *wu*" (*youwu xiangsheng* 有无相生) (chapter 2), by which it is meant that *you* and *wu* are mutually defining and conditioning as well as mutually forming and producing. In this, one sees what is described in the *Yizhuan* as the alternation of the *yin* and *yang* in the *dao*.

One way to reach the state of *wu* and hence the state of natural functioning of the *dao* is to have no desires (*wuyu* 无欲) and no actions (*wuwei* 无为) on the part of a person. This is important for the Daoist theory of reality, for the theory is not a matter simply of abstract speculation; rather, it is a matter of close embodiment of *onto-cosmological* and life experience. In fact, without such an embodiment, Laozi would not be able to describe so vividly the reality and creativity of the *dao*. From this, one may very well think that for the Daoist any human being could come to an intimate knowledge and understanding of the *dao* if one is to reduce one's desires and knowledge and even actions to a state of oneness (*Daodejing* 道德经, chapter 39). This also means that at a minimum one should not let one's desires and knowledge block the open vision of the whole process of change and transformation in the *dao*. That one's vision could be blocked by one's desires and knowledge is no doubt a result of a close observation of reality. Hence, Laozi advises that one should keep oneself free from diversions of senses and the burdens of learning, for the *dao* reveals itself to those in a free state of mind or in an open state of non-fixation of belief. This point is also strongly stressed by Zhuangzi.

We come to a third feature of the Daoist theory of reality. Reality in the name of the *dao* is always a matter of return (*fu* 复) and reversion (*fan* 反). It is said: "To reach for the ultimate of emptiness and to abide by the utmost of tranquility, ten thousand things will agitate at the same time. I would therefore be able to observe the process of return. There are many things, and each would return to its root. To return to the root is called 'tranquility' and this is called 'return to destiny'" (反命 *fanming*) (*Daodejing*, chapter 16). It is interesting to note that whereas the *Yizhuan* approach to reality stresses the ceaselessness of the productive creativity (*shengsheng buyi* 生生不已), the Daoist approach to reality stresses the constancy of return. In this sense, the *Yizhuan* approach is dynamic and the Daoist approach is static. However, the Daoist note on return as a distinctive feature of reality was already implicit in the symbolism of trigrams and hexagrams. One can see that the relationship between the *yin* and the *yang* in the Qian and Kun trigrams and hexagrams demonstrates such a return when we see this relationship in a temporal process of alternation of one *yin* and one *yang*. If the *dao* begins with the *yin* and moves to a stage of the *yang*, then the only way it could go is to return to the *yin*. Similarly, from the *yin* it would return to *yang*. But if the root of being is non-being in the sense described above, one can see that the root is closer in nature to the *yin* than to the *yang*. This observation led the later Neo-Confucian philosopher Zhou Dunyi to speak of a state of the ultimate less (*wuji*) as logically if not temporally prior to the state of the great ultimate (*taiji*) in his famous work *Taiji tushuo* (太极图说 *Discourse on the Diagram of the Great Ultimate*). In this work the idea of the return of things to their root is also articulated: for, according to Zhou, not only has the *wuji* given rise to the *taiji*, which produces all the things in the world, but the whole world is always a unity of the *taiji*, and the *wuji* is no more than the beginning state of the *taiji*. From an ontological point of view one could regard *wuji* and *taiji* as two alternating states of the *dao*, which exist at the same time and form a mutually defining unity. On this view, then, there need not be a temporal sense of return, and we can speak of the reversion of the *dao* from one state to another and vice versa. In fact, this is what is also observed by Laozi in the *Daodejing*.

It is said that "reversion is the motion of the *dao*; weakness is the function of the dao" (*Daodejing*, chapter 40). As return is a temporal reversion of the *dao*, reversion is a non-temporal return of the *dao*. They can be regarded as referring to the same action. On the other hand, it might be suggested that reversion is a more fundamental characteristic of the *dao*—as the *dao* always exists in opposites, and reversion can be logically considered to be the exercise of opposition within a unity. But then we would have to consider return as a different function of the *dao* as well, namely, the function of going back to the unity of the *dao*. This would make return and reversion two different functions of the *dao*. But, although we can see *wu* and *you* as two opposite and yet mutually related processes of the *dao*, there is no good reason to see reversion and return as dualistic rather than as one process described under two forms—a process that has its opposite in the process of ceaseless productive creativity in the *Yizhuan*.

The fourth feature may be stated in brief. Given the pervasive nature of the *dao*, one can observe the *dao* both outside oneself and within one's own person and thus understand the *dao*; moreover, one can further cultivate the *dao* so that one can participate in the *dao* or imitate the *dao* to achieve or reach for a desirable and ideal state of life. For the Daoists, just as for the Confucians, there are ample grounds for speaking of the unity of humanity and heaven or the unity of the human person and the *dao*. This unity is important for both schools insofar as ethics, social action, and political life are all dependent on it.

We now have a composite picture of reality in classical philosophy by way of the *Yizhuan* approach and the Daoist approach. Their different points of emphasis should not overshadow their common roots and common vision of reality as a world of interrelated things in a creative process of change and transformation. At a later time there arose both the Neo-Daoist and Chinese Buddhist philosophies in which reality was either presented and articulated on the basis of the Daoist model of reality or presented and articulated on the basis of the Buddhist theory of illusive consciousness and its emancipation in enlightenment. It is not until the rise of Neo-Confucianism in the Song period that the *Yizhuan* model would become the standard and norm. Yet the distinctive features of the Daoist model of reality together with some features of the Chinese Buddhist model of reality were absorbed into the Neo-Confucian system. This leads to a theory of reality presented not only in terms of mutual production of *wu* and *you*, but in terms of new categories of *li* (principles) and *qi* (vital force).[4]

Divinity without Theology: Chinese Approach to Divinity

Any theory of divinity must be grounded on or must presuppose a theory of reality. Historically, a notion of divinity might appear on the scene first, but in time it must disclose the theory of reality presupposed by it. It may happen, of course, that when a theory of reality is first suggested, a theory of divinity could be founded on it. It also must be pointed out that a theory of divinity could attempt to give the ultimate grounding to a theory of reality and therefore would overrule the theory of reality as its consequence. Yet, on the other hand, a theory of reality could also replace a given original notion of divinity and thus provide a new interpretation and new understanding of divinity in light of the theory of reality. We can see the development of Christian religion in the West as a classic example of the former case of the development from a theory of God to a theologically grounded theory of reality, whereas we can see the development of Confucian and Daoist metaphysics as an example of the latter case of development from a theory of *tian* (heaven) or *di* (Lord/Source on High) to an *onto-cosmology* of reality that traces and reveals the activity of the divine in the creative productiveness and transformativeness of things.

In the Christian case, the ontologization of God makes God the foundation of all reality in a theology, or Onto-theo-logik following Heidegger. Hence, this is always the leading theme of theological interpretation of reality in the Western religious traditions. On the other hand, it is the "daoization" of *tian* as God that replaced the *tian* with the *dao*, and therefore a theory of reality has subsumed a potential theology or "*tianology*" of divinity in the Chinese philosophical tradition. This tradition is therefore one in which we see processes of the depersonalization, the naturalization, and the humanization of the *tian*, without, however, giving up the spiritual meaningfulness of reality. Thus we have what may be said to be a notion of "divinity without theology." This "divinity without theology" is best expressed by the statement in *Xici* of the *Zhouyi*: "Divinity has no form and change has no substance" (*shen wufang, yi wuti*).

As early as the beginning of the Xia era in 2000 BCE, there was already reference to the Lord on High (*di*) who would supervise and oversee human affairs and who controls human destiny from above. This notion of the *di* could be regarded as a spiritual projection of a powerful and venerated ancestor who had played the role of a ruler or a governor in his lifetime. The word "*di*" is also said to symbolize the bud of a flower and hence the source of life. It is clear, then, that the Lord on High as mentioned in the *Book of Documents* (*Shujing* 书经) and the *Book of Poetry* (*Shijing* 诗经) is a supreme being who combines source of life and source of power in one person and who cares for the well-being of people (as his posterity) and the ordering of the state. He was thought of and worshipped as a personal god who could issue commands and mandates. In time, however, the notion of the *di* fused with the notion of the *tian* (heaven, sky, a term to be understood spatially rather than temporally). The *tian* too is to be conceived of as powerful and life-giving, and it is further conceived of as infinite. In *Shijing* it is said, "The great heaven has no limit." It is probable that a deeper and wider sense of reality made possible the transformation from the worship of the *di* to the worship of the *tian*, and that this took place as Zhou conquered the Shang people (who were known for their faith in ghosts and spirits and naturally *di*) around 1200 BCE.

This deeper and wider sense of reality diluted the personified character of *tian* as a supreme ruler on high and as a supreme creator of life. As this sense of reality focused increasingly on the unity of humanity and heaven, understood in terms of a common bond of creative activity, the *tian* eventually came to be regarded as the way of heaven (*tiandao* 天道), which is manifested in nature and is to be realized as a moral command in man. We find this depersonalization of the *tian* already in Confucius, although Confucius still occasionally spoke of the *tian* as if it were the Lord on High or a supreme moral being. The full naturalization and depersonalization of the *tian* occurs in Daoism, where the *tian* is seen as having arisen from the great *dao*, not the *dao* of something but the *dao* by itself as a creative process and reality that generates things in the world and imparts to them the power of self-autonomy and self-transformation with inherent dynamics of the *yin-yang* alternation and complementation.

The transformation of the *di* to the *tian* and then to the *dao* demonstrates a movement from a theory of personal divinity to a theory of depersonalized reality. Even though a personified notion of divinity is lost, which accounts for the fact that China, unlike the West, has not sustained a monotheistic religion, the sense of divinity is still preserved in the form of a profound understanding of reality as the process of creative change and as the inexhaustible source of novelty and life. This is what I have labeled the "divinity without theology."

What, then, is divinity in Chinese philosophy? The Chinese term *shen* is used to refer to all natural spirits, which may be conceived as personalized entities vested with life and special powers. In fact, *shen* is the living presence of power that may be said to exist in all of those living things of nature that can exert their influences upon other things. More specifically, the term *shen* applies to human persons in their possession of this living presence of powers to influence others. Thus, a person who accomplishes great deeds and achieves exemplary virtues, and who is consequently respected and wields great influence during life, leaves upon his death his *shen* (or influence, heretofore referred to as "spirit") to be worshipped or sought after. In this sense, the *shen* of a person is the natural extension of his life and the power of his influence projected into the present and the future even after the physical person is no longer present. When an unworthy person dies, however, his spirit is not to be sought after but rather to be avoided, and he is known not as a *shen*, but as a *gui* or ghost—something belonging (one hopes) only to the past. As *shen* is to be explained as the beneficial power of a person extending to the future from the present, *gui* is to be conceived of by contrast as the traces of a past human life. Even if the *gui* of a person may come back to affect the present, its coming back to the present would be a surprising and alarming event.

This conception of *shen* is well developed in both classical Confucian and classical Daoist philosophy of the constitution of a human person. (This basic theory is found in the texts of *Mencius*, in the *Xici* of the *Zhouyi*, and in the texts of the four chapters of the *Guanzi*, in *Laozi* and *Zhuangzi*. This theory is developed into a basis for alchemy and the search for immortality by the Neo-Daoists in the third century.) The human person is thus conceived of as formed of three or four levels of existence. On the first level, there is the physical reality, which is the body (*shen*).[5] On the second level, there is the essence of life (*jing* 精) or the essential elements of life as an organism. On the third level, there is energy and the circulating powers of life, which are referred to as vital breath (*qi*). Finally, there is the level of *shen* (spirit), which can be regarded as the quintessence of life and vital energy or the *ling* (efficacy) of *qi*. It is the freest element of life, but an element that also survives physical life in a free manner, as it can be expressed in the arts and deeds, the work and the word of a person.

According to this conception, human existence is not a conjunction of mind and body, as Cartesian dualism would have it, but rather a holistic unity of interpenetrating life elements, each of which is to be conceived of holistically. The holistic conception of life differs from the atomistic conception of life in that there are no absolute, simple elements postulated, but rather nebulous wholes with basic organic parts interactively supporting each other. Thus, it is not simply that the higher level depends on the lower level but that the lower levels also depend on the higher levels. In this sense, any lower level of existence could have a higher level, which would be its *shen*. Whether the *shen* stands out or not depends on the special influence or presence of power possessed by a thing. Thus, for the ancient Chinese, all major mountains and rivers have their *shen* or spirits, which are worthy of worship or respect. On the other hand, the *shen* of a human being who achieved great power of influence would be more vividly entertained in the minds of the relevant people and thus would become even more of an object of worship.

With respect to the last point, it is interesting to note the following saying of Confucius in the *Analects*: "[I] sacrifice to the spirits as if the spirits are present. If I am not engaging myself in the sacrifice, it is like not holding a sacrifice" (3.12). How does one feel that the spirits are present? One feels the presence of the spirits by using one's sincere feelings and vivid imagination in a projection of the known person or object. In the case of the unknown person or object, it is to think deeply of the person or object in worship. It is a total engagement of one's person for the projected construction of the object, and as a consequence the object becomes the subject because it is infused with the best spirit and essence of life of the person engaged. A person who does not engage in sacrifice in such a manner is not considered to have genuinely performed a sacrifice.

When we enlarge and extend the notion of *shen* as explained above, we shall see that the whole universe has its *shen*, particularly when we reflect and observe the life-generating and life-preserving power of the universe conceived of as an organic whole. The whole universe is then seen as a progenitor, maintainer, and preserver of life. As we have seen, it is in this way that the notion of the way of heaven was developed, in which heaven is both a concretion and an abstraction of the whole of nature focusing upon its influence and power of life generation and life maintenance. The *tian* is conceived of as both the whole of nature and the whole process of life production, in which both birth and death are regarded as part and parcel of the life-maintaining and life-generating process. In this sense, death is absorbed into the larger process and circulation of life and must be faced by a person with equanimity and peace of mind. This is a point specifically stressed by Confucianism and Neo-Confucianism.

Zhongyong (中庸): *Cheng* 诚 as Source of *Shen* 神 and *Sheng* 圣

When we speak of the *shen* of the whole of nature or the universe, we speak of the divine. The divine in this sense is an elevation of the spiritual, because in becoming the divine, the spiritual is no longer confined to any projected or formerly existing person or thing, but pertains to the ever-present and ever-active life and vitality of the whole of nature. In essence it pertains to the ever-creative creativity of the source of life. Therefore, the power of influence of the spiritual becomes the power of generation and transformation of life. We find this sense of divinity presented in the writings of Mencius and the *Zhongyong* (*Doctrine of the Mean*). Mencius says: "What is desirable is goodness. One holding to oneself [in self-knowledge] is integrity. To fulfill one's potentiality is beauty. To have self-fulfillment and shining out [and being influential] is greatness. Being great and capable of transforming life is called sagely (*sheng*). When the sagely power is beyond the measure of knowledge, it is called the divine (*shen*, in the deeper sense of the spiritual or creative)" (*Mencius, Jinxin Xia* or 7.B.25). It should be noticed that the spiritual creative power, which is the divine, is to be built up from the basic desires of life whose fulfillment is a form of goodness, according to Mencius. Only when one attains goodness based on one's genuine desire for goodness, will one achieve integrity in the sense that the self is not just a physical event but a value of importance. This integrity would then be the base or starting point for enlargement and extension of a transforming power that raises other beings and persons onto a higher level of existence. The key phrase for this transformation is "great and transforming," which is taken as the mark of the divine.

The divine is conveyed by the notion of sagacity (sheng 圣), which culminates in the limitless influence and transformation it may entail, and one will thus have the full measure of divinity still known as *shen*. The combination of the "sagacity" and "divinity" in the term "*shensheng*" (divine and sagely) can be said to capture the meaning of the sacred or holy in the best spirit of the Western religious tradition without assuming its entrenched concomitant theology. Thus, there are two forms of divinity without theology: the Confucian and the Daoist.

According to Mencius, the divine is rooted in human life and is continuous with human life, and hence there is no transcendent state of the divine outside of life. For this reason, Mencius even suggests that "a genuine person (*junzi* 君子) is capable of transforming people and preserving his spirit in such a way that he is in the same vein with heaven and earth [with regard to its creative and transforming powers]" (7.A.13). The reference to heaven and earth is meant to underline the analogy between the creative and transforming power of the divine over things in nature and the power of a ruler over his people.

The Confucian has taken the political power of a ruler very seriously and sees in it the same creativity as in heaven and earth, because life and death and transformation of people's lives are vested in such power. Hence the analogy was suggested. But this analogy is also literally a reflection of the underlying cosmology of the unity of heaven-and-earth and the human person that comes to the fore at about the time of Mencius, namely, in the period of Warring States, when Confucianism has achieved a new stage of development based on the pristine insights and cosmic experiences of the second and third generations of the Confucian School. This is how we come to the positions of the *Doctrine of the Mean* (*Zhongyong*) and commentaries of the *Zhouyi* (*Yizhuan*).

In the *Doctrine of the Mean*, it is said:

> A human person of utmost sincerity is capable of fulfilling his own nature. Capable of fulfilling his own nature, he is capable of fulfilling the natures of others. Capable of fulfilling the natures of others, he is capable of fulfilling natures of things. Capable of fulfilling the natures of things, he is in a position to participate in the creative activities of heaven and earth. Being in a position to participate in the creative activities of heaven and earth, he is posed to form a trinity with heaven and earth. (*Zhongyong* 21)

This important passage is again a testimony of the inner and virtual divinity of the human person in the sense of participating in the creative activities of heaven and earth. If we understand this to mean that a human person engaged in government could make decisions bearing on the life and well-being of people, it is quite clear how he could be creative and transformative just like heaven and earth, which bring forth things and regulate and preserve them. This means that there is a functional unity between humanity and heaven. But of course there is a deeper level of unity in the *Doctrine of the Mean*, namely, that the human person is endowed with human nature from heaven. (It is said that "what is endowed and mandated from Heaven is called the nature [of man].") This means that human creativity is derived from heaven, and thus the human person is capable of forming a unity with heaven and earth. Such is the vocation of humanity, and such is the ideal state of human existence in a political community and family of heavenly mandated order. This is not to equate humanity with heaven, for the human person is not to create things in nature like heaven, but can preserve them, just as modern ecologists would endorse. In so doing, the human person creates and preserves one's own life and well-being as far as the human community is concerned.

What the *Zhongyong* stresses is that when a human person exhibits the utmost sincerity, that person becomes creative and thus divine in the sense described above. But when the *Zhongyong* says that "the utmost sincerity is like the divine" (24), there is a special meaning attached to this use of "divine," namely, the ability to foretell the future or to have foreknowledge (*xianzhi*). This may refer to a diviner's act of divination using tortoise bones. But there is no doubt a sense of divinity which pertains to a power of knowing the future. One would know the future if one were able to grasp the totality of things and the direction of the whole process of change in addition to being able to participate in the change. This, then, defines the meaning of *zhicheng* (至诚 utmost sincerity). The utmost sincerity is real in the utmost, and this means to know the real and participate in the real as much as one can. This means, according to the *Zhongyong*, to devise the great principles of governing the world, to establish the great ground of right action, and to take part in the nourishing process of heaven and earth. In essence, it is to fulfill the heavenly virtue of creativity as a sage (32). Insofar as this creativity is interpreted as profound love (*ren*), it is directed toward and based on the Confucian ideal of human and self-cultivation of a human person.

In this way, one sees as well how divinity in the sense described would result from cultivation of a person in *ren*.

We need to elaborate on the key concept of "sincerity" (*cheng*) in the *Zhongyong* in order to understand the creative and transformative power of humanity. We read in the *Zhongyong*: "Next, to fulfill the hidden and subtle [desires of a man], one can be sincere in one's desires. Being sincere, there will be form of action. Action being formed, it will become conspicuous. Being conspicuous, it will be illustrious. Being illustrious, it will move. Moving, it will change. Changing, it will transform. It is the utmost sincerity of the world that can transform" (23). I would identify "the hidden and the subtle" with the genuine desire for change in a person. It follows that if one really desires change, one is able to effect the change because one will act on one's sincere desires, which will provide a base for the change. This process of transformation is how an inner motive leads to an outer result.

Sincerity as the motivating force is therefore a self-making and self-creating force. But *cheng* is not merely for self-making but also for the making of others, and is identified by the *Zhongyong* as the most fundamental force of origination and transformation in the world. In this sense, *cheng* is no more and no less than the root source of all beings, and the human experience of sincerity is only a manifestation or sign of the creativity of reality itself.

Based on its understanding of the divine, the *Zhongyong* maintains that when a person is able to achieve centrality and harmony, there will be a proper positioning of heaven and earth and nourishing ten thousand things. This centrality (*zhong*) and harmony (*he*) are derived from the divinity of heaven and earth, which perfects a person, a community, and the relationship between human community and natural environment. We need to see the centrality and harmony operating on two levels: the human and the cosmic. On the human level, centrality is described as the state of human emotion not yet issued in response to things outside, because things outside have not called for any response. If and when such a response is called for, because there is an unbalanced situation in need of being balanced, then the restoration of equilibrium would be the task of the emotions. The emotions lead to action and interaction between the subjective and the objective, which produces a new state of balance, and this is harmony. But this also means that there is a primordial state of harmony and balance of things derived from natures (or propensities) of things. In the primordial state everything follows its own nature, and thus this state can be described as the way of nature. Because not only the human being but all things have their natures, centrality is both the inner state of a thing and the totality of natures of things. This leads to the description of centrality on the cosmic level. Centrality is the state of nature in which natures of things are not engaged in response to outside situations. Cosmic harmony, on the other hand, is a matter of actions and interactions among things and events being balanced so as to allow their natures to function naturally. Here we can see, then, how in centrality and harmony there will be a proper ordering of heaven and earth as well as nourishing of all things therein. We might also suggest that centrality is a form of harmony, harmony in stasis. And harmony is a form of centrality, centrality in dynamism.

We may regard centrality and harmony as two aspects of the same thing along the lines of the *onto-cosmology* of the *yin* and *yang*. Thus we can speak of the centrality as the nature inward-directed state of a thing, while we can speak of the harmony as the relation outward-directed state in which a thing is situated. A thing may at one and the same time exhibit two forces at work: it may centralize itself so that it maintains its given nature, and it may harmonize itself with other things in its development or growth. The former is inward-and-self-oriented equilibrium and balance, whereas the latter is outward-and-relation-oriented equilibrium and balance. These two principles are opposite and yet interdependent and complementary with regard to both the development of the individual and the development of a larger system in which the individual is situated. But when we ask how this centralization and harmonization (as two processes or two states) are possible, and how they are ontologically grounded, we have to go back to the texts of the commentaries of the *Zhouyi* for an answer. And in connection with this, we have also to take into consideration the Daoist views of Laozi and Zhuangzi as expounded above.

3

The Trinity of Cosmology, Ecology, and Ethics in the Confucian Personhood

Introductory Remarks

There exists, in recent philosophical literature, a quest for an environmental ethics, no doubt generated by a heightened awareness of the ecological crisis. Philosophers and ethicists have been quite outspoken regarding the harmful consequences for the environment of Western humanism or humanistic ethics.[1] Some critics simply see humanism or personalism as embodying a human-centered rationalism, as a form of "anthropological egoism" or "human chauvinism" that seeks what is good and of value in satisfying human interests and concerns, and confines morality to activities engaged in by humans alone.[2] There is no denying that humanism can be either deontological or utilitarian in orientation and goal setting, but the ultimate goal for a utilitarian or deontological ethics in humanism is human goodness and human satisfaction, individually or collectively. Humanism thus is seen as a device for the exercise of "group selfishness" by or on behalf of humankind in the world of nature. It could be pointed out that, since a humanistic ethics might incorporate the Golden Rule, the Kantian "categorical imperative," and some law of comprehensive love as part of its content, humanism need not be considered exclusively human-centered. The ethics of humanism can be extended to all living sentient beings that are capable of pleasure and suffering in light of these moral principles.[3] It could even be specified that one might imagine oneself to be a wriggling worm in order to decide what one should do with regard to the worm. Or, one might require oneself to act in such a way as to treat other life forms as ends, not as means. Or, one could simply decide to love all animals in order to protect their natural life activities and processes. This would constitute a humane-society approach to the ethics of the treatment of birds and beasts, but it does not answer the question of the human-centeredness aspect of humanistic ethics. Nor does it answer the question why a human must extend those universal principles of morality to the animal kingdom.

Clearly, when humanistic principles of morality were developed, they were intended to apply to the human world. In extending humanistic ethics to the animal kingdom and on to other life-forms, it is obviously, yet implicitly, assumed that this extension is necessary, if not sufficient, to ward off the ill effects of a human-centered morality and thus prevent humanity from causing an ecological breakdown. Though this justification for a humanistic ethics is, on reflection, more holistic and totalistic than other such considerations based on an awareness of the ecological crisis, it is still derived from implicit utilitarian considerations of human welfare.

Uncovering the underlying utilitarian considerations of the extension of humanism or humanistic ethics means undermining the ethical or moral validity of such an extension. One might imagine that, if circumstances require us humans to forfeit or rescind this extension for even more sophisticated reflective utilitarian considerations, we would still end up being human-centered in our ethical thinking and moral actions, which could either benefit or harm the world of nature and our environment as a consequence. In view of this, three very basic questions must be raised: Is there a different formulation or understanding of humanism that might moderate its human-centeredness? Are there criteria according to which things in nature and in the human world can be equally and properly treated, based on considerations of the world of nature and humanity together rather than merely on considerations of a single human being or on the human world alone? If any such criteria exist, how might a human apply such criteria so that he or she might act morally within the world of nature and develop an ethical attitude or habits that would preserve such criteria? I intend, in this article, to explore these three questions from a point of view deepened by Confucian and Neo-Confucian philosophy.

Inclusive Humanism as Cosmo-Ethics and Eco-Cosmology

In the intellectual journey that humankind has made in the last 2,500 years, two types of humanism can be distinguished: an "exclusive humanism," which exalts the human species, placing it in a position of mastery of and domination over the universe, and an "inclusive humanism," which stresses the coordinating powers of humanity as the very reason for its existence. The West has for the most part followed an "exclusive humanism" since the beginning of the modern age. Although we need not regard Descartes's rationalism as the very prototype of "exclusive humanism," his rationalistic philosophy has no doubt provided a solid foundation for this type of humanism in the modern West.

Descartes developed the notion of an essentially deistic God who provided the single foundation for our knowledge of the external world. To have this knowledge also means using it to conquer nature, and there exist, then, no ethical restrictions on how we explore and use nature on the basis of our knowledge of the external world. Descartes's dualism of matter and mind, or body and soul, in fact further develops a logical basis for the domination of mind over matter and soul over body. The traditional Creator-God reigns in Heaven but also relegates his power of dominion to man on Earth. The modern rational person, unlike the artistic Renaissance person, is a free spirit liberated from the shackles of the Dark Ages (or Cage), able to taste the sweet fruits of power and relish the sense of domination by displaying his intelligence through invention and employing cunning in industry. To use Nietzsche's metaphor, the modern person is like a young lion set free after being transformed from a camel. Thus, modern science and modern capitalism as the lion's claws arose at the same time to provide modern persons with weapons for both play and prey. These two were linked through the Cartesian vision of knowledge as power or domination. In this sense, humanism in the modern West is nothing more than a secular will for power or a striving for domination, with rationalistic science at its disposal. In fact, the fascination with power leads to a Faustian tradeoff of knowledge and power (pleasure and self-glorification) for value and truth, a tradeoff that can lead to the final destruction of the meaning of the human self and human freedom.

It is in this development of the human being where the natural world loses its enchantment and its inherent moral worth for humans. Rather than as a natural abode for the soul of the modern person, the natural world becomes instead a hunting ground on which a skilled marksman may pursue and collect fortunes. Hence, it is not science and rationality that deprived nature of its moral worth or of its intrinsic significance to humankind: the post-medieval human will, as a surrogate for the authority of a Creator-God, accomplished this. Unlike God, however, modern humanity is devoid of the goodness of God. This humanism is thus human-centered and exclusive of any real connection or intrinsic link with anything else in the world. This dominant exclusiveness results in an increased control over natural resources as well as in an accelerated development of technology, and it is a demonstration of the ability and talent inherent in an invincible human urge for power supported by the successful functioning of human instrumental rationality. Humanism in this exclusive sense is a disguise for the individualistic entrepreneurship of modern man armed with science and technology as tools of conquest and devastation.

There is, however, a second kind of humanism, an "inclusive humanism."[4] As the term suggests, humanism in this sense focuses on the human person as an agency of both self-transformation and transformation of reality at large. As the self-transformation of a person is rooted in reality and the transformation of reality is rooted in the person, there is no dichotomy or bifurcation between the human and reality. There is always an underlying connection between the two. How to conceive of and configure this underlying connection is a metaphysical task to be carried out, not only in terms of the imagination, but also in light of a deep sense and wide experience of the organic connection defining both what the real as the human is and what the human as the real is. With regard to this connection, there is no essential opposition or conflict between the human as a subject and the world of nature as an object, nor is there any opposition or conflict between the human as an entity and nature as another entity. In fact, both the human and nature belong to each other in a continuum of the whole reality. Because this whole reality (to which both the human and nature belong as parts) must be conceived as a dynamic and creative process of change and transformation in order to allow the mutual transformation of the human and nature, it should be clear that the very actuality and creativity of the transformation provide the required underlying link. We can see, then, that inclusive humanism is a view of the human as a creative process of self-fulfillment of reality, in reality, for reality, and from reality.

What needs to be addressed immediately in inclusive humanism is the basic recognition or understanding that nature, or even the whole of reality, whether in the form of a moving universe or in the form of the totality of things, has an interconnecting or interlinking context of being as value. This implies that not only that a single reality is a common source or common ground for human beings and all things, but because of this reality-source or reality-ground, each and every thing has intrinsic value, value in the sense of being able to form a mutually enriching or mutually strengthening relationship among things contributing to the total unity and harmony of things in reality. This amounts to saying that an ideal projection of harmony among things must always be a basic consideration for human action. This will always cause a natural strain in the development of a relationship among things. There is no transcendent God separate from the world and there is no delegation of power to humankind as the representative body of God in the world of nature, because God needs no such delegation. Humans have, from the beginning of their existence, participated in the sharing of the power of transformation with other things in the world.

Humans and nature are already intrinsically related when a human individual comes to know his or her role and station, and this is realized as an innate sense of being in the human individual, perhaps forgotten in transition but never eliminated. Although, under some historical circumstances, an emergent desire for power, in its quest for self-assertion, self-aggrandizement, or self-glorification, could lead to an inner split of the human self and a loss of the sense of the common source of being, and although this loss would inevitably result in the restlessness of strife and struggle for conquest and possession, this innate sense of being can always be cultivated and restored or reinstated. This reemergence of an ever-present sense of being is the transformation from an exclusive humanism to an inclusive humanism, a form that does not make the human the center of the world but instead makes the between-ness, or among-ness, of the human and things in the world the center of the world. We thus come to see that for inclusive humanism the defining spirit is the will for harmony—the transformation of the will for power into a spirit of friendly love and support. The human being thus stands for the way of creative transformation, interrelating, coordination, and integration or mutual identification among things in the world. The whole process of the creative change of the human is meshed with the process of the creative change of the world. There is no permanent gain or permanent loss but a dynamic balance of the best efforts of the human for the dynamic balance of the possible and the actual, the positive and the negative, in a conscientious exertion of heart-and-mind. Inclusive humanism might also be called "cultivational humanism," or a "humanism for cultivation," based on the metaphor of the cultivation of the land so that it yields fruits that both benefit humankind and enrich the land at the same time. Exclusive humanism, by contrast, would be a human striving for domination of the land and possession of territorial rights out of a sense of alienation from an objectified world, perhaps best described as a nomadic tribe engaged in a perpetual hunt.

Because the basis of inclusive humanism calls for the inclusion of nature for there to be harmony, the object of moral action is not limited to the human world, nor is it derived solely from human concern. Anything in the world, animate or inanimate, can take on this role, for anything can be an integral part of the best possible harmony that may be achieved, considering both time and place, humans and nature, present and future, here and there. The human world and human concern are seen as presentations of the larger and deeper reality in the creative making. In this light, the entailed ethics cannot but be an ethics of the cosmos and an ethics of the creative change of the cosmos. This means that, as humans, we must think, act, plan, and decide with this vision of present and future harmony of nature always in mind. Thus, this cosmo-ethics is also an ecological cosmology that incorporates the values of being as creativity, creativity as harmony, and harmony as transformation.

I have called this cosmology of the life of the whole "onto-cosmology" in my earlier study of the metaphysical foundation of the *Yijing* as a way to suggest the harmony and unity of change and reality, or process and reality.[5] As reality contains resources of human values, which must be recognized as intrinsic values in the universe, the onto-cosmology of life-creativity is at the same time ecological, insofar as it presents itself in the natural environments of life processes and life-forms in the world and is also a basis for human ethical considerations and moral action. Hence, the onto-cosmology also becomes a matter of cosmo-ethics, or ethics based on the recognition and consideration of the nature of the reality as creative change.

It is evident that inclusive humanism marks a starting point in the axiological transformation of cosmological reality due to human participation, reflection, innovation, and renovation in humankind's ceaseless efforts to overcome obstruction and misunderstanding and find the way to achieving a dynamic equilibrium and harmonization of being, becoming, and non-being.

If Descartes can be singled out as the founding father of exclusive humanism in the West, Alfred North Whitehead may be considered the spokesman for inclusive humanism in the West. Because Confucianism was founded on the same principles of inclusive humanism, we can see how the Confucian works in a partnership with all things in the universe to establish not just a humane society but also a harmonious universe.

Onto-cosmology as the Inner Core of the Confucian Trinity

Confucianism is humanism in the inclusive sense. Often Confucianism is perceived only as human centered or human relations centered. It is often perceived as merely a philosophy of morality and ethics. Its ethics of *ren* (benevolence/humanity) is seen as lacking a rational and transcendental foundation, whereas its ethics of *li* (rites/propriety) is looked upon as polished conventions governing social relations or rules of behavior intended for optimizing social utility. Even its ethics of *yi* (righteousness/rightness) is taken to be merely a matter of doing right in a human and social context. I would not dismiss these perceptions simply as naive misconceptions, but they are nevertheless misleading because they are based on incomplete and superficial understanding. Such misunderstanding arises from a failure to appreciate the underlying discourse of onto-cosmology as the basis for Confucian ethics. Even though the classical Confucianism of the *Analects* appears to consist primarily of virtue ethics and its political application, one cannot ignore the broad underlying onto-cosmological discourse that gives vitality and spirit to the values and ideals of Confucius and his followers. As made amply clear in the works of Neo-Confucians of the Song and Ming periods, classical Confucian philosophy presents itself—and should therefore be seen—as a comprehensive unity comprising every single aspect of reality and humankind. This is particularly evident if we realize that the relevance of the onto-cosmological view is implicit in the symbolism and texts of the *Zhouyi* and becomes explicit in the *Yizhuan* (Commentaries) of the *Zhouyi*. I suggest, therefore, that we should not base our understanding of Confucianism on Confucius's *Analects* alone, or, even on the Four Books. It is important to relate Confucian morality and ethics to its onto-cosmology in the commentaries of the *Zhouyi*, among other works.[6]

Aside from the need for acquiring a comprehensive and balanced understanding of Confucianism, there is another critical reason to examine these works: unless and until we read Confucian ethics and morality as practicality (praxis) and practical reason, we will not fully understand this ethics and morality as a discourse unified with, and thus requiring, a metaphysical and onto-cosmological source and grounding. Many terms suggest the presence of such an onto-cosmological grounding and reference: *tian* (Heaven) is the center of moral concern for value; *dao* (the Way) is the basis for *de* (inner power/virtue) and *ren*; *xing* (性) nature/naturality) and *ming* (command/ destiny) reveal the experience of the polarity of the reality of the human individual as a moral being. The discourse becomes even more complete and more structured when we take into account the *Daxue* (大学), the *Zhongyong*, the *Mencius*, and the *Xunzi* (荀子). Once we encounter the *Zhongyong*, there is every reason to turn back to the *Yizhuan*, which gives a full disclosure of the onto-cosmology of the Confucian Way presented in forms other than morality and ethics. But one must still heed the subtle difference between the *Zhongyong* (together with the *Mencius*) and the *Yizhuan*: whereas the *Zhongyong* focuses on the practical and moral activation of the Way in a human being, and even in human society, one sees that the *Yizhuan* evokes very powerfully a heightened description of how the Way operates, how the world unfolds, and how the human being emerges with moral destiny and creative mission. What I wish to stress, in light of this discourse, is that we not only see a fuller picture of Confucian ethics as praxis focused on the *Yizhuan* onto-cosmology, but that we also realize that unless we have such an onto-cosmological worldview, we will not be able to effect real changes and transformations in the conditions of our existence and being through ethics and morality.

The onto-cosmological worldview in the *Yizhuan* consists of the following basic points. First, there is an inexhaustible source of creativity, which is one and undifferentiated but which is always ready to be differentiated into concrete and individual things. This notion of *taiji* (the Great Ultimate) represents a reflective insight into the dynamic unity of the reality of things: it combines the elements of unity and multiplicity and their dynamic connections in a process of development and involution. The most important thing about *taiji* is that it is the constant fountainhead amidst all things and provides the integrative and purposive unity of any type or any individual token while, at the same time, it also serves as the impetus for the diversity of things as types or tokens. In other words, it is both the starting point and the ending point of all things, and it always sustains connections among all things rooted in it as the origin.

We may thus see in *taiji* an intrinsic power of initiation leading to an intrinsic power of completion and fulfillment that gives reality and value to whatever is evolved or created. Furthermore, *taiji* can be seen as the state of equilibrium of non-differentiation before or after any concretion of things; therefore, it subsists as an ultimate level for all things. Apart from being the creative source, it is the source of harmonization among things and provides the basis for harmonization of the differentiations among all things whatsoever. Harmony, or harmonization, here means that all things mutually support and complement one another; harmony is conducive to fostering a renewed creativity and future development. In this respect, *taiji* can also be said to be the *Dao* (the Way) and, together with the *Dao*, signifies both a process and world qua the totality of things in which there is a profound equilibrium from the beginning and a pervasive accord or harmony among all things at any time. Humans, like everything else, are founded on this profound equilibrium and are included in this pervasive harmony. But, unlike everything else, the human being rises above everything to embody *taiji* and the *Dao* in his or her potential ability to create higher orders of equilibrium and harmony through culture and art. We come now to the second observation on the nature of creativity as a process.

It is said in the *Yizhuan*: "The alternation of one *yin* (the shady) and one *yang* (the bright) is called the *Dao*. What succeeds is the good and what completes is nature."[7] This statement underlines the polar nature of creativity during the process of producing all things in the world through *taiji*. What, then, is *yin*? What is *yang*? Clearly, the phenomenologically defined *yin/yang* can be realistically understood in a world of things and ontologically understood in the process of the creative production of things. The phenomenal paradigm of *yin/yang* presents a unity of contrast, a wholeness of complementarities, as well as a natural process of mutual transformation. It is the completion and return (one might call it creative circulation and recycling) illustrated in our aesthetic feelings and the felt qualities of things. Similarly, one may also see things that are congregations of qualities and dispositions exhibiting the same relationship and dynamic as the *yin/yang* interaction and integration.

Not only are things created out of the interaction of *yin/yang*, but all differentiation and unification of things, which then give rise to new things, can also be explained in terms of *yin/yang*, such that *yin/yang* could be ramified on different levels of being. An understanding of the relativity and multiplicity of *yin/yang* is, therefore, the basis for a reflective explanation of the natural processes of things. And *yin/yang* is also an onto-cosmological principle suggesting the unity and mutuality of the ontological and the cosmological. The *yang* is the visible, bright, changing, or moving cosmological process, whereas the *yin* is the invisible, hidden, and constant ontological reality. The interdependence and interpenetration of both give rise to the phenomenal reality of nature. We can therefore regard *yin* and *yang* as two inseparable and mutually transformable moments of the ultimate reality (*taiji*), which, by being the ultimate and unlimited source, gives rise to the two moments of creative concretion of things. This process, in turn, completes the creative concretion of things in the fold of the oneness of *taiji* as the source.

These dialectics of the creative transformation of the ontological into the cosmological, and vice versa, assures the ceaseless creative activity of the *Dao* as the underlying process/reality revealed in a description of the dynamics of the *yin/yang* interaction. Zhang Zai provided an apt characterization of this process of interaction in terms of *taiji*, embracing both the oneness of the *yin/yang* polarity and the *yin/yang* differentiation of *taiji* oneness: "Being one, it is creative; being two, it is transformative."[8]

We need to illustrate, in this connection, the important proposition that all things in reality are things generated as value, for value, and toward value. What is realized is real and the real is value. A value is value, not just because it is created real, but because it has an intrinsic position in the scheme of things and is capable of being related, developed, and intensified. Value also has a special relationship to the human mind: value is embodied in a feeling as well as in the felt qualities of things; moreover, it is an object of enjoyment, recognition, affirmation or negation, exploration, and development or reconstruction. Every thing has value because it arises from a creative source and is achieved in a creative process. Hence the saying "What is accomplished is nature and what succeeds is good." Good is a presentation of nature and can thus be a basis for understanding the holistic nature of the world or can be an ideal form of value. Given this understanding of value, it is up to the human being to discover the real value of things and situations so that he or she can be engaged in a creative construction and reconstruction of values.

In light of this polarizing process of the creative initiation and completion of things, we can see how Heaven and Earth must be formed in the creative process of *Dao* or in the creative realization of the oneness of *taiji*. In the *Zhouyi*, Heaven and Earth are the most basic cosmological concretions of the *yin/yang* from which other cosmological concretions are derived, as indicated in the *bagua* (Eight Trigrams) system or in the *wuxing* (五行 Five Phases) system. We may, in fact, conceive of Heaven and Earth in the whole symbolism of the *Zhouyi* as the basis for the creative evolution of the natural universe and as the basis for the further creative evolution of the human world. One can see how Heaven must be correlated with Earth in presenting the primordial creativity of *taiji* oneness via its polaristic moments of *yin/yang*. This is how the creative power of Heaven (*Qian* 乾) and the receptive power of the Earth (*Kun* 坤) work, where *Qian* and *Kun* are simply cosmic designations of *yin/yang*. It is interesting to note that in the symbolic text of the *Zhouyi*, the names of "Qian" and "Kun" are given to the icon-indexical symbols of Heaven and Earth, indicating the original oneness of *taiji* and its creative structuring of its moments into the polarity of *yin/yang*. Therefore, the way to reach *taiji* cosmology, which I call the onto-cosmology of *taiji* and the *Dao* in the *Xici*, and which later was further elaborated in the *Taiji Tu Shuo* (*Explanation of the Diagram of the Great Ultimate*) of Zhou Dunyi, is not arbitrary but logical.

When the Daoist philosopher Laozi speaks of the one generating the two, the two generating the three, and the three generating the ten thousand things,[9] he clearly has in mind the scheme of *taiji* producing the polarity of *yin/yang*.[10] But Laozi also says, "The *Dao* generates the one." This underlines the dynamic creativity of the ultimate reality, which, nevertheless, has the form of oneness.[11] If we see *taiji* as the source of the world, the *Dao* would be the same as *taiji* in generating the world of things as a whole system. But when Laozi says that the three generates the ten thousand things, the three is also seen as the third, that is, the resulting offspring of the interaction of the two. We may see the whole world of things and life-forms springing from the *yin/yang* interaction of Heaven and Earth. But we might also see the two as any two forces or things and hence see the three as any three forces or as a third force or as things derived from the two forces or things.

In this context it is clear that the human being is the most unique and outstanding third in the production of Heaven and Earth. Together with Heaven and Earth, the human being forms a ternion, or triad, with the whole universe. The interesting thing about this ternion is that a human is capable of doing what Heaven and Earth do, namely, nourishing life and helping things to grow. But a human is not exactly Heaven or Earth, although he or she possesses the virtues of Heaven and Earth in order to achieve higher orders of value. It is in this sense that the human creations, such as culture and art, should be treasured as products of human creativity. But what humankind creates has to be conducive to the continuation of the natural course of Heaven and Earth, not detrimental to it. Therefore, it is in this spirit of preserving our heavenly and earthly virtues that we should at no time act against such virtues that are not endowed in our human selves by nature but that are primarily exemplified in Heaven and Earth. In this way an ecological ethics can be constructed, as I shall explain in the next section.

What, then, is the position of the human being in this onto-cosmological process of creative production? In the *Yizhuan* it is said:

> [The sage] is similar to Heaven and Earth and therefore his conduct would not violate Heaven and Earth. His knowledge is comprehensive of all ten thousand things and his way will save all under Heaven. Even in acting in terms of special considerations, he does not deviate from rectitude (*zheng*). He enjoys the principles of Heaven and knows the limitations of destiny (*ming*). Therefore he has no anxiety. He is settled on the land (*tu*) and devotes himself to the sincere practice of benevolence (*ren*) and therefore he is capable of love.[12]

Zhuxi, in his commentary on this passage, says that this is a statement about fulfilling nature (*jinxing*). But *jinxing* means to practice *ren*, the way of Heaven and Earth, deeply and widely. Zhuxi even comments on the comprehensive knowledge of the sage as a matter of Heaven, and he comments on the saving grace to the world as a matter of Earth.[13] In this sense the sage is an apt representative of Heaven and Earth as benevolent rulers, not just an offspring of Heaven and Earth as parents.[14]

As a representative of Heaven and Earth, the human is not to conquer and exploit nature for his own comfort and private enjoyment because he has knowledge. Rather, it is this comprehensive knowledge that enables the human to care for other life-forms and to appreciate and protect nature. In like manner, a human is able to institute ways of governing in accord with what Mencius called a "government of benevolence" (*renzheng*).[15] As a child of Heaven and Earth, the human should have even more empathy with and sympathy for other living things in the world and so cannot bear to see, for example, the suffering of an ox or a sheep.[16] It is in this sense that the notion of *jinxing* applies. *Jinxing* is a complex notion, which in a narrow sense involves fulfilling one's own nature but in a broad sense involves fulfilling the natures of others and the natures of all things in the world apart from fulfilling one's own nature. Thus:

> Only the most sincere under Heaven are capable of fulfilling their own natures. Once capable of fulfilling their natures, they are capable of fulfilling the natures of others. If they are capable of fulfilling the natures of others, they are capable of fulfilling the natures of things. If they are capable of fulfilling the natures of things, they are capable of supporting the transformation and nourishment of Heaven and Earth. If they are capable of supporting the transformation and nourishment of Heaven and Earth, they are capable of forming a triad with Heaven and Earth.[17]

Who is this most sincere person? It is the person able to preserve and reveal the genuine virtues of Heaven and Earth so that he or she is not only able to realize and complete himself or herself but also able to realize and complete others. As the following quote from the *Zhongyong* notes, sincerity involves both *ren* and *zhi* (comprehensive knowledge as wisdom): "To accomplish oneself is *ren*, to accomplish things is *zhi*. Both are virtues of the nature. Sincerity (*cheng*) is the union of outer and inner ways (meaning *zhi* and *ren*). It is the fitness of timely action."[18] It is also in this sense that Confucius says: "It is the human being who is capable of enlarging the *Dao* and not the *Dao* that enlarges the human."[19]

It is clear, then, that the human being is related to Heaven and Earth in origination. If Heaven embodies the spirit of incessant creativity and the development of life and Earth sustains the everlasting receptivity and consistency of love, then the human must embody their combination in a harmonious fusion and should apply both in appropriate measure in thought, emotion, and conduct. Heaven is a symbol of the cosmology of creativity and development; Earth is a symbol of an ecology of comprehension and harmonization; and, finally, the human being is a symbol of the combination of the two, thus producing the ethics of integration and fulfillment of values.

Hence, we see in the Confucian sage the trinity of Heaven, Earth, and human that embodies the unity of cosmology, ecology, and ethics. It is important to see that the unity of the three is based on and unified in the onto-cosmology of the *Dao* and *taiji*. The relationship of the elements in the trinity may be diagrammed as follows:

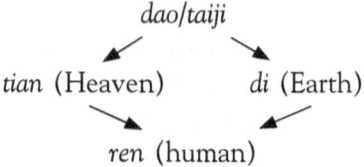

The concept of the trinity is derived from Christian theology, in which God the Father, God the Son, and God the Holy Spirit form a triad and yet are considered one, though as three positions within one.[20] As this trinity is historically soteriological, the question of how a trinity may be applied to cosmology, ecology, and ethics is a subtle and challenging question. In the *Zhouyi* interpretation of the trinity, explained above, we might see God the Son as the ideal human, God the Father would be Heaven (the creative spirit), and God the Holy Spirit the earth (the receptive co-spirit) or agent of the world that testifies to the accomplishment of the divinity. As I noted above, unless the transcendent notion of God is an immanent notion (immanent on Earth, immanent in humans, even immanent in Heaven), humankind's dominion of the earth becomes the domination of the earth in the name of God. Humankind then is enslaved by its own separate freedom and becomes the victim of its free will in isolation.

Finally, I now turn to an interpretation of the onto-cosmological base of Confucian cosmo-ethics and ecological ethics in terms of the organismic cosmology of Whitehead. First, the open creativity and continuity of creativity of Whitehead is well suited to the principle of ceaseless creativity in the onto-cosmology of the *Yizhuan*. The very way in which creativity takes place, which Whitehead describes as "Many are one and are increased by one," signifies the unity and harmonious integration of differences into an emergent whole as a realization of novelty and value. As an open process of creative advance, the integration of the many in one is both an increase by one and a decrease by the many regarded as an intrinsic characteristic of the dynamic balance and harmony of the process of *yi* in terms of the *Taiji Tu* (Diagram of the Great Ultimate). In the *Taiji Tu* a creative and correlative process displays the comprehensive harmony and dynamic transformation of the *yi* in terms of the ontogenesis of the many, which can be described as

"One are many and increase by many." This is the process of division and multiple divisions of *yin* and *yang* in the generation of sixty-four hexagrams and beyond. We may see this as a process of differentiation of novelty and value forming the Whiteheadian ingression of possibilities into concrete reality of actual occasions. What also needs to be noticed is that, whereas many are one and increase by one, they are one and decrease by many as well. Similarly, whereas one are many and increase by many, they are many and decrease by one as well. This internal balance of "give and take," "come and go," "increase and decrease" exhibits the rich texture of harmony and balance of reality as a creative process of novelty and value.

Second, Whiteheadian cosmic creativity is ultimately conceived in terms of the polarity of the primordial and consequent natures of God as two modes of the ultimate creative force. This suggests, no doubt, a strong analogy with the *yin/yang* polarity of the Great Ultimate in terms of its movement/rest and firmness/softness in which the concretion and individuation of things arise. Although one may note in Whitehead a certain transcendence of the primordial nature of God relative to its consequent nature, it may also be said to be a form of immanence with regard to the whole open process of the creative advance. The very inception of movement from the state of rest of the Great Ultimate can be seen as representing such a transcendent, yet immanent, power of the Great Ultimate and is therefore both an eternal source and an open process. The very fact that identity could negate itself to give rise to difference, and difference could negate itself to give rise to identity, so that we have both difference of identity and identity of difference, shows how immanence can become transcendence and transcendence can become immanence. It shows how in the very action of creative change both transcendence and immanence exist simultaneously. This must be the dialectical element in any effort of the mind to think about creativity and is conspicuously present in both the *Yizhuan* and Whitehead. Hence, dialectically, the primordial nature of God as *tian* and the consequent nature of God as *di* not only cannot be separated but are equally required for the evolution of all things in the world, including humans. That the human being can reflect on this creative process reveals the internal relationship existing between the human and the creative process of the world and indicates the source of human creativity.

Finally, we can see how a potential ecological ethics congenial with the *Yizhuan* can be developed from Whitehead, although Whitehead did not specifically address this issue. In his *Adventures of Ideas* (1933), Whitehead spoke of five values of culture that serve as a benchmark of the achievement of human civilization: truth, beauty, adventure, art, and peace.[21] It is obvious that these five marks of a civilized society are both descriptive and normative, applied to our thinking and conduct as both a standard and as a goal of our valuation. What is important is that they cannot be regarded in isolation but must be appreciated in conjunction, so that each will be reinforced and restricted by the others to form a truly harmonious and intense unity of values in a concrete sense. This harmonious unity of values can be called the supreme goodness, which ultimately defines human creativity as well as cosmic creativity. This is precisely the original goodness of the source of reality that is enlarged by the creative efforts of the successive stages of development—what is referred to as *jizhizhe shanye* (what is being succeeded is goodness) in the *Yizhuan*. For action with regard to ourselves, to others, and to the whole environment, there is simply no other goal or standard than this integration of values addressed to the whole of reality and to the future development of the whole reality. This is the essence of the cosmological-ecological-ethical imperative of *ren* and *zhi* expressed by both the *Yizhuan* and Whitehead.

Cosmo-Eco-Ethics and Moral Decision-Making

With the place of the human in the onto-cosmological framework of the *Yizhuan* understood, one may draw distinctions in the approach to environment and nature between the Confucian sage and the traditional Daoist, on the one hand, and between the Confucian and a modern technologist, on the other. The Daoist believes in the natural and spontaneous action of nature and reality and advocates following a course of natural spontaneity as the ethical way of a good life. In order to reach the state of "doing nothing," or "doing nothing unnatural," that defines or is regarded as a method for following natural spontaneity, a common version of understanding implies, however, that one has to be cut off from both desire and knowledge so that one will not be stirred by desire or knowledge and thus act in ways detrimental to the equilibrium in which humankind and nature exist. On reflection, not only is this an unrealistic goal to attain, it is also not the principle according to which the *Dao* creates and moves in the world. The *Dao* is a creative impulse that finds intrinsic joy in the creation of the world. There is no creation if there is no vitality of life, and from the vitality of life come life-forms, with their naturally endowed desires and instinctive zest for learning and experience.

The human being, like any other life-form, belongs to the creativity of the *Dao*, but unlike other life-forms, the human is endowed with a far greater capacity for knowledge and a far greater ability for action. Thus, what is natural for a human is not that he or she should lead the life of a plant or a simple animal; rather, the human should accomplish a state of value befitting his or her capacity for knowledge and ability for action, but without twisting, damaging, losing sight of, or violating the larger harmony and equilibrium between himself or herself and nature, on the one hand, and among things in nature, on the other. The human being should have the wisdom to accomplish this and should strive always to develop such wisdom. This wisdom is an integrative wisdom composed of both a reflective reason—knowing and understanding the relationship between humankind and the environment—and a practical reason—acting to maintain the relationship between humankind and the larger world of nature. Insofar as humans are able to do this, they will also be able to extend their knowledge and preserve their vital desires.[22]

On many occasions in the *Daodejing*, Laozi has envisioned this more enlightened version of following natural spontaneity (*ziran*). He speaks of the "non-selfishness" (*wusi*) of the sage that leads to his self-realization by way of the realization of others.[23] He also speaks of the Daoist principle of non-action (*wuwei*) as that of "creating without possessing, doing without being arrogant, and growing without dominating."[24] This principle of non-action constitutes a new approach to natural spontaneity that could be broadly applied to human creativity generally and to environmental ethics specifically. Its general application is important and necessary for humans in order that they reflect on the extension (scope) and intension (meaning) of their thinking and knowing and on the motivation and consequences of their actions.

This first type of reflection could be called Questioning the Adequacy and Depth of Knowledge and the second type, Questioning the Adequacy and Depth of Action. It is only when questions on the adequacy and depth of knowledge and action are raised that we can gain a critical assessment of our knowledge and action according to value. Such considerations demand an understanding of the nature of things and the world of nature from a holistic and long-term point of view.

They demand, especially, an intense critique of the inner self and the final good of human life. It is with such considerations in mind that any scientific knowledge must be examined from the perspective of a system of reality and value that transcends knowledge; and similarly, any action must be evaluated from a perspective taking into account the interaction, reversal, equilibrium, and harmonization of things in a whole system or process that necessarily transcends the action. Keeping this understanding in mind, it is clear that the onto-cosmology of the *Dao* and *taiji* provides a meaningful and fundamental model for such assessment and reflection.

On the one hand, the cosmology of Heaven should provide a model for human creativity in which cultural and scientific activities must be conducive to the preservation of life, not only of the human species, but of the whole of nature. For human life would be cut short were it not to be sustained on the basis of the continuing creativity of nature. On the other hand, the ecology of the Earth should provide a model for human non-action and natural spontaneity in which one must contemplate and reflect on one's creative activity so that it matures to a real fulfillment of value at large. As a final requirement, human ethics must combine the wisdom of Heaven and the wisdom of Earth in order to incorporate knowledge and action in a holistic context of equilibrium and harmony. Whether knowledge warrants action and whether action verifies knowledge are not considerations on the level of simple knowledge or on the level of simple action: they require the reflection and insight of the cosmology of Heaven and the ecology of the Earth. It is on the basis of the synthetic wisdom of a cosmo-eco-ethics that we are able to fulfill our lives as human beings by fulfilling the values of our lives as the fusion of Heaven and Earth. On this point, the Daoist of the *Dao* and the Confucian of *taiji* coincide and reinforce each other in mutual support. The conceptual scheme of reflection for human creativity may be summarized as follows:

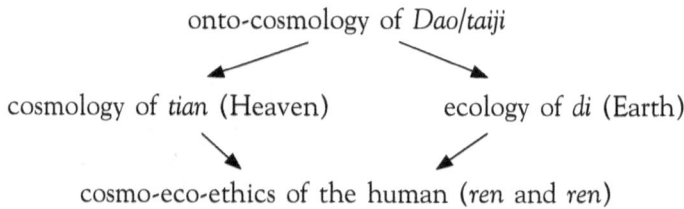

I turn now to the issue of scientific and technological development. The evolution of science and technology makes a difference to human knowledge and human action. Modern science sheds light on humankind's place in nature, but it need not determine humanity's destiny or define what the good life ought to be. It is technology that actually changes human life and human society to an unpredictable degree. It is also technology based on industry that leads to environmental crisis. The question inevitably arises: Should we regard technology as a harmful activity of human culture that should be abolished from the start? It seems clear how Daoists would answer this question: Laozi regarded modern technology as a "weapon of harm" (*xiongqi*) in the sense that not only could it be applied to further war and destruction, but it could lead to "galloping and hunting which makes people crazy at heart."[25] *Zhuangzi* also expresses his disapproval of technology as a means to promote the "artful mind" (*jixin*), which should be stopped before it takes root. The Daoist perspective on technology is that it does more harm than good, because it destroys the purity and innocence of the human self, leading then to a vicious cycle of the pursuit of desires following upon the pursuit of knowledge, and so on. Although Heidegger may not share exactly this same stance, his critique of technology could be construed as one concerning the ontological alienation of human from Being. It is not, therefore, simply that technology could be damaging to humankind's environment: it may actually obstruct the ontological integrity and authenticity of the human being.

According to the onto-cosmology of the *Dao* and *taiji*, human creativity is not limited to one level of activity but is founded instead on the basis of both cosmological and ecological creativity. In this sense, both the world of nature and the world of culture form a continuum and a hierarchy of both embeddedness and ascendence. Insofar as human creativity functions in view of the cosmological creativity and takes into consideration the values of equilibrium, sustainability, harmonization, and a healthy constructive reversible cycling, there is no limitation on human creativity. This means that any technological development must be assessed and understood within a framework allowing for the interplay of knowledge and value, part and whole, past and future, and human individual and the world of nature. It is because of these considerations that we may state that the Confucian who thinks and acts according to the imperatives of cosmo-eco-ethics by using his or her abilities and capacities preserves the human value as a whole. It is with this understanding that the *Yizhuan* speaks of "opening things and forming new affairs of culture," of "preparing things for extending functions, establishing utensils for the benefits of the world"—statements that can be understood as technologically oriented and pro-technological.[26] It is with the same understanding of the actuality of both human and nature that Whitehead's organismic philosophy likewise allows for the development of technology in an open and creative context of interchange between the possible and the actual, with human self-reflection on the fulfillment of important values in a prospective course of time.[27]

In the *Zhuangzi* it is suggested that there must be a true man (*zhenren*) before there is true knowledge (*zhenzhi*). But what is a true man? What is true knowledge? The *Zhuangzi* considers true knowledge as knowing both the function of Heaven and the function of man. How, then, could one have knowledge of Heaven and of man if one does not establish in one's own mind a creative vision and a creative attitude? In fact, the *Zhuangzi* describes the true man as one who does not harm the Way with his mind and does not assist Heaven by being a human being. Furthermore, the true man is one who sees Heaven and man as a unity in which there is no opposition between Heaven and man (*tian ren bu xiang sheng*).[28] This emphasizes the fact that the true man and true knowledge mutually ground and presuppose each other, and there is no separation between the two. But a different sense of knowledge and a different sense of the human being may be intended here. It also means that, in order to change knowledge and its use, one needs to change the person who has the knowledge. Similarly, in order to change the person, one needs to change the knowledge that person might have. Given the danger of environmental ruin and the urgency of the current environmental crisis, it is certainly not too great a demand to advance true knowledge and to cultivate the true person. My analysis here has demonstrated the need to raise up both the true person and true knowledge. An understanding of the trinity of cosmology, ecology, and ethics is such knowledge, and the cosmo-eco-ethical combination of the three in the accomplished Confucian personhood is such a true person. For the true person who holds true knowledge has a practical wisdom that may be mediated by technological reason but will remain rooted in the reflective and meditative reason of ontology and cosmology.[29]

4

Toward an Integrative Pluralism of Religions
Embodying Yijing, Whitehead, and Cobb

Pre-conditions of Integrative Pluralism

A religion once it is recognized as a religion has three components: it has a history and hence is founded in some past events of particular concretion; it has a goal directed toward its future realization, whether it delivers the individual or a nation from a human condition or finite fatality or promises a state of grand benediction or eternal bliss for a community of people; and it is also active in terms of theoretical justification, doctrinaire conversion, and institutional organization at the present. All three aspects combine to reflect how the human person and human society are constituted and serve a human purpose of transforming (in life) or transcending (in death) humanity in humanity. Whether this explanation of religion fulfils many other requirements of religion as defined by historians, sociologists, or philosophers and theologians of religion, however, is another question. But it has at least brought out the minimally shared characters of present world religions such as Christianity, Buddhism, and Islam. Based on this working perception of what religion is, one can immediately identify a core of subjectivity in any religion, which is the self-identity of what it says it is destined to achieve. One can further identify how a religion perceives its origination and which ways it offers, or persuades people to follow, in order to achieve the goal that it promises or professes to promise.

It is clear that despite the fact that a world religion has a particularity of historical beginning and development, its futurity is not bounded by its historicity; instead, it has embodied a universal claim, which is to be applied to all people in order to vindicate its message of final deliverance and spiritual conversion. In this sense it is intent on transcending time and space in establishing a power of being or presence at any moment. Hence the roots for spreading a doctrine and establishing an institution by a world religion already become inevitable. This is to be seen again in Christianity, Buddhism, and Islam.

Although each world religion may have made its universalistic claim, as a historical fact or in light of a theoretical reflection, it will have to find its doctrine being contradicted or rejected by other religions of different historicities. In this regard, conflicts of religions must take place insofar as each lays an exclusive claim on truth. This situation of religious conflict is in one respect like the case of conflict of philosophies that would lead to arguments and debates and disputes. In another it could be different, because it is linked to a populace in a way in which philosophy does not, and could claim a power over society and share an interest in politics. Hence religious conflict could lead to wars because it could involve claims to power of influence and possessions of resources and people.[1] Thus, in speaking of religions we have to recognize not only their rootedness in history, but also their vital realistic interests in the present. This would make religious understanding and religious harmony especially important. If all major religions find that they could peacefully co-exist, have mutual respect for each other, and honor the other's right to preach its own vision of truth, then there is no worry about a clash of arms among them, and consequently they could learn to co-develop and could even learn to assist each other toward better development.

When such circumstances arise, we must say that each religion must see the other religions as equally valid and equally credible, and thus each could consider the others as equal members of a free association or a great council of religious faiths, which in turn would recognize the others as equal partners and would make efforts to provide services to facilitate the sustainable development of each religion in their own ways without conflict or clash. This of course does not mean that world religions would not compete with each other. They could still compete as they actually do in terms of their persuasive powers and the appeal of their programs of deliverance. They may also cooperate with one another to achieve a large role in serving humanity when there are calamities.

The above is a scene of what I come to envision as a comprehensive harmony of world religions founded on the principles of Integrative

Religious Pluralism or an Integrative Plurality of Religions, which would recognize the following propositions as universally valid:

1. Each religion has its own particular and uncommon (peculiar) history and is rooted in a time or location of limited scope.

2. Each can have its own view of the origins of the world and the origins and conditions of humanity (particularly in reference to meaning and value of life and death), which could be formulated in universalistic terms.

3. Each could have its own universalistic teaching of salvation and self-discipline and self-transformation of people and the world.

4. Each has its vision of transcendence whether in the form of a personal God or Buddha or in the spirit of an impersonal Nirvana or Dao.

5. Each has its own community of preachers, teachers, believers, and followers.

6. Each agrees to recognize and respect the same rights of others to persuade, to preach, and to offer religious beliefs to the world.

7. Each agrees to disagree with others on religious beliefs and resolves to use reasonable and peaceful means to resolve conflict of interests or influences.

8. Each refrains from attacking, abusing, defaming, or distorting the others violently or physically, orally or in writing, even though philosophical argument and ethical critique are allowed.

9. Each has at least a minimal good will or good wish to understand each other for eliminating bias and/or learning knowledge and wisdom.

10. Each cultivates, cherishes, and makes efforts to maintain inter religious harmony and the common good once achieved as a result of such harmony.

Given such a scenario, which we may say "Harmonize Without Being the Same," in the words of Confucius, or, still better, "Let Being Different Lead to Harmonization," as I would say, and we wish to ask whether the teachings of the religions may be justified in terms of a comprehensive theory of religious truth that is directed toward understanding humanity, the human condition, human deliverance, and reality in general. In other words, once we have religious pluralism, we need to ask philosophical questions about their truth-value as well as their value of truth. This is how the philosophy of religions becomes most relevant for today, because we do have a de facto scene of religious diversity. I also take this to be how and why Alfred North Whitehead set out to mediate the diversity of two world religions, Christianity and Buddhism, that is, to relate them or to transcend them in light of an emerging understanding of what the world is and what human beings are. Whitehead has provided his own framework for accommodating all religions against a background understanding and a new interpretation of being and human being. But I like to interpret his purpose in terms of three levels of understanding pluralism in the following terms:

1. See the theoretical and practical differences of existing religions such as Christianity and Buddhism.

2. See the theoretical and/or practical complementarity of different existing religions in light of an underlying philosophy of being and becoming.

3. See all religions (including both present and future religions) as off-springs of a comprehensive philosophy of being and becoming and the related understanding of humanity and the world.

Given these three levels of understanding, we may say that there are three forms of religious pluralism: The first kind is *differential pluralism*, which is set on recognizing the difference between all existing religions or even future religions; the second kind is *complementary pluralism*, which is set on seeing all existing religions or future religions as complementary forms of religious practice or believing; and the third kind is *integrative pluralism*, which is intent on showing that all religions are to be regarded as integral parts of a holistic developmental process of humanity and its understanding of the world. This integrative form of pluralism is important because it would provide a philosophical basis for differential religions in terms of their histories while also providing an open and creative vision for relating their differences to a creative whole so that they can be seen and encouraged to develop further and learn from each other to achieve their ultimately proper places in light of an overarching vision of human understanding and human practice. In this light, I wholeheartedly appreciate John Cobb's and David Griffin's work in developing the *complementary pluralism*, but I also wish to stress how this complementary pluralism must go one step further toward *integrative pluralism* in light of the Whiteheadean philosophy of creativity, to avoid relativism while preserving uniqueness, to embrace the whole while achieving the part, to realize the global while enjoying the local.

In the remainder of this chapter, I discuss four interrelated topics for understanding the importance of developing an integrative pluralistic view of religious truth and beliefs: (1) how the Whiteheadean framework should integrate with the framework of the philosophy of *Yijing* in order to meet challenges of a global religion of the East and West, which would also simultaneously cater to local and relative needs of humanity; (2) how the inherently open issues of relativism could be both overcome and allowed in a world religion, so that they may help the religion continue developing; (3) how humanity has acted as a root metaphor for divine personalization, which leads to the enrichment of the onto-cosmological view of creativity and God as creator, and which can be seen at the same time as deeply rooted in a background *Yijing*-Whitehead philosophy of creativity and creative change; (4) whether the integrative harmonization of Christianity and Buddhism as two world religions based on the historical model of the integrative harmonization of Confucianism and Daoism is possible; whether Confucianism and Daoism should be regarded as religions, and why they are important and instrumental for achieving a future transformation of the world religions into a state of integrative harmonization of different religious beliefs and practices.

Integration of Creativity: Whitehead and Yijing

How do we understand Whitehead's notion of "creativity"? The primary understanding is that creativity is the ultimate that makes any and all things possible or in virtue of which actuality realizes itself and expands into a world of things. Without the production of things, there is no creativity. If creativity is an ultimate category for describing the world, it has to describe the continuous formation and transformation of things in the world, which no doubt includes production of new things, such as new plants and new human babies. Hence creativity must pertain to the ceaseless productivity of things, and it should hold without cessation in any place and at any time. As to how production of new things takes place, is it a matter of coalescing many into one? Or is it a matter of differentiating one into many? Observations show that both are common ways for producing new things, which we may refer to as fusion and fission respectively. Oftentimes a production of a new thing involves both fission and fusion; for example, the formation of an embryo is a fusion of egg and sperm, but it immediately involves fission (mitosis) of cells to grow into what it is. Or take the formation of a storm: it is a separation of water particles from the ocean and then gathering momentum and speed by accumulating more of the same under tropical heat. In this sense, creativity can have many modes of being and becoming: a simple mode of fission or differentiation, a simple mode of fusion or integration, or a complex of fusion/fission or fission/fusion. It is interesting to note that for Whitehead creativity is the principle of novelty, which consists in advancing a unifying entity from a diversity of many entities:

> Creativity is the universal of universals characterizing ultimate matter of fact. It is the ultimate principle by which the many, which are the universe disjunctively, become the actual occasion, which is the universe conjunctively. It lies in the nature of things that the many enter into complex unity.[2]

> Creativity is the principle of novelty. An actual occasion is a novel entity diverse from any entity in the many which unifies. Thus creativity introduces novelty into the content of the many, which are the universe disjunctively. The creative advance is the application of this ultimate principle of creativity to each novel situation which it originates.[3]

However, there is no reason why a novel thing may not be an entity resulting from differentiation of an existing entity in the first place. In fact, to mark out this as a mode of creativity is extremely important because we have to see how creativity as the ultimate of all things and the universal of the universals must guarantee the origination of the originating agency of all things, which is God. The very coming into existence and actuality of God is the first and the foremost and the most powerful act of creation from the principle of creativity, for without God there is no further creativity, and without God creativity would not become a principle that can be recognized by the human mind. Here the use of the term "God" is both conventional and unconventional: it is conventional because "God" is designated as the "Creator" or the source of creativity for all things moving in the world, including the world. It is also unconventional because we do not have to identity "God" by any historical account of any world religion or any other theological view. We can instead identify "God" entirely by its creativity and creativeness, which consists in the creation of things by modes of fission or fusion. We could equally well use the word "*dao*" or "*tian*" or even better still "*qianyuan*" (the powerful originator) from the *Yijing* (*Book of Change*), which expresses the idea of "power of being" or "power of origination."[4] In this sense God is the embodiment of creativity and the initial and real/actual fulfillment of creativity as a principle. Whitehead has given the following description of how God is related to creativity: "The true metaphysical position is that God is the aboriginal instance of this creativity, and is therefore the aboriginal condition which qualifies its action. It is the function of actuality to characterize the creativity, and God is the eternal primordial character. But, of course, there is no meaning to creativity apart from its creatures, and no meaning to the temporal creatures apart from creativity and God."[5] With God so conceived, it is clear that God is oneness arising from itself as an infinite creativity to itself as a source of the power of determination, motivation, inspiration, and efficient causation against a background that is both itself and not-itself. In its arising as a sui generis power of being and becoming, the mode of creativity may be conceived as a fission or separation from itself, which may also be described as being for itself in being not for itself. In so conceiving it, we may think that God is both a creative power from nothing and a creator creating the world from nothing. We may even think of God as both being and non-being because it transforms being into non-being and transforms non-being into being. In this sense, Whitehead's concept of God in combination with his concept of creativity needs not be seen as conflicting with the traditional view of God as the creator who performs *creatio ex nihilo*. In fact, it is due to the coming into existence of the creative power, such as God, that there comes to be the distinction and differentiation between being and non-being. Hence God marks both the difference and identity of being and nonbeing, as well as the dynamical process of creativity between the two.

In this light we can see how the Whiteheadean view of creativity and God approaches and actually could merge with the view of the onto-cosmology of the *Great Appendix* (*Xici*) of the *Yijing* and the *Taiji Tushuo* (*Discourse on the Diagram of the Taiji*) of the great Neo-Confucian philosopher Zhou Dunyi (1017–1073) in the Song period. Without going into great details, it suffices to cite two fundamental insights from the *Yizhuan* (of which *Xici* is a part) that would lend a base for claiming the complementary plurality of things in the world and their underlying universal oneness.

In the section 5 of the *Xici*, it is said that "One *yin* and one *yang* is called the *Dao*." This statement is based on comprehensive observation (*guan*) of both the outer universe and reflection on the human condition, which may be regarded as a most comprehensive induction of human experiences as well as the rational intuition on what any process of change would have exhibited.[6] The key notion here is the *Dao* and the key assumption is that the world is seen as a process of change (*yi*). The change in the world is observed to move from one state to another state, which is different from the earlier state, and the two states must be different and yet connected in terms of time. What becomes visible and explicit is the *yang*, and what remains invisible and implicit is the *yin*. Insofar as change is concerned, one must see the transformation of the explicit into the implicit and vice versa. No doubt there are degrees of such change in terms of the degrees of explicitness and implicitness, which can be related to degrees of brightness and darkness, degrees of firmness and softness, and degrees of motion and rest. To see changes in these dimensions and their relatedness requires common experience and perception, which, however, need not be simply located or atomically identified. Therefore the experience of observation (*guan*) need not be simply sensationalistic, but could be apperceptional and holistically intuitive and reflective.

With this experiential basis, one can see how the *Dao* as the whole and universal process of change must be an alternation of *yin* and *yang* in the sense suggested. Apart from seeing the temporal alternation of *yin* and *yang* as the paradigm for describing the experience of the *Dao*, it is also to be understood that *yin* and *yang* constitute two ultimate categories of reality insofar as their alternation is to be seen in a spatial sense; namely, there exists in the world diversity of things, many of which are found to be related side by side in *yin-yang* relationship. The relationship of the cosmic heaven and earth is such an example. Other examples include the female-male relationship and ruler-people relationship, along with many other social relationships (or the Whiteheadean nexuses) that form wholes of polarities. This suggests that the *yin-yang* conception can be used as a metaphor to understand all different kinds of relationships relative to different contexts or conditions that share the basic pattern of a dynamic contrast. What follows from this is also the perception that the *yin-yang* relationship forms a dynamic field of forces that can be seen as related in simultaneous opposition and support, interdependence, mutual stimulation, and reciprocal enrichment. It is in light of these experiences that we can see the *yin-yang* relationship not only as phenomenologically open but also ontologically allusive: they form open clusters of percepts and concepts that can apply to things and events on different levels in different contexts. As ontological concepts, they define not only what a dynamical wholeness is but also what complementarity in a whole process is.

The relationship of *yin-yang* constitutes a whole field and a whole world (or a whole reality) that can be seen as complying with our primary experiences of change in terms of the polar (or dialectical) dynamics. In other words, the *yin-yang* relationship defines a wholeness and a unity, or oneness, in which the *yin-yang* dynamics can be said to be meaningfully observed. There is also another sense of the *yin-yang* relationship in light of our experience, the *yin* and *yang* being those basic elements or forces that when linked in an appropriate way would lead to the emergence or creation of novelty or new entities. This defines the *yin-yang* relationship as a creative process and gives a meaning to the assertion that creativity of the *yin-yang* consists in production and transformation of all things in the world. It also gives a meaning to the notion of complementarity: *yin* and *yang* are complementary insofar as they find each being conducive to the change of the other; together, they are conducive to the production of novelty because of their interaction and merging. This sense of creative complementarity is different from the whole-producing or holistic complementarity in that the latter leads to a hypothesis on how diversity and novelty, which are exemplified in most of the life phenomena, could come into existence, whereas the former can be found in many structurally organized phenomena of physical nature, such as the famous wave-particular dynamics of light.

In light of these two senses of complementarity, we find the *Yizhuan* stating the following in regards to the holistic complementaries: "The *yi* (change) has the *Taiji* (the Great Ultimate), and *Taiji* produces the two norms (*yin* and *yang*), two norms produce the four forms (*old yang/young yang/young yin/old yin*), the four forms give rise to eight *trigrams*" (*Xici shang* 11). The so-called eight trigrams *(bagua)* are also forms standing for large clusters of natural phenomena just as the four forms stand for still larger natural phenomena, whereas the two norms of *yin* and *yang* would underlie these two levels of phenomena as the basic structure of dynamic change that leads to or creates these differentiations of forms.[7] Consequently we may note the following nine points:

First, the process of differentiation and integration are both observable processes, but they could be projected as metaphysical principles of the formation and transformation of reality. Thus, the difference of *yin* and *yang* works both ways: it leads to the positing of the unity of *Taiji* to which both *yin* and *yang* belong, and it also leads to the positing of the diversity to result from the interactive dynamics of the *yin-yang*. Hence we find that the *yin-yang* principle leads to an ontology of the power of being in oneness, which is *Taiji*, and a cosmology of many things generated from processes of the *yin-yang* on different levels and throughout different periods of time. Because both the ontology of being and the cosmology of things are pivoted in the creative integrating/differentiating process under the agency of the *yin-yang*, we have an onto-cosmology of *Taiji-yin/yang*-diversity of forms. The whole world is seen as a procession and process of creativity working in both the direction of integration into oneness and differentiation into diversity. It is to be noted that the positing of the *Taiji* could be related to the observation in the *Tuan Commentary*, which posits the great creative force called the Creative (Qian) and the great receptive force called the Receptive (Kun), which work together to produce the world. *Taiji* as the great unity and source of the *qian* and *kun* serves as both the efficient and material cause of all things, which in the process of its production of things also endows things with different forms and subjective aims (*telos*). Hence the Qing critical Confucian, Dai Dongyuan (1724–1777), says, "To be creatively creative is the source of transformation. To be creatively creative and yet at the same time providing patterning and ordering is the flow of the transformation."[8]

Second, with both integration and differentiation we have a creativity that is creative in both ways. This is referred to in the *Yizhuan* as the process of creative change or change by creative creativity (*sheng-sheng*). It is said that "[T]he creativity of creativity is to be identified as the *yi*" (*Xici shang* 5). From this it can be seen that the principle of creative unity or wholeness leads to the principle of oneness in Whitehead, whereas the principle of creative diversity leads to the principle of plurality (many) in Whitehead. Both "one" and "many" are principles of creativity, and they are exhibited in the process of the integration of the many into one and the differentiation of the one into the many. God is the ultimate one, and there is no ultimate many, as creativity is an open process that has its sources in the ultimate one, which is *Taiji* and God. Here I identify *Taiji* with God in the sense I have explained. Perhaps from a philosophical point of view it is better to see God as *Taiji* rather than *Taiji* as God. But on the other hand, there is no reason why *Taiji* when endowed with personal traits other than pure creativity may not be called God. This renaming in fact involves a process of onto-hermeneutical interpretation; namely, one has to interpret something abstract and philosophical from a historical, social, or religious point of view, which is often rooted in experiences of a particular concretion. But it is equally important to hold that one must become aware of the possible reference in light of an understanding of reality. In this sense, the *Yijing* and Whitehead together provide a framework of reference, reidentification, and onto-hermeneutical re-interpretation in light of our new experiences and new insights learned from other traditions.

Third, there are other important messages conveyed in the onto-cosmology of creative change of the *Yijing* that would give a clear sense of complementarity. Complementarity implies wholeness to which complementary parts belong as parts related in an organic way. It also implies creativity that gives rise to novelty and new development in an open future. Insofar as Whitehead is concerned, his idea of seeing Christianity and Buddhism as complementary would imply both even though he did not clarify the contents of either in detail. But in calling his 1926 book *Religion in the Making*, one can see many meanings implicated: a new religion from interaction of old religions would arise; a new view on ontology and cosmology could inspire such a new religion or provide a mediation for such a new religion. His 1929 book, *Process and Reality*, was clearly intended to provide this function of interrelating and mediating.

Fourth, in light of what is said above, it is clear that the *Yijing* philosophy of creative change would lead the complementary plurality of truths or things into an integrative plurality of truths and things.

116 | The Philosophy of Change

One need not go too far to find support of this view in Whitehead's *Process and Reality*.

Fifth, for completing the work of onto-cosmology of the *Yijing*, we must introduce the work of Zhou Dunyi, in whom we see a merging of ideas from Daoism, Buddhism, and Confucianism, which is manifested in the extension of the notion of *Taiji* to *Wuji* (the ultimateless). It is said in Zhou's *Taiji tushuo* that "*Wuji er Taiji*" (The ultimateless and then the great ultimate). What then is *wuji* (the ultimateless)? What does this sentence mean? In the first place, "*wuji*" is a negation of the existence of any limit or any property, or any force, that can qualify as any character or any characterization of being. As things are to be characterized and qualified in one way or another, "*wuji*" therefore stands for voidness (*wu*) of characters or nothingness in the Daoist sense. We may simply say that *wuji* is equivalent to *wu* (void/ emptiness), although Zhu Xi in the twelfth century tried to make *wuji* a qualification for *Taiji*, namely, indicating the infinity of the Great Ultimate. But Zhu Xi was obviously mistaken, because the sentence "*Wuji er Taiji*" does not suggest any qualification of *Taiji* by *wuji*. On the other hand, the syncategorimatic word "*er*" indicates that *wuji* is actually being qualified by *Taiji* (the great ultimate). This means to say that in the first place there is a non-being or non-existence of anything, and then there comes into being the Great Ultimate, which is the power for creating or generating the world of things.

Sixth, as to how nothing becomes something is to be considered a matter of creative creativity of the non-being in the Laozi's writing *Daodejing*, where it is asserted that the *wu* (void) begets *you* (being). The *you* begins with the one, which should be the *Taiji*, which gives rise to *yin* and *yang*, which are the two norms, which then give rise to everything in the world. From this we can see that there are two kinds of creativity: creativity for the rise of the *Taiji* from the *wuji* and creativity for the rise of the cosmic world of things from the *Taiji*. It can also be said that without things in the world we would not come to see the two forms, and without two forms we would not make the intuitive projection of the source of the complementary creativity of *yin* and *yang*, namely the *Taiji*. Without *Taiji* there could not exist a way of speaking of *wuji*, for if there is no quality to speak of, there is no way of referring to anything whether by language or by action (each of which is a qualifying character), as there would be no language or action. With *Taiji* we can refer to *wuji* as the negation of characters of things;

thus, *wuji* comes to be known only by way of the *Taiji*. Consequently, one can come to see that even *Taiji* and *wuji* can be associated in a complementary relationship of creative action—namely, *wuji* gives rise to *Taiji* as a positive force of being that shows in contrast the creativity of the void, which is *wuji*. In this sense, one may see *wuji* as a symbol for primordial creativity, which is creative of creativity.

Seventh, the question may be raised whether *wuji* may be related to the Buddhist notion of *kong* (emptiness or *śūnyatā*). There is no simple answer to this question, for we have to trace the complex history of how the Indian Mahāyāna concept of *śūnyatā* was first interpreted in terms of the Daoist concept of *wu* (void) in the fourth century, how it gradually acquired its original meaning of nonattachment and non-substantiality, and finally how, by the seventh century, it became reconstituted and understood as naturally leading to the world of things and life as it is in the Chan writings on enlightenment (*wu*). In this sense the Buddhist *kong* has to be understood in a context that in fact does not depend on the Indian Buddhist negation and extinction of world and life (*nirvana*, the de-creative nothingness) and could become exchangeable with the Daoist *Dao*, which is the creative void. As a matter of fact, the Buddhist co-origination (*pratītya-samutpāda*) theory of the formation of things in the world needs to be explained as a principle of natural transformation of the *Dao* with its inherent ordering, not just as simply a matter of karmic recycling. In this analysis we can see that *wuji* in Zhou Dunyi actually acquired a meaning in a post-Buddhist age as involving a reformation of the Buddhist *kong* not as quietude or extinction but as creativity and as origin of the originating power.

As the eighth point to be noted, it may be also mentioned that for the *Yijing*, onto-cosmology, the sense of time, and the sense of temporal process are important, because creativity is creativity in time and real in time and thus is related to the sense of becoming and transformation. The *Yijing* onto-cosmology presents a creative unity of ontology and cosmology in time and change in which one and many, *yin* and *yang*, being and non-being become dynamically one. This requires an insight of mind into the creativity of time and unity in time, for at any moment, one needs to see all differences and disparity as resolved in a harmony of complementary forces without necessarily losing their individualities. This quality of harmonization in time is also a feature of Whitehead's philosophy, as we can see in the following quotation: "The doctrine of the philosophy of organism is that, however far the sphere of efficient causation be pushed in the determination of components of a concrescence—its data, its emotions, its appreciations, its purposes, its phases of subjective aim—beyond the determination of these components there always remains the final reaction of the self-creative unity of the universe."[9] The "self-creative unity of the universe" is regulative of the creative advance of the world in which differences will be harmonized in the sense of a creative unity of the world, if we keep in mind the creativity of time, which is the creativity of the *Taiji* itself in sustaining the world of things and in both bringing new things into being and dissolving old things.

The ninth and final point to be noted is this: in contrast to the preceding discussion of time, we could speak of a timeless order of harmony whether pre-conceived or pre-established in the sense of the ontological identity of the state of *kong* (emptiness) and the state of dependent causation, which would also logically give rise to a state of interdependent events and things. This is the final perception or conception of the world-reality described as the state of "non-obstruction of all things" (*shishiwuai*) or the state in which "one is all and all is in one" (*yijiyiqie, yiqiejiyi*) as in Huayan Buddhism, a state of "perfectly accomplished reality" (*yuanchengshi*) as in Weishi Buddhism, or "the perfect fusion of three truths" (*sandiyuanrong*) as in Tiantai Buddhism. The point of making this remark is to show that Buddhism has a tendency to reduce time to timelessness so that harmony could be realized in an enlightened understanding of mind, whereas for the *Yijing* Onto-Cosmology what is realized in a timeless perception of the self-creative unity in the source has to be realized in a temporal process of ceaseless harmonization of the world. In the latter case, the world has to be real and has to be realized through co-participation of the human mind and human action together with the creative force of the *Taiji*. This point is important, as we shall see, because the pluralistic differences of the religions must be resolved in the creative evolution of the religions themselves in a process toward harmonious unity and integration. The self-imposed universalism in a religion is merely abstract and needs to be given meaning in a concrete process of creative adaptation, dependent co-origination, and co-definition, even though in another mode a sense of transcendent satisfaction can be derived from a sense of immediate self-sufficiency and universal consistency in one's own mind.

We may now sum up the above briefly described Onto-Cosmology of the *Yijing* in light of Zhou Dunyi's philosophy as is expressed in the following four propositions cited directly from the *Yizhuan*:[10]

1. "The change and transformation of the world has originated from the originating power titled 'the great ultimate' (*Taiji*)."

2. "The *Taiji* has its emergence from *wuji*, which becomes known only when the *Taiji* is formed."

3. "All changes are composed of two sides derived from the *Taiji*, the *yin* and the *Yang*, which are found in contrastive opposite qualities and forces but which are also creatively complementary so that they form the sources for the formation and transformation of the world."

4. "The processes of change are always creative, ceaseless, and sustainable."

It is clear that the basic propositions of Whiteheadean metaphysics are onto-hermeneutically interpretable or re-interpretable in terms of the *Yijing* onto-cosmology of creative change. Furthermore, Whiteheadean discourse could receive a clearer meaning with regard to the concepts of Cosmic Epoch, Creativity and God, Concrescence, Novelty, Creative Advance, Actual Occasions, Prehension, Complementarity, God and World, Primordial Nature and Consequential Nature of God, One and Many, Super-Actuality, Dipolarity, Being, and Nothing. This means that all of these Whiteheadean concepts, particularly those related to non-being, or nothing, or origins of creativity, could receive a creative re-statement in the *Yijing* and Daoist philosophy of onto-cosmology. On the other hand, it can be equally possible to show that the *Yijing* concepts of the *dao*, the *Taiji*, *wuji*, and *yin-yang* can also be given a Whiteheadean meaning and re-interpretation in terms of the analytical details of Whitehead's organismic philosophy of being and becoming. In light of this implicit reciprocal re-interpretation of each other, a comprehensive framework for understanding the creativity of reality and human life could be presented and applied as a philosophy of religion or as a mediation for different philosophies of religion, East and West.

Overcoming Relativism in Integrative Pluralism

Now I address the views of John Cobb in regard to his efforts to overcome relativism in his complementary pluralism of religions. Based on what has been described in the lucid papers on Cobb by David Griffin,[11] it is obvious that Cobb has shown great insights in seeing the equal relevance and importance of both Godhead (from Christianity) and emptiness (from Buddhism) in describing the Ultimate Reality and hence affirms the universally claimed truth of both religions as equally valid. His point is that the Ultimate Reality that a world religion has made efforts to embody can enjoy many characteristics, which can be realized or revealed individually or severally to different world religions, perhaps, because of their different conditions of historical origins. Although I do not know how Cobb explains the different approaches taken by different religions, we might suggest that different ecological, social, cultural, and historical conditions induce different religious needs and provide different ways of satisfying those needs. If we want religion to provide a holistic solution to the problems of life, we also want to see religion explained holistically on the basis of life. It is the forms of life that determine the religious experiences we have, just as religious experiences determine or conduce to a form of life. In this fashion, we find good reason to say that religion cannot be explained by a single science or social science or by any combination of them. We may have to include the self-fulfilling abilities and self-creative abilities in human individuals and human collective life for understanding the creative functions of religion for human evolution and human cultural development.

As Cobb recognizes that different religions could yield different insights into the ultimate reality, dialogues among religions can only increase the width and depth of the self-understanding of a religion. It may also enable religions to enrich each other in the way Cobb calls "complementary." It is by this way that Cobb has moved from a Christian-centered point of view of religion to a point of view that would put any two religions on an equal basis for seeing how they may benefit and enrich each other.

Although it is not immediately clear how different religious claims of truth can be reconciled as complementary and in reference to which framework of reconciliation, Cobb has suggested that one way to do so is to find reasons to see two different and apparently contradictory assertions of religious truth as truly non-contradictory and instead complementary. It seems to me that there are two steps involved in this process of transformation. The first step is to see contradictories as contraries by saying that they do not completely describe the ultimate reality. The second step is to see that contraries are in fact sub-contraries, being descriptions of different properties of the Ultimate Reality. In this process of transformation, one has to develop a concept or a view of the Ultimate Reality with regard to which one can perform transformation of contradictories into contraries and then perform transformation of contraries into sub-contraries. What is this Ultimate Reality that enables Cobb to do the transformation work? The answer is that it is his understanding of Creativity and God, the notions of which are suggested in Whitehead's philosophy of organism.

I agree with Cobb's analysis of the Whiteheadean notion of creativity as two ultimates (creativity and God) or even three ultimates (creativity, God, and the world) insofar as they are to be seen as interconnected. If they are not holistically connected or integrated in some theoretical and philosophical fashion, we shall not be able to see how the Buddhist truth of Emptiness and the Christian truth of Godhead could be related as parts of a whole. But then the question of integrating the three ultimates is an urgent task, which needs to be confronted. Although Whitehead has provided a basic theory of creativity, God, and world, their interrelation still can be justified in the framework of the *Yijing* and the Neo-Confucian theory of the *Taiji* and *wuji*, as carried out in the above section. The significance of doing this newer interpretation is to see how emptiness can be linked to the Godhead in light of how *wuji* is related to *Taiji*. This is an important task of philosophy of religion, which is implicit in Whitehead, but which has been brought to the surface by Cobb.

Given Whitehead's framework reinforced by the Yi-Onto-Cosmology, one will be able to bring a deeper sense of complementarity than simply recognizing particularity in a universal whole. One would also see how complementarity could be the condition for future and further creativity, production of novelty, and renewal of the cosmos. For we have to see the rich suggestiveness of the paradigm of the *yin-yang* interaction and inducement in order to see how different religions could learn from each other, renovate each other, and then bring out their own fruits of innovation. It is in this sense that a religion could receive a new life and have a new content based on integration of its old content and new experience of the world in which other religions are resourceful parts. The interaction between emptiness and being, just like the interaction between world and God, is the fountainhead for the transformation of our beliefs and concepts of world, God, and ourselves as human beings. In reference to a Whitehead statement quoted above, Griffin quotes

Cobb as saying, "without a cosmic reality there can be no acosmic one and that without God there can be neither. Similarly, without both the cosmic and acosmic features of reality there can be no God" (Griffin 14; Cobb, TCW, 121). The interdependence of the three demonstrates an integrative creativity, which is only to be realized in the ongoing creative advance of the world in which everything including the *human person* has a creative role to play.

Neither Whitehead nor Cobb seems to identify creativity as emptiness, nor do they explain how emptiness fits into a framework of creativity. If the Buddhist view on reality as emptiness is truly insightful of the ultimate reality, this notion should be explicitly brought into the structure or framework of the theory of integrated creativity. What has been given in the earlier section has shown how the *Yizhuan* and Zhou Dunyi and Daoism have formulated this theory, which even integrated the notion of Indian de-creative emptiness with the creative void of the Daoism to allow creation of the *Taiji*-God and a creative cosmos and humanity. (I shall discuss the human factor in the next section.) This suggests again that the complementary pluralism of Cobb could benefit from the *Yijing*-Whiteheadean Onto-Cosmology of Creativity (creative origin of being and creative becoming of being) not only in gaining a substantial meaning of complementarity but could become logically more enriched in becoming an integrative theory of plurality and hence transform into the integrative pluralism as I have formulated in the above.

It must again be recognized that this integration of plurality also leads to reconciliation with the traditional view on God as performing creation out of nothing (*creatio ex nihilo*). The question here is how one understands "*nihilo*." In a sense, God is self-created from *nihilo* and co-exists with *nihilo* as creative resources. The traditional view of God as the eternal and infinite power of creation does not bar God from maintaining its own order of creativity, which is revealed in a way in which the world is organized and in a way in which the human person is endowed. There is more reason to believe that reason has a power from the whole process of creativity than from something not falling into the pattern of ordering as revealed in the world and the human person.

In the process of recognizing the need for integrating religious differences into a creative totality or whole, what is independently meaningful as a term or concept has to be inevitably modified in the context of the whole, as this is the necessary implication of the philosophy of organism. Hence epistemologically speaking, one must recognize that to hold that the

Buddhist and the Christian truths could be reconciled in a holistic theory of creativity is to hold that each has to subscribe to such a transformation of meaning. The epistemology of recognizing independent contributions leads to the epistemology of integrating differences and affirming meaning in a context of the whole. This is the methodology of moving semantic clarification of specific features to onto-hermeneutical re-interpretation. What is referred to here as "onto-hermeneutical" re-interpretation is to find or define a framework of the ultimate reality in which every feature worthwhile would be accommodated in a logical and epistemological order. In this sense, any assimilation and transformation of a religious insight into the underlying philosophy of creativity must see that the semantic meaning could have to be changed in the context, and one's belief has to adapt or adjust to such semantic and onto-hermeneutical change. In this way the doctrine of "*creatio ex nihilo*" is to be tested against a whole theory, not on piecemeal projection of possibilities.

One difficulty of relating one religion to another, even in the complementary and integrative pluralistic framework, is that one usually does not wish to give up the standard of truth one maintains in one's own religion; consequently, one does not wish to perform semantic clarification and/or onto-hermeneutical re-interpretation. But if one wishes to do so, there is also the problem of understanding what religious truth could mean in a pluralistic framework. The fundamental question is that one wishes to maintain a pluralistic position without giving up an absolutist or universalistic standpoint. The reason is that pluralism often leads to relativism, and relativism leads to a closed-door self-complacency and loss of universal or objective standards and therefore loss of universal values, which human beings are expected to cherish universally. Hence the problem is how to maintain an open system of religious pluralism without diminishing the universalistic values of one's own religion.

As a theoretical and philosophical issue, pluralism does not need to lead to relativism in the sense that universal standards and universal values need to be given up. It is quite possible that all members of a free association could be subject to the same standard of objective merit and organization, but may differ in many ways of implementation and evaluation or renovation or development. The problem of recognizing a common core of truths and values need not conflict with different styles of expression or different strategies of achieving secondary goals. As the Confucian motto indicates, there could be harmony and difference at the same time. Of course, genuine harmony may require some creative unity, which binds all different parts into one, and each part would have to contribute to the maintaining of the central harmony as its universal principle and value. In this case, one can have both plurality and unity, existing in the form of unity in plurality and plurality in unity. This no doubt underscores the importance of identifying the right core values and universal standards for emulation and evaluation.

In order to maintain this unity in plurality, one needs to distinguish the ideal goal of understanding from the actual understanding one presently has with regard to the ultimate reality. If this distinction is made, one may see how differences in the other religion may be stimuli and lessons for one to improve oneself in theory or in practice, so that one may get closer to the ideal goal of one's religious standard of achievement of perfection. This is not to say, of course, that one need not hold one's own self-understanding as authentic, genuine, and as a basic standard for identifying truth. But to focus on this as the exclusive standard and the source of all inspiration will close one's mind to possible concrescences of novel truth about the ultimate reality. The very concept of the ultimate reality must be maintained in an open and creative manner so that one can derive openness from it and thus one can learn from others or come to see one's prejudices in reflection. This also means that one must maintain oneself in an open manner that makes learning from others possible. With this said, the universal claims of one's truth could be modified and enriched in the course of the creative advance in time and new encounters with the other religions of the world. In this sense, there is an intentional universal truth and a realized yet still enrichable universal truth in accordance with temporality. The *Yijing* motto that one should grow with time (*yu shi juxing*) applies here as a solution or as a way of reconciling universal claims with specific encounters, including encounters with another universalistic religion.

David Griffin has performed a service in contrasting Cobb's pluralism with that of another Whiteheadean theologian, Schubert M. Ogden, which Griffin calls Semi-Pluralism. For Ogden, according to Griffin, if a Christian religionist is to accept the truth claims of another religion, he has to find that "the truth in any philosophy not only has to confirm that in any religion, but also to be confirmed by it."[12] It is possible that all different religions find the truth of other religions confirmed in that way and reach an accord of mutual understanding. In this sense, all religions are merely different expressions of some great religious truth and thus cannot be said to be pluralist in an enriched sense. Griffin in fact wants to call this position "semi-pluralism" or "identist pluralism." According to this view, universality is the commonly shared truth of two different relations, even though one may differ from the other in other respects. Those differences that two religions do not share in common are to be regarded as relative or relativist by implication. On the side of Cobb, one sees a genuine pluralism that consists in recognizing the truths of other religions even when they are not confirmed in one's own religion. As explained above, the two different truths belong to the same ultimate reality as aspects that could give rise to a better understanding of the ultimate reality. Now we wish to raise the philosophical question as to which is a better way of preserving universalism and pluralism at the same time or whether the two could be related as identist or separate as pluralist.

Clearly we must see both as two different approaches to universalism in pluralistic contexts, and there is no reason why we cannot have both. Ogden's approach, as Cobb's, would enable us to discover our truth in others and other's truth in us and thus reach a common core of minimal common values. On the other hand, Cobb's approach would enable us to discover new truths about the ultimate and expand our scope of understanding by combining the different aspects of the same reality. We need both because we need find the common core and because we also need to explore new territories. Hence we need to integrate Ogden's approach with Cobb's. Of course, Cobb is much more open than Ogden, for in the case of not being able to identify a core, Ogden will remain enclosed in his own circles and lose touch with a larger reality. For Cobb, on the other hand, a genuinely rooted religious truth will get his attention and will be included in his system so that he can form a larger circle of association or understanding of religious truth if others are doing the same. But he needs not nor does he have a reason to reject Ogden for his approach for discovering a common ground of religious truth. In other words, there is no reason to reject identist pluralism as a part of the complementary pluralism. We may regard identist as the lower limit of reaching universality and complementary pluralism as the upper limit of reaching universality. Both can be integrated in the integrative pluralism as the lower and upper limits of an integrated understanding of the ultimate reality or ultimate creativity.

Besides, we need to take Whitehead's principle of universal relativity seriously. According to Whitehead, every actual being is a potential for every becoming of another actual being. In other words, any item of actuality is to be formed from all actual and potential items in a process of becoming.[13] In fact, this principle defines the philosophy of organism as well as the ontological principle of the philosophy. For according to this principle, an actual entity is present in every other actual entity, as all entities are dynamically related in a process of becoming and self-achievement in such a way that every entity becomes the potential ingredient for the formation and transformation of a given entity. In Whitehead's words, "The principle states that it belongs to the nature of a being that it is a potential for every becoming. Thus all things are to be conceived as qualifications of actual occasions."[14] This means that for the rational explanation of any actuality, one must appeal to every other actuality and hence to the whole universe.

The principle of relativity is rooted in the ontological principle, which says: "No actual entity, then no reason."[15] Whitehead has formulated this principle more explicitly in the following way: "Every proposition is entertained in the constitution of some one actual entity or severally in the constitutions of many actual entities."[16] From this he draws the following conclusion:

> It follows from the ontological principle, thus interpreted, that the notion of a common world must find its exemplification in the constitution of each actual entity, taken by itself for analysis. For an actual entity cannot be a member of the common world, except in the sense that the common world is a constituent of its constitution. It follows that every item of the universe, including all the other actual entities, is a constituent in the constitution of any one actual entity. This conclusion has already been employed under the title of the principle of relativity.[17]

This means that every part of the reality must be understood in reference to other parts of reality. Even though there could be different degrees of relevance according to Whitehead's "Principle of Intensive Relevance" (in the sense of having a gradation of relevance of more or less, important or negligible), a part of reality must be defined in terms of other parts in our understanding. By thus relating the ontological principle to the principle of the constitution of actuality, and then to the principle of relativity, one can see how each reality is organically defined and understood in a whole set of other actual beings and in a process of mutual transformation and interaction.

The so-called relativity is to simply identify that every entity is understood and defined in relation to or relative to what is constituted from other entities. It cannot be defined or understood apart from other actual entities or nonfactual forms of reality, which are potential or eternal objects by way of compatibility and contrariety. What the ontological principle stresses is the importance of the concrete analysis of actual entities and our experience of them, for understanding of reasons must derive from such analysis and experience of actuality and nothing else. The Relativity Principle describes the inter-prehensional relations of actual entities, which contribute to our apprehension, definition, and understanding of entities. The Ontological Principle indicates and requires that we take reality as only those entities that follow the principle of relativity. Relativity defines ontology, and ontology reveals relativity: these two principles are equivalent and are found to be so via our direct experience of reality and reflection on what would constitute reasons for experience of reality.

A consequence of such equivalence not only blurs the distinction between the subject and the object, which is another subject or superject, but it also blurs the distinction between the universal and particular as understood since Aristotle. The traditional universal is now a potential form, which has its unique particularity that can enter into the description of an actual entity, whereas the traditional particular now becomes an actual entity that enters into the description of other actual entities.[18] I take this to be a matter of the interpenetration of the universal and particular in the mutual defining processes of actual entities in regard to other entities, actual or potential. The theoretical implication of this mutual defining and interpenetration is that an actual entity is relationally and relatively definable. An actual entity can be conceived in relation to and relative to other actual entities in different dimensions and on different levels; thus, any universalistic claim of truth could simply reveal one or two universals among others and could also be regarded as a particular projection resulting from the actual entity itself.

On the other hand, the ontological principle allows that one can discover others in oneself just as one can see how others discover oneself within them. If one does do this, we have a case for Ogden's thesis of reciprocal confirmation of truth. If one could not do this, namely, if one could not for the moment find such reciprocal confirmation of truth, the differences between two religious truths could be seen as contributions to a re-definition of one's truth and the growth or enrichment of one's belief. This would be the thesis of Cobb, who believes in a process of growth in an ever developing future of one's theology by which one would overcome the particular limitations that one may see in one's own religion when confronted with religious truth and values of other traditions.[19] It is in reference to this possibility of overcoming one's particular limitations and incorporating new truths about one's faith that Cobb speaks of "fundamental changes" to be effected within the Christian religion.

We have indeed seen how fundamental changes have been effected within the Buddhist religion in the sixth-century China, which has further led to fundamental changes in other traditions such as Confucianism and Daoism. Indeed, in this present era, one may regard globalization as a process of religious change and religious reform. It is also correct for Cobb to recognize that when religions become more globalized, their teachings, whether theological or non-theological, will become both global and local. They will become global, for they must face universal issues and values, for which all humankind wishes to have an understanding and solution. They will retain localizable identities as well, for they will have to address the particular needs of local cultures and peoples, to which they belong.

In light of what is said about universals and particulars above, religious pluralism could be both universalistic and relativistic in that the religious truth of any mature religion must be seen as proposing a universal truth and a particular form of life embodying that universal truth. Both the universal truth and the particular form could be enriched and changed in light of encountering difference from other religious truths.

In connection with the concept of religious truth, we may make another important observation, namely, religious truth is a matter of trust based on an understanding and interpretation of what the ultimate reality is. If one loses vision of what the ultimate reality is, a trust would lose its ground and become blind. Since the Enlightenment Age, the Western mind is engaged in an enlightenment project of understanding the world by way of reason and science. In this sense, a religious truth must be consistent with what science enlightens. It must extend to what one's heart could reasonably trust based on scientific knowledge and a comprehensive reflection on one's experience of life. In this sense, a reasonable religion by its nature must be both scientific and experiential, which should include one's experiential understanding or re-understanding and insight into historical origins. As different persons may have different nuances of life experiences, there is always a personal side to one's religion or lack of religion. It is unreasonable to reduce religion to dogmatic teaching without an understanding that is mediated by one's experience. A blind trust is trust devoid of such understanding and therefore devoid of experienced truth.

In speaking of integral and complementary pluralism, we are open to the possibility of transformation based on learned insights into the ultimate reality. We therefore avoid the relativistic complacency therewith, but we are also open to the possibility of achieving a blind trust in rejecting experiences and insights from other traditions and become enclosed. An enclosed universalism is as problematic as a complacent relativism. An open-minded relativist need not be considered less worthwhile than a dynamic universalist: both are ready to seek universal identity and recognize relative differences.

Given the above discussion on integrative pluralism, we can now see that to overcome complacent relativism and enclosed universalism in religious truth, a religious tradition needs to seek what is in common with other religious traditions and at the same time recognizes what is genuinely and insightfully different in other traditions. Both provide a reason and incentive for religious renovation and reform whether in theory or in practice, in style or in content. It is always important to establish common ground for inter-religious communication, and one way to seek common ground is to have communication, dialogue, and understanding. From a static and substance point of view, two religions may be radically different, but from a dynamic and process point of view, two different religions may share a few things and ideas in common or may have resources of interpretation that induce such common understanding. What is incommensurable is often a matter of looking at things from a static and substance point of view, but the incommensurable can become commensurable if we relate to things in a process and interactive matter. We have to find mediation in order to see and realize complementation between two religions, and that is why an onto-cosmological philosophy such as the Yijing and Whitehead is extremely important.

For relating two different religious traditions, one may have to work with two basic principles of understanding: the principle of achieving common ground by creating maximal common parts both religions share, and the principle of achieving common ground by creating a minimal understanding of the reality comprising their radical differences. The first principle is one of intersection and the second principle one of union. The first I call the "Principle of Maximal Signification" and the second I call the "Principle of Minimal Comprehension," in view of the assumption that we should desire the least difference and the most significance in a coherent system of understanding. This is also the principle on how an onto-hermeneutical understanding and interpretation are to be performed. We need both principles so that we can move on from a common ground to a greater and more enriched vision of the ultimate, which in turn will increase the cohesiveness and congruence of the two different religions in a unified whole. The theoretical and philosophical model, which exemplifies a combination of these two principles, is precisely the Yijing-Whitehead, or should I say the Yijing-Whitehead-Cobb, system of onto-cosmology or process philosophy of organism that we now have at hand. Not only is it most significant and least differentiated, it is also methodological for creating and achieving such a system from two or more religions according to the system as a methodology.

The Role of the Human: From Ontological God to Ethical God

In describing the integration of the onto-cosmology of the *Yijing* and the philosophy of organism of Whitehead, we have identified the *Taiji* (the great ultimate) with Whitehead's God as an ultimate of creativity. But the term "God" as used here clearly is an ontological God or more specifically a Creator-God without implying that God is personal or has powers and faculties of mind and spirit. But it is not to say that the *Taiji*-God may not embody or contain such powers and faculties in some deep potential form. This may be the basis for the suggestion and formulation of some form of the anthropic principle by some physicists since the later part of twentieth century, which allows the development of human intelligence and human mind. But still it is apparent that it is only when human beings come around that the notion of God or the creator was formed. It is also clear that human beings have been able to attribute to God many other qualities such as love, kindness, justice, wisdom, knowledge, goodness and righteousness. In other words, God as a pure ontological creator could be considered a perfectly ethical power and entity like a person on an infinitely expanded analogy to human powers, not merely argued from anthropic principles. Although I am not in a position to sort out which ethical and moral qualities have been attributed to which named ultimate reality in the traditional world religions, it appears clear that we would normally conceive God as upright and just and yet with the ability to love and be kind or merciful, so that God can be a moral model for people to worship, if not to emulate. In general, it is conceived that God must be good in some generic sense apart from being a creator and a sustainer of being and life.

Now it appears to me that we need not mix up these two kinds of God-concepts, the concept of an ontological God, or *Taiji*, or *Dao* and the concept of an ethical or good God. The former is impersonal and the latter personal. The conception of the former does not require the existence of a person, but the conception of the latter does. We would not have a conception of a person, however, until we have become persons and are conscious of and know that we are persons. Hence the existence and self-awareness of the human person are the keys or the turning points of the formation of the conception of an ethical God. In other words, the formation of the conception of an ethical God presupposes the formation of the conception of the human person. It is by appropriating features that we experience as human beings that we come to see God as a creator who possesses moral and ethical qualities. The notion of the human person thus can be said to act as a metaphor and provides a model for understanding what God would be in terms of possessing these or those moral qualities.[20]

One may raise the question why we normally conceive our personal God as a necessarily moral power. The answer is that we find morality to be desirable for us and would like to become moral if we want to be human. Nietzsche even takes the position that for the survival of the poor and weak there comes into being the morality of the slave, which requires God to be just, caring, and compassionate in order to be worshipped by the poor and weak. But Nietzsche fails to note that it is sufficient to justify attribution of love and justice to God if this attribution does express the feeling and sentiment of the believing people in some way. The question of the rise and genealogy of morality can be complex and controversial, but at least one can see that if morality were humanly describable and significant for human purpose, to conceive of and believe in God as perfectly moral in some sense would be absolutely justifiable on the human ground. Besides, a personalized and moral God does satisfy a human and moral purpose for human morality, for it provides a standard and a justification for our belief and respect when morality is founded on theology and God becomes moralized. In this sense one sees how God has been humanized before we come to see how a moral and powerful God could uplift people morally and maintain a goal of justice because he himself has perfect morality and power.

We can simply put our point this way: the human person creates the image of a personal God so that a personal God can be said to create the human being and cherish the human hope in his image. Because moral qualities in a divine entity are derived from the human self-experience and self-imaging, which moral qualities need to be chosen and attributed to God the creator also depends on our experience of what constitute the most desirable perfect moral qualities. Of course, we must also admit that the conception of these chosen qualities could also derive from our experiences and understanding of the ultimate reality. Thus, the Buddhist Buddha could have different ethical qualities from the Daoist True Person (*zhenren*) and the Confucian Sage-ruler (*shengwang*), and these are also different from the Saint in Christianity. Similarly, the Confucian Heaven as a Divine Person is different from God in Christianity and Allah in Islam. Although we still have to admit that among all the major world religions the moral qualities of a personal God or even of an impersonal ultimate reality such as the *Dao* or nirvana are different and even respectively unique, these world religions may still share some generic or common qualities of morality such as compassion, love, kindness, or responsibility. Ontology or theology has conditioned and founded ethics. Ethics, on the other hand, could be said to personalize the Creator-God or ontology of creativity. Special ethics brings out special moral qualities of God, whereas general ethical qualities bring out general and often commonly recognized moral qualities of God. Once our ethics becomes more global, so our conception of God would likewise become more global. A global ethics may bring out a global theology, but a global theology need not lead to a global ethics, as ethics has to be practiced and known before it can be easily attributed to God as a creator.

Not only do we wish to see God as a person based on our own self-knowledge of personal and moral qualities, but we wish to also see God as a savior so that we can be morally strengthened or improved. Better yet, we want God to be our savior because we feel sometimes we need to be saved or protected. The finitude and fragility of human life put human existence on the vulnerable side, and it seems natural for the human person to wish to be saved from such compromising or limiting situations such as sickness and death. Besides, even as a moral person, a person may suffer from a weakness, which needs forgiveness and spiritual purification. In this case one also needs a savior. As a savior, the more powerful God is, the more hope and confidence a human person may have regarding the salvific function of God. In order to make this inner wish true, it is inevitable that a person could start to conceive of God as an indispensable infinite savior. To believe in a God as a savior and also as morally good (so that He may punish the bad) comes to the full circle of religious belief.

One may ask the question whether a non-theistic religious believer may have taken the view that even if there is no salvation in a creative *Taiji*-God, there is salvation in terms of self-cultivation and self-enlightenment as we have seen in Confucianism, Daoism, and Buddhism. Ethical or moral virtues may be seen as emerging from understanding the ultimate reality in our selves.

The above distinction of ontological God, ethical God, and salvific God makes it easy to solidify our argument for an integrative pluralism of religions. All major existing world religions could be found to share an ontology of God as the creative force, as made explicit by the *Yijing*-Whitehead ontology of process and change, and their assertions about the creativity of God as a creator could also be interpreted and given a meaning in the *Yijing*-Whitehead system of understanding. Hence all such religions could be said to be universalistic in their claims about the ultimate reality. In this sense they are united and integrated in a medium or language of the philosophy of process and change. But as concrete belief systems and practice systems they can also be found to contain different personalistic, ethical, and soteriological understandings of God based on historical, social, and psychological reasons or causes. These differences are relative to their historicities and are unique individually due to their perceptions of the values of human life and means for human cultivation or transformation.

In these regards, we must take a pluralist stand to allow comparison, interaction, mutual learning, and mutual enrichment among them. This means that even though we see a differential side apart from an integrative side in these religions, we can hold them together in light of their underlying ontology of *Taiji*-God as a creator and further in light of their capability to learn and understand. With regard to ethical and moral differences, very often we may see more convergence of values after a process of interaction and mutual adjustment than with regard to soteriological differences. For after all, the human nature we share in common in some sense may provide a basis for unification of human virtues and human rights. The process of globalization in which interaction and learning take place would also facilitate the exchange and sharing of human understanding of humanly and even divinely desirable ethical and soteriological qualities. Given these considerations, to speak of a globalized or global ethics (not necessarily regional and local levels based on cultural needs) is not far-reaching. Soteriological needs and routes, perhaps, we could leave to personal choices, which are both a matter of relativity and a matter of relativism.

In sum, we can and must distinguish the ontological God as the impersonal creative force, which we may come to know on philosophical grounds, from the ethical-moral God whom we may admire and emulate, and distinguish both from the salvific God whom we wish to believe in for redeeming purposes and for hope of our future. Because we attribute our moral qualities to God in our personal manner, it should not be expected that all religions would embody the same ethics. Whatever we attribute to God on the basis of our hope for our future well-being, salvation, or purification, we again do not expect that all religions have the same appeal in regard to the problem of salvation. In this manner we can see how religions could differ on the ethical and personal salvation levels and yet share a purified understanding of the ontological Godhead as the creative force embodied in these religions. In this way, we see how a plurality of human religions could enjoy their differences and share the same core of an onto-cosmology of creativity. It is nevertheless hoped not only that the *Yijing*-Whiteheadean philosophy of creativity and organism provides a universal basis for all religions that value creativity and originality, but also that a closely shared and overlapping ethics and soteriology could develop among all religions in reference to their shared underlying onto-cosmology of process and change.

Reflections on Four Religions: A Historical Model of Integrative Pluralism

To recapitulate in a different way, there are two principles at work in Integrative Pluralism: the Principle of Integration in terms of which an integrative philosophy of dipolar creativity (being and becoming) will function as a basis for integrating two different religions in the same ontological paradigm; and the Principle of Differentiation in terms of which the differences of the two religions are realized as two complementary polarities. The philosophical inspiration of this methodological approach is derived from the *Yijing* philosophy itself, which is well illustrated in Whitehead's philosophy of God/World dipolarity. It is further crystallized in the saying of the Neo-Confucian philosopher Zhang Zai (1020–1077): "Oneness leads to divinity, twoness leads to creativity" (*yigusheng, liangzehua*).²¹ But can we cite any factual or historical example of this theory of integrative pluralism based on integration and differentiation to show how it works? The answer is affirmative, because we can point to the developed working relationship of Confucianism and Daoism in Chinese philosophy as an excellent example.

Without getting into details, it can be shown that Confucianism and Daoism have accepted the basic philosophy of creative change as the core onto-cosmology. This is because both philosophies have drawn their origins in a common way of thinking from the philosophy of creative change in the *Yijing*. Even though this point of common heritage may not be clear until later times, it is still significant to see how their explicit ways of thinking point to the same ontological grounding. This becomes obvious in light of a close comparison of the underlying views of the ultimate reality in the major classical texts of classical Confucianism (*Yizhuan*, *Zhongyong*, and even *Lunyu*) and Classical Daoism (*Daodejing* and *Zhuangzi*). As we have discussed earlier, these two Chinese schools of philosophy have come to share the same ontology and cosmology in the onto-cosmology of creative change of the *Dao* and *tian*. This view became even more systematized in the Song Ming Neo-Confucianism of *li/qi* and *Taiji/wuji* in the texts of Zhou Dunyi, Zhang Zai, the Cheng Brothers, Zhu Xi, and Wang Yangming. But to say that in the Classical period the Confucianism and Daoism, or in the Song-Ming period the *Li* Neo-Confucianism and the *Qi* Neo-Confucianism, or the *Xin* Neo-Confucianism, shared a common core of onto-cosmology and accepted the same canonical texts is not to say that they may not still have somewhat different interpretations of the underlying philosophy or somewhat different readings of the same canonical texts. In particular, it is not to say that they have shared the same ethical, moral, and political philosophies. They did not.

If one takes what Confucius and Laozi have respectively taught about how human beings should live and behave, or compare what Mencius and Zhuangzi have said about self-cultivation and government, one will be struck with the vast difference between the two sides. This would hold with regard to moral philosophies of life of the Cheng Brothers and Zhu Xi on the one side, and Lu Xiangshan and Wang Yangming on the other. Despite these differences and even despite their mutual criticisms, they do appear to respect each other and each other's views and appear in a way that naturally and gradually forms a sense of complementarity in their own writings. From an objective point of view, one can see how each side has influenced the other even without knowing or acknowledging it. This seems also to have happened between the Song-Ming Neo-Confucianism and Chinese Buddhism as well as between Daoism and Chinese Buddhism. We can see influences and enrichments as well as remaining differences. Those enrichments and differences have been achieved through a long process of interaction, learning, examination, reflection, and rethinking. Without this process, such deeply inspiring complementary differences simply could not take place. One would also see that in this context of dynamical interaction, differences become complementary, and complementary differences become sources for novelty and creative advance, or adventures of new ideas, in Whitehead's sense.

With this integrative pluralism based on complementary integration, one can see how its exemplification in Confucianism and Daoism is of great benefit to people in practice. Why cannot a person be a Confucian in public life and a Daoist in retired privacy when he can afford to enjoy mountains and rivers? Why cannot a person be an enthusiast for national politics when young and take a contemplative and even emptiness-oriented Chan view of life and death when old? It appears that there are different times, different tasks, and different challenges of life or in a person's life that invite different goals, command different interests of life or in one's life, each of which needs not contradict one another, but rather fulfill each other—thus is the creativity of the central onto-cosmology of *tian/ren/dao/de*. Life is able to accommodate different forms or styles of life with one central onto-cosmology, not only for many different people, but also for different times or stages of one's life.

Now with science and technology well developed in today's age, there are different skillful professions, which yield different stations and require different roles for a person, apart from different times and stages, to perform one's duties and demonstrate one's abilities. It is not only necessary but also desirable to have different and even incompatible forms of professional life and professional ethics for social and community life so that humanity may continue to thrive and flourish in division of labor and in cooperation or competition for excellence. But with regard to the understanding of an underlying onto-cosmology of creativity and creative change, this abundant multiplication of forms of professional life and professional ethics will learn not to contradict each other but would rather come to cherish, complement, and enrich each other and even communally lead to an achievement of the common good. This central core philosophy would become an ever-refreshing source for one to go back for repose and an inspiring stimulus to move on to the future. This is what a philosophical or religious globalization should be: an integration, or a will to integrate, with a willingness to transform differences into complements without yielding one's rightful place and identity in the process of doing so. The ideal goal should be "Harmonize without being the same" (*he er butong*); the ideal norm to follow is "Let being different lead to harmonization." (*butong er he*). A great religion needs this Confucian insight and will have achieved it by reflecting on the essence of creativity in the ultimate reality and process of life.

One may argue that Confucianism and Daoism are not religions, and their integrative and harmonious complementary differentiation may not apply to established and organized religions such as Christianity and Buddhism, the possibility of whose real integration and creative complementary differentiation in a whole needs to be proven. The answer to this criticism is this: It is true that Confucianism and Daoism are not quite the same religions as Christianity and Buddhism, but their moral and spiritual values and their embodiment in personal practices have sustained vast numbers of people for thousands of years, as early as Buddhism and as solidly as Christianity. There are no Confucian churches or priests, but there are Confucian temples and Confucian scholars. In the case of philosophical Daoism, the Daoist teachings do get absorbed in the religious Daoism; Daoist temples were built and Daoist priests flourished. The whole point of this description is that we could identify the religious sides of Confucianism and Daoism apart from their philosophical sides just as we also need to identify the philosophical sides of Christian theology and the Buddhist a-theology apart from their religious sides. I believe that this is precisely what Whitehead has intended to do, and his process philosophy of organism could be said to embody his vision of a complementarily well-differentiated integration of Christianity and Buddhism as two major religions of the world, respectively representing the East and the West. I do not know whether he has any idea of the integrative harmonization of Confucianism and Daoism in China, but the historical fact of the integrative harmonization of Confucianism and Daoism in China does provide a strong example, model, incentive, and hope for the development of such integration among other world religions.

We might suggest that if Confucianism can be interpreted as leading to Christianity, as this has been done by James Legge in his translations of the Confucian Classics such as *Book of Poetry* (*Shijing*) and *Book of Documents* (*Shujing*), Christianity can also be interpreted as leading to Confucianism. Theoretically there is no reason why there could not be mutual and equal interpretation of ancient texts in different religions or religious schools. The philosophical hermeneutics of Hans-Georg Gadamer has stressed the possibility of achieving a meeting ground and fusion of horizons via dialogues and reflective understanding. In my own Onto-Hermeneutics, which is developed in light of both Gadamer's insights and the *Yijing*'s onto-cosmology, a mutual but creative recognition of each other's ontological assumptions and reflective understanding of timely and creative change will lead to creative sharing of insights and enlargement of onto-cosmological visions in two different systems of beliefs and ideas.[22] A comprehensive and profound understanding of significant differences in one single ultimate reality could be developed subsequently, as has been indicated in my earlier discussion of integration. In the spirit of both philosophical hermeneutics and Onto-Hermeneutics, we can see how Confucianism and Christianity could be unionized or intersected and move on to a consensus on the personalization of Heaven and God as well as the formation of a virtue ethics of self-cultivation and self-sanctification in the context and in the spirit of *Yijing*-Whitehead onto-cosmology of creativity and creative change.

Similarly, Daoism and Buddhism could be mutually interpreted by each other. In fact, when Indian Buddhism was introduced in China in the third century, it is by way of a Daoist interpretation that it became understood and accepted in China. In later times there were Buddhist monks who would also undertake a Buddhist interpretation of the Daoist texts. This mutual interpretation and interaction between the two finally led to the formation of the great school of Chan Buddhism, which has combined the Daoist freedom of creative spirit and the Buddhist wisdom of non-abiding or non-clinging into one onto-enlightenment philosophy of the ultimate and the ultimateless.

With such philosophical and hermeneutical alignment for both Confucianism-Christianity and Daoism-Buddhism, we can now see how a well-developed harmonization and integration between Confucianism and Daoism could also take place between Christianity and Buddhism. In this harmonization and integration, Christianity and Buddhism will become truly complementary and interrelated in a holistic unity of creative understanding as the one between Daoism and Confucianism. The spirit of harmonization and integration, and yet at the same time the well-adjusted complementarity between the two, will hold on and pass on to the relationship between Christianity and Buddhism. There is no need to worry about differences in styles of life and in differences in ethical norms arising from such differences of styles of life. Insofar as they are harmonized and justified in light of the onto-cosmology of creativity and creative change, they should maintain their distinctive identities, which will be basis for future creative transformation.

With the model of Confucian-Daoist harmony in view, we shall find a Christian God more humanized under the influence of a Confucian view of life, and a Buddhist emptiness more naturalized under the influence of the Daoist natural philosophy. We shall also find a Confucian individual more rights-oriented than traditional virtue ethics-oriented under the Christian influence and a Daoist recluse more compassionate and world-caring than Laozi under the Buddhist influence. In different ways, but with the same insight and spirit of creativity, we come to a consummation of integrative pluralism among the four religions, which would pave a still wider road toward integration and harmonization of all the religions in the world.

5

On Neville's Understanding of Chinese Philosophy

The Ontology of Wu (无), the Cosmology of Yi (易), and the Normalogy of Li (理)

Introduction

Robert Neville's understanding of Chinese philosophy is profound and comprehensive. It is not only that he has worked his way diligently into various aspects of Chinese philosophy, but he has also acquired a special feel and insight for Chinese philosophy in his interpretation of the Chinese philosophical concepts and systems. Even in his own philosophical speculation on the most fundamental issues in philosophy, one cannot fail to detect a fine sense of the *Dao* at work. Is it because being a consummate *Taijiquan* master, his sensibility has penetrated to the very heart of his own being and thinking? Or is it because being an open and creative thinker, his thinking has come to encompass a logic and a dialectic one would naturally find in the creative philosophies of Plato, Whitehead, Laozi, and the *Yijing*? I must say that Neville has both the sensibility and the reflective wisdom to absorb Chinese philosophy and to be absorbed into Chinese philosophy.

It is hence interesting to note that while one could approach Neville from a strictly Western philosophical and theological perspective and find him speaking good sense and making good points in the enterprise of reconstructing fundamental Christian theology or Greek value theory, one can equally approach Neville from a strictly Chinese philosophical and perhaps the Daoist perspective and find him also speaking good sense and disclosing a level of understanding that can only be identified in the experience of enlightenment of a great Daoist or a great Chan master.[1] Consequently, I find it possible even to interpret him thoroughly along the lines of Chinese philosophy of the *Dao* (the way), the *yi* (change), and the *li* (proprieties and rites) just as he is totally at ease in interpreting Chinese philosophy and recovering a hitherto unfathomed depth of meaning from his understanding of God or being, becoming, and justice.

One possible way to understand Neville's view on Chinese philosophy is to understand Neville's efforts in the construction of a system of being, value, theory, and norms. What Neville has in mind is to construct an architectonic philosophy that would comprehend and accommodate everything in the universe and explain the creation and rise of the universe from the very beginning as well as the continuous striving for achieving value and excellence on the part of humans. We may indeed agree that there is a Whiteheadian background in Neville's speaking of quantity, quality, and value in his reconstruction of human thinking,[2] yet one must also point out that there is also a determination to overcome the polarity of the Whiteheadian God in order to guarantee an unbounded and infinite source-fullness (not just the resourcefulness) of creation and creativity. There is no doubt, Neville's effort to expound and justify the worldliness and humanity of the human person so that the human person will have both the freedom to express himself in culture and the ability to see a plenitude of differences of cultural histories.

Neville is at his best when he aims to preserve genuine creativity on four levels of being: the ontological, the cosmological, the socio-cultural, and the individual-personal, each with its qualitative features and yet each related to the others based on a dialectic of being (conditions and harmonies of being). As I have suggested, Neville is a disguised master of the *Yijing onto-cosmology* with a truly profound vibrating consonance between his own philosophical system, derived largely from Western sources, and the Chinese philosophical wisdom. In fact, one must be amazed at how he could so easily reach a rapport and develop a common measure between Chinese and Western views. To do so, Neville has truly mastered the Chinese wisdom of both Daoism and Confucianism at the same time. The creativity of the *Dao* transcending culture and the creativity of culture immanent in the *Dao* work in great harmony to exhibit a framework of thinking of multifaceted creativity. Without such philosophical depth and hermeneutical creativity, I do not know how Neville, or for that matter anyone, could reconcile the radical differences in essential issues between Confucianism on the one hand and traditional Christian theology on the other.[3]

Consequently, I must conclude that Neville has been imbued with a Chinese philosophical spirit in constructing his systematic works equally derived from his spiritual and rational reflections on Chinese philosophy and from the Western sources, the combination and synthesis of which again lead to his insights into both Chinese philosophy and Western traditions. In what follows, I shall explore Neville's contributions to the understanding of Chinese philosophy in three areas that are essential to his system-building, namely, the area of ontological creativity, the area of systematic creativity, and the area of creativity in the cultivation of the human person and human society. I will elucidate relevant points for the purpose of clarification and elaboration so that one can see how various strains in Chinese philosophy are important for Neville's construction of a comprehensive and fundamental philosophy of reality and value and how they in fact must be important for any construction of a measure of truth in the comparative study of world religions.

Ontological Creativity and Ontology of *Wu*

One of Neville's major insights occurs in his revival of the argument for creation ex nihilo in the context of Christian theology. In reviving this argument for a necessary understanding of the fundamental creativity of God, he also has introduced new meanings and relevance for any understanding of creation of the world in other great world religions. Neville's reconstruction of the argument ex nihilo has the following five highlights:[4]

1. Creation ex nihilo is a three-term relation of the created world, the ground, and the act of creation. No term of this triad can be separately conceived or known.

2. The created world includes all determinate things, which must be ontologically grounded.

3. The determinateness of a thing is a harmony of essential and conditional properties.

4. Nothingness or emptiness in the creation ex nihilo bespeaks the contingency of everything in the world and the world itself.

5. Everything determinate, being a harmony, has a value of a certain kind and a certain degree.

We can see that all these five points are either explicitly verified or implicitly assumed in writings of Daoism and the *Yizhuan* and hence can be said to contribute to a systematic understanding of Chinese philosophy at large. In this regard I see Neville's reconstruction of the theological argument as a reconstruction of a metaphysics of creativity that has an even greater significance for contemporary persons and society in a cross-cultural perspective.

It is a great insight to insist on a fundamental form of creativity in the creation ex nihilo, from which other forms of creativity become possible. In general, we understand creativity in terms of creation of something new from something old and preexisting. This is true not only of physical and biological evolution; it is true also of human cultural activities including scientific theorizing, philosophical speculation, and poetic and artistic composition. The new in creativity is based on the old, and yet it goes beyond the old. When we see life regenerated, we see creativity at work where new form and new structure, hence new function, are being developed, and yet the old form or structure is preserved to sustain the new.

Human creativity, on the other hand, involves things and actions of the human person. It is an exhibition of an ability to synthesize and to organize a new form, a new structure, and a new function, yet it must be done on the basis of knowledge of the old and understanding of experience. Hence we can see that creativity in general must presuppose something in the past and present in order to present something new. But then we must face the question that if there is nothing to presuppose, could we have creation of something totally new? Furthermore, is there any reason to suppose that we must have something to begin with or rather that we cannot presuppose anything and something has to come into existence by itself? There is no end to the argument for and the argument against a positive or a negative answer to these two questions. For in the nature of logic, there is nothing necessary or universal in the following possibilities:

1. Something produces something. (Something dependently comes into being.)

2. Something produces nothing. (Something remains the same.)

3. Nothing produces anything or something. (Something independently comes into being.)

4. Nothing produces nothing. (Nothing comes into being from nothing.)

Without getting into extensive clarification of the meanings of "nothing" and "something" in modern logic, all four possibilities could be seen to be separately true as well as jointly true. It is clear that A and C are two basic forms of creativity. But then one may ask whether before something produces something, something has to be something in the first place. Hence the coming into being of something in C must be prior to coming into being from something in A. Hence creation ex nihilo is an even more basic form of creativity, which can be titled "ontological creativity." Once we have something in the beginning, one could then argue that all different new things are produced by the something in the beginning. This we can call "cosmological creativity." We can see from this where Neville's insight resides: in a strictly logical sense of presupposition "cosmological creativity" must presuppose "ontological creativity." This is precisely the point made by Laozi in the *Daodejing*. It is the formless and substanceless *Dao* that gives rise to everything (namely, every form and every substance) in the world. "The *Dao* gives rise to oneness, oneness gives rise to twoness, and twoness gives rise to threeness. Threeness gives rise to the ten thousand things."[5] But is the formless and substanceless *Dao* the nothingness or emptiness (*wu*) in ontological creativity? The answer is positive. As the *Daodejing* puts it, "*Wu* (non-being) is to name the beginning of heaven and earth; *you* (being) is to name the mother of the ten thousand things."[6] But of course such a name is not a constant name and hence the *dao* we speak about is not the constant *Dao*. What is constant and therefore pervasive is the ground of all activities and all existence and this can be neither named nor spoken of, because in naming and in speaking we will make the *Dao* a thing or an object. Hence it is not even proper to identify the *Dao* as the emptiness (*wu*), because in speaking of *wu* we would objectify the *wu* into a thing. Insofar as the *Dao* gives rise to oneness and so on, it is the primordial source of a limit and a development of a cosmos and a plentitude.

How does the *Dao* come into being? This question cannot be really answered because it cannot really be asked. If one comes to understand the *Dao*, the question and the answer will be self-dissolved.[7] Logically we could perhaps say that the *Dao* is sui generis and self-created. But once there is the *Dao*, the creativity of the *Dao* is such that all things will fall in order. Hence we have the *Dao* as the ontological ground and source of everything. But this is not to say that there is no creativity of things and human persons insofar as they are coming from the *Dao*. The important insight of the Daoist is that there is creativity of things because there is creativity in things or because there is the *Dao* in things. The *Dao* is in things because things are in the *Dao*. In this sense, the *Dao* cannot be any thing, this thing, that thing, this nothing, that nothing, or any nothing, because it is any thing, and at the same time this thing, that thing, this nothing, that nothing. Yet the *Dao* is not a thing or nothing, but a relation of producing everything from a source. The creativity of the *Dao* is a relation involving everything, the source and the creative action. Hence we can also say that the *Dao* is both absolutely transcendent and absolutely immanent—transcendent beyond everything as the constant ground of activities of things and immanent as the very source of creativity in things.

It is also true that although we can speak of temporal change and transformation of things in the *Dao*, we cannot really speak of the temporal change and transformation of the *Dao* because it is the *Dao* that creates time and makes the temporal changes possible. In this sense it is constant and hence eternal. But eternity in this sense is not separate from temporality either. They could be seen as two sides of the same thing: as ontological creativity it is a-temporal and eternal, and as cosmological creativity it is temporal and changing. This is because the *Dao* cannot be simply self-produced and then self-destroyed. It has to be constantly self-produced from itself or from nothing (*wu*) so that it can be the constant ground of all creativities of all things, namely, the ground of cosmological creativities. In this sense we come also to another important insight of Daoism, namely, that ontology cannot be ontology alone but must be intrinsically linked to cosmology, and at the same time cosmology cannot be cosmology alone but must be linked to ontology as a consequence of ontological creativity. Hence we need to speak of the creativity of things as cosmo-ontological creativity, and of the creativity of the *Dao* as onto-cosmological creativity as well. In light of this creativity of the *Dao* we should speak of the onto-cosmology and cosmo-ontology of the world.

Although I am not so sure whether Neville will give such a rich meaning of creativity to his argument of creation ex nihilo, I feel that what is implicit in the Daoist view of creativity is fully compatible with his intention in bringing out the argument. What remains to be explored is the depth of meaning one may wish to attach to the notion of *nihilo*. Traditional Christian theology gives the appearance of abhorring a vacuum and thinking of *nihilo* as nonproductive or as being a symbol of negativity and darkness. But must we so think? To *bring* out the argument ex nihilo in terms of ontological creativity, cosmological creativity, and eventually in terms of onto-cosmological creativity and cosmo-ontological creativity mentioned above will no doubt endow the argument with a much richer meaning, an endowment necessary for a fruitful contemporary understanding of the world and humankind.

As a very important consequence of this understanding, one can see that the source of the creativity is always the ground of any creativity and is not really separate from the creative activity of any determinate thing. The transcendence of the source is made immanent by its continuous creativity, whereas what is immanent in a thing as ground of creativity is actually transcendent as timeless or time-transcending (or "eternal," to use Neville's word) power or source. It is clear that one cannot speak of transcendence without speaking simultaneously of immanence and vice versa. It would be wrong therefore to assume that there is no link between ontological creativity and cosmological creativity of either God or the *Dao*. Hence the issue raised by Keiji Nishitani, as mentioned by Neville, does not arise.[8]

It is in light of this onto-cosmological and cosmo-ontological creativity that we can then explain the creativity of producing something from something, or the creativity inherent in the nature of things, or the creativity of human mind and human imagination, for it is on all these levels that the original creativity of the *Dao* is at work. But this is not to say that the creativity of the *Dao* has determined the way things are. On the contrary, it is precisely the creativity of the *Dao* that lets things make themselves the way they are, for the *Dao* itself is undetermined and undeterminable: it is unlimited freedom from which self-discipline and self-limiting are possible. In this sense, things as determinate things, on the one hand, are subject to their formational and transformational conditions (referred to as "essential and conditional features" by Neville); on the other hand, they are free to realize what best possibilities they might have in terms of their creative potentiality and potential creativity. This is also where their value lies: they provide conditions for the realization of cosmological or cosmo-ontological creativity of other things, and they can also realize their cosmo-ontological creativity on the basis of their given conditions. It is in this light that Zhuangzi says that things are self-generated, self-created, and self-transformed, because things are in the *Dao* and the *Dao* is in things no matter how lowly in value they are.[9]

Neville speaks of the contingency of being of everything. Surely he would include the being of the great ultimate (*taiji*) as the Hebrew God (*Yahweh*) or the Neo-Confucian supreme principle. I believe that traditional theology would wish to prove the necessary existence of God in a conceivable sense. On the Chinese side, Zhu Xi certainly maintains the principle (*li*) of the great ultimate as a permanent and necessary given. How does the contingency of being as arising from non-being square with this aspect of God or the supreme principle? The answer is that the contingency of being is supported by the necessity of emptiness or non-being as creative. If being is contingent on non-being, and creativity as an aspect of emptiness is a transformation of non-being into being, then there is equally a necessity of being similar to the necessity of the non-being defined as creativity. That non-being can be so conceived is due to the fact that, in the tradition of the *Zhouyi*, the ultimate ground of being cannot but be "ceaselessly creative" (*shengsheng buyi*). This is very clearly expressed in the *Xici* of the *Yizhuan*: "To be productive of the productive is called the *yi*; to form forms is called the creative (*qian*); and to present lawfulness of being is called the receptive (*kun*)."[10]

This necessity of ontological creativity in the *yi* is no doubt characteristic of the Confucian metaphysical tradition that is continued in the *Zhongyong*, where the Zhou poetry of "what is mandated from the heaven is ceaselessly active" is quoted, and the *Mencius*. Together, they form the foundation of a creative metaphysics of onto-cosmology of the "the ultimate of non-being (*wuji*) and yet the ultimate of being (*taiji*)" in Zhou Dunyi's *Taiji Tu Shuo*. But even for the Daoists there is no other way of conceiving the *Dao* than conceiving it as a necessary or naturally necessary process or framework. Neville is correct to point out that there could be a sense of sequence from *wuji* to the *taiji*.[11] But if this is to be regarded as a statement of the original ontological creativity, as it should be, it cannot be a temporal sense of sequence but rather a logical necessity of entailment in light of the defining nature of the *wuji* or the *wu* as the creative.[12]

Neville speaks of the determinateness of a thing as the harmony of its essential and conditional features, an insight making a Confucian point. In fact, he even mentions that Confucianism focuses on the "harmonies among the elements of the primary cosmology, and cites attunement with the ontological creative act as the means to achieve that harmony."[13] But the question is how he understands harmonies as the determinateness of a thing, giving rise to both the being and the value of the thing. He has indicated that conflict and strife are elements of harmony that can work toward either loosening or tightening the pattern. Hence he does not see harmonies as always good. But it appears that these two senses of harmony, the axiological and the ontological, need to be subsumed in a larger theory of harmonization.

Perhaps we can explicitly define harmony as the unity of the polarity of *yin* and *yang* forces or elements in the process of cosmological creation. Any unity of the polarity of *yin* and *yang* is a harmony that carries with it a value. Its value is thus its own determinate existence or indeterminate existence in a determinate context. But whether the value of the harmony (or harmony as value) will last or should be broken depends on how a given thing or hence a given harmony may contribute to a larger harmony (both space-wise and time-wise) or whether it may hurt or damage a larger harmony such as harmony among harmonies or simply relationships among things. In this way we can see how harmony as ontological creativity and harmony as axiological value could remain the same even though harmony can acquire two meanings at the same time.

Given ontological creativity, although philosophically we must understand and analyze it in terms of a three-term relation, the inevitable question is how this relation is to be actually conceived or experienced in human history. Is it to be conceived in terms of its source, its act, or its resulting being? Apparently, the Daoist tends to think in terms of the source, namely the *Dao* as in Laozi, or in terms of its act in nature as in Zhuangzi, whereas the Confucian tends to think of it in terms of its creative being, the great ultimate from which an onto-cosmological process will ensue. In the actual historical experience, this great ultimate is embodied in the notion of the Lord-on-High (*shangdi*), reflecting the political sovereign on the earth. Later in the beginning of Zhou, *Shangdi* becomes the Heaven (*tian*), which is less personalized and more comprehensive in scope of influence. Similarly, Judaism also comes to think of ontological creativity in terms of its resulting being-power, which is further identified with the tribal protector God, Yahweh, for religious reasons.

It is interesting to note that while Judaism has retained the personified notion of God and made the hidden ontological creativity more abstract and more transcendent, the Daoist and the Confucian have gradually transformed the full personified notion of *Shangdi* into a less personified the notion of Heaven, and finally, has completely depersonalized this notion of Heaven into that of *Dao*. In this process of depersonalization there is also a process of immanentization that reaches its apex in the notion of the *Dao*.[14] It is good to see that Neville has distinguished "theological sources" from the "archeology of God" through which one can see how the same or similar notions could come across very different feelings, circumstances, and cultures, depending on the impact of different histories. However, it is through this retrieval of a god (in the sense of the great ultimate) that Neville is able to develop a framework of comparative religion in which he could vividly compare the Western religious tradition with the Chinese metaphysical tradition with regard to their cultural values.[15]

One can easily note that the transcendent personalization of the great ultimate in the Jewish tradition and the immanent depersonalization of the great ultimate in the Chinese tradition are processes that are the reverse of each other. The former leads to a transcendent God whereas the latter leads to an immanent *Dao*. Are they therefore absolutely incommensurable and completely exclusive of each other? The answer to this question is *no*. By closely looking into the nature of the transcendent God, as depicted by Karl Barth, we find God as beyond the grasp of human logic. Similarly, by looking into the nature of the immanent *Dao*, such as in Zhuangzi and Hui Neng, we also find the *Dao* as beyond the reach of language and logic. Hence, although being the reverse of each other, God and *Dao* still share something in common and thus could be regarded as extensions of this something in common. What they have in common is the unity of act, source, and result in the original ontological creativity, as suggested by Neville. The difference is a difference of posterior cultures, conventions, and histories, or, as Neville put it, the archeological difference of God and the *Dao*. The real God is also the real *Dao*, and the real *Dao* is also the real God.

Triology of Thinking and Cosmology of Yi

Neville has raised the question as to what the Chinese tradition can contribute to the philosophy of world religions. His answer is that it has brought out a version or versions of ontological creativity "devoid of difficulties of the theism-mysticism split characteristic of the West."[16] In making this answer, he has touched on a fundamental feature of Chinese tradition: Chinese tradition is primarily a philosophical tradition, not a religious one. But this is not to say that there are no religions in China in any sense of "religion." The point is that whether Daoist or Buddhist, a major Chinese religion developed its theoretical teachings in terms of philosophy, not in terms of theology, as Christianity has done. This may have something to do with the early and continuous effort of the Chinese mind, attuned to an enlightened pragmatism, to naturalize and depersonalize any spirit or god that has no origin in human affairs. Hence philosophy (whether called *weijizhixue*, study of self-realization; *xuanxue*, study of profundities; *dao xue*, study of the way; *lixue*, study of principles; or *xinxue*, study of heart-mind) via the community of scholar officials plays the same role as theology via a corps of church members.

In this regard one can see that Chinese philosophy in the above sense also functions religiously; that is, it provides a practical guide to life and presents a goal and a belief system for social practice and self-cultivation, as clearly exemplified in Song and Ming societies and individuals. In this light one can see how the Chinese tradition has presented a straightforward philosophical picture of the ontological and cosmological creativities without being encumbered by a heavy system of religious symbols and institutions.[17] Because of this, it is natural to see how ontological and cosmological creativities could be developed more articulately and more clearly in the *Daodejing*, which Neville's understanding suggests. Perhaps, it is not an exaggeration to say that after Neville's efforts, the combination of major strains in Chinese philosophy could provide a universal basis for understanding the issue of creation *ex nihilo* and understanding a basis for the study of world religions.

We can see that Neville's development of a systematic philosophy of religion is in fact motivated by the need to provide a basis for the study of world religions and their associated theologies or metaphysics. In so doing, he has been influenced by the great Western masters of theology and philosophy (such as Plato, Augustine, Whitehead, and Dewey) as well by the great Chinese masters of Daoism and Neo-Confucianism (such as Laozi and Wang Yangming). His effort from the very beginning has been to construct a solid universal foundation of Being and its creativity for the study of human beings and their cultures in their various historical engagements with that foundation. He has taken the challenge to reinterpret traditional arguments, to sort out nuances of meaning, and to explore and creatively propose a profound and comprehensive theory for synthesizing differences and accommodating them with a strong sense of justice in a theoretical framework.

In this light I can see Neville working not as a sectarian theologian, nor a Whiteheadian system builder, but as a truly reflective Neo-Confucian philosopher with a determination to seek the ultimate roots of human thinking that would cover and apply to all the ten thousand things under heaven and thereby inspire a creative life of moral practice at the same time. In this sense we might even say that Neville writes like a Zhu Xi and thinks like a Wang Yangming, particularly in light of his central motif, namely to resolve the problem of the one and the many by way of ontological creativity.

One might see that the Neo-Confucian principle of "one principle and many manifestations" (*liyi fenshu*) is in fact Neville's hidden guiding light and open challenge at the same time, which provides a key to understanding the development of his systematic views. From the early *God the Creator: On the Transcendence and Presence of God*, through his *Creativity and God: A Challenge to Process Theology*, to his *Eternity and Time's Flow*, one sees his concentration on the problem of the one and the many from the point of view of one source. Yet, in *The Cosmology of Freedom: Soldier, Sage, Saint*; *The Truth of Broken Symbols*; *The Tao and the Daimon: Segments of a Religious Inquiry*; and *Behind the Masks of God*, one can notice his concentration on the problem of the one and the many from the point of view of the many manifestations. The combination of these two points of view is, of course, finally revealed in his recently completed trilogy *Reconstruction of Thinking*, *Recovery of the Measure*, and *Normative Cultures*, in which one witnesses a systematic progress from a framework of metaphysics of thinking to the founding of a hermeneutical methodology for understanding nature and reality and finally to a theory of theorizing that would lead to a fruitful and harmonizing dialogue over cultural incommensurability. In these one also witnesses a Confucian practical reason at work, which makes Neville's philosophy truly ecumenical across time and space.

It is interesting to note that the way Neville developed his philosophy in general and his trilogy in particular can be best interpreted in the underlying philosophy of the *Yijing*, which is the living source and fountainhead of the development of the Song-Ming Neo-Confucianism. I shall make five points regarding this interpretation. This is intended to show that there is a deeper level of meaning in Neville's work, which demonstrates the significance of his work as a framework of cross-cultural world-thinking for the twenty-first century.

First, Neville's concern with the argument of creation *ex nihilo* is implicitly presented in the *Tuanzhuan* of the *Zhouyi* where the Active Originator (*Qian yuan*) is the beginner and creator of the ten thousand things and rules over heaven. If the *Qian yuan* is not the creative act in the ontological creativity, what could it be? When it is said that all things are created with its resources, it implies an *onto-cosmological* beginning of things, as mentioned above. The question has been raised as to whether the *Qian yuan* would form a correlative pair with *Kun yuan* (Conforming Originator) in co-creating the universe and thus lose its unique originating position. The answer is that the relation between *Qian* (activity) and *Kun* (conformity) needs to be seen with creativity as a three-term relation, as Neville has argued. *Kun* in fact is primarily non-activity or non-creativity from which creativity and action arise, to which all creations return, and at which all creations would reside. Hence the sequence from *Qian* to *Kun* reveals a relation that is implicit in the ontological creativity of the *Qian*. Even in the argument for creation ex nihilo we start with creation and then speak of the *nihilo* because of the nature of the creativity in the initial creation. It is clear that the first two *gua* of the *Yijing* text have established a paradigm for all other created *gua* (resulting from combination of *Qian* and *Kun*) to emulate, thus establishing the onto-cosmological nature of the creativity in a primary cosmology.

Second, we must see the symbolism of *Qian* and *Kun* as limiting archetypal symbols abstracted from all creative relationships and thus applicable to all creative relationships. In this sense we speak of Heaven and Earth as two concrete exemplifications of the working relationship of *Qian* and *Kun* because the former has suggested or disclosed the latter. Perhaps, along the line of a dialectic and semiotic of onto-cosmological creativity, we can see *Qian* and *Kun* as primary symbols that stand for the relation of ontological creativity and see all other symbols as logically subsequent interpretants of this primary symbolism apart from being primary symbols for a given reality. The *Yijing* can thus be regarded as both a methodology of interpretation of nature and an onto-cosmology of creativity. What is even more significant is the fact that *yi* (change and transformation) is best understood as representing both ontological and cosmological creativity.

Third, the primary cosmology of the *yi* as explained in terms of the great ultimate in the *Xici* is no doubt a demonstration of the process of cosmological differentiation and ramification with an implicit order derived from the ontological creativity. This *yi*-cosmology no doubt also illustrates how oneness gives rise to many and how many may also relate and return to the oneness in a symbolism far clearer than the abstract notions of Platonic participation or Hegelian objectification. Neville must have had this logic or dialectic of being in mind when he praised the Chinese contribution to his articulation of creation ex nihilo in *Behind the Masks of God*.

Fourth, in the *Yizhuan* one can see a framework of thinking that integrates reality and values in a single onto-cosmology of creativity. The very idea of the world as presence of the principle (*li* 理), which also forms a system in which all things basically can be positioned and thus harmonized in the order of complementation and mutual support for furthering creativity, is germane to valuational thinking.[18] In a system that caters to an individual's practical action, and regards human action as participatory and as both transcendently and causally effective, all situations are occasions for the valuation of understanding and the evaluation of action. It is not only that reality in a process of change needs be harmonized to avoid conflict and clash, but that even harmonies as a structure and as a relation are subject to change and transformation. Hence the question of how to preserve given harmonies and create harmonies in new situations becomes the challenging concern and burden (called the *youhuan*) of a creative person. It takes insight and knowledge as well as reflective understanding of the whole in order to reach a good decision and to strive for an end.

In other words, we cannot think of reality without knowing reality in some way, and we cannot know reality without valuing reality in some way. Similarly, we cannot value reality without evaluating our relation and action in regard to reality. Hence the cosmology of the *yi* entails or presupposes an axiology of the *yi* that in turn should give rise to a normative understanding of our action with regard to the knowledge and value of *yi*. For valuational and evaluational thinking, a correct measure based on one's own life purpose and intention and the whole context of a world philosophy must be entertained and followed.

Fifth, the *Yizhuan* philosophy of change could also be understood as a "theorizing of theories," as suggested by Neville himself. Neville's concern is to recognize the differences of civilized humanity and different ways or conventions embodying civilized humanity. But to integrate all these differences in an overall theory requires a deep understanding of the roots of the differences in the archeology of religion and the sociology of social practices. To recognize this is to start to think of a comprehensive basis for relating, interrelating, and even evaluating these differences. This should lead again to the ontological creativity and onto-cosmological creativity in which all levels and dimensions of reality and human activity can be accommodated and positioned. This would be the way of onto-cosmological thinking of the *Yijing* as a philosophy of reality and value. To be able to do this would be the basis for finding a practical reason to act in different situations with inherently different demands or norms. This is the wisdom that underlies the basic philosophy of divination for understanding and action in the *Yijing* system of thinking.

For the *Yijing*, to act in a given situation both wisely and in a timely way is to act in view of all the symbolic meanings and implicit values or disvalues of the situation. It requires that a person know the situation not only microscopically but also macroscopically and holistically across all possible situations and to know which goals of life and human responsibilities are allowed or mandated. Hence to act thus is to act creatively in an onto-cosmological sense of creativity. I believe that this is the essence of seeking theoretical wisdom across all theories and of seeking hypernorms across all norms in Neville's *Normative Cultures* (1995).

The above serves to show how Neville's philosophical-theological thinking as a whole, and his trilogy of thinking, understanding (interpretation), and normative decision in particular, could be deepened in meaning in an onto-hermeneutical understanding of the philosophy of the *Yijing*. One might also point out that while illuminated by the philosophy of the *Yijing*, the philosophy of the *Yijing* on the other hand might receive illumination from Neville's reflections on those fundamental issues. Specifically, his trilogy reflects a methodology of thinking, interpretation, and decision-making that can be said to be essential to the understanding of the *Yijing* in the modern or postmodern light. Together with his fundamental ontology of creativity, Neville can be said to have presented a profound and comprehensive reading of the *Yijing* even though he may not be aware of it. In this light he could also be said to have achieved a "fusion of horizons" across the Western and the Chinese or Eastern philosophical traditions and to have opened new ways toward a global philosophy of humankind in the future.

Confucian-Christian Comparisons and Normalogy of *Li*

As a philosopher, Neville can be best described as a Confucian-Christian or a Christian-Confucian. In terms of theological interests he is no doubt more a Christian than a Confucian and hence a Christian-Confucian. But in terms of philosophical interests he is more a Confucian than a Christian in the traditional sense of the terms and hence a Confucian-Christian. I have noted that Neville has changed his paper on Confucian-Christian incompatibilities into Confucian-Christian comparisons. I see this as a deepening of thinking inclining toward the Confucian onto-cosmology as embodied in the *Yizhuan* of the *Yijing*. But on the other hand, I do not think that he has completely avoided the incompatibilities that exist between Christian theology and the Confucian ontology on a level that still merits our serious consideration.

Neville's interest is not merely in comparing or eventually integrating the Confucian and Christian philosophical views. He is perhaps eager to establish a universal theory of human thinking and valuation in which all religions and all cultures can be rightfully appreciated and evaluated and, furthermore, in which relevant truths from each tradition can supplement and enrich each other. This is indeed a great task and a great vision, but it is nevertheless not whimsical or impractical insofar as we have no conclusive reason for a postmodern relativism of values, nor do we have a conclusive reason for a Western-oriented modern universalism. To avoid both, one needs to open up a deep understanding of world religions and world philosophies and to set one's mind to analyzing issues reflectively and creatively and to formulating frameworks. In this case, Neville argues for the portability of Confucian wisdom into the Western contexts (hence his slogan Boston Confucianism or the Boston School of Confucianism).

I wish to suggest that the portability of Western philosophical thinking apart from Western science has been argued for and in fact implemented since the days of May Fourth 1919 in China. Although there have been many debates on specific issues, the usefulness of introducing Western notions, categories, and methods or methodology cannot be denied in the interests of modernization, rationalization, and revitalization of the native tradition. Similarly, I believe that similar things can be said for the portability of Confucianism or Chinese philosophy to the West, even though the Western tradition is now at its height and the Western culture occupies a dominant position in the world today. Philosophically significant today are questions about how specific points can be made, how specific issues and difficulties of mutual interpretation can be overcome, and how specific issues of incompatibilities can be resolved. It is in this light that we can see how Neville has made his contribution toward a Confucian-Christian dialogue. Neville has located three specific difficult issues regarding the transporting of Confucianism to a modern Western social context: (1) the issue of Confucian filial piety as a holy duty in Christian religion; (2) the issue of Confucian ritual propriety as a moral requirement of Christianity; and (3) the issue of obvious Confucian objections to believing Jesus to be the Son of God in Christianity. How do we understand these issues, and how do we resolve them?

Regarding the first issue, filial piety is no doubt rooted in the ancient practice of ancestor worship and must be understood as a reverence toward life and the origin of one's life. It is consistent and necessary that one preserve the respect for one's parents or ancestors so that one can continue the tradition of the past and can look forward to the future as a continuity of the past. Hence for the traditional Chinese family, male progeny are considered part of the teaching of filial piety. It is true that in a traditional society in China filial piety as a virtue contributed to the care for the elderly, but it is certainly not the reason or even the cause for the practice of filial piety. In the *Zhou Rites (Zhouli)* and the *Book of Filial Piety (Xiaojing)*, glorification of the family name and honoring parents with one's official achievements are more the motivating reasons for filial piety than simply nourishing one's parents. Therefore, the issue of filial piety remains even in the present, despite the fact that parents do not normally need or wish to have their children's support. Then what is the ultimate value and justification for filial piety as a practice?

The ultimate value and justification for filial piety is derived from the cosmology of the creativity of heaven and earth in which the value of human existence consists. Parents give rise to the child just as heaven and earth give rise to humankind. The harmony and unity between heaven and earth and humankind endows and fulfills value in human beings. Similarly, filial piety toward one's parents would actually endow one with value and a sense of rootedness in the world. Hence filial piety is symbolic of the original unity and harmony between heaven, earth, and humankind and should be observed as a supreme norm. It is also true that parents love children without selfishness, and to return this love the children should be filially pious, which means care and love of parents without selfishness. In this sense filial piety is seen as an example of reciprocal care and benevolence (*ren*) and together with brotherliness (*di*) forms the root or the base for the practice of *ren*.[19] In this sense filial piety should be regarded as the very core of learning to preserve and extend one's humanity. It is with such understanding that paying respects to one's ancestral spirits and filial piety are linked together, and the meaning of doing this is so fundamental that nothing could really compete with it.

On the Christian side, Neville has rightly pointed out that to love God is not to abolish family relations but to transfer love from kinship to community under God. To love God is to love God as the common parent and as the supreme parent under whom all people are related as brothers and sisters. In the *Analects* Confucius has also said that "All men within the four seas are all brothers."[20] This means that all people should love each other because they come from the same roots. But the question is: Which is more fundamental, to love one's parents or to love God? Given the above explanation, I feel that this is a choice of faith, a choice of cosmology, and a choice of ultimate significance or ultimate commitment. It is conceivable that in Jesus's time, as in the modern period, a Western person from the Christian world would choose love of God over love of one's parents (demonstrated in certain crucial occasions). But this is again a begging of the question.

It ought to be pointed out that it is natural to love one's parents, just as it is natural for a parent to love his or her children. To give up this natural feeling for something else requires special consideration and special sacrifice, and it cannot be always the case. Hence Jesus's commandment to love God need not be a constant rule by which one would simply abandon one's parents for becoming Christians. Thus I see no conflict between the two requirements, and it would be wrong to assume that there must be a conflict. I have seen many Chinese Christian families in which obligation to parents and obligation to the church are well kept in harmony because each obligation is interpreted as part of the other obligation. Such is the way of harmonization from the Confucian view. It is of course conceivable that one obligation is exclusive of the other from another point of view. But again a meta-hermeneutical position based on a meta-ethical attitude is required to make a meta-decision of this sort.

There is no denial that the Christian church fosters a community independent of families but which is still a human family from which one could learn love and to which any (believing) individual could join as a member. The advantages of having church-centered communities are many, and God-inspired individuals can be great individuals. Perhaps, because of the Christian teaching and Christian community, individuals enjoy more freedom and assume more responsibility, face more challenges, and undertake more adventures, all of which have contributed to the promotion and implementation of the values of science, commerce, and democracy in the West. But, on the other hand, churches are no substitute for natural families, just as communes cannot substitute for natural families. Perhaps they would function best as surrogate families when natural families are broken. This is to assume that the genuine teachings of Jesus prevail. But once the teachings are lost, both communities and individuals are lost. Individuals become rough and tough self-interested and self-serving manipulators and macho entrepreneurs. Communities become lonely crowds of individuals who do not care for each other and who could become psychologically isolated nomads and disturbed eccentrics. In light of this, it is perhaps not accidental that in present-day America many leaders have campaigned for the promotion of family values. It is also not accidental that philosophers like Neville have also wished to introduce the Confucian proprieties (filial piety and the like) into America.

Neville speaks for the ideal Christian church and the ideal church member who would give love and teach love, with or without families, under any circumstance. Similarly, one could speak of an ideal Confucian family and an ideal Confucian person. It is important to note that the Confucian may extend his love of parents to love of community and then to the love of all people under heaven. Hence for the Confucian, family is the bastion for growing love toward society and even toward all the lives and things under heaven. Thus Mencius speaks of "loving my relatives, caring for people and being friendly to other beings."[21] Wang Yangming speaks of "forming one body with heaven, earth and the ten thousand things."[22] In the *Datong* chapter of the *Liji* (*Records of Rites*), one also envisions the ideal state of "grand unity" (*datong* 大同) where all less than fortunate people, the handicapped and orphans, widows and widowers, are to be cared for and nourished without fail. These ideal extensions and expansions of love must be seen as rooted in and beginning from the filial piety from a Confucian viewpoint. From this ideal development of love, one can easily see that the Confucian philosophy of filial piety could reach the same end as the Christian philosophy of love of God.

Perhaps we could say that the Confucian and the Christian have shared the same ideal goal of love. Their differences lie in their conceptions of means and methods for reaching such a common goal of human society, one through a family system and the other through a church system. These differences also are rooted in different conceptions of the ontology and cosmology as already mediated by history and sociology. We have discussed how, in terms of the pure consideration of ontology and cosmology based on creation *ex nihilo*, the West and the East have no disagreement, and Chinese ontology and onto-cosmology have specifically and thoroughly supported this thesis of ontological creativity. But then, history and culture have given different forms to this ontological creativity and have caused the great divide between them—the theology of God and the cosmology of the *Dao*.

Our discussion of filial piety as holy duty has led us to a recognition of the holistic character of the underlying philosophies of filial piety and holy duty. They are compatible as far as their ultimate social goals and understanding of creativity are concerned. Nevertheless, they are incompatible with regard to means and methods and to historical symbolism and belief systems requiring different practices and institutions. However, we must also note that in regard to means and methods, we could find some similarities, for example, between the self-cultivation practice of Confucianism and the self-sanctification theory of Christianity.[23]

The question can arise as to whether these two apparent differences make any real difference. The answer is both yes and no. It is no if the two communities or traditions do not meet, or when they do, they respect each other and make no attempt to impose one's system on the other. On the other hand, the answer is yes, if one community or one belief system tries to impose itself on the other, or if one believes itself be the ultimate truth and thus ignores or devalues the other. It is perhaps because of the nature of this question and answer that Neville shows a great interest in promoting the Confucian culture of ritual propriety (*li*) as a way of realizing concrete universalism.

As the *Analects* has it, the most precious function of *li* is its harmonizing function.[24] But the text also says that "Knowing harmony and harmonize without modulating it with the *li*, it is also not the right thing to do."[25] So here *li* at least has two important functions for relating people, to harmonize and to modulate, and both are achievable at the same time. This is because to *li* belongs the rules, institutions, and forms of behavior or relationships that embody respect for other persons, groups of persons, or even systems, customs, or practices that have been respected by people.[26] To have respect is to recognize the other's position, role, and what the other stands for. It is to do the right thing according to the rules for special behavior. Hence *li* involves a dimension of assumed understanding and trust in others. Finally, the question of how to show respect for others also depends on the concrete situation in which *li* is performed. One must take into consideration the relevant factors of time and locale in order to properly articulate one's *li*. Hence, to keep a promise and to keep it in a proper or fitting way is a matter of acting according to *li*.[27]

With this understanding of the *li* based on the *Four Books* and the *taiji*, I see Neville's reliance on Xunzi's explanation of *li* as basically correct and needed. For it is Xunzi who came to synthesize all the many factors into a coherent theory of the *li* in his essays "Lilun," "Zhenglun," "Wangzhi," and other related essays. Espousing a rationalist philosophy, Xunzi observes that human persons have rational minds to recognize, organize, and plan human ends and capabilities in connection with the given resources from nature. The system of *li* is precisely a result of rational organization and planning that would serve the advancement of human ends and development of human persons for both their individual and social needs. This rational and social utilitarian justification of *li* will also give it the proper authority and sanction for observation and implementation. *Li* is indeed what Neville calls "humanity-defining conventionality," for it is by *li* that a human person becomes functional in a human context and learns how to express herself or himself as a human person. Hence *li* can be seen as a catalyst for the humanization of the person and the society. But the question is whether we can understand the breach of order or the promise to God in the *Bible* as a matter of failing to observe *li*. In one sense it is, but in another sense it is not. Adam could ask God before acting on his own. Besides, he knows that God forbids him to eat the apple. It is a failure to observe an implicit *li*. But on the other hand, as a system of rules of behavior that have not been fully established and explained by God, Adam and Eve have no particular explicit rule to obey. To me their sinfulness lies in their violation of a specific order from God.

Neville has followed Xunzi closely to give a significant construction of the continuum of ritual conventionality. For Xunzi, as for Neville, *li* acquires a transforming power of cultivation and reformation. It is not simply a matter of harmonizing and modulating. It is also a matter of legislation and establishing norms and laws.[28] For Xunzi the setup of *li* in this sense is needed because he regarded human nature as basically selfish and greedy. But for Mencius, human nature, with the mandate of heaven immanently endowed, is not to be controlled in this fashion: *li* has to be understood as expression of the *yi* (rightness) from within the heart of humankind. For Mencius, *li* becomes more a matter of harmonizing social orders and realizing and maintaining the goodness of the human person. Perhaps, it is in Xunzi's strong sense of *li* that Neville can speak of "repairing the covenant" with God, but certainly not in Mencius's sense of *li* as expression of the *yi*. For in light of Xunzi's theory, humankind has to learn to obey institutions and orders from the sage-king in order to eliminate selfishness in its humanity and to avoid falling into chaos. I see how Neville may be attracted to Xunxi in light of Xunzi's theory of human nature. But one need not forget that before the Fall, humankind was supposed to have been given a good nature by God and hence need not have the system of *li* in Xunzi's sense. Xunzi's *li* is needed for reform only when man has become bad in nature or, for Christianity, only after he has fallen from Eden. Despite Neville's good intentions, unfortunately, there is an inconsistency in Neville's argument for compatibility or agreement between the Confucians and Christians by capitalizing on Xunzi.

At this crucial point we could come to see a more fundamental cleavage between the Confucian and the Christian in their understanding of ritual behavior as a system of observing *li*. Strictly speaking, for the Confucians in a classical sense the ultimate *li* consists in serving parents for filial piety, in serving ancestral spirits by paying respects at the family altars, and in serving heaven by worshiping heaven at the temples.[29] All of these are consistent with the doctrine of trinity of heaven, earth, and the human in a philosophy of onto-cosmological creativity. But all of these may actually run counter to the liturgy and ritual developed by Christians. Not only does the historically rich and culturally loaded symbolism of the Christian system run counter to the Confucian system, but also at the primary symbolic level, the respect for heaven and earth and the love of God are often intentionally interpreted to show difference rather than similarity. Hence we can see how the great Rites Dispute in the seventeenth century led the Roman Catholic Pope to forbid Chinese Christians to worship ancestors and how as a reprisal Emperors Yongzheng and Qianlong ordered all missionaries to be expelled from China in 1723 and 1747, respectively.

I have attempted to stress how things really stand, burdened as they are by history, archeology, and the various systems of social and religious symbolism and practice. Philosophically, we could still speak of an ideal system of *li* to which both Confucians and Christians could agree. We could further require or hope that both Confucians and Christians would reform their traditions and confront the need for communication, equal learning, and mutual enrichment toward reconciliation and integration. Perhaps this is the goal of Neville's trilogy, particularly as seen in the last book in the trilogy. We could establish common norms or norms of norms among different or even clashing normative cultures. We can do this because we share a foundation deep enough to go beyond our primary symbolism and historical differentiation. We also share the creative reason that would enable us to see and transcend our biases and show respect for and trust each other. It is perhaps in this that we find the deepest meaning of *li*, *li* as a way of realizing *ren* (unselfish love) and relating and reconciling even radically different and incommensurable traditions or communities in the interest of common visions and in view of common roots. This may take a long time to implement, but if philosophers do not begin to think, to persuade, and to articulate, who will?

In the interests of fulfilling *ren* and seeking development of the human potential, models are necessary. Neville is right in arguing for Jesus as a model of perfection of humanity. Similarly, we can say the same for Confucius as a model of perfection of humanity. I do not see any real objections to this comparison for either classical Confucians or modern Christians. This is because a model of perfection has to be understood in terms of actual exemplary behaviors. But when we come to theological and religious issues that bear on matters of faith and belief, we should not expect accord, which, perhaps, is what cultural and religious pluralism means. Neville has wisely appealed to a pragmatism of practical significance to resolve or cast aside the differences between the transcendent Christian models and the immanent Confucian models of perfection. We need to be aware, however, that historical, cultural, and even ontological differences do often make a real difference. The issue therefore remains unresolved.

6

Time in Chinese Philosophy

Western Paradigms of Time: From Plato to Heidegger

Time (*shi*) is a fundamental experience, category, and problem in Chinese philosophy. Not only is time deeply rooted in the metaphysical consciousness of Chinese philosophers, and thus forms the onto-cosmological cornerstone of almost if not all philosophical concepts, but it is also incorporated into the practical and cultural life of both individuals and communities and becomes the most well-considered notion and conscientious self-aware motive-force for moral action and cultural practice. One may thus say that time is a metaphysical principle of reality and existence and a principle of moral action and cultural transformation in Chinese philosophy. In a sense, concern with time and thinking on time constitute the very essence of Chinese philosophy on all its levels and in all its aspects. Chinese philosophy may be therefore characterized as the philosophy of time (on the metaphysical level) and the philosophy of timeliness (on the ethical and practical levels).

In order to comprehend the time-based and time-oriented nature of reality, truth, knowledge, morality, and art in Chinese philosophy, it is important to describe how time was discarded, transcended, and reduced—or even distorted—in the mainstream Western philosophical tradition. In saying this, time is here conceived in the primary or primordial context of experiences of "growth in time," "change in time," and "happening in time"; thus, it is conceived primarily and primordially in terms of "time as growth," "time as change," and "time as happening." As growth, change, and happening are matters of appearance or matters of "this-worldliness," they are not realities of lasting value and are therefore lesser realities than realities from a metaphysical point of view. The mainstream philosophy in the West, as initiated by the Greek philosophers of fifth century BCE, can be said to consist in a concentrated search for eternal truth transcending time or at least invariant with regard to time. This is to separate time from reality and truth, and it is to identify time with vicissitudes of life and world with all its indeterminate or inchoate contents. In this dualism of time and timeless, the world of time is considered an undesirable downfall or degeneration from the perfect order of timelessness and therefore either is by nature motivated toward restoring the perfect order of timeless forms or is pulled down as if by its own gravity toward an unexplainable and unintelligible state of chaos. This is the philosophy of time derived from the Socratic dialogues of Plato, which may be said to provide basic paradigms for understanding time in the Western tradition. One may also point out that this paradigm is well explored in the *Great Chain of Being* of Lovejoy and in the *Greek Thinking* of Heidegger. But there are some important observations that need to be made, observations that are made by neither Lovejoy nor Heidegger.

First of all, the Platonic paradigms of time become reinterpreted in terms of four causes in the Aristotelian metaphysics of primal matter and pure form, and thus acquired four aspects from the notions of the four causes: time is the prime matter of things from which things as substances are composed; it is also the forms of things in the sense that things acquire their forms in time; it is also the efficient cause because it provides energy for change and transformation; finally, it is the end cause, which provides direction and goal for movement of things in time. In this sense time is basically phenomenal and yet participates in the timeless as represented by form and end. We may indeed see time as primarily motion and movements of things in the world, which manifest an intrinsic motivating force as possibly inspired by the timeless. We may call this view "the transcendent-teleological theory of time." It seems clear that even though Aristotle has incorporated the timeless from Plato's doctrine of forms in his experience of time as a phenomenon, he has not metaphysically explained the origins of forms and ends, which consequently can be presumed to have a transcendent existence. His unique contribution is to demonstrate explicitly the teleology of time, and this of course became the very essence of the medieval theology and eschatology in Christianity.

Second, the "transcendent-teleological theory of time" has undergone a tremendous change in modern times, and this tremendous change takes two basic modes: the scientific mode and the transcendental mode. In the scientific mode, time loses its teleology as well as separates from material things as an independent substance of some sort. This is Newton's "theory of absolute time and absolute space." Although absolute space is regarded as the receptacle for things to be placed inside, time, like space, is conceived in the similar way in which things are supposed to move in time. The difference between time and space is that whereas space is rooted in the visual experience of extension, time is rooted in the invisible experience of duration. It had not occurred to Newton that time and space can be unified as a four-dimensional manifold and even become interchangeable as in the modern theory of relativity. But Newton has succeeded in making time, like space, an objective entity that has a dynamics of its own, but, does not move toward any goal as to be defined in terms of forms of things. The dynamics of time perhaps has been since the eighteenth century well represented in the second law of thermodynamics, the law of entropization of things. In essence, the modern scientific theory of time consists in a de-teleological objectification or reification of the notion or experience of time, and may be said to reduce our primary experience of time to the world of things as presented and represented by the scientific inquiry and methodology.

Perhaps, it is based on a reflection on the possibility of this de-teleological and objective notion of time that Kant is able to transform the objective-substantive notion of time into a subjective-nonsubstantive notion of time by way of his transcendental deduction. In this transformation, time as well as space are no more objective entities, but instead are revealed as the a priori forms of intuition of things as things in time and space.

No doubt this is based on the recognition that no thing can exist out of time and space, and therefore things have to be defined in terms of time and space. But this transcendental subjectification of time resulting from a creative act of imagination does not necessarily guarantee our empirical understanding of time; otherwise, Kant would have indeed achieved a unity of the world of sensation and understanding and therefore provided a unity for the objectivity of the scientific inquiry and methodology. In order to see the problematic nature of this position, we may ask the following question: What is the essence of time as a priori condition and form of intuition of things, or how is the intuition of time and space ontologically possible? There is no answer to this question in the Kantian framework. To make time and likewise space a priori conditions of intuition of the things in the world is to make time and space epiphenomena of the transcendental ego or to define the phenomenonality of things in time and space without really explaining what time or space is. The rich content of our experience of time is still left unexplained or would have to be explained in the manner of Newtonian physics.

However, Kant is able to raise a significant question concerning time in regard to human will and human action. In response to this question, many things regarding the ontology of time just as regarding the ontology of the moral self certainly can be said, but Kant has not said them. It is obvious that there should be ontology of time versus both phenomenology of time and transcendental epistemology of time, and in this ontology of time, time must be understood or grasped ontologically but not transcendentally. It is also clear that in the ontology of time, time is intimately related to human will, human action, and human freedom and therefore should present itself as an aspect of human existence. Then the immediate question is how time is presented in the human existence. Unfortunately, this question as well as the former question did not receive a systematic and explicit answer from Kant, and indeed they are not answered until recent times. And this is what I would regard as the third stage of development of the notion of time in Western philosophy.[1]

Third, it is Heidegger whose encounter with time forms the third stage of the development of the Western notion of time. According to Heidegger, time is neither a transcendental condition, nor an objective entity, nor a natural state of motion or movement of objects, but instead exists as a sense of care and anxiety with regard to the pure possibilities of human existence. In fact, for Heidegger time is an existential experience of coming-to-death of one's own existence, that appears in our anticipation of the future and in our fear about the end of future. Time thus revealed to us internally exists in the form of moods and emotions of the human self. In this sense time defines the human existence (*Dasein*) and in fact constitutes the very "essence" of human existence. From this view, the world as we live it is time-fused, as it is founded on the basis of our existential subjectivity. Human action and human freedom depend upon the confrontation with human self together with time as part of the human self. Time is to be lived by confronting one's finitude and by authenticating one's choices and actions. It is in this sense that we may even say that time is the condition of human freedom and human self-realization, and is expressed in human freedom, human efforts, and choices to make and remake oneself. Thus time is more defined in terms of morality and the human world called the *Lebenswelt* than it is in science or cognitive epistemology. This would be an answer to the problem of moral time in Kant. But then the Daseinization of time in Heidegger seems only to meet the problem of time in partiality, for we may raise the question as to whether we need time to understand time only in terms of times of anxiety and care in the human existence. Do we need time under the form of joy and hope? Do we need time in tranquility and overall development, cultivation, and transformation of the self, whether morally, socially, or aesthetically?

In fact, if we want to understand time, ourselves, and our life-worlds, we have to broaden the scope of time over many dimensions of human experience and across many levels of human existence, and we have also to reflect on the link, actual and potential, between the human world and the natural world, between subjectivity and objectivity. In fact, we have to penetrate into the intersubjectivity and interobjectivity of time, not just the subjectivity of time or just the objectivity of time, no matter how sophisticated each may appear. The total integration of time in terms of human existence and in terms of an enlarged unity of man and the world would be the next important task for our enterprise of understanding time. It is precisely in this area that we may see how Chinese philosophy in the traditional form and with its traditional concern has approached time and has therefore made very important contributions to the philosophy of time. But the importance of this approach and its resulting contributions cannot be adequately appreciated until and unless we see how the issues of time have been treated and concluded in the Western theories of time.

The Primary Paradigm of *Yi*: Comprehensive Observation of Time

The primary and primordial paradigms of time understanding come from the philosophy of the *Yijing* or *Zhouyi*. As the *Yijing* was one of the best-preserved Chinese classics from antiquity, and also as it is continuously the most commented on and annotated book by scholars of all persuasions throughout every stage of Chinese history since the Han period (first century BCE–third century CE), it is generally considered the fountainhead and spring-origin of Chinese metaphysics and for Chinese modes of philosophical thinking.[2] Why and how it is possible requires detailed and separate explanation. But one thing is surely relevant for explaining the exalted influential position of the *Yi*; namely, it reflects and speaks out a comprehensive truth of comprehensive being based on comprehensive observation of things over a comprehensive range (heaven/earth/man) and in a comprehensive period of time.

Apparently there is no philosophy in the world that is developed from such a method of "comprehensive observation" (*guan*) without any religious or philosophical presupposition, and because of this there is no philosophy so easily and readily adaptable and adoptable as a basic theory of reality insofar as reality is comprehensively and totally considered. But to comprehensively and totally consider reality is to see that things naturally undergo change and transformation from integration and coordination to differentiation, opposition, and reversion; that changes occur on different levels and across different dimensions of a system or a situation; that, comprehensively and totally speaking, there are patterns of change that can be described as balance of opposites and harmonization of differences. This means that the philosophy of the *Yijing* is in fact a philosophy of change (*yi*). This philosophy presents change in all directions, in all manners and with all possible combinations, yet preserves the fundamental unity and simplicity of change (*yi*) as we have directly experienced, whether consciously or unconsciously, and is capable of identifying and presenting the source and way of all these changes. Again, how this is possible depends on our understanding the non-methodized methodology of presuppositionless "comprehensive observation" (*guan*). It is the achievement of this methodology, not any a priori given idioms or norms, to have discovered the fundamental mode of change in all changes in time and all things in change in both macro-cosmos of nature and social cosmos of man through a long-term period of time. Thus one may even suggest that this *guan* consists in observing how time presents itself, not on one single level of linear changes but on many levels of nested nonlinear changes. Therefore, as a methodology, *guan* is able to present a "configurational theory of change" and consequently a "configurational theory of time." As reality is thus seen as change-in-time and time-in-change, there is nothing more real than changes and time, and the methodology of *guan* is co-extensive with a metaphysics of changes and time.

Before we deal with this "configurational theory," and "metaphysics of change and time," it is important to note that there is a practical side of the *Yijing*: the *Yijing* has been known popularly as a practical book of divination. In spite of this fact and perhaps because of this fact, one needs to look behind divinatory practice to see what has made it possible to lend itself to this divinatory use. Again, one will discover that as changes occur on different levels, changes are parts of human existence as human beings are parts of changes. How human beings and their surroundings configure becomes a concern that should have practical significance because human beings will be able to initiate and participate in changes, not just to receive or suffer from changes. Divination becomes used as a method for finding the configuration of interlinking human beings and their world, which would hence provide a basis for their action to meet or change their ends. But divination need not be the right or unique way of knowing this configuration. As Xunzi latter says, "Those who knows the *yi* will not divine." This is because once a person is able to see the whole field of changes and is able to appraise his or her own position in this field or map of changes, the person is able to take an initiative for adaptation or challenge.

This again brings out an important observation: namely, as changes are pervasive and comprehensive, changes are rooted in each and every individual thing, and this again means that each and every individual thing is a participant and initiator of change, because it has a direct link to the source of change that enables it to be a source of change by itself. This potentiality and agency for self-change not only explains an open universe of creative changes in the world, but would also make change a matter of individual freedom and a matter of coordination of the objective and the subjective. The former principle would provide an ontological explanation of moral freedom in Kant, and the latter explains why changes and time cannot be simply a matter of the objective or simply a matter of the subjective. Hence the underlying "configurational theory of time" in the "configurational theory of change" goes beyond both the scientific theory of time in Newton and the subjective theory of time in Kant and Heidegger. The fundamental question is then how to present change-time and time-change and their possibilities in a systematic metaphysical presentation for understanding.

Time as Change with Reference to Creativity

Based on the comprehensive observation of change and a consequent comprehensive reflection on the nature of changes, the *Yijing* brings out a hidden understanding of the source of time and change in the notions of the *dao* (the way) and *taiji* (the great ultimate). In order to understand these, we have to once again focus on the notion of change (*yi*) and then explain the *dao* and the *taiji* as two sides of the *yi* in terms of the following six observations:

1. Change (*yi*) is a process that can be regarded as the comprehensive activity of production, reproduction, and sustenance of things by an underlying force and the continuous manifestation of all things thus produced. In this sense change is creative (it brings out things from where things are not formed) and life-creative (it brings out things that are full of intrinsic life, namely capable of bringing out more life in virtue of their being rooted in the source of change). Thus the *Xici shang* in the *Yijing* says, "To be productive of production is called *yi*." This is strictly a remark based on the comprehensive observation of change as phenomenon. When the *yi* is thus phenomenonally observed, one may also see that change being creative does not obey any external order, nor does it concentrate on any direction or form any substance that is not subject to change. This of course is not to say that the *yi* may not bring out order internally and develop a pattern of its own accord. Thus the *Xici Shang*-4 saying: "The spirit of change (*sheng*, referring to the creativity and subtle initiations of changes that are profound and immeasurable) has no fixed domain and rule to follow and the change has no substance" has to be understood as a statement about the unlimited internal creativity of the *yi* and about how this creativity itself is creatively deployed. In fact, the *Xici Xia*-8 has a good description of this *yi*-creativity:

   > When the *yi* is considered in the book, it has examples close at hand. When it is considered as the way, it is always changing. It moves and stays nowhere. It circulates among six vacuities (referring to the six lines of the hexagram symbolizing six positions of the movement of the *yi*). It moves upward and

downward without constancy. It interchanges the soft with the firm and vice versa. Nothing is to be taken as a fixed norm. The change changes where it fits.

2. The underlying power of change, the activity of the power of change, and the resulted manifestations of change are not to be separated so that there is no absolute bifurcation between phenomena and reality as in Greek philosophy. In fact, the underlying power of change can be said to find its reality only in the things it produced, just as things finds their destinies only in being the productions of the underlying power of change. What matters are the process of production and the transformation of things. However, this is not to deny the importance of individuation of things, but instead to accentuate the fact that all things are interrelated in a process of production and transformation of the power of change, and in this sense each individual thing can be also said to be self-productive and self-transformative. The underlying power of change, which is invisible by itself and which is constantly creative in bringing about things, is called the *dao*, whereas things that are produced and transformed are called the *xiang*. *Taiji* is then the *dao* when conceived as the source and origin for all things or all *xiang*. In other words, *taiji* is when we focus on the *dao* as the source and origin or equivalently when we conceive the *dao* under the form of source and origin. Conversely, we can refer to the *dao* as the *taiji* when we conceive or focus on the *taiji* as a process of production and transformation. *Taiji* and *dao* are two sides of the same coin and are thus internally linked as a unity. This unity is the unity of process and source of the change (*yi*), for it is in the nature of change that change is a process from an origin, and an origin of change always gives rise to a process.

3. *Dao* as the process of change, even though full of infinite potentiality and obeying no external order, has an intrinsic order of its own, and this intrinsic order is expressed in terms of the differentiation, opposition, interaction, inter-

change, complementation, integration, innovation, and creation of two forces called *yin* and *yang* or alternately named *qian* and *kun*. All these terms are in fact descriptive terms, which refer to two aspects of the *dao* and signify the dialectical changes of differentiation, complementation, and integration. They also represent the results of such changes, which again perform such changes. This is how the formation of the cosmological world and things in it is to be explained. Thus in its infinite creative activities it makes cosmology of the world possible. In this cosmology of the *dao* everything will have its place and everything is intrinsically linked in the cosmological process of *yin-yang* or *Qian-Kun* interchange. Thus everything can be said to form a micro-cosmos of its own whereby all associations and complexes can be understood in a cosmos-making or cosmos-forming interaction or relation of the *yin-yang*. The *Xici shang* says of this cosmos-forming as the way of interchange of the *yin-yang*, "One *yin* and one *yang* in alternation is called the *dao*. To follow this is good (*shan*), to accomplish this is nature (*xing*)." Not only are things formed in this fashion, the individuality and the value of things, that consist in their cosmogenetic rooting in the *dao* and in the well-placing and positioning in the process of the *dao* are also given in their formation.

To speak of the goodness of a thing signifies the justification of the position of a thing and its potentiality for bringing about individual creativity and totalitistic harmonization (two primary goods of the *dao*). To speak of the nature of a thing indicates that each thing being brought out by the *dao* also has its own individuality and individual potentiality. Plurality and manifold of individual things are both independent and interdependent, and their individuality and interdependent are required for the creativity of the *dao*. As we shall see, it is on the basis of this recognized value and individuality of things that human beings as the most well-refined and the most well-endowed things have the full power like the *dao* to develop themselves and accomplish the works of the *dao*, and thus have the full power to form a creative trinity with heaven and earth, two complementary cosmological principles and powers of the *dao*.

4. Phenomenologically speaking, *yin* is a feature of darkness, softness, and rest that one may notice in things and states of affairs, but this feature is only symptomatic, for as a state and as a function of the *dao*, *yin* is actually the power and ability to contain, hold, and sustain. In this sense *yin* is called the principle or virtue of *kun* (the power of conforming). It is clear that the power of *kun* and thus the feature of *yin* can have many ways of manifesting, and there is no limitation to the way in which *yin* may manifest itself.

On par with the *yin*, there is the feature of brightness, firmness, and movement that we call the *yang*. As a state and as a function, *yang* is actually the power and ability of creativity, innovation, and leadership. In this sense *yang* is called the principle or virtue of *qian*. Again there is no limitation to the way in which the *qian* may function and act. Overall, *yin* and *yang* represent two functions and consequently two features and two states as well as two principles for the performance of the process of change called the *dao*. It is important to see that *yin* and *yang* are relatively determined relative to each other and thus constitute two aspects of the same reality. Besides, there is no atomistic reduction of things to *yin* and *yang*. On the contrary, it is things themselves that bring about a complex of relativities of *yin* and *yang*, as it is natural with the way of change. How *yin* and *yang* can bring their potential to bear and work together to form a whole requires considerations of individual situations.

Even essentially and in general *yin* and *yang* are complementary to each other and contribute to the unity of harmony of a situation. The difference and opposition of the *yin* and *yang* may be so great in individual cases that harmony and unity can only remain virtual. The important thing is that things and situations and any other relationships could be understood in the relativities and dynamics of the *yin* and the *yang*. With this as a base, then, we can speak of the *taiji* as the very origin of the change as well as the origin from which configurations of things can arise in terms of the combinations of the *yin* and *yang*. The cosmological production of all configurations of things and situations again proceeds according to the internal principles of differentiation and integration: each object is a product of both differentiation and integration. As this process has no ending, there is no end to the multitude of things that can be produced, and there is no ending to the levels-formation of things that can be understood or classified. Thus the *Xici Shang*-11 says, "Thus the *yi* has the *taiji*, which generates the two norms (i.e., *yin* and *yang*), two norms generate the four forms and four forms generate eight *gua* (trigrams)."

The symbolic system of the *yi* is thus well formed and produces a cosmological sequence of configurations of things in the form of trigrams and hexagrams. On the basis of the same principles of differentiation and integration, sixty-four hexagrams are formed and represent a new level of reality in distinction from but in connection with the level of eight trigrams. As far as the symbolic meanings of the eight trigrams and the sixty-four hexagrams are concerned, the level of eight trigrams represents the natural world, whereas the level of sixty-four hexagrams represents the human world. These two worlds are well connected in such a way that the human world cannot be fully understood without understanding the natural world, and the natural world cannot be fully appreciated without reference to culture and humanity.

5. The last statement of the above should lead to considerations regarding the place of human beings in the onto-cosmology of change. It is clear that human beings are a part and parcel of the universe. In view of the onto-cosmology of change, they participate in the creative change of the *dao* and form a *taiji* of their own. Occupying a higher level of reality than things and animals, human beings are endowed with a nature that can pursue goals,

accomplish tasks and perfect life, and a heart-mind that can form judgment and achieve understanding. It is because of human nature and because of the human heart-mind that human beings are able to act freely and creatively and to think, feel, and experience reality in its ultimate form. Human nature and heart-mind are that which make moral freedom possible. But human nature and heart-mind are what they are because they are embodiments of the *dao* and agency for the *taiji*. This makes human beings supreme vehicles for change and transformation, not only change and transformation of things external to human beings through the employment of intellectual mind, but change and transformation of the human intrinsically through activation of human nature. It is in this sense that the *Xici* speaks of the way of the sage (*shengren*). A sage is a man who has cultivated his nature and opens his mind and heart to the things in the world. A sage is capable of doing this because he lets out his nature and heart-mind without selfishness and obstruction and thus puts himself in the middle of change of things. In this sense a sage is like the *yi* itself, which "does not do anything; but being still without movement is responsive to subtle changes and thus comprehends reasons and causes of these changes" (*Xici Shang*-10). It is with this ontological sensibility that the sage is able to transform people and the world in terms of his resolution of doubt and consolidation of feelings, which are needed for achieving great deeds.

6. The onto-cosmology of change in the *Yijing* is marked by the creativity of the *dao* as *taiji* or *taiji* as *dao*, which leads to the creation of the self-creative human being. The high mark of man is not only that he is able to act freely but that he is able to act efficaciously and thus bring well-being and harmony into the world. In order to do so, he has to understand the change (*dongbian* or to comprehend change). But to understand change in the sense of *dongbian* is to penetrate change and master change so that one can correctly adjust oneself or transform oneself

toward a better or more facilitated realization of goodness as change. The latter effort and achievement is called in the *Xici* "*biantong*" (to change for going through). The *Xici Shang*-11 has the following explanation of the *bian* and *tong*: "Thus to close gate is called *Kun*, to open gate is called *Qian*. One closing and one opening is called change (*bian*); to go and come without limit is called *tong*."

It is clear that change is a matter of *yin-yang* interchange and that comprehension on the other hand requires harmonization, free passage, and efficacious interaction. Thus the *tong* will bring results such as presenting an object, forming a utensil, establishing a norm, and offering a method so that people can all use it. But without change there is no comprehension, and without understanding change there cannot be change. It is assumed that all persons can seek to understand change and therefore to realize the moral goodness and gain benefits and to do free and efficacious actions by changing. In other words, understanding change is the key to realizing order and harmonization in the world, and this means that human beings can achieve an ideal and desirable state of well-being in terms of timely change and transformation based on the comprehension of this. It is in light of this efficacious transformation due to comprehension of change that divination can be best understood. Divination (*bu*) is designed as a method to seek comprehension of change so that one may act to change efficaciously and thus to one's best advantage.

In the above we have presented a full philosophy of change (phenomenology of change and ontology of change) on the basis of the *Yijing*. As one can see, this philosophy of change is also a philosophy of time, as time is both disclosed and hidden in change. It is in change that we see and feel time come and go, and it is in time that we see and feel change in and out. But it is not just the equivalence between time and change that we wish to convey: it is the strict identification between the two that we argue and advocate because in both form and content they cannot be separated. With the philosophy of change depicted in terms of process, origin, and worldly structure, we can see that time must be understood as a process, as an origin and as a structure. As change is comprehensive and unrestricted on one level, so is time. As change can take place within changes, so there can be time within time. There is no sense and no way to reduce time to a simple one-dimensional entity.

Time in Relation to the Human Person

Regarding how time is related to human beings, it is again clear that people participate in process of change and can both understand change and change freely and efficaciously, so what is time is related to human beings in a similar way. Human beings participate in time and can both understand time and act with freedom and efficacy in timeliness. Now human beings are formed in change, but can we say that human beings are formed from time and made of time? The answer is affirmative. It is only in this sense that we can explain the creativity of human beings as well as the corruptibility of human beings. As the source-origin (the *taiji*) of change, time is no doubt the very beginning of human beings, and human beings can always go back to this source and become originative and creative. On the other hand, as the world is formed on many levels of time (change), so is the human thus formed. In the human as a world there are physical time in physical change, biological time in biological change, mental time in mental change, rational time in rational activities of consciousness, and transcendental time in transcendence of mind, which means time of timelessness or eternity if one's mind achieves this enlightened state, as many philosophers of religion have argued about. Even in greater detail we may speak of desire-time, emotion-time, will-time within the domain of mental time, or earth-time, sun-time, metal-time, electron-time, quark-time, quantum-time within the domain of physical time, and so forth.

To say that human beings are corruptible is to say that human beings live normally in mental time, that the human world of times could collapse onto the level of physical time for whatever external or internal reasons, and this would cause the human's loss of reason, thinking power, wisdom, and even life. In an opposite direction, it is absolutely possible that a human person can rise from a lower level of time to a higher level of time and achieve originative creativity. That human beings can move upward and downward on levels of time in a hierarchy of time characterizes the nature of humanity and the essence of human mind. Besides, a human is also endowed with the power of decision-making and making moral choice. But where does this power come from? It is from the total subjectification of time or subjective realization of time as a primordial source of creativity and thus from going back to the source of all changes (the *taiji*) in human beings' self-cultivation of the time-power given to them in the form of mind. In this sense not only the power of moral reasoning and moral choice come from time, but the moral freedom and the ultimate transcendental freedom of the human also come from time, depending on how and whether a person is capable of developing the time-power in his or her own existence. On the other hand, one is also capable of losing this time-power within oneself all through oneself or partially through oneself. All of these no doubt should carry many implications for the understanding and explanation of human behavior and human development for oneself, for others, and for the entire human community.

For lack of time and space (space is time on the level of physical change), we are not able to explore the greater details of the philosophy of change and time (or the change theory of time) as presented in the *Yijing*. It suffices to add that in reference to levels of time, one can make a distinction between content and form of time. Here one may point out that this distinction is always relative to a level of time. Time on a higher level can be seen as a form of time on a lower level. Finally, when this distinction cannot be made for any level, then time becomes timeless.

Comparative Analysis of Time

Now we can briefly compare this *Yijing* "change theory of time" with the four types of theory of time in the West. In the first place, it is important to note that there is a general trait and disposition among all major theories of time in Western philosophy to the effect that time is separated from the timeless on the one hand and from change on the other. This trait and this disposition have been clearly notable in Plato, Aristotle, Newton, Kant, and later in Whitehead and Heidegger. The timeless forms of Plato still remain in timeless forms in Aristotle, even though they reside in things and constitute the formal aspects of things. They are not to be identified with changes nor with the whole of time in any relevant sense. Similarly, in the classical physical theory of time in Newton or in the transcendental theory of time in Kant, time is separable if not actually separated from changes and remains an unexplained entity, which nevertheless differs from the timeless truth such as God. For Whitehead there are eternal objects that are timeless and could not be identified with actual occasions of change. For Heidegger the subjectification of time does not help to concretize time in change, but makes time an aspect (called *ecstasis*) of Dasein in the mood of care and anxiety. When Heidegger later came to speculate on time in relation to Being, he came very close to the *Yijing* position, as I have pointed out.³ He speaks of the Appropriation (*Ereignis*) as the origin and the moving force of heaven, earth, man, and gods. This notion of Appropriation no doubt reminds us of the *taiji*, though not the *dao*. Or one may say that it reminds us more of *taiji* than of the *dao*. It is in this lack of awareness in seeing the *taiji* as the *dao* that one may suggest that even in Heidegger there is a residue of Platonism in which the timeless is always separable from the time.

With this said, we may draw the conclusion that the Chinese theory of time as exemplified and also founded in the *Yijing* is radically different from Western theories of time in not only identifying the time with change but also identifying time with the timeless. In this manner one can speak of time of change as well as change of time, the timeless of time as well as time of the timeless. It is in light of the well-worked out philosophy of time that the character "*yi*" (transformation) acquires the meanings of change (*bianyi*), non-change (*buyi*), and simplicity (*jianyi*) all at the same time. This is not to deny that time, change, and timelessness cannot be separated in meaning, but only to underscore the fact that a theory of time need to be as extensive and as comprehensive and as profound as any comprehensive theory of cosmos, human beings, reality, and their interrelatedness.

At this juncture, it is useful and necessary to explore how the *Yijing* paradigms of time become embodied and developed in later schools, primarily in Daoism, Confucianism, Neo-Daoism, and Neo-Confucianism. But we cannot go into great details for each topic, for to do such would require a great length, which we cannot accommodate in the present chapter. We might also mention that the *Yijing* philosophy of time and its paradigms of time have even influenced the formation and presentation of Chinese Buddhism in regard to its views on time, change, and transformation of life and world (from the Madhyamika school to the Tiantai school, and from the Huayan school to the Chan school). But this is a subject-matter that we will not undertake to discuss in the present chapter.

Daoism

Even though the book *Daodejing* may come into existence later than the time of Confucius, the thoughts of the *Dao* as articulated by Laozi can be seen to have an earlier origin based on the *Yijing*. First of all, the idea of the *dao* is not explicitly spoken of as a central concept in the *Yijing* divination text (the original text of the *Zhouyi*), but the unfolding and the deployment of the *gua* in a timely sequence, which enclose all cosmological and human developments, exhibit the timely working of an underlying force and principle that cannot be defined or characterized in any form or image that it has produced. Hence the first statement of the *Daodejing* that "The *dao* that can be spoken is not the constant *dao*" betrays the understanding that underlying all changes there is the timeless, which is time as a whole and time as a creative power that motivates everything or enables everything to be moved by themselves. The unspoken and unspeakable *dao* is a very important understanding of the *yi*, for it signifies the understanding of the unity of change and non-change or the unity of time and timeless. Following this basic idea, all the Daoist ideas in Laozi, such as "All things hold the *yin* and embrace the *yang*," and "Do nothing and everything will be done," will naturally fall into place and present an implicit theory of time as the *dao* and the implicit theory of the *dao* as the process and substance of time.

The main contributions of Laozi, apart from the idea of the unspeakability of the *dao* (namely the idea that *dao* cannot be permanently defined, and once conceived in one way or another must encounter limitations and therefore must be transcended; nevertheless, this does not make the *dao* a transcendent or transcendental concept) consisting in bringing out the *wu* (non-having, non-being, void, voidness) aspect of the *dao* and in showing how *wu* gives rise to *you* (having, being, things, existents). Moreover, the idea of the unspeakability of the *dao* consists in showing how the action of the *dao* is creative and spontaneous, and thus capable of doing everything without doing anything specific (*wuwei er wubuwei*). Perhaps, we should note that *wu* should be considered a hidden characteristic of the *dao*, which consists in *dao*'s intrinsic resistance to be identified or characterized in any specific or general determinations of *you (being)*. In this sense *wu (non-being)* is simply different from *you*, yet is still opposed and complementarily related to *you*, as it is negatively defined in relation to *you* and thus forms a unity of mutual generativeness (*you wu xiang sheng*) with the *you*. It should be pointed out that this does not necessarily make Daoism idealistic in whatever sense of idealism. The use of the term *wu* may reflect our inability to catch a total and ultimate reality in its completeness, but again this does not prevent us from referring to this reality by using the term *wu*, as the term would suggest *dao*'s forever-transcending reality better than any other term. The essential point from Daoism is that we have to see this, that we are capable of seeing this, and that we are able to imitate and embody the *dao* if we void ourselves of desires, prejudice, and partial knowledge of the world, things, and ourselves.

To go back to the "change theory of time," this means that time has an aspect of voidness (*wu*), that we call no-time or timelessness, which makes time resistant to be characterized or identified in any reifying manner. Coincidently, this is the same conclusion, that W. H. Newton-Smith draws in his analytical study of time, *The Structure of Time* (London, 1980). In this book, Newton-Smith concludes that time should be considered a theoretical framework with regard to which no internal questions on the nature of time can be raised.[4]

After Laozi there is Zhuangzi to take account for classical Daoism. Again, without doing full justice to his philosophy, it suffices to say here that Zhuangzi has shown that the *dao* can be seen and should be seen as the self-identity and self-transformation of individual things, that there exist relativities of perspectives and existential values among all things, and consequently that there exist ontological equality and cosmological interrelatedness among all things. He did speak of the beginning of the not-yet-beginning of beginning of time (*you wei shi you fu wei shi you shi ye zhe*), which means that there is no absolute beginning of time, as every moment of time is a beginning of time for life and death, and hence for being and non-being. He says in *Qiwulun*: "There is now life, there is now death; there is now death, there is now life." The best way of understanding time and being is to "reach to the center or axis of the circle which is the *dao* and respond to infinity in infinity (*de qi huan zhong yi yin wu jiong*)." One important implication here for time is that we think of time and hence of everything in a linear fashion, but in actuality, reality is non-linear (namely resisting linear characterization), and our thinking on reality or time would come to itself in a circle; thus, we would fare better if we reached for and resided in the center of this circle of thinking so that we can be freed from limitations in our exercise of creativity. Understanding the circle of thinking, which is essentially a circle of the *dao*, in this way, we are certain that we would not have to meet the Kantian antinomy of time.

Confucianism

Confucius does not say much that is specific about time. In the *Analects* he says of the flow of a creek that it flows away so fast. What he says of course can be applied to time. The remark on the fast flow of a creek is essentially a remark on the fleeting nature of time as the *dao*. Time creates, and as it creates it also flies away. That means that a human person should cultivate himself and create as many values as possible so that he can realize and lead a worthwhile and significant life. Confucius says of himself that he studies hard and sometimes even forgets to eat, knowing not that old age will arrive. It is true that if one works hard and concentrates on a significant project, time would cease to exist for that person. This means that one would transcend time and reach a state of timelessness in terms of one's activity and achievements, which exist in time in a different sense. It is in light of this unity of time and timelessness that we can speak of the timeliness of one's action and one's work, with timeliness (*shizhong*) understood as penetrating into the core of things in a situation and reaping or bringing out their potentiality toward a fruitful achievement of good, including achievement of desirable transformation, harmonization, and uplifting.[5]

In this light we can see Confucius's efforts for teaching disciples to attain virtues and cultivating themselves toward bringing peace and harmony to people as efforts for teaching self-realization and realization of others, which are two forms of time/timelessness-realization in a timely manner. These two forms of time/timelessness-realization are the core of personal morality and social morality, as morality is no more than reaching self-realization and others-realization in time toward timelessness. In order to do this, Confucius speaks of realizing *ren*. What is then *ren*? *Ren* is to discipline oneself for consideration and respect toward others. It is the effort to preserve a harmonious and humane society or community so that civilization may flourish. *Ren* is therefore the effort to extend humanity from oneself to others and to create an environment in which all people may fulfill good lives. But in acting out *ren*, one has to do things right on time and to respond to people with sensibility and care again in timeliness. For to care and understand people is to understand people in terms of time-relations and time-consequences. Thus to worry about one's parents being old, to respect one's elder brother, and so forth can all be said to be a matter of considering time-values in human relationships. Hence acting according to time is a moral imperative for Confucianism. When Confucius accounts for his own life, he gives his personal development in stages of his life and age. To put it in an abstract manner, we may see *ren* as giving one's time-potentiality for benefiting others, and as such transcending oneself and therefore one's life-time in an effort for reaching values of timelessness.

Classical Confucianism cannot be completely understood without discussing Mencius. The importance of Mencius's contributions to classical Confucianism lies in his disclosing a self-motivating nature of the human person for moral action. Morality in both duty-performance and virtue-comprehension is in line with and also derives from human existence. It is Mencius who clearly states the need for both teleology of goodness and virtues and deontology of justice and duties. Again, morality is to be considered in terms of doing the right thing, at the right time, in the right place. His example of saving one's sister-in-law by giving her a helping hand illustrates the principle of exigency in time. In fact, one has to take into consideration the specific circumstances of time in a situation in fulfilling one's duty and demonstrating one's benevolence (*ren*). One may even see Mencius's distinction between "nature" (*xing*) and "destiny" (*ming*) as full of time-significance in this sense.

Ontologically, one must see that "nature" comes from activity of heaven—a principle of creativity of time (to be called *tiandao* or *Qiandao*), whereas "destiny" results from the passivity of earthly life—a principle of receptivity of time (to be called *didao* or *Kundao*). Human life and human existence are made of both "nature" and "destiny," which accounts for human creativity, including efforts made to perfect oneself and benefit others, on the one hand, and human limitations and vulnerabilities, including mortality, on the other. But a human person can always use his creative nature to overcome his limiting destiny, precisely in the sense of developing one's nature in time so as to transcend time and to achieve values of timelessness, even still being bound by time on the physical level where his possibility and limitations lie. Mencius has the insight that man's nature is naturally creative of goodness, and this should be regarded as a manifestation of the natural and spontaneous creativity of time, on the basis of which man can use time to achieve the timeless value and to apply the timeless value for the creativity of time in a timely manner. To be timely is a matter of profound wisdom, which comes from seeing the intricate relationships of things and events in a situation being interwoven and produced in time, from time, and from the ultimate reality (the *dao*) behind them. Mencius has titled Confucius "a sage of time or timeliness," and this no doubt betrays Mencius's own profound understanding of time in the spirit of the *Yijing* tradition.

More could be said about classical Confucianism in regard to the philosophy of time. Apart from other things, it is necessary to mention that Confucianism develops first with moral insights and understanding

of man and society and then grows into a full metaphysical and ontological understanding of man, heaven, and their potential unity on the
level of heaven, which man has to actualize on his own level. The full
metaphysics of man and heaven is reached in Confucius's reflections on
the original texts of the *Yijing* in his later life. What has been quoted
and explained in reference to the *Xici* of the *Yijing* belongs to the results
of these reflections, which are elaborated and articulated by his disciples.
Thus the *Yijing* philosophy of time, as based on the *Xici* and the rest of
the commentaries in the *Ten Wings*, can be said to be both a disclosure
of the pristine wisdom of the *Yijing* authors and Confucian testimonies
on their own experience, and in this sense provides the primary and
foundational understanding of time in the Chinese indigenous tradition
and native Chinese mind.

Another relevant document in this connection is the *Zhongyong*
(*Doctrine of the Mean*) from the *Liji*. Like the *Xici*, the *Zhongyong* sees
reality in terms of creative transformation and self-fulfillment in time, of
time, and by time. The human in particular is given the time-potentiality
for realizing his or her own nature, the nature of others, and the nature
of all things. If a person can fulfill this time-potentiality in an authentic
way (*cheng*, genuinely desiring and making utmost efforts to do this),
the person is able to form a trinity with heaven and earth, and hence is
able to participate in the creative transformative process of heaven and
earth. In other words, a person is to be one with the *dao* and achieve
full freedom and unlimited creativity in the unity of the time and
timeliness in the origin-time. In fact, this ideal of developing a person
is also confirmed and embraced in the *Tuan Commentary* of the *Yijing*.

Neo-Daoism

Neo-Daoism developed during the second to fourth century CE as an
intellectual and philosophical response to the needs and times of the
Wei-Jing society. The Neo-Daoist philosophers and poets deepened their
studies in the *Zhouyi*, *Laozi*, and *Zhuangzi* for the purpose of both freeing
and escaping from worldly worries. They called their studies "learning
of metaphysical profundities" (*xuanxue*). It is clear that they explicitly
deal with the metaphysical problems of *wu* and *you* from the very start.
For our purpose here I shall merely mention two contrasting positions of
Neo-Daoism and assess their philosophical implications for time. First,
we should mention Wang Bi (226–249) as the foremost Neo-Daoist

philosopher. His philosophical thinking concentrated on arguing for *wu* (void, emptiness) as foundation and source of all things in the world. It is with this fundamental thought that he made his epoch-making commentary on the *Zhouyi* and also went on to reinterpret the *Laozi* and the *Analects*. He argues that all things must come from oneness and return to oneness, and this oneness must be conceived in terms of *wu*. For it is only from *wu*'s lack of characteristics that the diversity of things can be said to be originated. The innovation of Wang Bi is that he points out why *wu* by its very nature of not being any *you* (things) must be origin of all *you*. From this Wang Bi may be said to have attained an insight into the natural creativity of the *wu*. For this reason he sees *wu* as an essential characteristic of the *dao*, *dao* being the name given to focus on the all-penetrating characters (*wubutong*) of the *wu*.

On the basis of the *wu*, Wang Bi stresses also the original quietude of the *dao*. It is by spontaneous creativity that rest gives rise to motion, and yet because of the original quietude of the *dao* all things will return to rest, which of course is oneness. He further speaks of the substance (*ti*) and function (*yong*) relation between *wu* and *you*, *dao* and things, and emphasizes their inseparability, which means that *you* always has *wu* as its sustaining source. In this light, we may say that time as the *dao* and as the *taiji* is thus the *you*-originating *wu*, but also still remains in the *you* of all things. This means that time can be considered as having two sides, the substance side of *wu*, which is the formless and infinite origin of things, and the function side of *you*, which is always a matter of producing diversification of things (inclusive of the so-called "biodiversity of nature"). These two sides of time are not separable from each other and may be said to function like *yin* and *yang* in the unity of the *taiji*. It is clear that Wang Bi's philosophy of *wu* has brought out very vividly the creativity of time and its ontological nature of self-emptiness and self-emptying.

Guo Xiang (d. 312), a Neo-Daoist later than Wang Bi, attempted to contradict Wang Bi by pointing out that because *wu* is *wu*, *wu* cannot give rise to *you*. Apparently, he insists on the logical understanding of *wu* and refuses to see *wu* as dynamically and spontaneously creative as Wang Bi sees it. In order to make an explanation of diversity of things, Guo Xiang instead appeals to *you* in the sense of *qi*. Although Wang Bi also refers to *qi* (vital breath, vital force, and energy of all forms) in his annotation on Laozi, he did not elaborate on the unifying and transformative nature of *qi*. It is Guo Xiang who seizes upon the notion of *qi* from Laozi and Zhuangzi (certainly more from Zhuangzi than from Laozi) and makes it a principle of creativity and transformation for diversity of things.

Like Zhuangzi, Guo Xiang would consider life and death, formation and destruction of things as results of the gathering and dissipation of *qi*. As *qi* is always in change, so all things are always in change. Yet things can be also said to be formed and transformed all by themselves (*duhua*): things transform and change according to their unique natures found in unique situations, and there are no external forces that can be cited as the cause or causes of their generation and change. This of course amounts to affirming the intrinsic self-creativity of things derived from the *qi*, and makes *qi* functionally equivalent to the *dao* and the *taiji*, even though we cannot quite make *qi* the ultimate source of all things. Perhaps what Guo Xiang has in mind is that the *qi* provides a universal context for the arising of *yin* and *yang* opposites, which then give rise to diversity of things in terms of mutual generation of opposites (*xiangyin* and *duisheng*) on different levels. This of course returns Guo Xiang's philosophy on birth and change to the fundamental philosophy of the *Yijing* as explained above. But in terms of the significance of Guo Xiang's philosophy of *qi* for time, it is clear that even though *qi* can be used to identify time as change, one must specify the timeless in terms of the self-transcendence of *qi*, but not simply in terms of its permanent presence in all things, for the timeless is a notion in which time has voided its own existence in any concrete form. This problem then leads to the development of the position called Neo-Confucianism.

NEO-CONFUCIANISM

Neo-Confucianism contains far more rich resources for thinking on being and time than philosophers in previous periods in Chinese philosophy. It is also remarkable that the Neo-Confucians conscientiously sought inspiration from and were inspired by the philosophy of the *Yijing* almost without exception. In fact, many of them have contributed directly to the enriched interpretation and development of the philosophy of the *Yijing*, apart from having their own philosophical systems inspired by the *Yijing*. Here we shall briefly mention three important Neo-Confucians among others for their everlasting contributions to the philosophy of time in terms of their innovative understanding of reality and man.

First of all, it is necessary to mention Zhou Dunyi (1017–1073) as the founder of the Song Neo-Confucian philosophy, who developed the diagrammatic system of the *taiji* as an illustration of the cosmogenesis and the homogenesis. But his *Discourse on the Diagram of the Taiji*, however, cannot be regarded simply as a cosmological theory of time-transformation, but must be also seen as an ontological reflection on the nature of reality of time-change. He affirms the subtle creativity of the *wu* (called *wuji* or the ultimateless) toward *taiji* (the great ultimate or the primary *you*) and incorporates the theory of five powers (*wuxing*) into the philosophy of *yin-yang* for the onto-cosmological explanation of the creation of all things and man. But he also speaks of the return of the *taiji* to the *wuji*, *dong* (motion) to the *jing* (rest). In this sense he sees the ontological reciprocity, duality, and unity of *wu* and *you*, being and non-being, motion and rest just like Wang Bi. But he also sees everything as a *taiji*, and therefore all things can be said to change and transform by themselves. In this he thus shares the same insight on individual creativity as Guo Xiang.

It is in combining these two aspects of Neo-Daoism that Zhou Dunyi is capable of showing how the human person can achieve creative transformation of himself and thus reach the unity of the human with heaven or the *dao*. A person has to be absolutely sincere (*cheng*) in the sense of exercising his innermost creativity in order to bring forth the creativity of the *dao* for his or her self-transformation and the transformation of others and things in the world. Thus the message for becoming a sage is basically Confucian and related to the *Zhongyong*: a person has to know one's nature and use one's heart/mind for the realization of self and the reality. This means that one has to become conscious and conscientious of one's existence in time and act in a timely fashion based on understanding of the creativity of time and the time-nature of one's efforts of self-transformation. He specifically speaks of the moral virtue implied by the cosmological principles of *yin* and *yang*. He says, "Heaven generates all things by *yang*, and accomplishes all things by *yin*; generation is a virtue of benevolence (*ren*) and accomplishment is a virtue of righteousness (*yi*)" (*Tong Shu* 11). One may see in Zhou the reciprocity, duality, and unity of the human and heaven in terms of the two realms of time, which are metaphysically bound together and which function as complementarities of each other.

Zhang Zai (1020–1077) continues the thinking of the change/time and *taiji/dao* in regard to their reciprocity and duality and unity. He even reaches a point that might be described as the Heideggerian (or even Hegelian) identity of difference and identity. For the duality and unity of the change and the *dao* are themselves one. This dialectical identity is the very basis for the self-creativity of time-origin (*taiji*) and self-transcendence of time. He thus says, "In oneness (the *dao*) thereby becomes unpredictable (*sheng*); in twoness (the *dao*) thereby becomes transforming (*hua*)" (*Zheng Meng*). To say that the *dao* becomes *sheng* is to say that time transcends to the timeless and cannot be gauged by things in change; but on the other hand, when time is transformative, it sets itself in the form of the *yin/yang* reciprocity and duality. The process of time-change is well elaborated by Zhang Zai in terms of the basic sequence of mutual attraction of the *yin/yang* and their contrast, opposition, and final reconciliation and harmonization. An important development of Zhang Zai also consists in his combining the position of Wang Bi and the position of Guo Xiang in terms of the unity of the notion of "great void" (*taixu*) and the notion of "great harmony" (*taihe*). Zhang Zai has applied these two notions to the notion of *qi* and thus produced a philosophy of reality in terms of the unity of time-being (namely *taixu*) and being-time (namely *taihe*). He is also able to argue for the intrinsic structure of ordering and resulted patterns of order (*li*) of *qi*, so that one may say that time is by itself pregnant with self-growing order structures, and the process of change is a matter of self-fulfillment of time itself in terms of order-generative activities. In this connection, one may note that Shao Yong (1011–1077) has very much concentrated on the formation of structures and rational patterns of change and time-transformation in the philosophy of the *Yijing*. He has tremendously enriched the form-number (*xiangshu*) interpretation of the *Yijing* process of onto-cosmological change and transformation. This interpretation no doubt gives time a mathematical and symbolic representation in abstract structures of forms and numbers.

With both *qi* and *li* being developed by earlier Neo-Confucians, Neo-Confucianism advanced to a new stage of development in terms of Cheng Yi (1033–1107) and Zhu Xi (1130–1200). Both Cheng Yi and Zhu Xi have written commentaries on the *Yijing*, and both their philosophies thrived on the interplay of *li* and *qi* as two primitive onto-cosmological categories and principles of reality. Although *li* and *qi* are not to be reduced to each other as if they are separate entities, they are always in close coordination and unity in producing the world of things with intrinsic orders. Without going into details, it is important to note that for Cheng Yi and Zhu Xi, *li* is basically a principle of unity and integration, whereas *qi* is basically a principle of differentiation and diversification. Thus their thesis that "Principle is one and things are many" (*liyi fengshu*) can be understood as a statement on the creative unity of *li* and *qi*, which is significant for the philosophy of time. While *li* suggests the timeless and *qi* suggests time, this means that the timeless is to be always found in time and time always shows a constitutive timeless. This may be also regarded as a reinforced statement on the unity, duality, and reciprocity of substance and function of time along the line of *yin/yang* thinking. As the *li/qi* theory pervades human existence in terms of the composition of human nature (*xing*) and heart/mind (*xin*), one may also see why and how man should and can reach for the unity of man and heaven in the sense of reaching for a higher level of realization of time, namely, the level of realization of time-creativity and timeless-unity in the human person and through the human person.

The discussion on the *li/qi* relationship and their relationship to *xing/xin* has continued from the time of Zhu Xi and Lu Xiangshan to the time of Wang Yangming and the time of Wang Fuzhi. It even has continued into contemporary Neo-Neo-Confucian efforts on rethinking and reconstructing Confucian philosophy for the modern and postmodern world. But the views by Xiong Shili, Liang Shuming, and Xiong's speculative disciples such as Mou Tsung-shan and Tang Zhunyi and their significances for the Chinese philosophy of time need separate treatment. Yet it needs to be pointed out that their views have taken inspirations from the primary paradigms of time in the philosophy of the *Yijing* and thus have inherited a distinctive wisdom related to the classical Chinese understanding of time.

Time and Chinese Ethics

It is often suggested that Chinese ethics in the tradition of Confucianism is an ethics of situations, which means that perception and action of right and good are results of one's consideration of a given situation without any unchanging principles involved. Thus, ethics of situations are contrasted with ethics of principles in which what is right or good has to be determined according to principles, which are absolute commands to the individuals involved. However, both the understanding of Chinese ethics in light of Confucianism as ethics of situations in the proposed sense and its contrasting with the ethics of principles are mistaken, and these mistakes should be exposed by giving a close analysis of the Confucian ethics in Chinese philosophy. But a correct and full understanding would not follow until we are able to constructively reveal the underlying philosophical ground of the Confucian ethics.

The key to the prime model of Confucian ethics is stated by Confucius in his saying "Do not do to others what you do not wish others do to you" (*Analects* 15). In this so-called "silver rule," one uses oneself as a measure to determine what is undesirable for others and what one should not do to others. But the content of what one does not want others to do to oneself has to be specified. How are we then going to specify what we do not want others to do to ourselves? We have to go by our natural feelings and desires (desire not to get hurt, for example) as rooted in our nature. But more than that, we have to go by our understanding of a situation and what we specifically want to avoid in a situation. What therefore will enable us to determine what we do not want others to do to me is twofold: something stable and standing in our common feelings based on our nature and something varying and changeable in our situation.

There is nothing absolutely arbitrary in reaching a moral judgment in a given situation, and therefore there is nothing absolutely relative in a situation. It is a mistake to think that a situation determines what one wants to avoid and what one desires and that the subjectivity of an individual has no role to play. But morality always relies on the subjectivity of an individual, for it is the subjectivity of an individual who gives value-content to a judgment or action, and the subjectivity can be considered autonomous and yet universally shared among all individuals, as experience and history have testified. In this sense, we will have universality of subjectivity or intersubjectivity among persons, and morality thus cannot be said to be merely relativistic because of its relation to situations.

One serious philosophical point is in fact regarding how to apply moral principles to situations. The application is not simply a matter of mechanical procedures, but involves complex considerations (weighing) for establishing understanding and appraisal of a situation. As situations always involve an element of open indeterminacy and a veil of ambiguity, they sometimes make perception and cognizance of the situations a matter of hypothetical work. As situations also are subject to change, the input from the situations to agents therefore fluctuates, at least theoretically speaking. Therefore there cannot be a matter of sole determination by situations. On the contrary, it is still the subjective elements from the agents that determine the meaning of moral judgments and moral actions. This of course does not prevent us from seeing the relativity of moral judgments based on considerations of situations. But this does not prevent us from seeing the autonomy and universality of subjectivity in moral judgments either. One may therefore have to encounter the apparent contradiction or conflict between relativity and conditionality on the one hand and autonomy and universality of subjectivity on the other. But is this apparent conflict also a real one?

If real conflict cannot really exist because of the law of contradiction, the apparent conflict can be only at most a potential one, one who can develop into a real one. But then in doing so one side of the conflict must win out so that the moral judgment finally must be either merely universalistic or merely relativistic, or, as the case stands, must be *both* universalistic *and* relativistic in a certain sense, and consequently neither merely universalistic nor merely relativistic. This means also that one has to resolve the apparent contradiction between relativity and universality in moral judgment in a time process of dialectical development and/or hermeneutical rethinking. The net result of this discussion is that a mature moral judgment is always a matter of seasoned practical wisdom, which stands on its own ground and is not subject to vague or generalized characterization in one determinate category.

Going back to the question on what we wish others not to do to us, we would know what we will not do to others on the basis of our humanity. But does this ensure what we should do to others in a situation? Clearly it does not. To find what we should do to others, one also cannot rely on what we want others to do to us. Because what we want others to do to us may not be what others want us to do to them, and it would be a mistake to assume that this is the case. Why is this the case? Again, it is because there are many indeterminacies in a situation, that make many differences even if we assume that human feelings and desires are basically and normally the same and universally shared. The Golden Rule of Jesus apparently makes this assumption. But the Confucian principle in the Silver Rule has its unique point: It is a principle of no harm, and it is a principle of minimal protection of humanity as well as an invitation to maximal exploration into what is positively right and positively good for one person to do.

To determine what to do to others, Confucius in fact suggests quite a few possibilities for practice. This falls into his positive theory of cultivating and practicing *ren* (benevolence). To cultivate and practice *ren*, one has to love others, or one has to discipline one's desires for the purpose of practicing established proprieties (*li*), or one has to establish and help others (of course according to the legitimate wishes of others) so that one will establish and help oneself. The whole point of the Confucian principle of *ren* is to hold a vision and develop a common community and a common destiny in which others and one can share and in which actions not only conform to but enhance interests of both. In the *Daxue* (the *Great Learning*), the principle of reciprocity (*jiezhu zhi dao*) is suggested for positive moral action in the same Confucian spirit. The principle of reciprocity is a principle of putting oneself into others' place in order to develop genuine insights and authentic empathy into what others want us to do. This same principle is very much stressed and vividly described in Mencius in terms of his "to think of others in terms of others' feelings" ("*nai ruo qi qing*") and in terms of his "feelings of unbearability" (*bu ren ren zhi xin*).

In both Confucius and Mencius, many virtues are stressed as principles of moral action. Although *ren* forms the core virtue in Confucius, in Mencius it is both *ren* and *yi* that define the centrality of the Confucian ethics. As expounded by both Confucius and Mencius, *yi* is righteousness, fairness, and justness all combined. *Yi* makes the performance of *ren* and other virtues necessary and also constitutes a requirement on preservation of social dignity of man. For Mencius the feeling of sympathy and empathy is the beginning of *ren*, and the feeling of being ashamed or being not worthy of oneself is the beginning of *yi*. Hence one may regard *yi* as a principle of self-dignity and self-respect (which in turn may be regarded as the very basis for all legitimate human rights) and hence a principle of respecting others. On this basis *yi* can be the ground for preserving and enhancing well-being for others: it is a principle of recognizing distinctions and differences in things as real and as worthy of respect and consideration. If human beings have potentialities for development, to recognize this and assist in the realization of human potentialities would be also *yi*. But in this regard *yi* would coincide with *ren*. This also shows that *ren* requires *yi* for its realization and rational justification, whereas *yi* requires *ren* for its purpose-setting and holistic justification. Perhaps, some sort of this relationship of complementation can be said to apply to *ren* and *yi* on the one hand and other virtues (such as propriety, *li*) on the other.

Based on this consideration of the Confucian ethics, it is clear that it is not true that the Confucian ethics is an ethics of situations only, nor is it true that the Confucian ethics is an ethics of principles only. The Confucian ethics in fact has taken into account both considerations of situations and considerations of principles. The outstanding and remarkable point of the Confucian ethics is that a person should develop considerations for both situations and principles, and this means that one has to develop and cultivate oneself into a moral person (*junzi*), and then not just a moral person, but must strive toward becoming a sagely person, the person of comprehensive wisdom (*shengren*). This should bring us to the consideration of *time* in the Confucian ethics in reference to a person's cultivation of self-discipline and virtues in himself as well as his cultivation of a general understanding of world and therefore a general understanding of situations that he encounters in the world. Both considerations involve time and understanding time in a profound sense.

The moral cultivation of a person requires a process of time and should be maintained continuously throughout one's life. Confucius stresses the constant efforts that are required for cultivating oneself into a virtuous person and the sincere heart with which one must make these efforts. This process is long and its mission is heavy, as his disciple Zengzi would say, but one has to undertake this task under whatever difficult circumstances. This is because one has to consider cultivation of one's nature and developing one's character a most important work, that one should feel naturally and morally bound not to give up. If one loses this sense of self-duty, one would lapse into a life of what Mencius calls "self-violation" (*zibao*) and "self-abandonment" (*ziqi*). One has this sense of self-duty by nature, and this sense of self-duty would always come back to oneself under normal circumstances; at least, this is what Mencius insists. In fact, he calls this sense of self-duty "innate knowledge of good" (*liangzhi*), which in being so called points to the pursuing of what is good and right in one's life and thus leads to a cultivation of one's nature.

The point about this identity of sense of self-duty and the Mencian *liangzhi* is that any virtuous act one performs has two aspects: the correct and moral treatment of others and the realization of one's moral nature. Unlike the duty performed in the Kantian ethics, the Confucian ethics makes the duty performance a growth of the moral person and thus makes moral duty a matter of virtue, perhaps to be called "virtue of duty," to be contrasted with Kant's notion of "duty of virtue." Thus, there is always a historical and temporal significance for the performance of moral virtues in a person: It demonstrates how the whole person has morally grown and developed in time and how the person has used time (as concretized in events and occasions) to develop the self. One may even explore deeper into the meaning of this effort of self-cultivation by performance of moral and virtuous acts: The effort of self-cultivation is a manifestation of the ultimate time-reality as realized in the human person and thus the self-manifestation of the onto-cosmological creativity in the self-sufficient individuality of a person, that is both particularistic and universalistic at the same time. The moral performance of virtues and the cultivation of a person together would therefore bring out a hierarchical interaction of levels of time.

Confucius says of his life that he has progressed through a sequence of moral self-cultivation efforts and their results. He has dedicated himself to learning at age fifteen and became established in community and society at age thirty. He reached a state of firmness and freedom from temptations in heart at age forty. At fifty he came to know the mandate of heaven (*tianming*). At sixty his ears became pliable and he came to understand well people and things in terms of their causes and reasons and knew how to respond to them. It is however at seventy that he became fully and truly morally free so that whatever he does naturally would not trespass against righteousness, and he can do whatever his heart dictates. It is clear that this sequence represents a temporal process of moral maturation, and there is no way to skip over a necessary stage in this process. This means that a temporal, timely build-up in one's moral cultivation is essential for moral development and moral achievement of a person.

Onto-cosmological Theory of Time

Given Confucius's ethics of moral cultivation with regard to himself and others, we may now move to the question as to how to morally respond to situations one finds oneself in. Again, the answer is that one has to command a deep understanding of time as a motivating force and as a rationale for moral action in such situations. This means that one has to understand things in the world in terms of their formations and transformations and to understand the latter in terms of changes as time and time as changes. This is a view that we may label the "onto-cosmological theory of time" or "time theory of onto-cosmology" as represented by the implicit and underlying philosophy of the *Yijing*. To say that time is onto-cosmological is to say that time is rooted in the onto-cosmology of the world, and one has to see the onto-cosmology of the world as a substantive embodiment of time and that time presents itself in many stages and on many levels as well as in a manifold of things. This is exemplified by the twelfth-century Japanese Zen master Dogen when he says, "Dogs and tigers are times." We may also say that times are dogs and tigers.

In fact, this last point brings us to the other assertion of the above, namely, onto-cosmology is temporal or time-based and time-derived. This is to say that time is the origin and source of all things, and as such time can be also seen as timeless in its own self-transcendence. But timeless time is the same as temporal timelessness, so that time and timeless represent two aspects of the same thing, which we may call the great ultimate (*taiji*) or the way (*dao*). It is in the great ultimate or the *dao* that time and timeless are unified as one. This unity is also present in all things which time gives rise to, but also if one does not have this onto-cosmological vision, one would be unable to see this unity of the time and timeless in things, and thus one would not be able to act in timeliness by applying this time-onto-cosmological insight to events and situations. I have shown that *Zhouyi* contains such an "onto-cosmology of time" and "time theory of onto-cosmos (the whole of things with their ontological grounding)," which enables us to interpret onto-cosmos in terms of time, and interpret time in terms of onto-cosmos so that we may reach a dynamical identification between the two in a hermeneutical fusion of horizons. In light of this understanding of time, we may now make the following summary of the salient points of the "onto-cosmology of time."

1. The *taiji* or the *dao* (as timeless time or timing timelessness) gives rise to all things in the world in orders of increasing differentiation and individuation, whereas things are transformed in terms of concentration and dissipation of the *qi*, which can be regarded as the substance of the *taiji* or the *dao*.

2. All things are natural combinations of natural forces (generally represented by the Five Powers, Eight *Trigrams*, and *yin/yang* in orders of increasing or decreasing phenomenality) and are embedded in processes of transformations such as being represented by sixty-four hexagrams, which

form the progressive order of changes describable as creative manifestation of the timeless (*buyi*) in organic unity and interpenetration of cyclic changes (*bianyi*, on different levels) as well as conic changes (*qianyi*, ascent or descent through different levels).

3. From the *Yijing* system, which presents a framework of time changes of things, eight trigrams generally represent natural things and forces, whereas sixty-four hexagrams generally represent transformations or situations that are combinations of events or forces in change, in terms of which the true nature of things (which involves the unity of past/present/future) can be understood. Therefore each trigram or hexagram can be said to stand for a form-structure or image (*xiang*) of things as well as for a phase-structure of process-change (*yi* or *yaobian*) of things.

4. Thus understood, each trigram or hexagram represents a microcosm of internal change-relations with its internal dynamics of opposition/unity, balance/imbalance, support/suppression, harmony/disharmony, creativity/non-creativity, etc. But each trigram or hexagram also has a place in the system of hexagrams, and thus forms part of the totalistic transformations of the whole system of hexagrams, which can be described as the macrocosmos of inter-hexagrammic changes in terms of which the three ecstasies of time (history, present, and future) can be analyzed. It is to be noted that the dynamics of opposition/ complementation, unity/ disunity, etc. is to be found on this level of inter-hexagrammic changes. A third form of change relations is to be found in the cross-level co-dependency between levels of systems of forms or situations such as between *trigrams* and hexagrams. It is clear from the very beginning that the *taiji* or the *dao* differentiates itself into things on different levels, and thus imparts individual onto-cosmological history into each thing. The *taiji* or the *dao* also sustains each thing and its transformation so that they will have their proper places among all things and all transformations at all times. This is why time in its ultimate sense is both ontological

and cosmological. The cosmo-genesis and ontogenesis are basically one, yet ontogenesis may transcend cosmo-genesis through the human mind.

5. Sixty-four hexagrams are used specifically for representations of human situations in which human beings participate and into which transformations of human beings can be analyzed and understood. This understanding is a matter of relating a human person to a situation, confronting him in terms of the situation's impact on him, and his response to the situation.

6. A human person can understand a situation in terms of the time-formation and time-change structure and system as described by the onto-cosmology of time, and this understanding is effective in being the starting point of participating in the natural transformation of the situation and changing the changes through one's creativity. In general, understanding is the possibility of self-transformation and transformation of situations external to a self. This understanding of a situation leads to a reflection on oneself and therefore a transformation of oneself for participating in the natural transformation of a situation and the creative initiation of changes in the natural transformation of a situation.

7. When a person deeply understands his situation in this sense, he can respond by acting in conformity with the situation with self-control, self-reduction, or even no-action. To act with no action is a Daoist idea in which one responds like the *dao* and thus lets the *dao* take care of the change through *dao*'s innate or intrinsic creativity, which has the capacity to do everything (*wuwei er wubuwei*). Other Daoist virtues are developed along this projected ideal state of non-action: i.e., desirelessness, knowledgelessness, thoughtlessness, willessness, humility, quietude, innocence, simplicity, etc.

8. A second mode of responding to a situation consists in mobilizing one's moral abilities in developing oneself in terms of acts of benevolence, righteousness, diligence,

active participation, cultivation of consonance and harmony, hard work, prudential cautiousness, etc. These Confucian virtues are particularly relevant for situations involving other human beings either individually or collectively. They are bases and resources for harmonization of changes as well as for inspiring consonant and synergic efforts toward solution of problems and management of crises.

9. In both Daoist and Confucian responses to a situation, time-energy and time-changes in both situation and the human person are fully employed. This employment may be described as using time to control or overcome time, or as using time to adjust time, or harmonize with time as time has individuated on many levels and in many periods. The principle and essence of human action is to respond to time in a timely fashion with the understanding of the time onto-cosmology as a foundation and as a ground. It is in this sense that moral action, whether Daoist oriented or Confucian oriented, can be described as time-oriented, time-fitting, time-based, and time-valued, and this is how the Confucian notion of timeliness (*shizhong*) of a moral action is to be understood. In fact, we can see that all moral actions are and must be a matter of *shizhong*, for it is only in seeking *shizhong* that a moral action can be considered moral.[6]

Morality is by its deep nature a matter of onto-cosmological creativity with both holistic and individual significances. It is in this light that we can see how Confucius and Mencius seek out moral cultivation of a person, as this moral cultivation consists in understanding oneself, others, and the world as well as consists in thus applying this understanding to achieve creative harmony by way of timely actions. We may also see how the Daoist virtues can be similarly explained. This actually applies to all major ethical theories in the modern West as well. It is in terms of the timeliness based on time onto-cosmology that all major Western theories (such as the virtue theory, the duty theory, the rights theory, and the utility theory) can be evaluated and even synthesized or integrated for a more sophisticated understanding of moral decision-making and moral evaluation.

10. The philosophy of the *Yijing* provides a classical example of the ethics of timeliness in terms of the above explanation. Although the original texts of the *Zhouyi* use evaluative words such as fortune, misfortune, prosperity, advantage, firmness, regret, and mistake for evaluation of a situation in which one may find oneself, these words of evaluation have to be properly analyzed and understood in terms of the underlying philosophy of time-onto-cosmology. With this underlying philosophy properly understood, there would not be simple-minded conclusions regarding the nature of ethics in the *Yijing*. It is not an ethics of situations in the sense of making solely relativistic or purely utilitarian responses to situations. What is shown here is that the responses as prescribed by the texts to each *gua* (symbolic form of a human situation) is a reflection of time-onto-cosmological principles as well as a reflection of human transformation toward a greater self-realization, a greater harmonization with others and environment, and a greater identification with nature and the *dao*. Hence the ethics involved is not an ethics of situations as commonly and partially understood, but an ethics involving both principles and individual subjectivity through the power of understanding in time and of time. This may be perhaps called the "ethics of timeliness."

11. It is not denied that there is a vulgar use of the time-cosmology in Chinese society even up to this day. But this application belongs to the area of popular culture as well as the area of traditional agriculture-based social ethics, social climatology, and popular astrology/astronomy. By this I mean that the popular Lunar Calendar (*huangli*) as published by institutes of astronomy and calendar describes for each and every day of the year what is fit to do and what is not fit to do. What is fit to do and what is not fit to do should be determined in terms of

the place, time, nature, and potential of the day as found in the complicated system of five powers and yin-yang cosmology tailored for timely and fruitful farming life. In fact, the twenty-four occasions of climate-change (jieqi) are objectively and empirically based on observations of time-changes in connection with the Lunar Movement. Even in this concrete case there is no ethics of situations, but an "ethics of timeliness," except that here time is not consciously understood in a philosophy of time and that creative time-power in human beings has not been fully recognized and employed.

Grounding the above Considerations in the Yijing

We may now summarize the procedure of a person's response to a situation in an action of moral significance according to the philosophy of the Yijing.

1. Identify or find out one's situation in which one finds oneself (although traditionally and in popular folkways people find out their situations via divination [pu], but, because the Confucian Commentaries have made the implicit time philosophy in the Yijing explicit, one need not grasp one's situation by way of divination. One can come to know one's situation by knowing the dao and what one actually encounters in life).

2. Apply the time onto-cosmology of the Yijing to the given situation so that we can see it as a phase structure of the gua.

3. Analyze and understand the inter-hexagrammatic structure for a given situation in terms of dynamics of time relations in relative positions of time and further see how the given hexagram transforms into another hexagram or other hexagrams.

4. In terms of this understanding, one can see the time-fitting action, which is called for, for the sake of achieving the maximum harmony and transformation toward creativity.

5. One acts with freedom of will, and his action will make a difference to both the human world and the world of nature from a temporal point of view.

Given the above explanation, we can now see how the philosophy of change in the *Yijing* actually argues for recognizing the time-meaning and time-significance in human action as against a background of the philosophy of the time-onto-cosmology (or the philosophy of the *yi* in the *Yijing*). In the above, I have discussed and elaborated on the time-onto-cosmology in terms of the *Xici Shangn* the *Yijing*. It may be said that the *Xici* has developed as a result of philosophical reflections on the original texts of the *Yijing* and its divinatory uses in the past. Apart from the *Xici*, the present *Tuan Commentary* and other commentaries such as *Wenyan, Xiang, Shuogua, Xungua,* and *Zagua* can be also regarded as results of similar philosophical reflections. These philosophical reflections are possible because time has arrived for an overall query for the meaning of change and transformation in the world and thus for a justificatory explanation of divination. This query is no doubt set in motion by Confucius in his effort to lay a foundation for his humanistic ethics. Thus, one may see the *Xici* and other commentaries (particularly *Tuan* and *Wenyan*) as an explicit elucidation of the implicit philosophical onto-cosmology and methodology of time in the original texts of the *Yijing*.

It is important to point out that in virtue of the Confucian background, the *Xici, Tuan,* and *Wenyan* have come to provide a moral application of this implicit time-philosophy of the *Yijing* as made explicit in the *Xici*. Hence there is a close link between the time-philosophy of the *Yijing* and the moral philosophy of Confucius. This link in fact is historically justifiable because the *Yijing* system was originally intended for practical applications, particularly with regard to human actions. Hence the moral application of the time-philosophy in the *Yijing* would consist in the application of the time-philosophy to the analysis and understanding of a situation and the associated human response to the situation, as we have shown. As a consequence, the *Xici* and the related commentaries may be said to effect both a metaphysical and moral transformation of the original texts of the *Yijing*. Hermeneutically speaking, this twofold transformation is possible because the time-philosophy and its moral application to human action are implicitly presupposed in the original texts of the *Yijing*. In this light we can see the original texts of the *Yijing* as providing an "applied ethics" for human action and see the practical judgments of the *gua* as providing normative ethical statements in this applied ethics.

It is in the *Tuan* and *Wenyan Commentaries* of the *Yijing* that we find many indications of explication of the time-philosophy in the *Yijing* and its applications to the individual *gua* as a representation of a situation. Let us take the first and the primary *gua* (*qian* and *kun*) for examples. With regard to the *qian*, the *Tuan* says that "By understanding the beginning and ending of the creativity of the *dao*, one can see the six positions (as represented by the six lines in the hexagram) as accomplished by time. It is on riding these six dragons in time (or in timeliness) the sage practice the way of heaven." This clearly indicates how ontologically a situation is formed in time and of time and how morally one can apply knowledge of time and become creative in following the norms suggested in the six lines. Each of the six lines has a judgment advising the person to act in a certain way (within the framework of the situation as provided by the six lines). To understand the proper moral meaning of the advisory statement, one has to apply his understanding of the time-philosophy in the *Yijing*.

Thus, for example, in regard to the first line, "The hidden dragon, do not use it," the message is that the right time has not arrived for acting out one's beliefs. To the second line, "Seeing the dragon in the field, it is good to see a great man," the message is that right time has arrived for seeing an important person for advice. To the third line, "A gentleman works hard every day and takes precautions in the evenings. Danger but no blame," the *Wenyan* says that the gentleman needs time to cultivate his virtue and learning and takes precaution because of consideration of time (*yin qishi er ti*), and thus there is no blame even there is danger. To the fourth line, "(The dragon) sometimes jumps in the deep water. No blame," the *Wenyan* suggests that in order to cultivate virtue and advance deeds, the gentleman must strive and reach for time (*yu qishi*). To the fifth line, "The dragon flies in the sky and there is advantage to see a great man," the *Wenyan* says that what originates from heaven is close to the above and what originates from earth is close to the below, for everything follows its own class. This is a statement of the full realization of time in changes of things, and everything in following its own class follows its own time and time-change. The time-change embodied in the sixth line, "High dragon has regrets," means that the gentleman has separated himself from people and friends and thus in moving comes to regrets. This again means that time is running out for maintaining one's high position, and therefore it is time to retreat and step down.

Wenyan has used two important phrases to indicate very clearly the time-content and time-motif in the human action: "To move with time (*yu shi xiexing*)" and "To reach the limit with *time* (*yu shi xieji*)." These two important principles are clearly applied in the explication of the sixth line (yao 爻) of the *kun gua*. Terms like "arising from time (*shifa*)" and "moving from time (*shixing*)" are used to suggest that all *kun* actions, like the *qian* actions, are fundamentally based on time and considerations of time. Hence, the morality of an action can be clearly seen as a matter of consideration of time in light of our understanding of time in the time-philosophy of the *Yijing*.

Apart from the *qian* and the *kun gua*, there are many *gua* in the original texts of the *Yijing* that have explicit statements or judgments concerning the meanings of actions or norms for actions in terms of considerations of time and understanding of the meaning of time. We may indeed briefly enumerate the following *gua* as having their *tuan* respectively enunciating the "greatness of time" (*shizhida*) in the *gua*, the "greatness of the meaning of time" (*shiyizhida*) in the *gua*, and the "greatness of the function of time" (*shiyongzhida*) in the *gua*:

1. For the "greatness of time" in the *gua*, we have *daguo, yi, ge, jie*.

2. For the "greatness of meaning of time" in the *gua*, we have *ke, lu, you, shui*.

3. For the "greatness of the function of time" in the *gua*, we have *gui, qian* (obstruction).

There are many other *guas* that have *tuan* referring to the "having time" (*youshi*), "moving together with time," "not losing time" (*bushishi*) or "losing time" (*shishi*), "following time" (*suishi*), or "rising and resting together with time" (*yushixiaoxi*). The most significant statement seems to come from the *tuan* of the *gen*: "When it is time to stop, then stop; when it is time to move, then move; moving and resting should not lose the time to do so. Consequently, one's way will be bright." This clearly illustrates both the "meaning" (*yi*) and the function (*yong*) of time. "Meaning" (*yi*) of time refers to the substance and principle of time, whereas "function" (*yong*) of time refers to the interaction between a situation of time and the person in the situation, which gives rise to an action as a consequence of the person's understanding the time in the situation and the time in himself. One cannot understand the principle, the substance, and the function of time and thus cannot understand time unless one comes to grips with the time-philosophy of the *Yijing*. By the same token, therefore one cannot achieve a moral action in a situation unless one comes to apply the time-philosophy to oneself and to the situation in question.

Concluding Remarks

In the above, we have discussed why and how time is most essential in Chinese ethics as represented by the primary paradigms of the classical Confucianism in Chinese history. With similar analysis, we may also show how time-philosophy is essentially relevant for determining human action and conduct in other systems of philosophy such as Daoism, Neo-Daoism, Neo-Confucianism, and even contemporary Chinese philosophy based on the Chinese tradition. The basic key to this point is that there is a common heritage of the time-philosophy among all these philosophies, and the understanding of time is a basic requirement for understanding all these philosophies.

7

On the Hierarchical Theory of Time with Reference to Chinese Philosophy of *Dao* (道) and *Qi* (气)

Introductory Remarks

The nature of time has been a profound mystery to humankind from time immemorial. Although human beings have experienced time, to explain time and even to explain the experience of time are difficult things to do; for this reason many philosophers have chosen to deny its reality or regard it as less real than space and objects which are open to a person's overt sensible inspection. The mystery of time is often due to a sense of paradox inevitably arising from our reflections on time: Does time have a beginning and an ending like everything in time? Where is past and where is future? Are past and future real? What is the nature of the present? Does the present point to one direction rather than another? All these questions are difficult to answer. In answering them we end up in puzzles and perplexities.

Among all these questionings, the question regarding the beginning and ending of time is particularly significant and perhaps most difficult to answer. This is because we have no experiential basis for answering this question. Yes, we have experienced time—in the sense that we have experienced the passing and hence the past (in some sense) *of* or *in* time as well as the coming of time from futurity and hence the future (in some sense) *of* or *in* time. We have par excellence experienced the nowness of the present in a direct and vivid sense. But could we ever experience the beginning and ending of time? How could we ever identify the beginning and ending of time? We may have identified beginning and ending *in* time, but never *of* time. When we speak of beginning and ending in time, we of course refer to the beginning and ending of an event or a process in time. Such a beginning and an ending is inevitably concrete, or involves concrete things or concrete qualities. It seems that when we speak of beginning and ending of time, we have already identified time with a concrete event or a concrete process. This is a logical inference from an implicit analogy or model: we are to understand time after processes and events in time. But we cannot therefore speak of time *in abstracto*. *Abstract time does not have a beginning and an ending*. Beginnings and endings are concrete; when we simply speak of beginning and ending of time, we already make time as a concrete thing, based on concrete beginnings and endings of events and processes. Thus time in a real and experiential sense must be always *event* and *process*. Time must be *times* or concrete processes and events whose beginnings and endings must be concretized: not even in our limited experience, at least in our philosophical conceptualization about time. But how do we conceptualize this beginning and this ending? Again, I believe we can draw some conclusions from a deeper analysis and understanding of the beginnings and endings of times *in* time.

In speaking of beginnings and endings of times, we are presented with concrete events and processes. But what are concrete events and processes? Whitehead has suggested, through his comprehensive philosophical system, the concept of "actual occasion" for naming concrete events and *processes*. An actual occasion is a unity-nexus of happenings, which interrelates and relates to all things in the Universe. Without entering into an elaboration on the Whiteheadian Philosophy, which we have done elsewhere,[1] what is important to see is that an event or process constitutes a whole and is based on a whole entity or a nexus of related entities.

The notions of wholeness and relatedness are essential for the understanding of events and process: they are the basis for individuating and identifying one event and process from another. If there is no wholeness and no relatedness in an event and a process, there is no single event and no single process. Perhaps a better way for describing this wholeness and relatedness in an event and process is to say that a process or an event is a change or a result of change and transformation of things in the world. This change and transformation may be regarded as integrative and organizing or re-organizing insofar as it leads to a more integrated whole and a new nexus of relatedness from a less integrated whole and a given nexus. Since we do notice through our experience and observation that integration of wholeness and relatedness occurs at different levels of organization and involves emergence of different qualities, it might be postulated that events and processes are motions and changes that take place on different levels. Perhaps, they could be said to advance from one level to another, or to degrade from one level to another under the perspective of long-term evolution or de-evolution.

The net result of such a view is that if we wish to speak of time as having a beginning and an ending, time is necessarily embodied in a structured and many-leveled hierarchy of motions and changes, which are reflected in the integration and disintegration of the individual whole and related things and also reflected in the integration/disintegration of the generic whole and related specimen of things that carry emergent qualities defining them. In this view, the beginning and ending of time are not confined to one thing or one sort of things, nor do these concepts imply a unique direction, for the beginning of time need not always be integrative rather than disintegrative and vice versa. The beginning of one event or one process may be one of disintegration, and the beginning of another event or process may be one of integration or reorganization. This appears to be the case especially for individual things in light of their wholeness and relatedness.

In individual things such as the life cycles of living beings, there is integration as well as disintegration. The events of integration and disintegration form an apparently unending cycle of change. What is the beginning of such a cycle? The answer is: Unless we can regard this cycle as an event or a process in itself, we cannot conceive what the beginning of such a cycle is. Insofar as we can conceive this cycle as an event taking place in the long chain of events in the past, and insofar as we seem to have basis for making such an assumption, we can indeed speak of the beginning of such a cycle and even describe it as the emergence of a new integrative level of being, or for that matter a new organization of time itself. By the same token, we can speak of the possible ending of such an unending process and describe it as the disintegration into a lower level or a rise to an advanced level.

Modern evolutionary theory has led to the philosophical hypothesis and theory that time in this larger sense is inherently evolutionary. Evolution explains the historical development of life from matter, intelligence from life, and to the speculation that superhuman intelligence will arise from human intelligence, as is argued by Teilard de Chardin in his book *The Phenomenon of Man*. Nietzsche of course has already hinted at such a position. Philosophers such as Bergson, James, and Dewey have also embraced the evolutionary position, which traces the evolution from matter and brains to consciousness and intelligent minds. Philosophers such as Samuel Alexander argue from this view, in which god, mind, animal life, and inanimate matter together form an ordered structure.[2] Perhaps Aristotle may be said to be the first philosopher to suggest such a view. For him, however, the evolution seems to be a completed process; a purposive force inherent in all activities that are related by way of teleology as well as efficient causation. Time for each philosopher carries qualities that should distinguish each philosophical system from the other.

A hierarchical theory of time, where time begins and ends on different yet nested levels, is best exemplified by J. T. Fraser's work on time. In his recent work *Time as Conflict*, Fraser argues that there are several levels of events and processes in the world and consequently several levels of temporalities, each of which has a beginning and an ending.[3] Six basic levels of processes and events and thus six basic levels of time are distinguished: the atemporal, the prototemporal, the eotemporal, the biotemporal, the nootemporal, and the sociotemporal. Each level represents a structure of wholeness and relatedness and a certain degree of integration. On each level, time has its occurrence implicit in and in fact identifiable with the occurrence of an activity on that level. In this sense, Fraser has treated time simply as a quality or a qualification of events and processes of a certain integrative structure. The beginning and the ending of a time are respectively attributed in the initiation of an integrative structured whole, on the one hand, and the termination or collapse of such an integrative structured whole, on the other. Because it is assumed that evolution explains the hierarchical differentiation of integrative levels, there is the beginning of the emergence of each integrative level in the evolutionary sense. Because it is also assumed that conflict between opposing forces of growth and decay, or between opposing forces of organization and disorganization, is inherent in each integrated being on a certain level, the dissolution of such a conflict via a collapse into a lower level or via an uplifting into a higher level represents a natural ending of time on that level. Apparently, for Fraser there is generally an evolution of beings from lower level to higher level,

On the Hierarchical Theory of Time | 211

and therefore there are times found in a hierarchy of levels of beings. *Time with beginnings and endings is nested and localized in (or confined to) individual events and processes.* What is interesting and noteworthy is the fundamental view that beginnings and endings of time grow out of things, represent and reflect natures of things in their organization, re-organization, and transformation, from disorder to order and vice versa.

Based on the general hierarchical view of time by Fraser, we can make several critical observations and accentuate several important topics concerning the nature, the beginnings, and the endings of time.

First, it is correct to see our thought about beginning and ending of time as basically human-oriented, or, more precisely, as human-mind-oriented, for it is through the point of view of human mind as an integrated unity that things are perceived or understood as having beginnings and endings: beginnings and endings receive their meanings from the mind. Because mind is a development after life in general, and life presupposes ordered and organized processes, the very meanings of beginnings and endings the mind sees in things are hierarchy-theoretical; i.e., they are founded on presuppositions of level-specific stages of integration. *The conclusion to draw from this is that the language of beginnings and endings of things and events is always teleological and that the higher the stage of integration obtained, the more precisely teleological time becomes. By the same token, the lower the stage of integration, the less teleological time becomes.*

Fraser regards the lowest stage of being as atemporal, a stage where there is no order of events ands no perception of such order. Whether the temporal *Umwelt* may be said to be a world of total order or a world of complete entropy is not quite clear from Fraser's own description. Perhaps a distinction between the atemporal as timeless order of eternality and the temporal as complete randomness or chaos should be made. Once this distinction is made, it is apparent that the atemporal world that Fraser intends for his first level of time-world is that of randomness and chaos, for it is in this world that not only no beginning and no ending of time can be recognized, but also no order whatsoever can be recognized. It seems to me that Fraser may have not closely examined the nature of atemporality. Due to the lack of the distinction mentioned earlier, he may have not paid sufficient attention to the problem of the timeless in the sense of eternal order as first clearly articulated in Plato. Consequently, one may always raise questions such as what the primordial nature of the chaotic atemporality is, what place eternality or the timeless as a form of atemporality occupies in the total scheme of the theory of hierarchical structure of time, and how each of them links and relates to other levels of integration or contributes to the formation of such levels. These questions remain unanswered in the present hierarchical account of time.

Second, following Fraser, it seems correct to hold that different levels of temporality do not constitute the whole time, and thus the beginnings and endings of a level-specific temporality need not be the beginnings and endings of time as a whole. But then what is time as a whole? And what is the beginning and ending of time as a whole? In my discussion earlier I indicated that beginnings and endings of time accrue in things, forming nexuses of wholeness and relatedness. Without formation of such wholeness and relatedness, and in absence of reference to wholeness and relatedness, there cannot be beginning and ending of time as a whole; hence, there cannot be time as a whole in an ordinary sense. But this is not to deny existence of time in a primordial sense, nor is it to deny existence of time in a comprehensive sense. We have to understand time either analogically or in a metaphysical system under proper intelligible assumptions. For this purpose we have to examine time in its fundamental context—the context whereby time is identified with motion and change.

We have argued earlier that time must be conceived in a concrete way. Insofar as motion and change are time-oriented concrete experiences, and times are motion and change-oriented concrete experiences, time in its basic and primordial sense can be simply said to be motion and change. Although things that we generally observe provide a sense of direction and order from motion and change, there could be conceivably motion and change without direction and order. In other words, time in a primordial sense can be conceived to be chaotic change and motion of things that do not have thinghood and do not provide a context for orientating time or time sequence. Time is just that motion or change per se or the force of such. Perhaps this motion or change can be positively regarded as creativity per se, for seeing in a larger perspective and taking into consideration the evolutionary emergence of levels of integration of things, motion, and change as primordial time is the source and matrix from which all things grow and develop.

Given this view, time in general can be then identified with the creative potentiality for integration of things, processes, and events. Time can be said to be essentially rich and powerful in creating things, for it is in time that time-levels of integration are created. There is even no limit to this potentiality, since there could be always higher and higher stages. Perhaps we could posit a limiting stage, the stage where beginning and ending of processes are both one in the epistemological and the ontological (metaphysical) senses, and where in contra-distinction from the primordial atemporality, there is perfect order of things. This stage of evolution perhaps must be based on the understanding of mind and derive validity therefrom. This is the stage of the time-less: the stage of eternal objects and ideas—the stage of Aristotelian God where all things are completed, and creativity becomes fully realized and potentiality fully actualized.[4]

If time is conceived to be composed of a sequence of stages and to have all these stages in either actual or potential forms, we may be said to reach a comprehensive notion of time in general. In this notion, time has many beginnings and endings; moreover, it has a unique general beginning in the stage of perfect potential creativity and a unique general ending in the stage of perfect actualized order of eternality.

Third, according to Fraser, each level of integration of beings is maintained by the tension and conflict between opposing principles: the principles of decay and entropy and the principle of order are crucial to the existence of beings on an integrative level. One may suppose that the reason for this is as follows: when a certain integration of being occurs under optimum conditions by way of evolution, it is always opposed by random motions of the atemporal world, which represents forces of chaos to the effect that decay will always set in and the given integration will gravitate toward the lowest level of energy distribution. Under analysis, the conflict that Fraser regards as inherent in an integrative level of being seems to me to be no more than the opposition between the force of the integrative organization and the force of the disintegrative diffusion of order and organization derived from the chaotic base of the temporal world. This state of opposition is the reason and cause for the submergence, rather than emergence, of an integrative level. It is, in other words, the cause for leveling down integration, rather than the cause for lifting up the integration. The conflict, therefore, does not account for the rise of the integration of elements from a certain level, nor does it account for the equilibrium and stability of such integration.

Furthermore, Fraser thinks that there is no resolution of the conflict on the same level. According to him, the resolution must come from a higher level or must reduce to the collapse of the given level into the primitive level of being: the evil of chaos. If we look carefully into the resolution in the sense of advance and evolution into a higher state of integration, it is clear that the working principle for this resolution is not conflict; rather, it is the principle of integrating more conditions into more complicated structures and organizations. It is the principle of more advanced creativity that introduces more order and structure into the integrative process and produces more subtle and advanced forms of being. The very evolutionary process from inorganic matter to organic matter, from organic matter to life-forms, then to human minds and human society, illustrates this process of creative integration that opposes and conquers conflict. This principle of creativity that opposes and conquers conflict on a level, and that leads to higher forms of existence itself, is not a principle of conflict. On the contrary, it is a principle of enriching organization and advancing integration. As such, it overcomes conflict on a certain level and produces a new unity of wholeness and relatedness. This principle may be called the "Principle of Harmonization," following the theory I introduced in an earlier article of mine.[5]

The basic idea of harmonization is this: opposing forces or elements are coalesced to form novel unities and structures in which opposing forces or elements become reciprocally supportive and mutually complementary. Such a unity of complementation and interlinking of opposing forces is a state of the dynamic harmony rather than a state of conflict. Insofar as the opposing forces are fundamentally polaristic, the state of harmony in question is one of unity and polarity. It is natural, therefore, to assume that harmonization is the very force of creative integration by which new higher forms are generated as well as maintained. We may also assume that for different integrative levels, there are different specific principles of harmonization; thus, there are different specific paradigms for harmonization. It is also clear that harmonizations on all specific levels share the same general characteristic of producing balance and organization.

Given this understanding of harmonization, we may regard the very origin of organic and biological forms of being and their associated temporality as an outcome of creativity under guidance and restraint of principles of harmonization that are inherent in the root creativity of things. Things on different levels arise because conditions of harmonization exist or obtain for harmonization to take place. Hence, matter leads to organic material, which in turn leads to life and mind under conditions of harmonization—the optimum conditions of occurrence of integration. Indeed, the very obtaining of the conditions of harmonization may be regarded as naturally derived from the creativity of the elementary forces or elements on the lowest level: the level of the chaos or atemporality of pure change and motion. Even though it may be admitted that the conditions for harmonization may not be always stable and are subject to the opposing process of decay and disintegration in both the individual and generic cases, there is no reason not to see the ever-obtaining of such conditions and existing hierarchy of advanced forms of being as indications that creativity inherent in the elementary forces are oriented toward ordering or re-ordering of beings and a hierarchical development of beings to higher structures. The very metaphysics of harmony would posit a comprehensive unity of creativity in uniting all opposing forces into productive and creative processes.

Fourth, there remains the problem of nowness. According to Fraser, nowness becomes definable only when the integrative stage of life comes into existence. Nowness is defined as the time required to secure and maintain the biological simultaneity of the biological organism. In this definition, relative to biological existence, nowness seems to be an objective experience. Yet it is very much confined to the level of biological existence, and is not in consistency with the experience of nowness through direct intuition and other forms of perception in the human mind. Human experience of nowness can be that of a time-span admitting flexibility of duration. The now can be a short span of time; however, a relatively long span of time in a human life can be *felt* to be like a *now*. Even the long history of human civilization can be poetically addressed as a *now* in comparison with the long process of evolution of the cosmos. Can we therefore make sense of the rich ambiguity of the meaning of "*now*," as we have experienced?

One important point to make in this connection is that nowness of time depends on, and is relative to, different conditions of experience and perception. It may be granted that a conspicuous sense of nowness is related to biological simultaneousness within a biological system. Nevertheless, nowness may be also experienced or conceived under the conditions of simultaneities in other systems. Of course the better defined the system is, which forms a nexus of wholeness and relatedness, the more pronounced the nowness in that system will become. The converse is also true if a system requires a long span of time (in a conventional sense) to constitute simultaneity for it, then the long span of time becomes a now for that system. In the human situation, minds can dwell on different levels and therefore experience different durations of now; on different levels there could be different simultaneities relative to different needs and whims. Particularly with reference to human mind-oriented temporality, there is no reason why a mind may not conceive a simultaneity that covers events of distinct localities, as if the present perception or experience of mind comprises events of different pasts and futures for differently spaced individuals. Even though modern communication technology makes it possible for a person to enjoy nowness in different earthly localities, so that nowness for the experiencing mind can be said to cover future and past in relative sense of pastness and futurity.

The relativity of simultaneity and the extendability of simultaneity no doubt suggest that mental experience of nowness can be both different and richer than nowness experience relative to the norm of biological simultaneity within an organism. Given mind as a pivotal point of reference, that which is composed in a conceptual system and exhibited in terms of ideas and referring acts of mind can all fall within the framework of a mental nowness or conceptual nowness. In this sense, insofar as mind can contemplate and achieve a mental picture of what is contemplated, it is not difficult even to conceive "*now*" as extending over all the happenings in time or all the possible happenings in time in a generic sense. "*Now*" becomes possible to compress both the past and the future of time through the contemplative and referring powers of mind: time in fact becomes extended and completed before an indefinite and unlimited view of mind's eye.

This description of the mental nowness leads to two further important observations. In the first place, nowness can be achieved by intuition of mind, "*now*" links past and future into a unity, a unity given meaning and purpose by mind. In this sense, mind might be said to be linking between past and future. In the second place, the *now* in the ideal conceptual experience of mind can be eternity or the timelessness, which transcends the physical and biological presentness or simultaneity, and displays an order of non-change and stability and even primal actuality. A sense of completion and perfection may accompany such an experience of the *now*. This seems to be what is precisely intended by the metaphysical world of ideas in Plato's philosophy and the world of intellectual love in Spinoza, suggested in his motto of seeing things under the form of eternity. That mind can see things under the form of eternity is precisely what makes mind a transcendental entity above the biological time of duration and nowness. Time and the timeless or eternity belong to two different levels of integration, and they show two different levels of creativity, yet they are related in view of the ambiguity and extendibility of the human experience of nowness.

The above discussion of time in connection with Fraser's hierarchical theory of time has revealed that time must be conceived as a concrete process of many layers and sub-processes, and the beginnings and endings of time must be consequently conceived to have a hierarchical structure of nested contexts, which do not allow simplification of reference. At this point we may still wish to provide a metaphysical explanation of time and its beginnings and endings. To achieve this goal, let us consider the Platonic suggestion: Time is the moving image of eternity. As eternity is achieved by conceptual experience of mind, the moving image of eternity must be experienced by life and all things in the world of motion and change. It is clear that one cannot separate time from what makes motion possible: namely, the moving force, the force that essentially leads to the creation of many integrative levels of beings and times. Time hence can be succinctly conceived to be essentially the same thing as creativity as revealed in constant motion, change, and life-activities of beings in the world. But if time is also an image of the order of eternity, time also produces the order in its creative flow, duration, and advance. In this sense, time can be even said to make time-space and things possible.

Space is a reflection of time, for space exhibits a model and structure of completed order. It is in the very outcome of time as creativity that the time-space manifold of things becomes possible. In this light it is not difficult to see how philosophers sometimes find it easier to talk about space than time and wish to reduce the conception of time to that of space.[6] Perhaps, it is also because mind wishes to see creativity as completed, rather than in the process of making, or mind has the ability to make such a transcendental jump. What is completed in space can be open to public inspection; it can be measured with more intersubjectivity and with less interference than the workings of mind. Hence the view of time as space flourishes among those who demand a measure of scientific objectivity. Yet time remains both a creativity—a creative force and flow and an outcome of such creativity—and the displayed worlds of things and beings. In this enlightened synthesis on the true nature of time, the beginnings and endings of time can be understood with simplicity without losing adequacy.

To conclude this argument, I have discussed the hierarchical theory of time in terms of the hierarchical levels of time, generality of temporal reality, harmonization and harmony as bases of time-specific levels of being, the relative projection of nowness and transcendental extension of the mind-oriented timeless, as well as time as creativity. These topics and problems seem to me to cover the full range of a hierarchical theory of time in which important dimensions of time are revealed, and in which the questions of nature and the beginnings and endings of time can be adequately answered. In the following I shall show how these fundamental topics concerning time have been already suggested and explored in Chinese philosophy. Specifically, I shall explain how Chinese Neo-Confucian metaphysics of *li* and *qi*, the Daoist philosophy of *dao*, as well as the Chinese Chan Buddhistic theory of enlightenment (awakening) all provide views or bases for developing views on time that reinforce our points discussed above. In point of fact, Chinese philosophy in these areas has evolved a view of time that we may also refer to as hierarchical.

Dao and *Qi*: Creativity and Generality of Time

One of the most important insights that the *Book of Changes* (*Yijing*) develops is that all changes and motion in nature exhibit the power of the creativity of life. Thus it is said that "To produce life is the nature of change" (*shengsheng zhi wei yi*).[7] Because change is considered universal and comprehensive, as well as constituting the ultimate reality, this means that creativity of the creation of life underlies all strata of beings. This assumption is based not only on the specific observation that life is the actual product of transformation of things in the course of nature, but also on the general observation that the larger universe is full of lively processes and elements, which should suggest the potentiality for living and for creative life activities. In fact, our very experience of change and transformation is considered an experience of creativity. That change and transformation are creative of life and order is called the *dao*: the *dao* is hence simultaneously nature, power, and process of creative and universal change as well as transformation among things. As nature and life exhibit orderly patterns and belong to a principle of ordering, so the ultimate reality of the *dao* has its power of intrinsic ordering, which explains how things come in a certain order and how changes follow a certain order.

The ultimate reality of the *dao* is specifically referred to as the Great Ultimate (*taiji*). The Great Ultimate or the *dao*, because of its intrinsic power of ordering, is described as producing the interaction of the *yin* and the *yang* in an opposing, yet dynamically complementary, unity. The *yin* and *yang* are forces or principles indicating positive and negative, active or passive changes or states—they need not be considered entities or substances as such. In other classical texts, and later, specifically in the texts of the Neo-Confucian philosophy, they are regarded as the prototypes of *qi*, the vital force or the vital energy pervading the whole universe.[8] In this connection, the *dao*, or the Great Ultimate, is largely identified with the primal *qi*—the ultimate vital energy that has neither shape nor visibility. But in due course the creative nature of the *dao* makes it possible for the *qi* to differentiate into the *yin* and the *yang*. Then from the interaction of *yin-yang* all things in the world emerge and develop, following the order of natural elements, natural objects, plants, animals, and human beings with a highly cultivatable mentality.

The very ordering of life-producing power of the *taiji* or the ultimate *qi* is indicated by the cosmological statement: "The change has its great ultimate, from which two norms of [*yin-yang*] are produced. The two norms produced the four forms. The forms produced the eight *gua* (symbols or phenomenal manifestations)."[9] The whole book of the *Yijing* is devoted to showing how the primordial unity of the *dao* or *qi* leads to all things and situations in a creative yet orderly manner. This cosmogenesis is further succinctly developed in the works of the precursor of the Neo-Confucianism, the philosopher Zhou Dunyi (1017–1073). Zhou Dunyi's essay: "Discourse on the Diagram of the Great Ultimate," gives the following order of development: "The Ultimateless; the Great Ultimate; Yin and Yang; Movement and Rest; the Five Processes and Agencies of fire, water, metal, wood and earth; the Female way and the Male way; and the production and transformation of all things in the world." The Ultimateless (*wuji*) in this passage indicates the non-substantiality and the inexhaustibility of the source nature of the *dao* as the Great Ultimate. This cosmological picture is elaborated in other Neo-Confucians such as Zhang Zai (1020–1077) and Zhu Xi (1130–1200), although with variations.[10] The creativity of the *dao* is similarly stressed in the *Daoist* philosophy of Laozi and Zhuangzi. In the *Daodejing* it is asserted, "The *dao* gives rise to one, one to two, two to three, three to ten thousand things."[11] The one, two, and three refer to gradual differentiation of the elementary forces or energy that should constitute the ultimate reality of the *dao*. The orderliness and the potentiality for creative production are inherent in the conception of the *dao*. Of course, it takes more than simply one level of creativity to achieve everything. The complexity and multitude of things must be based on supporting forces derived from various levels of creative activities of the *dao*. Thus *Daodejing* says, "The *dao* generates them (things); the virtue (*de*) nourishes them, the nature of things shape them and the situation perfects them."[12]

The *Dao* as the source of creativity is not an entity, nor is it to be identified with anything tangible. It is in fact described as the void (*wu*). In this sense the *dao* is the vast unlimited energy from which all things originate, and the originative power is inherent in this origin per se. The best description of this creativity is given in the following terms, "The *dao* always does nothing and hence everything becomes done."[13] What this means is that the creative process of the *dao* is intrinsic and spontaneous and natural. Totally of its own accord and by its own nature everything comes into being. The order and life from the *dao* are all natural and spontaneous manifestations and expression of the *dao*.

Now it is clear that in the framework of the creative cosmology of *dao* and *qi*, time must be ultimately conceived as the *dao* or the ultimate *qi* itself. Time is the essence of things and their formation and changes, just as the *dao* or *qi* is the essence of things and their formation and changes. Time thus can be identified with the principle of creativity in the *dao* or the ultimate *qi* insofar as it not only gives rise to everything but also produces them in an orderly fashion. The integrative levels of being, which will be discussed a little later, are all due to gradual concrescence of time. In this sense time is not just the Kantian sensible form of understanding how things are things, but has a definite content in terms of the base energy of formation and transformation. Indeed, it is precisely because of the creative and active nature of time that time can be felt as a form of knowing on the level of intelligent mind at all. But the basic experience of time must be one of concrete reality of change and creativity, which can be metaphysically and cosmologically explained.

In the light of the Neo-Confucian and Daoist Philosophy, it is also clear that time, as the creative power and process of creative transformation of things, is never to be conceived only negatively. The orderly interaction of the *yin-yang* shows that the destructive or disintegrative change is always accompanied by creative and constructive change. Therefore, there cannot be principles of decay apart from equal principles of construction. There is always the relativity of decay and generation within a total process of change based on the creativity of the *dao* or the ultimate *qi*. As the ultimate *qi* is the most fundamental level of reality, even the relative atemporality in terms of free activities of the *qi* need not be said to be void of time. Time at this level is identified with creativity itself, which is formless and directionless, yet it is the base from which form and direction arise. Hence, there is potentiality for explicit time as it is inherent in the *dao*. The *dao* is the source from which things arise, but it is also the ends to which things return. Even mind-oriented virtues and qualities may be said to inhere in the *dao*. The return to the *dao* is for the purpose of continuing creative advance of formation and transformation of things, which shows that time is inexhaustible and unlimited. In other words, time is the pivotal point of being and non-being and the everlasting foundation of the world.

Given this view of time, it is clear that there is no beginning and no ending of time in the ultimate and fundamental sense, because the *dao* and the ultimate *qi* by itself has no beginning and ending. Beginning and ending are terms applying to things that have shapes and forms and undergo processes related to wholes and the nexus of relatedness. The *dao* and the ultimate *qi* in the *Yijing*, Neo-Confucianism, and Daoism are pure ultimate energy of creativity that contains neither wholes nor nexuses of relatedness. It is the foundational level of energy for all differentiation and integration. It exhibits only the *qi* tendencies of the *yin* and the *yang*. Even though we may describe the *yin* and the *yang* as interacting or alternating, they are mutually intertwined, and neither can be said to be a beginning or an ending. Thus it is said by Zhou Dunyi, "One movement and one rest in alternation, they are mutually rooted to each other."[14] Even though the *dao* or the Great Ultimate of the *qi* may not be said to have a beginning and an ending, it can be properly said to be the beginning of all things in the sense of being the foundation of all things. Because all things also return to the *dao* or the ultimate *qi*, it can be also said to be the ending of all things. Yet to say this is not to deny that all things have their individual beginnings and endings as they are formed on different levels and in different stages of transformation of things. Thus Shao Yong (1010–1077) says: "There are two types of beginnings (*yuan*): That beginning which generates heaven and earth is the Great Ultimate (*taiji*); among ten thousand things, there are respectively individual beginnings: these are roots of their individual generation."[15] The relation between these two beginnings is that the ultimate beginning of things in the *dao* is also the ultimate ending; in the *dao* all beginnings and endings of things are creative transformations and expressions of the *dao*. Even heaven and earth, insofar as they are considered things in shape, have a beginning and an ending according to Shao Yong. We may therefore conclude that time in the ultimate sense comprehends all beginnings and endings of times through the creative self-transformation of itself.

Hierarchy of Generation and Harmonization in Time

In the light of the above-discussed cosmology of the *dao* and the *qi*, the nature of time and beginnings and endings of its transformation are clearly illustrated. There remains the question as to how things are produced and generated in the orderly fashion, as being comprehended in the *dao* or in the ultimate *qi*. The order of generation of things as conceived by Chinese philosophers in the *Yijing* and the Neo-Confucian-Daoist Schools generally follows this sequence: The *Dao* or the Great Ultimate, Heaven and Earth, the Five Processes and Agencies, the Ten Thousand Things, Human Being and Mind. Apparently this order of generation indicates a process of hierarchical formation and transformation pointing to the end of formation of human species.

Even though there are qualitative differences for each stage of development, the whole process of generation is explained in terms of the activity of the *qi* (the vital energy). Not only do large phenomena such as heaven and earth represent the concentration of *qi*, but the subtleties of *mind* are also expression of *qi*, albeit the finest and most refined product of *qi* transformation. In Zhang Zai this comprehensive process of *qi* is given the most systematic expression; here, *qi* is described as having powers of concentration, expression, contraction, and stretching: these all being the creative functions of *qi*. Similarly in Zhu Xi and other Neo-Confucian philosophers, *qi* is conceived as the basis of all phenomena of a hierarchy, inclusive of the material universe and the universe of mind. Even in *Zhuangzi* we see a sequence of development and generation of things semi-metaphysically described as the process of development from the ultimate *qi* (which is called *ji* by Zhuangzi—subtle beginnings of things) to *zhong* (seeds of natural kinds), to fish, to none, to man.[16] This may be indeed the earliest statement of an evolutionary theory of species.

It is noteworthy from above that the creative power of the *dao* or *qi* produces things by way of harmonization rather than conflict. The idea of harmonization is again tied to the metaphysics of the creative *dao* or *qi*.

The *dao* or the ultimate *qi*, as we noted earlier, generates the interaction of the *yin* and the *yang*, which functions to produce all things in the world. Now the working together of the *yin* and the *yang* is a matter of harmonious unification of two opposing differentiating forces that complement and support each other, even while opposing one another in virtue of their converse natures. Why does the opposition of the *yin* and the *yang* suggest more the concept of *harmony* than that of *conflict*? The reason is not far to find. The opposition of the *yin* and the *yang* is always grounded in the unity of the *dao*, and is always contained in the framework of the unity of the *dao*—the opposition exhibits the unity of the differentia more than their tension and mutual aversion. The opposition of the *yin* and the *yang*, therefore can be said to be a cause of harmony, attraction, and stimulation rather than conflict and struggle.

It is not the case that only the very existence of the opposing forces *yin* and *yang* is premised on the underlying harmony between the two, the harmonization of all elements and forces in the creative process of the *dao* is the very reason for the formation and evolution of the novel organization of things and integration of beings. In other words, harmonization is the very mode of operation for the integration of things toward higher and higher stages. This process of operation indeed can be titled the Dialectics of Harmonization.[17] It can be contrasted with the Dialectics of Conflict whereby the absolutely warring elements of forces have to be overcome on a higher level of synthesis, lest the warring and struggle between the opposing forces or elements lead to destruction or annihilation.

The *Book of Changes* has provided the basic model for the Dialectics of Harmonization. It speaks of the origination (*yuan*), development (*heng*), flourishing (*li*), and holding firm (*zhen*) of a process or an event. It also speaks of the mutual attraction (*gan*) of heaven and earth as the cause for the transformation of things. The abilities of *gan* (attraction) and *ying* (responding) indeed become the guiding principles for the Neo-Confucians. Thus Cheng Hao (1032–1086) says: "Within the heaven and earth there is merely one relation of attraction and response (*ganying*). What else is there?"[18] It is on the basis of this observation that the development of things is always considered a matter of harmonization than conflict. It is also on the basis of this observation that the creativity of *dao* can be said to function by way of the Dialectics of Harmonization and necessarily and universally exhibit the spirit of life and vitality among things. Thus Cheng Hao remarks: "The living air of all ten thousand things is most remarkable to note."¹⁹ Zhou Dunyi, Zhang Zai, and Shao Yong, in their studies of the *Yijing*, have all contributed to an enrichment of the Dialectics of Harmonization.

In the *Daoist* writings, the Dialectics of Harmonization as a procedure for generation of things is equally emphasized. *Daodejing* says: "All ten thousand things bear *yin* and embrace *yang*."²⁰ But the Daoist also emphasizes the idea of return (*fu*) or reversion (*fan*) as elements of the Dialectics of Harmonization. The principle of return is indeed called the movement of the *dao*. In the *Yijing* this same idea is also introduced but not stressed.²¹ Apart from the idea of return, Zhuangzi further introduced the idea of self-transformation (*zihua*) to the Dialectics of Harmonization. This seems to be a natural extension of the principle of spontaneity and non-action (*wuwei*) in *Laozi*. The net result of all these ideas is to make the process of harmonization a natural process of self-realization of the *dao*—there is no element of struggle and conflict whatsoever in the evolutionary creation and transformation of things.

The very concept of harmony (*he*) is dominant in the Chinese philosophical tradition. Confucius has spoken of the importance of *he* in the performance of proprieties (*li*). In the *Yijing* the idea of *he* is indirectly expressed in terms of the above mentioned *yuan, hen, li, chen*, as well as in the orderly pattern for formation and transformation of *yin-yang* and all things. It is called the nature (*xing*) of things and the consequential goodness (*shan*) of change. In fact, the whole symbolic system of the *Yijing* seems to display and illustrate the idea of harmony and the process of harmonization.

It has been mentioned that in the *Daodejing*, all the ten thousand things bear the *yin* and embrace the *yang*. Following this, the *Daodejing* concludes that "Hence [all the ten thousand things] unify the *qi* to achieve harmony (*he*)."²² In *Zhuangzi* the idea of harmonization is also outstanding. To harmonize (*he*) is to harmonize with natural principles of the heaven (*tian*), which are nothing more than the spontaneous self-transformation of things and orderly unceasing creativity of the *dao*.²³

However, the most celebrated passage that explains the nature and import of harmony belongs to the *Zhongyong*. It discusses the idea of *he* in terms of human feelings and emotion. It says:

> When [feelings of] anger, joy, sorrow and happiness have not yet been aroused, there is centrality (*zhong*) (of mind). When they are aroused and are expressed with right measures, there

is harmony. [In the same spirit], [the principle of] centrality is the great basis for all things in the world, the harmony is the perfect path for all things in the world. If centrality and harmony are reached, the heaven and earth will be well-positioned and all ten thousand things will be well-nourished.[24]

This passage clearly indicates harmony as an ideal state of being in perfection and harmonization, as well as an ideal path for actualizing the potentiality of the world. Hence, the evolution of the integrative levels of times must be conceived as oriented toward, as well as guided by, the principle of harmony and the process of harmonization inherent in the creative process of the *dao*. It can be also concluded that time in different contexts and on different levels must be defined and described with reference to an activity and a goal for harmonization. Time in general as well as in particular is, therefore, no more than timeliness (*shizhong*) (as mentioned in the *Yijing*) for realizing the creative richness of the *dao*.

Cultivation of Mind and the Insight into Nowness

We have seen that in the hierarchical development of time, mind-time or mind-oriented time occupies an important position. The importance for mind-time consists in this: that time is more distinctly perceived and is given a structure and a form, which does not obtain on lower levels. Moreover, the beginnings and endings of time in terms of the events and processes are recognized and given meanings in terms of the meanings of the events and processes. That mind can perceive and give meaning to events and processes so that their beginnings and endings stand out is not necessarily a subjective reflection of the mind; it can be considered a reflection of the objective structure in reality or in time itself. It simply takes mind to reveal the inner content and overt form of time. As time, as we have argued, is metaphysically ambivalent, the meaning of time is logically ambiguous.

It might be also suggested that mind provides an occasion for time to individuate to a high degree of complexity and refinement in both its content and its formal precision. In regard to content, time can contain as much information as mind can, and time can produce as much information as mind can. Here the content in the sense of information is simply an example. The content of time on the level of mind in general can be as creative as mind itself if we can speak of the creativity of mind. In a cosmological sense, consistent with our theory of the evolution of time in hierarchical stages, mind itself embodies the very creativity of time. In fact, it is through the creativity of time that mind becomes mind and mind becomes creative. For time reaches its apex of integrative development in the emergence of mind and therefore makes mind a vehicle for its own creativity. The creativity in mind relieves creativity of time in a manner different from other forms of creativity. Mind-time is simply one form of mind-creativity or creativity of time in mind. Art, philosophy, language, science, and even religion are products of mind-time or time-creativity by mind.

Another area of time-creativity of mind is the precision that mind gives to the beginning and ending of time. Objective time as measured by precision instruments is a mind-product—for it takes the mind to design and make the measurement. Even though the objective time applies to physical universe, it contains a component of the subjective—namely the creativity of time as revealed in the dimension of cognitive activities of scientific mind. The interesting thing to note is that through the design of clocks and computers we can speak of so-called nanoseconds—hair-splitting of time into shortest possible moments. With regard to these shortest possible moments can we still speak of the beginning and the ending of time? Is the beginning also the ending? Is the ending also the beginning? The answer is: insofar as mind can perceive or find an event or process concreted in such a moment, and insofar as the event and the process can be said to have a distinguishable (basically intellectually distinguishable) beginning point and ending point in a meaningful context (such as an execution of an order in a computer program), we can speak of the beginning and the ending of the shortest moment and even give it a meaningful content as rich as mind can distinguish. This example shows how mind may expand the horizon of the time sequence and its beginnings and endings. This leads to the question of the nowness we discussed earlier.

Inasmuch as mind has the capacity to recognize a shortest possible moment as having a meaningful beginning and a meaningful ending, it has the capacity to recognize the longest possible duration of time as having a meaningful beginning and a meaningful ending. The condition for such recognition depends, again, as in the case of recognizing the shortest moment, on mind's being able to provide a meaningful content, meaning structure and direction for such a duration. That mind can be said to be able to do so is precisely part of our conception of mind. If mind may not actually perform its creative function of this sort to a satisfactory extent, there is no reason why it may not have the potentiality to do so. Hence what type of a theory of mind we will have will decide how we determine and identify events and processes and their temporal beginnings and endings.

In the earlier discussion I have suggested that insofar as mind can provide an organized content of ideas or concepts for a duration of time, the duration of time in question can be given a meaningful beginning and a meaningful ending. I have suggested that mind can reach the timeless by developing a cosmological and an ontological theory that should apply to time as a whole through an analogical extension of the now. In metaphysical words, mind determines the duration of the now relative to its ideological activities insofar as mind can be considered distinguishable in its wholeness and relatedness from other entities on other levels. In mind the *now* of mind-time need not be determined or dominated by the *now* of body-time or matter-time. In fact, mind has the capacity to give nowness to events and processes on different levels. On the level of mind, events and processes simply become displayed as ideas of such or as exhibited as completion of activities. Hence we have the theory of ideas in Plato and Spinoza's motto on seeing things under the form of eternity. Nowness for mind can be thus regarded as relative eternity: Once it is extended indefinitely through mind by the creativity of time itself, it will approximate to absolute eternity. This means, metaphysically at least, that time reaches eternity through mind.

In Chinese philosophy, mind is given a role to reach the timeless and eternal order in and of things. Mind is considered the supreme achievement of the time-creativity of the *dao* or *qi*, and as such it embodies the ultimate function of creativity of the *dao* or the Great Ultimate. But this does not mean that mind in its emergence is endowed the fully factual power to penetrate the full reality of time itself. It has to be *cultivated* so that the function for penetration into reality can be fully fulfilled. When mind fully reaches the ultimate reality, mind can be said to enhance the *dao* and can be identified as the creativity of the *dao* itself. At this stage mind can be said to transcend the time, for it exhibits the full content of time. The beginning and the ending of time are met in a circle. Yet mind's transcendence of time is together with mind's immanence in time, for mind achieves its transcendence by fully identifying with time and the creativity of time—the *dao* or the Great

Ultimate. This state of mind is self-actualization of the Great Ultimate or the *dao*. This state perhaps can be aptly described as "the ultimateness and yet the great ultimate" in Zhou Dunyi's "Discourse on the Diagram of the Great Ultimate." It is a state whereby rest and movement become one and creativity is creatively completed. This is also the state that characterizes the nowness of the ultimate reality or the ultimate nowness of reality. It is the state that a Neo-Confucian would call the full realization of mind (*jinxin*) and the full realization of nature (*jinxing*). When the content of the ultimate reality is considered, it is a state where *li* (principles) of all things are fully displayed and understood. It is also a state that the Chan Buddhist would call enlightenment or awakening (*wu* or *satori* in Japanese).

In classical Confucianism, Mencius has spoken of "fulfilling one's mind and knowing one's nature."[25] Zhu Xi comments on this in response to the question on whether "The wonderful use of mind has a limit?"

> What inheres in heaven is the destiny (*ming*), what inheres man is *nature* (*xing*). What masters the nature is mind (*xin*). In fact mind and nature share in one thing—the *dao*. If mind can penetrate to the *dao*, how can it have limit? There is nothing outside the nature. If there is limitation [of mind and nature], it must come from the fact that there are things outside nature [of man].[26]

Zhu Xi spoke of the function, not the form, of mind as limitless, because he sees it as basically identifiable with the *dao*, and he thinks that one can cultivate one's understanding and mind to realize the identity of mind in the *dao*. One's mind reaches this understanding and acquires illumination concerning one's nature and mind. This illumination is an insight into the *dao* and hence an insight in the ultimate nature of time. This I consider as an insight into nowness of time.

Mencius has indicated the importance for cultivation of mind in terms of "nourishing the *qi* of heaven and earth." This is highly significant. For in light of our theory of time as *qi*, to nourish the *qi* of heaven and earth is to refine and sharpen one's creativity in a larger universe. It is to let creativity become fully active and open so that it relates and integrates all things in the world. As Zhu Xi clearly states, "Mind is *qi*." "Mind is the quintessence of *qi*."[27] It is the highest integration the evolution of *qi* (or creativity of the *dao*) has achieved. Thus it is where time reveals its fullest creativity. That is why mind is called void (*xu*), subtle in activity (*ling*), illuminating (*ming*), and perceptive (*jue*). Concerning the cultivation of mind, Zhu Xi has this to say:

> Regarding the perceptiveness of mind, it can know things, and all things in the world have principles (for their existence). It is because principles are not thoroughly surveyed, so the knowledge of mind is not exhaustive. Thus the *Great Learning* (*Daxue*) at the beginning of its teaching, makes the learner reach for the full understanding of the principles of things, and to do this to the utmost. After one has made efforts long enough, there will be a time of full penetration whereby all nuances and aspects, inside and outside, will be clear, and the total function of my mind will be illuminated.[28]

When the mind is thus fully cultivated, one might follow Mencius in saying that "All ten thousand things are complete in me." In the same spirit Lu Xiangshan (1139–1193) says, "My mind is exactly the universe and the universe is exactly my mind."[29] These need not be considered as idealistic statements. In light of our theory of time and the timeless, these statements indicate how mind as the highest expression of time-creativity comprehends and comprises things like time itself in mind's unique way. This indicates how time links to eternity or the timeless via mind or precisely via the nowness of mind.

In the cultivated sense of mind, mind is considered to be the Great Ultimate by Shao Yong.[30] This shows the recognition that mind provides an origin and an end for time-processes to run its full course. It also shows how mind may gain insight into the nowness of reality. As the Great Ultimate, mind indeed perceives and comprehends all things in totality and full wholeness. This perception is indicated clearly by Cheng Yi (1033–1108) as well: "With readiness of spurting (like water) and vastness of expansion, there is no beginning [and ending], all ten thousand things are already sublimely presented. Not responding is no priority of time, already responding is no posteriority of time. It [the total order of things in time] is like a tree of a hundred feet, from its roots to its branches and leaves, there is one thread of unity."[31] In seeing time in its totality via cultivated mind, one should not forget that mind arises from time. This is where the creativity of time ultimately lies. The words of Zhang Zai are therefore good to remember: "From the Great Void (*taixu*), the name "heaven" (*tian*) comes into existence, from the transformation of *qi*, the name "*dao*" comes into existence; by combining the void and the *qi*, the name "nature" (*xing*) comes into existence. By combining nature and perception, the name "mind" (*xin*) comes into existence."[32]

8

Leibniz's Notion of a Universal Characteristic and Symbolic Realism in the *Yijing*

A Universal Characteristic and Its Purpose

Leibniz argued for improvements of science based on reason, which means that we can reason to truths by way of using a good system of symbols, which he calls characteristic symbols (abbreviated hereafter as CS). An essential requirement for such CS is that they correspond to precise concepts that allow demonstration and demonstrative certainty. According to Leibniz in a paper of 1684, the only existing system of CS is that of numbers.[1] It is in a number-corresponding symbolic system that we can reason precisely and with demonstrative certainty. Perhaps it is because humans first come to discover the rational nature of numbers that we are able to invent a convenient system of symbols for reasoning in numbers, which must correspond to our concepts of numbers. By the time of Descartes, it was found that we should algebraize geometry in order to represent and demonstrate truths in geometry. Algebra is a system of CS that corresponds to numbers or has numbers as its basic model. It is not difficult to see that, even over 400 years after Descartes, we still have to rely on a numerical system and number theory as the foundations of all mathematics and that our scientific knowledge still aims at exactitude, certainty, and demonstrative clarity. This means that Leibniz's quest for a universal system of CS to advance knowledge has basically remained a quest to this day.

Why is this the case? Have we learned something from this? My answer to the latter question is that we have learned that we have simply two different kinds of truth, numerical and non-numerical, neither of which can be an adequate substitute for the other. This fact would then provide an answer to the former question: namely, we cannot hope to find a numerical system of CS for non-numerical truths without knowing what the numbers stand for. Of course, there is still the question on whether Leibniz actually intended to find a numerical system of CS for non-numerical truths or whether he intended to find a universal system of CS, either numerical or non-numerical, which would cater to both numerical and non-numerical truths (similar to a numerical system of CS with regard to numerical truths).[2]

Based on Leibniz's work, it can be shown that he is ambivalent on this question: his study of mathematical analysis led him to believe in something like a universal calculus or general analysis of human ideas that is to be founded on two principles: the principle of contradiction and the principle of sufficient reason. Both principles apply to both necessary and contingent truths, a distinction he makes in analogy to commensurable and incommensurable numbers. It is to be granted that we could analyze contingent truths on the basis of these two principles, but this does not amount to a full calculus of ideas, for we can neither establish contingent truths with certainty nor in a finite number of steps. Leibniz acknowledges this and speaks of an infinite analysis to be performed by God. It is in this latter sense that we can say he denied the possibility of a universal system of CS with finite symbols. Instead, he can only speak of a calculus of "estimation of degrees of probability," the "weight of proofs," suppositions, conjectures, and criteria.[3]

In order to formulate such a calculus, one needs a formal language defining terms and relations and a system of operations such as in algebra. Hence, we shall have some sort of universal system of CS that proposes to reach clear and distinct reasoning and to avoid obscure and confused thinking. It is also intended to achieve adequacy of proofs or inferences and to uncover inadequacies whenever they occur, to render what is intuitively symbolic and what is symbolically intuitive for the purpose of clarity and distinctiveness. But there are still limitations: we can neither formalize all truths nor symbolize them in any finite formula of our calculus.[4]

In light of this intellectual background, what would the symbolism, structure, and system of the *Yijing* symbols signify to Leibniz? Can it be considered a universal system of CS containing the truths of both numbers and non-numerical entities? Can it be an algebra for both necessary and contingent truths?[5] In this chapter I shall develop some answers to these questions and come to the conclusion that we should recognize two kinds of systems of CS: one is used for inferential and analytical purposes, the other for interpretative and decision-making purposes. The former would provide a system of pre-established principles or axioms of consistency, whereas the latter would suggest or invite us to recognize a system of post-established norms or actions of harmonization. We can thus move from a universe defined by a closely set rationality to a universe opened up by a dialectical rationality, which is adaptive to an ever-developing universe. We can even come to a better appreciation of a cosmology and ontology, like the one proposed in the Neo-Confucian Zhou Dunyi's *Taiji Tushuo*, after we have seen both the strength and limitations of Leibniz's metaphysics of God and contingent truths in the *Monodology*.[6]

Truth and Existence

Leibniz takes an individual substance, which he called "monad" in his 1714 treatise *Monadology*, to have contained relations with all other individuals, and thus it takes an infinite analysis to see or demonstrate the truth of any contingent proposition about matters involving individual substances. Individuals are designated by individual concepts or particular terms, whereas properties and relations are connoted by general concepts or terms. It seems clear that the distinction between necessary and contingent truths is not just one between truths concerning relations on the one hand and truths concerning individuals on the other. For among general concepts there are necessary relations versus contingent or synthetic ones. The concept of four contains the concept of larger than three, but the concept of saltiness does not necessarily contain the concept of solubility. From this point of view, which conceptual relationships are necessary and which are not requires analysis and construction. Mathematics and logic are fields in which efforts are devoted to discovering the necessary relations of general concepts once certain general concepts are established. But Leibniz wants to extend this analytical approach to certain general concepts, not only to all general concepts but also to individual concepts, which can be regarded as composed of a non-finite number of general concepts, so that we could come to apply analysis to both contingency and necessity. This is an interesting though confused approach, for questions can be raised as to whether we could equate contingency with necessity from God's point of view or equate contingency with infinite relations or general concepts. For Leibniz, God is an entity or mind for whom all predicates of an individual should be contained in the concept of the subject individual. Thus, to know the individual is to know all its properties and relations according to the principle of sufficient reason; hence, it is to know what would necessarily happen and why certain things happen to one individual rather than to another.

Contrary to Russell, who opposes Leibniz in his earlier critical account of Leibniz's philosophy, I personally found this analytical approach equally appealing and challenging. Rather than holding that the principle of sufficient reason would lead to the assertion of final causes according to which God has to create things according to his best will, it could lead to the view that an analytical account of any contingent truth could be given once we construct a theoretical explanation of it. The point of giving sufficient reason is to construct a theory in which an individual concept is to be explained by deduction according to presupposed or known laws of nature. This is the way in which scientific knowledge is theorized and scientific theories are logically formalized.

According to Couturat in his *Logique de Leibniz*, the principle of sufficient reason is the principle that all truths are analytical, which is the converse of the principle of contradiction, in that all analytical propositions are true.[7] As the converse of the principle of contradiction, we have to define truth in such a way that unless it is analytical, it cannot be truth. But to be analytical can be an open concept, it may simply mean being made analytical according to the principle of contradiction, and hence it is not to be conceived as false. But for Leibniz, as existence of a thing involves all things in the world and the world is infinite, the contingent truth of any thing would require an infinite analysis in terms of the infinite relations it has with other things in the world. Hence, no analyticity can be granted without such a grasp of the infinite analysis, which only God is capable of performing. This is, of course, a kind of analytical truth different from anything that has been suggested before, because the emphasis is put on the contingency or contingent existence of the thing, whereas what is usually suggested is analyticity of the essential or conceptual content of contingent propositions that are general in scope and nevertheless could apply to individual things. According to Leibniz such statements and laws of nature are contingent and not necessary to our minds because we could conceive their being false, and an alternative possibility could hold.

We have to separate the question of the principle of sufficient reason for constructing truth into analytical truth in a theory, from the question of taking existence as a predicate. It can be argued that in Leibniz's mind, existence is a predicate or similar to a predicate, which is required for making a possible world the best of all. According to E. M. Curley, Leibniz may have made contradictory statements about his position.[8] There are three significant passages quoted by Curley, namely:

> If existence were something other than an exigency of essence, it would follow that it has a certain essence or adds something new to things, concerning which it could be asked in turn whether this essence exists, and why it rather than another (GP,VII, 195n). Just as existence is conceived by us as if it were a thing having nothing in common with essence, which nevertheless cannot be the case, because there must be more in the concept of the existent than in that of the non-existent, i.e. existence is a perfection, since there is really nothing else explicable in existence than that it enters into the most perfect series of things; so in the same way we conceive position as something extrinsic, which adds nothing to the thing placed, though it does nevertheless add the way in which the thing is affected by other things (C, 9).

In the last quotation, by comparing existence to position and therefore implying that existence adds nothing to the thing that exists, just like position adds nothing to the thing that is placed, Leibniz is not saying that existence is not a predicate. On the contrary, the way a thing *is* affects how it relates to other things, and therefore it can be a perfection that makes a difference. For him, existence is a relational predicate or perfection, namely to cause the thing to exist as part of the series of things that exist. The existence of a thing makes it possible to say that things exist in a pre-established harmony: namely, that things come to exist rather than not, that there must be a sufficient reason for this, and that the world as the totality of all things must contain all the reason there is for the existence of things. One may even suggest that the principle of sufficient reason necessitates existence as a condition of the best. On the other hand, the idea of best implies a sense of good-will or a choice from a good-will, and hence the predicate of existence is precisely a matter of creating things according to God's best will. In this latter sense, Leibniz could be said to also originate the proposition that existence is not a predicate, because without God's good-will, there could be no best possible world.[9]

However, one may take issues with Leibniz in the following way:

1. We may point out that precisely because existence adds nothing to the thing itself, but makes a difference between its existence and non-existence, it is essential that it is not caused by our notion of the thing, which necessarily implies its existence, for we cannot identify a quality of existence except through our experience rather than through thinking. (This is the Kantian anti-ontological argument.)

2. Whether a thing exists by its own essence or its compossibility with essences of other things, it takes a creative effort by itself or an external cause with other things to make it exist, which is not to be determined by whatever notion we have of the thing. The notion of a thing serves to identify or designate a thing, but whether it succeeds or not in doing so depends on whether there is the objective existence of the thing. Leibniz fails to make a distinction between a notion of a thing prior to experience, or knowledge in the real world, and a notion of a thing when we have gathered all knowledge of it in the real world. As we are not God, we may not have a complete perfect notion of a thing in the world. Even though we may presume that the thing in the world involves relations with all things in the world, without experience we would not know which relations there are. Leibniz may be said to have spoken from the point of a perfect, omniscient God and hence from that point where all things can be seen to have completed their run of fate and have everything determined one way or another, and this would include existence as a peculiar perfection of their being what they are. But still one can ask whether such a world would be an idea of God if God does not cause it to exist. In other words, one still has to distinguish between conceiving or knowing a world conceptually, in which case the world need not exist, and knowing the world in existence apart from conception.

3. The existing world need not be conceived as compatible, compossible, or optimally so. Again one has to look into the world to see that it is full of radical differences, conflicts, and self-contradictions. One does not see a ready-made, pre-established harmony as maintained and required by Leibniz: differences and conflicts have to be resolved and harmony to be established in a contingent way and then perhaps conceptually presented or preserved. One has to see conceptualization and confronting reality as two separate efforts of humanity just as rationalization and creativity or creation are two separate efforts of divinity. The human or divine efforts in a process of reconciling or integrating the two is what makes humanity and divinity an everlasting creative agency.

When Leibniz overall argues for a position of all truths being analytical based on his principle of sufficient reason, he argues from the point of view of a justification of existence, not from the point of view of a discovery of existence. But we cannot justify things without first discovering them, which means without finding them existing first.

The *Yijing*: From Observation to Interpretation

Let us turn to the position of the *Yijing*. To begin, the *Yijing*'s position is totally different from Leibniz's position that all truths are analytical. For the *Yijing*, perhaps the opposite is true: all truths are results of comprehensive observation (*guan*) or consist of basic observed patterns. Hence all truths are observationally defined and observationally established, including even the necessary truths. We shall discuss this view of the *Yijing* in terms of considerations on four important aspects: observation, symbolization, divination, and interpretation.

OBSERVATION

As stated in the Commentaries to the *Yijing*,[10] we come to see the world as existent, and we have to understand how and why the world exists as it is observed, covering things above and below, near and far, within and without, and over a long period of time. It is in fact this comprehensive observation (*guan*) that makes our understanding of the how and why of things possible.[11] This is because comprehensive observation will generate sufficient experiences so that we can organize in patterns and use it to reflect on the converging source or sources of changes and transformations. We wish to preserve what we have observed in an effort to achieve maximum consistency of the observations as described in our common language. We may call this the "Principle of Sufficient Experience" in contrast to Leibniz's "Principle of Sufficient Reason." It is on the basis of comprehensive observation that we could even generalize on existing things as having sufficient reasons for their existence. In fact, what we have observed, including the consistency, compatibility, and congruence among all things, should provide sufficient reasons for their being what they are, provided they are observed to exist in the first place. But we cannot justify their existence prior to or independent of any observational ground. Hence, the reason for the existence of things is not simply found in how we conceive them, or how they represent the best possible world of compossible ideas. Instead, the reason for their existence is to be seen in how they originate from a source of formation and transformation (*shenghua*) and how they correlate with other things, which exist as reflection on our comprehensive observation. There are several passages in the *Yizhuan* that are extremely important in making a point as to how things are thought to be created from an ultimate source based on reflection on what is comprehensively observed:

1. There is *qian–yuan* (the Creative Source), which creates or produces things, and *kun-yuan* (the Receptive Source), which nourishes and cherishes things. Both *qian–yuan* and *kun–yuan* are notions we come to have when we see things in the world at large and when we see how things proceed and evolve as if from a dynamical unity of ceaseless creative and nourishing sources of beings. These notions are indeed conceptual constructions, and yet they are more than conceptual constructions because they are also ideas from our deepest experience and reflection.[12] It is on this basis that the *Tuanzhuan* says:

    > Great indeed is the *qian-yuan*. It is by which things form. Hence it commands heaven (the creative principle). By the moving of clouds and showering

of rain, different kinds of things flow in forms. Beginnings and endings are greatly illuminated and the six positions (of development) are accomplished in time. It rides on these six dragons of power in command of the heaven. The way of the *qian* transforms and makes all things follow their natures and destinies. The great harmony will thereby be achieved and protected. This is beneficial to divining.

The point of this is that based on one's observation and experience of things, one achieves a profound vision of an underlying harmony of all things, each of which could well be cherished.

2. Once we reach the *li* (pattern/principle) as the pattern and principle underlying all things, we can then organize our worldview in which all things will be positioned (*wei*). *Wei* (positioning) is important, and it does not come by itself but in a system in which all things are related to the creative activity of the *qian-kun*.

3. How do we come to have a general knowledge of all things? We come to know this again by way of organizing what we know through a comprehensive observation of things. We also come to know this through a deep understanding of how heaven and earth produce all things. Hence it is said in the *Yizhuan*:

> Being similar to heaven and earth, there is no violation of the existing order (*gubuwei*) in our thinking. Our knowledge will comprehend all ten thousand things, and our abilities and virtues will produce help for all people under heaven, and there is no deviation.[13]

On this basis of imitating heaven and earth, we are also able to exercise our love and perform our duties. The *Xici* also uses these phrases: "Trace the transformations of heaven and earth and do not transgress them; accomplish all things in diverse ways without missing any thing.

Penetrate the way of day and night and know the causes."[14] The above can also be said of the *dao*: the *dao* must not know how and why things came into existence, yet it produces things according to its power of intrinsic creativity, and in this sense the Daoists are even able to argue that things exist and transform by themselves and that the Dao is just the way all things exist and transform spontaneously and by themselves.[15]

In a similar spirit, we see the *Xici* maintains or concludes that "The spirit (*shen*) has no directions, and the change (*yi*) has no substance."[16] To say this is to say that there is no reason to predict or predetermine how things are. Creativity is beyond rationality, and this is not to say that creativity cannot be rationally or post-rationally justified. In this sense there is no need even to raise the question of whether the creative agency is aware of what is happening or whether it knows all happenings under the form of eternity or in accordance with a rational plan. Creativity is a performative act prior to or independent of cognition and reflection, and it is not necessarily confined or controlled by cognition and reflection.

Our conception of God need not be one of an epistemological subject; as a creative agent, God creates what is good and desirable according to the nature of God, and this does not necessarily imply that God has to justify his creative action or lay down his plans for creation in order to make his creation right. It is in this sense that the *dao* has performed the role of God without the necessity of being attributed foreknowledge or omniscience. In fact, the creative function of the *dao* forestalls the attribution of predictability and substantiality. Hence Mencius says: "Being sagely and yet capable of not being known is the spirit."[17]

With this understanding of the ultimate source of creativity, based on comprehensive observation and our reflection on it, the ideal goal a human being would aspire to attain is to identify with the reality of things in their totality within the framework of the creative activities of heaven and earth or simply the *dao*. Hence it is said in the *Wenyan Commentary* on the *qian* hexagram:

> The great man is one who identifies with heaven and earth
> in their powers and virtues, is one with sun and moon in
> their illumination, is one with four seasons in their orders,
> and is one with ghosts and spirits in their powers to cause

fortune or disasters. Thinking of what is prior to heaven and heaven will not deviate, and after the world is created things will observe orderly times. Even heaven will not deviate, how could man deviate? How could ghosts and spirits deviate?

In the hexagram *guan*, it is said in the *Tuanzhuan:* "Observing things from above, it is smooth and penetrating. One would also achieve centrality and correctness to observe the world. One preserves faith without making recommendation in an oblation. [Thus], one transforms by observing things below." It is thus through *guan* that one comes to act correctly and creatively.

SYMBOLIZATION

With this philosophy of *guan* in mind, we come to the question of symbolization. We shall see that the symbolism of the *Yijing* is conceptual yet highly realistic, idealistic yet highly empirically open, analytic yet highly organic, logical yet highly dialectical. It is not something invented in order to make calculations via a perfect design of things apart from things. On the contrary, the *yi*-symbolism is a creation of the sages who understand things via their comprehensive observation and who attempt to formulate the principles of change in the presence of things and changes. It requires a participatory and confrontational understanding of the things at hand so that we can see that things are to be viewed and understood in symbols and relations of symbols, and at the same time, how symbols and relations of symbols could be applied to things. This is derived from our capacity for interpretation, mediation, and finding meanings in the incessant exchange between the mind and the world (hence the importance of divination as well). From such a philosophy one therefore sees how symbolism works and how it constitutes a world of its own. Yet the symbolism is not designed to calculate, because it does not contain all the information and meanings in the symbols, but rather represents and interprets changes. The symbols are themselves indexes or icons for stages of development and transformation; therefore, their meanings have to be determined in a given process of transformation that we can observe.

We can see how Shao Yong has constructed such a process according to the statements of *Xici shang* 11 (see figure 8.1).

242 | The Philosophy of Change

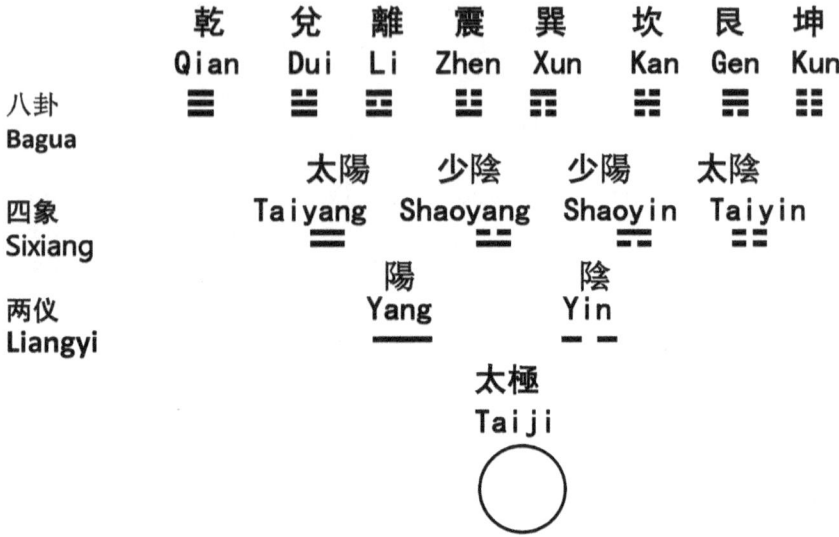

Figure 8.1. Fu Xi Trigrams Ordering-Diagram.

We should first note that in observing phenomenal changes and the transformations of things in the world, we come to be aware of an open process of changes and a field of indetermination; thus, we could differentiate a state of rest from movement, a moment of softness from firmness, and even a shadowy presence of powers and dispositions from clearly visible determinations of ostensible qualities. In a sense, we come to see the indeterminate in light of the determinate, the invisible in light of the visible. This observation can be said to be one of observing the background of things among all things and an insight into the source of the changes of things. Hence, we come to see the world as a manifestation or presentation of an ultimate source of creativity (namely, the *taiji*). But as we move to the two-norm level (*liangyi*), there would appear to be in our observation a marked distinction between the *yin* and the *yang* as the dark and the bright, the rest and the motion, the softness and the firmness. These three basic distinctions suggest a basic distinction of states of being or two forces in a field and process of constant changes and transformations that has largely been observed as the background of everything. We also come to see how *yin* and *yang* function as opposite sides of the same reality as well as how they interact and exchange, how they conflict and harmonize, how they separate and merge, how they oppose and complement, and how they give and take. This is how the two give rise to all further differentiations of things as manifested on higher and higher levels. Hence, we can see the level of *sixiang* (four figures) where there are 2x2 distinctions, the level of *bagua* (eight trigrams) where there are 2x2x2 distinctions, and the level of *zhonggua* where there are 2 to the 6th power or 64 distinctions.

Although the symbolization system of the *Yijing* stops at the level of the sixty-four *zhonggua*, there is no limit to the process of further differentiation, which can extend to a world of distinctions of 2 up to any nth power. Hence, the world as presented in the *Yijing* system is potentially infinite. This system shows how all individual things on any level are related to all other things on the same level or to anything on various other levels, including the ultimate source of the creative differentiating power. It can be seen that there are two kinds of relationships: the vertical and the horizontal. The vertical relationships trace the ancestral history of any differentiated position on a level, whereas the horizontal relationships derive from the relative positioning among positions of things on the same level. It is clear that any thing has a unique position in this framework of inter-level and intra-level relationships. It is also clear that the relationships can be logically understood so as to be capable of being classified into various kinds of oppositions and suppositions. We can also show that for any given position, a series of definable transformations exists that would transform one position into any other position. Hence, for any position we could be logically explicit about which relationships it involves, which taken together would determine the given position.[18]

Given this framework, one can see that the symbolization of the *yin-yang* positions by the broken line—and the unbroken line—captures the basic modes and qualities of being, namely *yin-yang*, *dong-jing*, *gang-rou*, and what is experienced along this line.[19] The combinations of these two basic symbols on each level would therefore give rise to determinate forms on that level, determinate in both quantity and structure. Thus, on the *bagua* level, we have the eight three-line *trigrams*, and on the *zhonggua* level we have the sixty-four six-line hexagrams. Each diagram represents a structure of internal ordering according to its history of origin from the bottom level, and at the same time each represents a well-defined position due to its structure in a horizontal series of related structures. This series could be considered both as a process of the development from one structure to another or as a field in which all structures co-arise as a result of the creative differentiation of the earlier level and the creative impulsion of the *taiji*.

Thus, given any hexagram in the form of six lines, we can visually detect its internal structure and determine its relative positioning in the circle and the field of all its structures of being. Specifically, we can consider any hexagram as a result of the interaction and fusion between the *qian* hexagram and the *kun* hexagram:

$$
\begin{array}{cc}
\text{———} & \text{— —} \\
\text{———} & \text{— —} \\
\text{———} & \text{— —}
\end{array}
$$

Given the cosmology of creative origination and transformation as present in the *Yijing*, all things in the world would arise as result of the creative differentiation of the *taiji*. There is no doubt that the *yin-yang* symbolism in the *Yijing* is capable of reflecting this cosmology of creative origination and transformation. One can see that it is not artificially designed to stand for the cosmological changes but rather naturally comes to represent the changes in nature and the human world by way of observation. As our observation of things primarily stems from our visual experiences, the symbols simply reflect how we visually perceive the states of being and the modes of changes and transformations. The resulting forms on whichever level in this sense also form our image of an event, a situation, or a thing in light of our observations of the simpler forms. There is no denial that there exists already an element of interpretation in identifying a complex symbol, such as any *bagua* (trigram), with a natural event or phenomenon, or a complex symbol, such as any *zhonggua* (hexagram), with a human situation or happening. Consider the trigram ☵. How do we identify it with water? How do we come to see it as a symbol for depth or abyss and thus as a symbol for danger? It is no doubt a result of the interpretation of our observation in light of our common experience. Similarly, considering the hexagram *guan*, how do we come to see the combination of wind over earth with pervasive viewing or comprehensive observation? Again, it is our interpretation of the relationship of wind over land in analogy to our understanding and experience of viewing a totality of things from a higher vantage point of view. Hence, we might say that the whole systems of *bagua* and *zhonggua* constitute not only a progressive differentiation of forms and structures, or a progressive integration of processes and transformations or developments, but also systems advancing meanings and interpretations corresponding to these forms and processes. More can be said about the principles of interpretation later.

Our question now is to see how the things in the world would fit into this pattern, how they are positioned, and their meanings and significance determined relative to our understanding of the world. But we must remember that it is not just this pattern of symbolization that organizes our perceptions of the world as a whole as well as of the relations between the things in the world, but that the way in which we understand concrete things and situations as well as the objectives we have in acting in a situation would also have to be specified in order to assess the meaning and significance of a thing or situation. What is required for such an assessment is both the cosmology of creative change and the method or mode of thinking according to which we come to know things and describe our knowledge. We need to point out that the cosmology of changes gives us not only a representation of the macroscopic framework in which the things in the world are originated and situated, but also a way of thinking and understanding the things that we encounter in our actual life. Hence, one could describe a concrete situation in terms of the *yin-yang* symbols or even identify a situation as one of our *gua* symbols. We may see that this identification may be relatively simple insofar as natural events are concerned, but is becoming increasingly difficult when we move on to human situations or human events. As far as the *Yijing* is concerned, such human meanings are developed as a result of our deeper experience and reflection on a human situation, and its structure is analogous or homographical to a natural situation or event. Traditionally, this has been called the extension of an image (*yanxiang*) whereby its meaning would also be extended. Obviously, such an extension of images and meanings must always involve insight, interpretation, and relevant measures of empirical and logical justifications.

I wish to make three points regarding this issue of symbolization. First, it is obvious that although *yin-yang* could be represented by the numerals 0 and 1, as could be done in the binary system of Leibniz, the sensible effects of the broken line and the unbroken line must be different from those of 0 and 1. The difference is that between a numerical and a non-numerical system in the universal language. In the above, I have discussed the point that Leibniz earlier in his career decided that there could not be any real UC apart from the numerical system. But it must also be pointed out that later in his career, Leibniz's enthusiasm for UC as a non-numerical system somehow re-kindled and re-flourished, particularly when he came to encounter the symbolic system of the *Yijing* and the Chinese characters via his correspondence with the Jesuit missionary Bouvet in China. Perhaps, in the *Yijing* system Leibniz has come to see the representational capacity of the *Yijing* as a cosmological system and its calculational component as a numerical system insofar as the symbolism can be translated into the binary system. However, I am not sure to what extent he appreciated the representational capacity of the *Yijing* symbolism and to what extent he realized the power of calculation in transforming the *Yijing* symbolism into the binary number system.[20]

It might be pointed out that although we could represent all situations in binary numbers, such as 111111 for *qian* and 000000 for *kun*, it is clear that we would lose the original representational efficacy of the *yin-yang* symbols. This no doubt would result in losing the intuitive meanings and much of the imaging power arising from the original symbolism. Hence, we might conclude that the representative power is perhaps reversely proportional to the calculative power, and vice versa. This is perhaps because in calculation we must rely on numbers that must be an abstraction of the graphic reality and its symbolization, whereas in representation we have to keep to qualities and relationships as we experience them, and which are not to be calculated as quantities but as qualities. Hence, Feng Youlan speaks of the "cosmic algebra" of the *Yijing*.[21]

In the tradition of the Xiang-Shu School (School of Form-Numbers), one has to maintain an interpretative system in which *gua* forms and xiang lines and numbers are to be correlated or implicated.[22] As to how the representational and the calculative capacity could be combined in a way as to serve the purpose of scientific inquiry for establishing scientific knowledge is still a challenging issue. It must also be pointed out that Leibniz's quest for a UC has also fostered his interest in the features of the Chinese language and Chinese characters. According to D. E. Mungello, although Leibniz rejected the Chinese language as a model for his universal language in a paper from 1679, he developed a new interest in the philosophical relevance of Chinese characters to his UC about twenty years later.[23]

Second, an important feature of the symbolic system of the *Yijing* is that for any *n*, the number 2 to the *n*th power must be a finite number, and this means that the number of the positions for things or things themselves must be a finite one. In this light, we could conceive the number of things in the world and also the number of human situations to be finite. Again, in light of the cosmic representation of the *Yijing*, the relationships of a thing with other things must also be conceived to be finite, although the finite number could be extremely large. Given this understanding, we can see that our analysis of an individual concept of a thing as represented by the *Yijing* symbols must be finite instead of infinite. In this sense it is within human capacity to grasp the truth of a contingent proposition, namely, a proposition that refers to a concrete existing situation or thing insofar as we could represent the situation or thing correctly in the *yin-yang* symbolism. This also means that we do not need an infinite mind like God in order to grasp the truth of contingent pro-positions. But on the other hand, it must also be pointed out that it is not easy to represent a thing or situation in the correct form because we do not know its *yin-yang* history or its relations to other things on the same level or on other levels.

A more serious problem is the way in which the symbolism of the *Yijing* is formulated. It is both intended for capturing the most universal aspects of things and identifying their most individual features. If a person is not able to identify individual things in their *yin-yang* structure, the system itself would not identify the individual thing for a person, for *gua* are not proper names but common names or general terms for positions or situations that things occupy. Because of this fact, one could attribute an indefinite number of characteristics to a thing, which would in turn lead to an indefinite analysis so that it cannot be said to be fixed in a definite number of steps. Nevertheless, one could still take the *Yijing* symbolism seriously, for one could impose one's own definite and finite analysis on a situation relative to one's purpose and in this way achieve a finite analytical-hypothetical understanding of a contingent proposition. One would then act on one's analytical-hypothetical understanding in order to achieve one's goal or avoid an undesirable consequence. In order even to do this, one first has to identify the situation. One has to face the world as a changing reality and take contingency very seriously, but at the same time one has to grasp reality for the purpose of conducting a good life or achieving a desirable goal. For these reasons, we can see how understanding *Yijing* symbols in the living context of life evolved into the practice of divination from a very early period onward.[24]

Third, a human situation is not simply a projection of the great ultimate as such but the projection of the human person as the great ultimate. The cosmology of changes in the *Yijing* is such that on each level of creative differentiation, any individual entity or situation has its own creative force that, together with the great ultimate as the ultimate source of creativity and with any other creative participation of presupposed levels of reality, is able to produce the human situation as we are confronted with it. In this sense, the analytical understanding of a contingency is within the capacity of the individual person himself, instead of being possible only on the part of God. This shows the fundamental difference between Leibniz's notion of God as the monad of monads that is the sole supporting base of all contingent things and the *Yijing* philosophy of the *taiji* or the *dao* in which each individual is an independent sovereign capable of cultivating himself into a state of identifying with heaven and the *dao* and thus acting in correlation or co-participation with heaven and earth in their creative activities.[25]

DIVINATION

Divination develops not just from people worrying what the future holds for them or searching for what they should do under some given circumstances, but because people in general neither know how to identify a given situation nor how to read significance from the situation in which they are currently involved. Although our commonsense and background experiences provide some helpful clues as to how the future will be for us, we do not know how events will turn in complicated situations that involve many variables, such as time, location, human conditions, human feelings, human decisions, and their combined effects. Hence, very often we need a more definitive way of evaluating a situation than that which is provided by common sense and our background experience, particularly with regard to critical situations that require immediate addressing or those that could turn from bad to worse and from worse to worst. It is obvious that divination based on the symbolization of the *Yijing* provides us not only with a way of identifying a situation but also with a way of reading the significance from the situation by reading it from the symbolism. Hence, the need for divination is essentially the need for knowledge, that is, knowing an effective way of understanding the significance of the situation and our way of acting on the situation. But to read significance from the symbol of a given situation still requires one's knowing its particularities so that the expected meaning would emerge from the interaction between the symbolism or sign of the situation as well as knowledge of the particulars of the situation that pertains to the objective or purpose to be pursued. In this sense, divination should be seen as a multi-dimensional strategy that involves situation identification, prediction, application to a given circumstance, evaluation, and judgment. Altogether, divination is to choose a sign for a situation and subject it to an interpretation under a system of readings, which in the case of the *Yijing* is derived from comprehensive observation (*guan*).

It is well known that divination based on the *Yijing* has been practiced in China since the earliest known history. In fact, the oracle bone inscriptions have been dated to around 1600 BC. It is on the basis of the matching of divinatory predictions against the actual events that turned up later that confirmed judgments were collected and appended to the symbols of the *yi* or the *zhonggua* system known as the *Yijing*. These judgments called *guaci* give explicit evaluative meanings to the symbolism in regard to human action and its consequences. They function as both descriptive and prescriptive meanings for a situation as identified by the symbolism. They are not just the cosmological meanings of the symbolism based on the comprehensive observation of natural events. But it is this process of divination that prompts the need for interpretation of a given situation with regard to human values, and consequently a new level of meanings arises that would then form the basis for the meaningful interpretation of the symbols. Not only does the *guaci* represent a new level of meaning, but later levels also arise through a more systematic interpretation of the symbolism with regard to human action and human prospects in the forms of commentaries, such as, notably, the *Tuanzhuan* and the *Xiangzhuan*.

In both commentaries, as we shall see, the naturalistic meanings of the combined trigrams are transformed into the humanistic and even moralistic meanings of the hexagrams. One can see from these transformations the fusion of objective reference and subjective feelings or intentions, which together form the basis for the evaluation and prescription of human actions with regard to human goals or human values, independently developed as one's holistic experience of the self in the world.

Divination loses its appeal and becomes obsolete when we are able to make out a situation and read its significance on the basis of our background knowledge or personal experience. If we were able to identify our present location on a map and see how the road we look for is leading to a certain destination, we would not resort to dice throw or random guess for deciding where we are located on the map. With scientific inquiry and accumulated knowledge, one will not rely on divination for decision-making. One can see that for a sagely person like Confucius, divination is not necessary, and the *Yijing* becomes a book of wisdom, showing where one's mandate of heaven (*tianming*) lies. Xunzi, the latter-day Confucian rationalist, simply maintained that the superior man (*junzi*) does not practice divination.

But we must also remember that by saying this we do not deny that divination has its own criteria of validity; as a practice under the veil of ignorance and exercising one's power of decision-making, divination is a means of randomly identifying a situation whose meaning is derived in three ways: the cosmology of change, the identified position, one's personal knowledge of the circumstances and purpose, and thus the consequent individual interpretative act for synthesizing all factors into a unified whole. When identification by knowledge is substituted for divinatory identification of a situation, the other factors still remain, that is, there is still the cosmology of changes, the personal knowledge of particulars. To read significance from a known situation is to read the meaning of the situation in light of one's personal experience and the cosmology of changes. This is nothing other than an act of interpretation, which requires creative insight and theoretical grounding. In the end, what will remain is interpretation in the absence of divination. The importance of understanding and interpretation increases as the importance of divination diminishes.

Leibniz's God would see the meaning of an event in his intuition of the event, and this intuition would amount to being an infinite analysis of the reasons for the existence or occurrence of such an event. As we have pointed out, there is no need to assume an infinite analysis of the occurrence of the event insofar as the event is an actuality, not a possibility, relative to the framework of the cosmology of changes. Yet, as God is also the final cause of things in the world, the human mind could be regarded as a finite embodiment of the divine mind and can thus be creatively enlarged insofar as God has the good-will to work through man. Hence, God can enable man to come to grips with things in the world of transformation. This would indeed be the view of the *Yijing* regarding the ontological relationship between heaven and man.

What comes out as most important is that instead of analysis, for the *Yijing*, observation and experience of reality together with a creative and attentive mind would be sufficient for an understanding of the truth of the contingency of the changes and transformations in the world.

Interpretation

What then is interpretation as a method or a way of ascertaining the truth of being as revealed in the contingencies of the world? First of all, it is obvious that interpretation is something to be accepted as an understanding of a given situation; it must be regarded as a conceptual construction that applies to a given situation by subsuming it to some general truth and bringing out its significance in light of the general truth. In the use intended here, understanding is the subjective intuition or awareness of the truth of a matter to be interpreted, whereas interpretation should be the objective presentation of an understanding, which inevitably involves conceptual thinking and conceptual theorizing in the form of language.

No doubt, interpretation is a far more analytical concept than understanding, for we could speak of the interpretation of something for a person relative to a specific goal. Interpretation as a theory, which applies to an instance in reality, can thus be analyzed as regarding its theoretical component, that is, that which interprets, and its factual component, that is, that which is to be interpreted as well as the interpretative act that enables the interpretation to take place. What is therefore essential to interpretation is the interpretative act that signifies the intuition of a whole meaning or a new meaning to be embodied in or to emerge from a given reality. This interpretative act can be regarded as a creative act arising from the human mind's ability to grasp the reality of the world. It has also an ontological dimension: the interpretative act is a form of the creative impulse of the great ultimate or the *dao* in which differentiation into the *yin-yang* and their integration are simultaneously realized. The resultant emergence of meaning is the presentation of the individuality of a new state of being or a new situation. Thus, one can neither speak of interpretation without presupposing an ontology nor speak of an ontology without recognizing interpretation as an ontological act.

The interpretative act, as an ontological and creative act, is nowhere more obvious than in the formation of the *Guaci, Tuanzhuan,* and the

Xiangzhuan. As has been indicated, these commentaries are individualized over different *gua*. In the case of *Xiangzhuan*, even individual lines are subject to interpretation.

What then are the basic principles of interpretation for the *Yijing* symbolism?

First of all, for any situation there is the need for human evaluation in regard to the consequences of action. Will the situation conduce to action toward the well-being or ill-being of the person? Which action is more beneficial? Which action is harmful? As action itself is considered as capable of altering the state of being and contributing to change and transformation and thus is considered as causative and creative,[26] one can see that some combination of circumstances would lead to beneficial results if further combined with certain actions while some other combination of circumstances would lead to harmful results if combined with certain other actions. One can explain this in terms of the compatibility or incompatibility of circumstances and actions, as actions are themselves contributing to circumstances, and circumstances are themselves potential agents for changes according to the cosmology of changes. If we conceive this in the Leibnizian language, we can see that the "best possible world" simply means the most compatible and compossible set of essences that is created or caused to exist for us by God.

Hence, an interpretative act means to see what combinations of ideas and circumstances are compatible or compossible and which are not. Of central importance for the *Yijing*, however, is the combination of real and potential circumstances that would come into being. It is not simply the combination of ideas as essences alone. What is also central is that a human person has the power to act out his ideas and wishes; thus, the person can have his own sense of agency and efficacy and a consequent sense of responsibility. For interpretation, this means that it could be based on an urgency for action and an awareness of our goals and values of action. Whatever leads to more life-preserving and life-fulfilling activity would be good, and what defeats that purpose is bad. A strong sense of life's activities and the fulfillment of life's potentialities underlie the interpretative act for understanding the meaning and significance of a given situation. This also explains how the *Guaci* arise in the process of divination. In sum, this is the principle of human action for interpretation in the *Yijing*.

The second principle of interpretation in the *Yijing* is that of the humanization of natural symbols based on the experience of life circumstances. This is precisely how the *Tuanzhuan* and *Xiangzhuan* arise. Consider the hexagram *song* (conflict), which is composed of the trigram *qian* (heaven) in the above and the trigram *kan* (water) in the below. As the *qian* sign has acquired the primary meaning of being strong or powerful from its standing for heaven, and the *kan* sign has acquired the primary meaning of being risky or danger inducing from its standing for deep water, the combination of the two with water below and heaven above suggests to us that the risky takes a strong position, and this further suggests the tendency to litigation and fights in human affairs. It is obvious that these insinuating suggestions would not take place if we had no experience of the risky taking a strong position or being situated in a strong position that leads to litigation and fight, and the further experience that heaven is strong and deep water is dangerous. To put it simply, if we had none of these experiences, we would not be able to read the *song* in this manner.

In fact, it might be suggested that all the names of the hexagrams are results of considerations of relevant background experiences of human persons, for all the names of the hexagrams are to be explained in light of the ordered combinations of the circumstances of two ordered trigrams. Take again the examples of the hexagrams *qian* and *kun*: the *qian* hexagram presents the combination of six solid lines, which suggests extreme strength; hence the name *qian* as power and firmness is used to name the combination. Similarly, the *kun* hexagram presents the combination of six broken lines, which suggests extreme softness and meekness; hence the name *kun* as passivity and conformity is used to name the combination.

In a sense, the whole commentary called *Tuanzhuan* is developed in an effort to give an interpretation of the meanings of the names of the hexagrams as well as to explore into those meanings could lead to a further understanding of the designated or identified position or situation in terms of effects on the human person and how the individuals would pose themselves in meeting such a situation. In doing so, it is obvious that it is not only the combination of the trigrams that is considered, but also the line-ordering and position relationship within the structure of the hexagram. Again, we could continue our example of the *song* hexagram. After explaining the rise of the meaning of litigation (*song*), the *Tuanzhuan* continues to say: "There is good faith in *song*; lacking caution but reaching middle is good fortune. For the firm comes in the central positions. In the end there is ill-fortune and litigation cannot be established."

This interpretation of the situation is guided by the structuring of the *yin-yang* lines and their relative positions in the *gua*, and the rules for understanding the meanings of the lines and their relative positions are determined, as it were, by the basic and extended meanings of the *yin-yang* in the configurations of the *gua* such as: A *yin* in a even position or a *yang* in an odd position is proper and harmonious and hence suggests good, whereas a *yin* in an odd position or *yang* in an even position is conflicting and hence suggests a problem. Again, the line in the middle of the lower trigram or the higher trigram is good because it is in a balancing and well-protected position, but the line in the middle of the higher trigram is better because it is in a higher position in the whole hexagram. It would be the best if there was further the *yang* line. How these are all possible is again to be explained in light of our general human experiences of life in community or society. Without such background experiences, it would not be possible to attach much meaning to such rules of interpretation resulting from using them.

Once an interpretation of the hexagram is achieved, one can see that what needs or what ought to be done should be apparent from the understanding of the situation. Hence, the *Tuanzhuan* of the *song* continues: "It is advantageous to see the great man, it is because it is a matter of holding to centrality and correctness. It is not advantageous to cross over the large rivers, because it would lead one to deep waters." This may be regarded as specific practical advice that is closely related to the understanding of the circumstances so that one would foster one kind of action for better combining with the given circumstances and avoid another kind of action for wrongly combining with the given circumstances. For the *Xiangzhuan*, a general moral advice is given as based on the same or similar observation of the nature and basic meaning of the *gua*.

We can see from this that this is a more extensive reflection than the specific practical advice or counsel generated from reading the *gua*, and thus it represents a deeper advance of the interpretation of the *gua*. Hence, in the case of the *song*, one reads the *Xiangzhuan* for it: "Heaven and water are opposite in processes. Hence, there is the conflict (*song*). A superior man therefore (upon knowing this) should think of doing the right thing in the very beginning." This means that a superior man should do things to avoid such a circumstance of conflict from the beginning. It is only a small step to conclude from this, pointing in the direction of the Confucian ethics, that one should cultivate one's virtues from the very beginning.

The third principle of interpretation for the *Yijing* symbols is the principle of the harmonization of wholes and parts. To achieve full understanding of a given situation, one has to look into the minutest parts and the largest wholes related to it. This would be a natural requirement from the cosmology of changes and transformations in the *Yijing*, as all things and all situations or positions are interrelated in space and time, in history and the world. This is why the superior man is advised to both observe the phenomena (*xiang*) and the change (*bian*). Both objects and changes can be macroscopic and microscopic and demand our close scrutiny and comprehensive review in order to see how they stand for themselves and how they are related to other phenomena and changes.

It is clear that both small and large things as well as small and large changes are relevant for the positioning and the future directions of a given situation; hence, the sagacious person would pay proper attention to both the microscopic and the macroscopic matters related to the situation so that the following can be said of him:

> He would function like heaven and earth, which will not violate the basic principle of incessant creation of life, and his knowledge would cover all ten thousand things and the way to help the world and would not go to the extremes. He can do diverse and indirect things without losing the right path. He enjoys his creativity and knows the limits of his strength and therefore remains unperturbed. He would settle in one place and devote himself to humane concerns, and therefore is able to love.[27]

This suggests that the sagacious person needs to extend and harmonize a knowledge of things so that the sage achieves a holistic vision of things that would enable him to move and act in correct ways, leading to the actualization of harmonization among things.

The *Xici* also explicitly says: "It is in terms of the cosmology of changes that the sage is able to reach for the profound and to study the infinitesimal. Because of reaching for the profound, he is able to understand the inner desires of people, because of studying the infinitesimal, he is able to achieve the great deeds for *the people*."[28] But what underlies all these activities is again to seek harmonization among changes so that the world will remain the most harmonious place in which things would relate to one another to induce harmony, which would in turn produce more harmony or continued harmony in the future. If any world is the best possible world, it is because it is the most harmonious world. This world of creative harmony, however, needs to be brought out by the participation of the human person who is endowed by heaven and earth with the creative power to participate and bring about changes in the world. One does not have to wait for the best combination of ideas to come into being by themselves simply because it is the best combination, and for a God to bring this about simply because God desires it. The key to bringing about the best possible world is to harmonize them and to participate in the changes so that one can creatively harmonize the world. Contingent propositions count on contingent events for their occurrence, and contingent events depend in turn on efforts of participation and harmonization on the part of the individual persons.

In light of the above, interpretation is simply a reflection of such efforts or the efforts to bring about harmonization in action by exploring large and small things as well as large and small changes. Harmonization as the goal of interpretation and action is the result of developing the original nature of the ultimate source of creativity: it is also a realization of the nature of the human person, as he is part and parcel of the whole reality. Hence it is said: "To succeed [the *dao*] is good; to accomplish it is nature."[29] In this sense the world that is harmonized is not a pre-established harmony but instead a harmony that is post-established.

Harmonization as a principle of interpretation is suggestive of the principle of the hermeneutical circle in which the meanings of the parts of a discourse depend on the meanings of the whole discourse and vice versa. But in the broad sense of harmonization, harmonization is to harmonize the parts and wholes of reality as we know them, as well as to bring out their potential power in order to organize and re-order it, as we are the co-creators of reality. Not only language is at issue, but also our ability to do things. Thus, meaning is not just a matter of language, but also a matter of reality as revealed in the dynamical symbolism for reality in the *Yijing*. Hence, the harmonization of which we speak as the principle of interpretation can be described further as the principle of the onto-hermeneutical circle.

Conclusions

In the above we have contrasted Leibniz's vision for a universal language and his views on the truth of contingent propositions with the *Yijing*'s system of a cosmology of creative transformation and its symbolism for the latter. It is apparent that Leibniz has taken a great interest in the symbolism of the *Yijing* and its meanings but has not explored philosophy behind such a symbolism. In our exposition of the philosophy covered by this symbolism, we come to see how the notion of the changing world and its contained contingent events differs vastly from Leibniz's own philosophy of contingencies, which stresses the pre-established harmony and the final causation by an all-knowing God.

The most significant difference lies in that for Leibniz, God seems to be directly involved in the creation of each and every contingent event and thus is responsible for knowing all the details of the truth of any contingent proposition in the world, whereas for the *Yijing* the *taiji* is evolving in differentiating into a world of hierarchical levels that are also involved in the presentation of any individual thing on any level, although the source of creativity is continuous with the ultimate one, namely the *taiji*. Besides, for the *Yijing* the constant creativity of the *dao* is vested in the inherent and ceaseless changes and transformations of things, and therefore the contingency of the world is to be seen as a process of creative change. But for Leibniz the world picture tends to be a stationary one in which every monad reflects everything in the world without considering the implication of their dynamical interactions and mutual influences. Hence God is solely responsible for the contingent truth of the world, whereas for the *Yijing* contingent truth of change is a matter of bringing out things by individual things as well as by different levels of being. The consequence of this view is that contingent truth cannot be said to be fixed on any point of the process of change and remains permanently independent of it, even to the mind of God: it is constantly changing, and for any proposition of contingency it is true with regard to a given level of being as revealed in the reflection of an individual. The cosmology of changes ensures an epistemology of finite analysis of positioning of any event, whereas the monadology of perception demands an epistemology of infinite analysis of the truth of contingencies.

Perhaps, the key difference between Leibniz and the *Yijing* is this: Leibniz focused on the epistemic consciousness of a state of the world as his paradigm of thinking, as this is nearly always the case since Descartes, whereas the *Yijing*'s way of thinking capitalizes on the cosmological paradigm of creative change, differentiation, and integration as a way of understanding things. Consequently, the key notion of the *Yijing* is comprehensive observation (*guan*), which would not only explain the rise of the *Yijing* cosmology but would also explain how the symbolization in the cosmological system would apply: it is a directive and presentational system to be completed by further observation and interpretation. The truth of contingent propositions is nothing but the reality of contingencies. Reality of contingencies is nothing more than what our observation reveals and our interpretation makes out in light of the cosmology of changes (which is again based and derived from comprehensive observation) with regard to preserving the value of comprehensive harmonization. In contrast to this, Leibniz would presuppose and predetermine a truth that is necessary in virtue of an all-knowing God. God comes to know the truth by an infinite analysis, which no human mind is able to achieve. Hence, we would not know the contingent truth but only its probabilities. But the assumption of a pre-determined necessary truth of contingency in God is only an assumption that is based neither in observation nor in anything, except when derived from the ontological argument for God in which existence is treated as a predicate.

The above shows that there are vast differences in the notions of existence and contingency, truth, and source of creativity between Leibniz and the *Yijing*. But to say the above is not to say that there is no common ground between the two systems. In point of fact, one can see that the idea of harmony is shared by both systems; the best possible world is a world of highly compatible and compossible essences or concepts, which is worth being implemented as actuality and is considered by Leibniz to be actually actualized by a benevolent God, whereas the "Principle of Harmonization" in the *Yijing* is the basis for the existence of the world, and it is interpretation as it is considered constitutive of the cosmological process based on comprehensive observation. As the essence of the transformation of the world, harmony is intrinsically present and urged to be extrinsically brought out by the man who is endowed with the creativity to participate and act. Hence, for the *Yijing*, harmony defines the best possible world to the effect that the best possible world is a matter of realizing the goodness of the cosmological process of change.

In terms of symbolization, it is also apparent that there is exchangeability between the *Yijing* symbolism and the binary system that Leibniz invented. The fact that Leibniz continues to search for a UC after his invention suggests that he wanted to develop or find a non-numerical system beyond the numerical one, that is, one that is able to represent the basic truth of the world but that can still lend itself to calculation or mathematical analysis. It is obvious that the symbolization of the *Yijing* would to all appearances fulfill such an expectation. But it is unfortunate that Leibniz has not been able to fully explore the *Yijing* system and its underlying philosophy in order to have something interesting and important to say about the relation between the numerology of the *yi*-symbolism and the onto-cosmological principles and ideas inherent and developed in the system as done by the Xiang-Shu School and the Yi-Li School since the time of Zhu Xi (1130–1200).

To say that there are differences between *Yijing* and Leibniz is not to say that these differences must be exclusive of each other. In fact, we can see that they could be suggestive of a possible integration of the two in a larger vision of reality. In fact, because of these differences, we could come to recognize that there are two kinds of rationality: creative-interpretative rationality and systematic-analytical rationality. Whereas the *Yijing* concentrated on the creative rationality, in which things are created in order and harmony and man participates in the responsibility for maintaining and increasing the order and harmony via his action and interpretation, how to systematically explain the world order according to or relative to rational norms or paradigms would be something left to a rational mind approaching an infinite dimension. We can approach or converge on this rationality by figuring out the reasons why God has for everything without abandoning our efforts to understand things by interpretation and improve them by action. No doubt, for scientific understanding and knowledge, we need to develop a logical and epistemic paradigm, which could then be used for our moral efforts in order to make improvements and advance amelioration. Consequently, we can see that logical analysis and creative interpretation are essential for each other and would compose a unity of a polarity of paradigms for the continuous advancement of human knowledge and well-being. Creativity and knowledge therefore have to work in a circle of interaction, interpenetration, and mutual embodiment in the spirit of comprehensive harmonization.

Appendix

Greek and Chinese Views on Time and the Timeless

Time, being the moving image of eternity, is already on the wrong side. But is time primarily a motion or an image? We are told by David A. Kolb that there is even timeless generation in the world of Platonic forms, which he calls "happening of definiteness." One is tempted to query about what sense we can attach to the notion of generation apart from a temporal analogue. Perhaps generation of forms from simpler unities (the One and the Indefinite Dyad) is simply a logical derivation presented to a timeless and yet perfect intelligence or mind, while this generation in the sense of logical derivation is even dispensable when viewed from the angle of a timeless perfect intelligence such as God. That generation means logical derivation or logical structuring is a natural explanation of generation of forms is reinforced by the suggestion that forms are numbers. If forms are numbers, then all forms can be numerically derived from the unity in a number-theoretic framework. Time indeed becomes logically irrelevant. But if forms cannot be reduced to numbers or such other mathematical entities as classes, then we have to assign a meaning to generation other than that of logical derivation. However, I see no possibility of such assignment apart from the analogue or model of temporal production or generation.

The same difficulty of understanding holds for the Greek sense of self-coincident activity in Aristotle and Plotinus. Apparently one has to understand such activity in time and then conceive of it out of time. Perhaps it might be suggested that such activity can be conceived of as occurring out of space like the self-thinking thought. But what does not seem to occur in space need not seem to occur out of time. From a logical point of view, it would be difficult to consider the timeless transcendence of activity and generation. For this amounts to conceiving of something as purely spiritual and supernatural, which nevertheless has characteristics of natural and concrete things attributed to it.

Similarly, it is difficult from the logical point of view to conceive that what has transcended time, namely, the timeless activity, will cause changes in time and indeed will cause the flux of time. Is time the inchoate primal non-being from which material things are made? Is it, theoretically speaking, totally devoid of form? Is the substance of time none other than Aristotle's matter and Plato's receptacle? I am inclined to a positive answer, although I could not prove that to be the case. But if the positive answer is the correct one, then we can see why time is the moving image of eternity and why change in time, which characterizes time, is highly perilous. The reason is that time is primarily motion and only secondarily an image: it is an image after eternity impresses its forms on matter or the flux of time. This of course leaves one to wonder how time and the timeless come to be linked or how eternity comes to impress its forms on the flux of time. If the link is due to an activity in time, then the timeless falls into time, which is undesirable in view of the Platonic intent. If, on the other hand, the link is due to the timeless happening of definiteness, then we are puzzled with the question of the independent meaningfulness of such a happening; hence, one finds the paradox of the relation between time and the timeless.

I think that this paradox in Plato and other Greek philosophers anticipates the formulation of the modern paradox of time: the McTaggart paradox. Is time an eternal order of things or forms? Or is time a process of constant change? Does time occur in a super-time? Or does time exist independently of the timeless? Finally, a minor question also arises. Early in Kolb's paper, he states, "when the flux of time and space is bound into stable patterns, temporal beings emerge." I wonder how time and space are related in the original writings of the Greek philosophers. Is space separable from time or not?

Shuxian Liu has correctly presented the essentials of Chinese views on time and temporality. In Chinese history as well as Chinese philosophy, time is regarded as a concrete reality not to be separable from the changing, growing, and developing processes of things. In other words, time is never treated as an abstraction, a concept, or a form, but is always considered a property of life activity, creativity, generation, and transformation of individual things. Time is indeed to be identified with change and transformation of things. Thus to experience time is to experience concrete events of change.

To observe time is to observe substantial happenings of the world. This similarly holds for the Chinese view of space. That the Chinese lack concepts of abstract time and space, I think, is well compensated by the well-developed theories of change and transformation of things such as one can find in the *Book of Changes* and the Daoist writings of Laozi and Zhuangzi. Although it may be inconvenient or impractical from a Western point of view, it need not be from an alternative point of view. The Chinese may adopt the Christian linear system of dating historical events. But this is clearly for the purpose of communicating with the West and comparing with Western historiography. A general Chinese view would be: if one merely knows the dates of historical events, that does not help him in understanding the historical events at all. To know time in any important sense is to know historical events in time.

Insofar as Chinese metaphysics holds that the ultimate reality is the source of change, and the world is a domain of creative transformation, there is no reality whatsoever that exists independently of time.[1] This simply means that there is no separate world of the timeless. The important point of this view is that there need not be such a separate world. There is no need for preserving perfection and various forms of value in a timeless heaven because events in time will always creatively bring forth and refresh forms of perfection and value in the world. This is the constancy of the creativity principle.

As suggested by the *Book of Changes*, on the other hand, forms of imperfection and such undesirables as decay and death, which we find in our temporal world and which Plato wishes to avoid in his construction of the ideal world of forms, are regarded as relative; in some sense, they constitute conditions for the good and are mutually transformable with those that are relatively good. This is the constancy principle of mutual and universal transformation as suggested by the Daoists. These two fundamental principles make it superficial and even unnecessary for the Chinese to construct a world of the timeless or to be even interested in the timeless.

If we follow this line of thinking, there is indeed no problem of transcendence of time, for there is no need for doing this. The great *Dao* (the Way), which is the totality of time, is not to be transcended but is to be identified with or to be participated in. If one can speak of transcendence of time at all, it is only to mean to identify oneself with the source of change or the power of change. The former is sometimes described as returning to the origin of change or as clinging to tranquility. The latter is sometimes described as participating in the works of creativity of Heaven and Earth. Liu may have all these in mind, but he does not make them clear to us when he uses the term "transcendence of time in the change of time," without explaining its meaning.

In connection with the transcendence problem, we must also mention the important problem of the immortality of a person. In Chinese philosophy, be it Confucianism or Daoism, there is no serious affirmation of soul separate from body. Mind and body, or soul and body, are organically one and are generally held to be generated from the same material called *qi* (vital force). Given this ontological view of human existence, there cannot be immortality of the soul, for that would entail immortality of a whole person.

Even religious Daoists have sought in vain to achieve immortality of the whole person in the form of personal immortals (*xian*). Certainly, no philosophical Daoists or Confucians or Neo-Confucians endorse this possibility. Individual life is limited, and death is a natural phase of transformation of life, therefore not to be feared or worried. However, this is not to say that man cannot be immortalized at all. Indeed, with a deep reflection on the essence of time in Chinese philosophy, one can at least come to see the existence of two forms of immortality for a person: (1) There is what I like to call intrinsic immortality of a person: when a man identifies himself with the source of creativity and the total way of change, as in the case of Daoism, or when a man develops and cultivates himself to the fullest extent of his natural potentiality, and thus is capable of participating in the creative activities of Heaven and Earth, as in the case of Confucianism, he has achieved a form of intrinsic immortality. He is immortal insofar as the source and the way of creativity are forever lasting. In other words, a person achieves immortality insofar as he becomes a subject and a vehicle of creativity. (2) There is what I like to call historical immortality of a person. A person is a metaphysical entity as well as a historical entity. As a metaphysical entity, he can achieve intrinsic immortality of creativity. As a historical entity, one can achieve historical immortality, which consists in making his achievement of value a matter of lasting influence and enduring significance in history for the benefit of humanity. It is in this sense of historical immortality that the Chinese thinker speaks of immortality of deeds, immortality of virtue, and immortality of words. As these immortalities are achieved owing to creativity of time, they are forms of intrinsic immortality as well. Properly, they can be said to be forms of immortality within time, not beyond time, precisely because they can be identified with the essence and creative power of time.

Finally, I would like to comment on the question of unity of principle and variety of manifestations of principle (*liyi feng shu*) in the writings of Neo-Confucianism. Unlike Plato, the Neo-Confucians in general recognize the necessity of embodying the universality of principles in the multitude of individual things. But nevertheless, such Neo-Confucians as Cheng Yi and Zhu Xi are confronted with the problem of deciding whether or not principle (*li*) is prior in existence to *qi*. Zhu Xi generally takes principle (*li*) to be logically and ontologically prior to *qi* and yet stresses the fact that they are temporally and phenomenally one and inseparable. As *qi* is the substance of time, this means that principles and time processes are organically one in reality. On the other hand, there is also the suggestion on the part of Cheng Yi and Zhu Xi that principle somehow gives rise to *qi* and change. If this latter view is taken seriously, one might say that *li* transcends time and yet creates time. This position may lead to a closer approximation between the Greek view and the Neo-Confucian view on the relation between time and the timeless. But in the light of the tradition of the *Book of Changes* and the Neo-Confucian philosophy as a whole, we might say that such Neo-Confucians as Cheng Yi and Zhu Xi do not really intend existence of a transcendental world of principles apart from the world of *qi*. Their ultimate view seems to be that *li* exists in the middle of *qi* or time and functions as the motor force of creation for *qi* or time. *Li* is, therefore, none other than *qi* in its constant movement.

Given the above view, the so-called universal and constant principles of reality, knowledge, and morality are simply and merely *matters of order and organization* persistently emerging and always renewable in the everlasting flux of temporal change. That time can do this and sustain this only testifies to the fact that, for the Chinese philosopher, time is none other than the ultimate and comprehensive reality of all things in the world of change.

In summarizing the Chinese view on time and the timeless, it can be said that time produces history, and history brings forth immortality of man in which the ultimate ontological nature of time and the timeless is shown.

Notes

Chapter 1

1. See Wen-wu, #2-8, 1986.

2. See *Kaogu Xuebao*, vol. 7, 1954; *Xinzhongguo de kaogufaxian yu yenxiu*, Wen-wu Publishers, 1984.

3. We see here the continuity from past to the present, and we shall see how continuity can be established from present to the future in the formation of the onto-cosmology of the *Yijing* tradition.

4. We may indeed speak of the Greek as rationally oriented and having developed abstract reason because their environment of ocean has challenged them to solving the problem of overcoming situational hardships, whereas the Hebrew has to survive a drastically unfriendly environment of desert and hostile neighbors by way of a faith born out of desperation and despair, and the Indian has to search for a state of total peace and tranquility of mind under the spell of tropical sun and forest. In all these three cases, the affective ties with nature are basically cut or transcended, and man has to face his "true" self or another transcendent world of value, be it *Eidos*, God, or *Brahma*. For a theory of primary orientations for major historical cultural traditions in the world, I have to wait for another occasion to elaborate.

5. See also my paper titled "Chinese Metaphysics as Non-metaphysics: Confucian and Daoist Insights into the Nature of Reality," in *Understanding the Chinese Mind*, ed. Robert E. Allinson (Oxford: Oxford University Press, 1989), 167–208.

6. This attitude toward divination is actually assumed in the "Hong Fan" chapter of the *Shangshu* where the official diviners are regarded as capable of communicating with spirits.

7. We must grant that as a historical reflection we note that no political form or system is able to contain or control social and economic changes. Hence the survivability of a political order depends on how open and how flexible the political order is. Perhaps, it is in this light that democracy may be said to be

the best survivable system of political control that allows smooth nonviolent self-transformation. But even democracy may lead to disorder if a stable social and economic order is not maintained and education toward independent thinking is not developed.

8. See *Zuozhuan* "Zhao Gong" first year and twentieth year.

9. I introduce this new interpretation of the *junzi* for capturing the vividly felt but generally academically neglected or overlooked substance of the notion of *"junzi."*

10. One can finally see the five virtues of the Confucian philosophy as forming a unity and circle of *ren-xing-zhi-yi-li-ren* or *xing-ren-zhi-yi-li-xing*. The pervasive quality of *xing* was particularly noted by Zhu Xi.

11. See chapter "Jie Lao" in *Han Feizi*.

Chapter 2

1. Chen Kuying has argued for such a position in his book *Yizhuan yu daojia sixiang* (Taiwan Commercial Press, 1994). In a broad sense, the idea of *dao* has pervaded the *Yizhuan* because the *Yizhuan* has contributed to defining and delineating what the *dao* is. The search for the *dao* was common among schools and scholars even at the time of Confucius. Hence the Daoist notion of the *dao* as we see it in Laozi and Zhuangzi is different in many ways from the *Yizhuan* notion of the *dao*, even though they could be said to share the same source or resources of understanding the *dao*, such as the texts of the *Zhouyi*.

2. See the chapter "Philosophical Significances of *Guan*: From *Guan* (观) to Onto-Hermeneutical Unity of Methodology and Ontology," in my book *The Primary Way: Philosophy of* Yijing (Albany: State University of New York Press, 2020), 119–48.

3. The meaning and origin of *ru* have been discussed by many modern Chinese scholars, notably, Zhang Taiyan, Hu Shih, Fu Sinian, Kuo Mouju, and Yao Zong. In a recent article, Zhu Gaozheng relates the notion and idea of *ru* to a few *Zhouyi* hexagrams to stress the meaning of the *ru* as a person of "relaxed airs" awaiting opportunities to put himself to public use ("Lunru," *Zhuantong wenhua yu xiandaihua* [Chinese Culture: Tradition and Modernization], no. 1 [1997]: 18–25). In the *Analects*, Confucius stresses ceaseless learning and self-cultivation as the main contents of being a *ru*.

4. For a basic understanding of reality in terms of *li* and *qi*, see my "Reality and Understanding in the Confucian Philosophy of Religion," *International Philosophical Quarterly* 13, no. 1 (1973): 33–61.

5. Though the term for body, "*shen*" (身), is homonymous with the term for spirit, "*shen*" (神), the former and the latter are merely homonymous characters with different semantic content.

Chapter 3

1. Since 1979, many publications on environmental ethics have been published. *Ethics and Problems of the Twenty-first Century*, ed. K. E. Goodpaster and K. M. Sayre (Notre Dame, IN: University of Notre Dame Press, 1979), seems to set the tone for the exploration of the interface between ethical theory and certain practical problems of an environmental and social nature.

2. See R. Routley and V. Routley, "Against the Inevitability of Human Chauvinism," in ibid., 36–59.

3. Cf. W. K. Frankena, "Ethics and the Environment," in ibid., 3–20.

4. I have, in earlier articles, used the term "intrinsic humanism" for what I mean here by "inclusive humanism" and the term "extrinsic humanism" for what I mean here by "exclusive humanism."

5. See "Chinese Metaphysics as Non-metaphysics: Confucian and Daoist Insights into the Nature of Reality," in *Understanding the Chinese Mind*, ed. Robert E. Allinson (Oxford: Oxford University Press, 1989), 167–208.

6. Although a few scholars have argued for the Daoist influence of Laozi on *Yizhuan*, it is likely that both Daoism and Confucianism shared a common onto-cosmological worldview that is derived from the time-worn tradition of the *Yi* view of its world and its use in divination. For more on this, refer to the chapter "Philosophical Significances of *Guan*: From *Guan* (观) to Onto-Hermeneutical Unity of Methodology and Ontology," in my book *The Primary Way: Philosophy of Yijing* (Albany: State University of New York Press, 2020). Even though Daoism and Confucianism share the same philosophical origin in an onto-cosmological worldview, this does not imply that their ethical, moral, and political attitudes must be the same. In fact, many factors influence the ways in which Daoists and Confucians interpret the same onto-cosmology and thus give rise to their specific approaches to life and politics. Besides, it could be the internal "ontological difference" in the *Yi-text* that leads to the difference in Daoist ethics and politics and Confucian ethics and politics.

7. *Zhouyi Benyi* of Zhuxi, *Xici shang*, section 5.

8. Zhang Zai, *Zhengmeng*, chapter 2. I translate "*sheng*" in "*yi gu sheng*" as being creative, because oneness is the source of creation and the motivating force behind the transformation of things. I translate "*hua*" in "*er gu hua*" as being transformative, because it is through the interaction of the *yin/yang* that things are formed and transformed. In the *Xici*, the term "*sheng*" in the statement "*sheng wu fang er yi wu ti*" also suggests being creative. Hence, the statement means that creativity is without confinement and change is without forms, suggesting how profound and vast creative change could be.

9. See *Daodejing* (Yan Lingfeng edition), section 42.

10. Laozi said, "The ten thousand things hold the *yin* on the back and embrace the *yang*, reaching the harmony by stirring and fusing the vital energy." Ibid., section 42.

11. Whether this *Dao* is equal to the notion of *wuji* (the ultimateless) is an open question. In light of Laozi's saying that the being (*you*) and non-being (*wu*) mutually generate, it is better to see the *Dao* as combining the two as two functions of the *Dao*.

12. Ibid., *Xici*, section 4; my translation.

13. See Zhuxi's *Zhouyi Benyi*, written after his essay on *ren* in which he explains *ren* as the virtue of heart/mind and the principle of love, which differs slightly from what he says in the *Benyi*: "*ren* is the principle of love and love is the function of *ren*."

14. Zhang Zai, in his famous "Ximing," precisely developed this parental relationship paradigm leading to the image of the universe as a large family.

15. Actually, this is the spirit of Chinese landscape painting, in which nature is represented as a place for joyful and peaceful wandering in the company of friendly birds and reposeful flowers or plants. This is a Daoist attitude derived, in fact, from the *Zhouyi* world outlook.

16. See Mencius's argument for the government of benevolence in the "Lianghuiwang" chapter of the *Mencius*.

17. *Zhongyong* (*Doctrine of the Mean*), 22; my translation.

18. Ibid., 25; my translation.

19. *Analects*, 15.29.

20. On the notion of positions (*wei*), see the chapter "Philosophy of Positions in the *Zhouyi*" in this volume. In a recent publication in Chinese, Professor Bang Bu reiterated his philosophy of "one divided into three," which he names Confucian dialectics. His book *Rujia bien zheng fa yen jiu* (originally published in Beijing in 1984 and reissued in Shenchen under the title *Yi fenwei san: Zhongguo zhuan dong si xiang kao shi* [Shenzhen: Haidian chubanshe, 1995]) explores the formation of two from base one and the unity of two on the basis of one or toward the development of one. He has stressed the division of one into three more than the union of three into one or their subsistence. In my view, we need to stress both instead of relying on one.

21. Alfred North Whitehead, *Adventures of Ideas* (1933; repr., New York: The Free Press, 1967).

22. A human being might also lose sight of the creative source and the holistic balance of the cosmos and act, therefore, with no consideration of the source and the interrelations among things. This creates a state of "unnatural" discord and disturbance that is bound to a cycle of self-defeating and self-destructing action. Hence, the question of human creativity is not a matter of simply following nature but a matter of participating in the natural course of creativity. It is a matter of exploring nature free from disturbing the fundamental equilibrium of nature and free from preventing the natural functioning of nature.

23. See *Daodejing*, section 7.

24. See ibid., section 10 and section 51.

25. See ibid., section 12.

26. See *Zhouyi, Yizhuan, Xici shang*, 11.

27. Cf. Joseph Grange, "Whitehead and Heidegger on Technological Goodness," *Research in Philosophy and Technology: Technology and Everyday Life* 14 (1994): 161–73.

28. See *Zhuangzi*, Inner Chapters, Chapter on the Great Master (*da zhongshi*), San Min version (Taipei: San Min Book Co., 1974). English translation mine.

29. Apart from Confucianism, even Aristotle can be interpreted as treating "theoretical reason" (contemplating eternal objects) as a part of human life rooted in practical reason (without, however, touching on the technological use of the theoretical). It is obvious that for Aristotle, the human being must combine the theoretical or the philosophical with the practical in order to do the right thing. See Richard Kraut, *Aristotle on the Human Good* (Princeton, NJ: Princeton University Press, 1989), chapters 2 and 5.

Chapter 4

1. Without this side, religious conflict could be reduced to philosophical conflict. One notices that war is seldom caused by mere philosophical difference. Perhaps when religions are reduced to philosophies there would be no religious conflict because there would be no religion as such. This of course raises the question of the difference between religion and philosophy.

2. See Alfred North Whitehead, *Process and Reality*, corrected and edited by David Ray Griffin and Donald W. Sherburne (New York: The Free Press, 1978), 21.

3. Ibid., 21.

4. This is not to say that people may not dress up or project and configure the notion of the creative originator as a perfect mind or a divine person of infinite knowledge, supreme good, absolute power, and universal presence that is found in the notion of God as the Savior. I believe that in speaking of God, Whitehead himself is both conventional and unconventional in this sense. It can be also shown that when we take God as the source of subjective aims, God still plays the role of an initiator or a creator. Even for matters of evil, we may also conceive that God has intended good in the sense of providing initial conditions that are good in a human sense, and that may lead to evil in a human sense under certain circumstances, which in turn may be corrected or overcome by way of the creativity in us as originally derived from God the ultimate creator.

5. Ibid., 225.

6. See my article "Philosophical Significances of *Guan* (Contemplative Observation): On *Guan* as Onto-Hermeneutical Unity of Methodology and Ontology," *Guoji Yixue Yanjiu* (*International Journal in Yi Studies*), Beijing: Huaxia Shudian, 156–203.

7. All the quotations from the *Yizhuan* are from the standard *Yijing* text under Zhu Xi's commentary.

8. See his essay *"Yuan Shan"* (*Inquiries into Goodness*), translated by Chung-ying Cheng (Honolulu: East-West Center Press, 1970) and *"Mengzi Ziyi Suzheng"* (*Commentaries on Words in Mencius*), in *The Complete Works of Dai Dongyuan* (Beijing: Qinghua University Press, 1911), Part 1.

9. Ibid., 47.

10. All these are quotations from the *Xici* part of the *Yizhuan*.

11. These two papers are "Whiteheadian Philosophy and Genuine Religious Pluralism: Rationale for a Conference," and "Cobb's Whiteheadian Complementary Pluralism."

12. See David Griffin's second paper 25, Ogden IT 72.

13. See Whitehead, PR, 22, the 4th principle in the 27 categories of explanation; also see 50.

14. Ibid., 166.

15. Ibid., 19.

16. Ibid., 147.

17. Ibid., 148.

18. Ibid., 48.

19. See page 38 of Griffin's second paper, and reference to TCW 45.

20. We need not to necessarily conceive of God as having moral qualities. One may accuse God of having no moral qualities or being immoral by human standards, but this is possible because we have projected the image of a human person onto the existence of creator God or God as a creator. Any argument for the existence of God on anthropic or analogical grounds must consider reasons why God must be necessarily always moral, and could not be both moral and immoral at different times like a human being. Besides, when we come to see God as lacking admirable moral qualities, the appeal of God as an object of worship and reverence would lessen.

21. See Zhang Zai's well-known treatise *"Zhengmeng"* (*Rectifying Obscurations*), first chapter.

22. See my article "Confucian Onto-Hermeneutics: Morality and Ontology," *Journal of Chinese Philosophy* 17, no. 1 (2000): 33–67. See also my Chinese articles in *"Benti Yu Quanshi"* (*Ontology and Interpretation*) (Beijing: Sanlian Publishing, 2000), 15–62, and *"Benti Quanshi Xue"* (*Onto-Hermeneutics*) (Beijing: Peking University Press, 2002), 1–14, 25–30. I have edited both volumes.

Chapter 5

1. I know that Neville sees himself as a scholar-official in the best tradition of Confucianism as indicated in his explanation of the workings of the Boston Confucianism.

2. See the first book of his trilogy, *Reconstruction of Thinking* (Albany: State University of New York Press, 1981).

3. One sees the changing of the title of his recent paper on Confucianism and Christianity from "Confucian-Christian Incompatibilities" to "Confucian Christian Comparisons" in about a year, 1994–95.

4. Neville has formulated the logic of creation *ex nihilo* in his various writings, but the most pronounced statement of it is given in his 1991 book *Behind the Masks of God* (Albany: State University of New York Press, 1991).

5. See *Daodejing*, section 42.

6. Ibid., section 1.

7. *Daodejing* says that "The *Dao* follows the nature (*ziran*)," which in a sense means simply that the *Dao* exists and functions of its own accord, without any external or internal restriction or limit.

8. See Neville, *Behind the Masks of God*, 94–95.

9. Although Neville has referred to Zhuangzi a couple of times in his book *Behind the Masks of God*, he does not recognize the importance of pervasive presence of the self-creativity of the *Dao* in the sense of onto-cosmological/ cosmo-ontological creativity. See Zhuangzi's essay "*Qiwu Lun*" ("On Equalizing Things").

10. See *Yijing*, *Yizhuan*, *Xici*, section 5.

11. See his recent paper "The Dialect of Being in Cross-Cultural Perspective," a typescript.

12. I think that when one recognizes creativity as a defining nature of the *wu*, *wu* would become the ultimate of the *wu* and hence the *wuji*. But this is not to say that *wu* must be so conceived, yet as an ontological intuition it has been so conceived from the earliest founder of Neo-Confucianism to the founding father of the contemporary Neo-Confucian Xiong Shili. Another point is: Why cannot the ontological creativity be both contingent and necessary, just as it is both transcendent and immanent?

13. See Neville, *Behind the Masks of God*, 83.

14. For the process of transformation of depersonification from *shangdi* to *tian* and then to *Dao*, see my article "Dialectic of Confucian Morality and Metaphysics of Man," *Philosophy East and West* 21, no. 2 (1971): 111–23.

15. Neville has recognized the abstract nature of the ontological creativity in the argument of creation *ex nihilo* and considered religious symbols and significations far more interesting than an abstract theory of God as ontological act or source and outcome. But I disagree with this evaluation: the abstract analysis of the divine creativity sheds light on the hidden nature of any major religion and reveals common ground or differences among all major religions. Furthermore, the three-term of the creativity as a relation illustrates the hidden relationship of the terms of the trinity of God the Father, God the Son, and God the Holy Spirit, which can be reinterpreted as the creative act, the created result, and the implicit ontological ground or source. Similarly, the trinity of

heaven, earth, and the human can be also identified as that of the ontological creative act, the ontological creative ground or source, and the created result, which is endowed with the ability and the nature to act creatively in the environment of heaven and earth.

16. See Neville, *Behind the Masks of God*, 83.

17. Despite fancy names being given to directions and states of reality, it remains basically a matter of philosophical understanding. However, this is not to say that the lack of an organized transcendent religion with its theology in traditional China must be an absolute blessing. On the contrary, one might argue that this lack deprives traditional China of a balancing power against the despotism of emperors and prevents forces in favor of the development of science and democracy.

18. See the chapter "Zhouyi (周易) and the Philosophy of *Wei* (Positions 位)," in *The Primary Way: Philosophy of Yijing* (Albany: State University of New York Press, 2020), 245–73.

19. See the *Analects*, 1.

20. See the *Analects*, 12.9.

21. See the *Mencius*, 7A45. Zhang Zai also speaks of "treating people as my brothers and things as my companions" in his well-known essay "*Ximing*" (Western Inscription).

22. See his essay "*Daxuewen*" ("On the Great Learning").

23. See discussion on this subject in Neville's *Behind the Masks of God*, 116–25.

24. See the *Analects*, 1.12.

25. Ibid.

26. Mencius simply puts it: "The heart/mind of respectfulness is *li*." See the *Mencius*, 6A6.

27. I have enumerated eight senses of *li* in my earlier comments on Neville's book *Normative Cultures* (Albany: State University of New York Press, 1995).

28. See Xunzi's essay "*Wangzhi*" ("Institutions for a Kingdom"), which certainly goes beyond what Confucius and Mencius explicitly would articulate.

29. In traditional China it is only the rulers who are to perform the *li* of worshipping heaven or *jitian*.

Chapter 6

1. There is no denial that after Kant, Hegel has made a dialectical-historical re-presentation of time, and McTaggart has tried to show how time can be unreal because there are apparent contradictions in understanding time of time. But no philosopher in this group has concentrated on time as an ontological reality or as a rich human experience that needs an ontological account. Because no

such account appears to explain the rich complexity of time-concept as well as time-consciousness as focused on by Husserl, the overall tendency seems to ignore time or to treat time as unreality or to reduce it to a space-like entity as in Weyl. The present-day discussion on time made possible by the efforts of Fraser seems to suggest a deeply seated uneasiness of the Western mind regarding time as a problem and as a mystery. See Fraser's book *Essays on Time*.

2. Indeed, one can go through every major system of philosophy in Chinese history to show its relation to the way or paradigms of thinking in the *Yijing*. It suffices to point out that all major and minor philosophers of the Song-Ming Neo-Confucianism have been consciously linked to the *Yijing* either by using the *Yi* to interpret/justify a system of thinking or to interpret/justify the *Yi* in terms of a system of thinking or to do both. This also happened to both Daoism/Neo-Daoism and Chinese Buddhism, including Chan Buddhism. See the chapter "Chinese Metaphysics as Non-Metaphysics," in *Understanding the Chinese Mind*, ed. Robert E. Allinson (Oxford: Oxford University Press, 1989).

3. See my paper "Confucius, Philosophy of the *I Ching* and Heidegger," *Philosophy East and West* 37, no. 1 (1987): 51–70.

4. See his book, 239–42.

5. See chapter 12, "On Timeliness (*Shizhong* 时中) in the *Analects* and the *Yijing*: An Inquiry into the Philosophical Relationship between Confucius and the *Yijing*," in my book *The Primary Way: Philosophy of* Yijing (Albany: State University of New York Press, 2020), 353–426.

6. Ibid.

Chapter 7

1. See my articles "Chinese Philosophy and Symbolic Reference," *Philosophy East and West* 27, no. 3 (July 1977): 307–22; "Categories of Creativity in Whitehead and Neo-Confucianism," *Journal of Chinese Philosophy* 6, no. 3 (1979): 251–74.

2. See Samuel Alexander's book *Space, Time and Deity*, 1950.

3. This book by Fraser is published by Birkhauser Verlag, Basel, in 1978, preceded by his earlier study of time, *Of Time, Passion and Knowledge* (New York: Braziller), 1975.

4. J. N. Findlay, in a recent article, has discussed how eternity relates to the temporal and has correctly indicated the eternal as a limit of the temporal or the time. See his article "Time and Eternity," *The Review of Metaphysics* 32, no. 1 (September 1978): 3–14.

5. See my article "Toward Constructing a Dialectics of Harmonization: Harmony and Conflict in Chinese Philosophy," *Journal of Chinese Philosophy* 4, no. 2 (1977): 209–45.

6. See works by J. T. Smart and W. V. O. Quine.

7. Cf. translation of the *Yijing* by Richard Wilhelm, *The Book of Changes* (Princeton, NJ: Princeton University Press, 1967).

8. See my unpublished article "*Li* and *Qi* and the *Yijing*," presented at the First International Conference on Chinese Philosophy, Fairfield University, June 5–11, 1978.

9. See the Great Appendix in the Yijing.

10. Cf. Wing-tsit Chan's translation of the Neo-Confucian Philosophy Anthology—*JinsiLu* by Zhu Xi, published under the title *Reflections on Things at Hand* (New York: Columbia University, 1967).

11. Cf. D. C. Lau's translation of *Daodejing*, section 42.

12. Ibid., section 51.

13. Ibid., section 37.

14. Zhou Dunyi's "Discourse on the Diagram of the Great Ultimate," in translation (mentioned in note 10).

15. See Shao Yong's *Guanwu Waipian*.

16. See *You Yen* and *Ji Wu* in the chapters in *Zhuangzi*.

17. See my article mentioned in note 5.

18. See chapter 1, in *Jinsilu* (mentioned in note 10).

19. Ibid.

20. *Daodejing*, section 42.

21. The judgment on the Tai trigram in the *Yijing* says: "There is no going which does not return. This is what happens between heaven and earth."

22. See *Daodejing*, section 42.

23. See the *Youyan* and *Jiwu* chapters in the *Zhuangzi*.

24. See chapter 1 in the *Zhongyong* (the *Doctrine of the Mean*).

25. See the *Jin Xin*, chapter 1, *The Mencius*.

26. See *Zhuzi Yishu*, book 18.

27. See *Zhuzi Yulei*, vol. I.

28. See Zhuzi Shi Shuzi Zhu.

29. See Lu Xiangshan's *Complete Works*.

30. See his work *Guanwu Waipian*.

31. See *Jinsilu*, chapter 1.

32. See Zhang Zai's work *Zhengmeng*, chapter 1, *Taihe*.

Chapter 8

1. See his paper *On the Universal Science: Characteristic*, partially selected in *Leibniz: Monadology and Other Philosophical Essays*, trans. P. Schrecker and Anne M. Schrecker (Indianapolis: Hackett, 1965), 11–21.

2. It is important to note that a numerical system of CS could be used to represent non-numerical truths under sufficient theoretical interpretation, such as reading financial indexes in economic analysis or physiological texts (in numbers) in medical-clinical diagnosis.

3. See *On the Universal Science: Characteristic*, in Schrecker, 15.

4. As modern set theory has shown, we have more truths than we could express in our language. On the other hand, we could formulate even contradictory statements in our language that would have no reality corresponding to it. It is apparent that there is no single correspondence between language and truths. Moreover, the Gödel Incompleteness Theorem can be interpreted as demonstrating the impossibility of the formalization of all truths in any theory accommodating natural numbers.

5. There could be other relevant questions to be asked: What would Chinese language mean to Leibniz? Could the Chinese language fit in with his idea of a universal characteristic (abbreviated hereafter as UC) because of its iconic and representative character?

6. It is not clear whether Leibniz knew much about Zhou Dunyi (1017–1073), who is considered the founder of Song Neo-Confucianism by Zhu Xi (1130–1200). But, judging from the correspondence between Leibniz and Bouvet, there is no doubt that Leibniz acquired a basic and essential understanding of Song Neo-Confucianism at the end of the seventeenth century.

7. As discussed in E. M. Curley's article *The Root of Contingency*, in *Leibniz: A Collection of Critical Essays*, ed. H. G. Frankfurt (New York: Anchor Books, 1972), 69–97, 78.

8. Ibid.; in Curley's paper the question is raised as to whether God as the final cause should be the real reason for an essence to come into existence or whether it is sufficient that the essence's compossibility with other essences in the best combination is judged to be the reason for its coming into existence.

9. Leibniz seems to have sufficiently recognized this truth in 1714 in his *Monadology*; see propositions 38 and 39.

10. Here, I use Zhu Xi's well-known book *Yijing Benyi (Original Meanings of the Yijing)* as the standard text of the *Yijing* for reference and quotation.

11. I have explained the notion of guan as "comprehensive observation" in my article "On Guan as a Method of Onto-Hermeneutics of Understanding," in *International Yijing Studies* 1 (Beijing 1993): 1–25.

12. Similarly, many Confucian and Daoist metaphysical concepts must be regarded as coming from concerted efforts of thinking and feeling, instead of thinking alone. Hence, for example, *zhi tian* (knowing heaven) in Mencius comes from *zhi xing* (knowing one's own nature by reflection) and *jin xing* (fulfilling one's own mind or heart-mind by searching one's thinking, feeling, and willing), both of which are efforts made on the basis of deep personal reflection and feeling.

13. *The Book of Change*, Xici shang, section 4.
14. Ibid.
15. See for example the position of Zhuangzi in his famous *Qiwu Lun* (Equalizing all things).
16. *The Book of Change*, Xici shang, section 4.
17. Mencius, 7B25.
18. See my article "Zhouyi and Philosophy of *Wei* (Positions) in the Philosophy of Zhouyi," in *Extreme-Orient Extreme-Occident* 18 (Paris 1996): 149–76.
19. These qualities form a similarity class that is open to additions from experience, as indicated in the diagnosis list in Chinese medicine.
20. Leibniz corresponded with the Jesuit Bouvet in Beijing from 1697 until 1702, i.e., a total of five years. He was introduced to the *Yijing* by Bouvet and saw the "Prior Heaven Hexagram Order" (*xiantian guaxu*) as late as 1701. But prior to that period, a mirror-image square table of 64 gua (figures) was available as early as 1658 and an *Yijing* order of the 64 *gua* was available as late as 1687, and there is no evidence from the literature that Leibniz was not familiar with either of them. To say the least, with his intense interest in Confucian philosophy and the Chinese language, there is no evidence that he would not come to know something about the underlying philosophy of the *Yijing* symbols or the philosophy contained in the *Yizhuan* or the *Ten Commentaries* to the *Yijing*. But the trouble is that the source of the knowledge of these subjects was the missionary Jesuits in the mid-seventeenth century, whose zeal for spreading Christianity and background training prevented them from a thorough and authentic reading of the native philosophy, which in itself has a rich history of commentarial development. Bouvet himself may have been influenced by a Xiang-Shu school of mysticism in reading the *Yijing* symbolism, which is further reinforced by his hermetistic interest in the Figurist interpretation of ancient Chinese texts as containing Christian sacred truths. Under the circumstances it is difficult to see whether Leibniz could come to a full understanding of the philosophy of the *Yijing*. But there is no doubt that he was pleased with the confirmation of his discovery of the binary system in the symbolism of the *Yijing*. Leibniz's further enthusiasm about the Chinese language can be explained by his intense interest in finding a universal language from a source dating back to antiquity, which has also been a common concern of many European scholars since Francis Bacon (1561–1626).
21. See his discussions of the nature of the *Yijing* philosophy in his *Revised History of Chinese Philosophy*, vol. 1 (Beijing, 1981).
22. The school of Xiang-Shu interpretation of the *Yijing* was well developed and flourishing in the Han period from 206 BC to 52 AD. But it is interesting to note that there is no speculation on Xiang-Shu in Leibniz.
23. See D. E. Mungello, *Curious Land: Jesuit Accommodation and the Origins of Sinology* (Honolulu: University of Hawai'i Press, 1988), 195–96. As we

shall see, we could still raise this question as a philosophical issue in light of Leibniz's notion of a UC.

24. I have held that the *Yijing* is first of all a book of cosmological mapping. It is only on the basis of such cosmological mapping that divination as a practical art of reading warnings for the present or the future could develop. One cannot say that the *Yijing* is merely a book of divination, but only that divination is one of the uses to which the *Yijing* is put.

25. This is the well-known doctrine of the unity of man and heaven or returning to the *dao* in which there is no transcendence of *dao* from man.

26. Being causative is a form of being creative when the source of causation is located in the cause itself and no earlier or antecedent cause is to be posited.

27. *The Book of Change, Xici shang*, section 4.

28. Ibid., *Xici shang*, section 10. In this section, the *Xici* also lists the four ways of the sage: language, action, institutionalization, divination. These four ways are also the ways of interpretative action: how to express change in language, how to act to make change, how to lay down rules to regulate change, and how to identify change

29. Ibid., *Xici shang*, section 5.

Appendix

1. A good example of Chinese metaphysics, which sees reality as a process of transformation, stresses unity of the source and material of transformation and identifies time explicitly with phenomena (process and product) of change, is provided by the philosophy of Zhang Zai (1020–1077), one of the great Neo-Confucians in his time. Zhang Zai says:

> The vital force (*qi*) has *yin* and *yang* dimensions. When it realizes itself in orderly sequence, it transforms things. When it moves in unity with things and becomes unpredictable, it is spirit-like in power. In the case of man, (the *qi*) makes it possible for man to know righteousness and use utilities, both the transforming power and supremacy of spirit are accomplished. In the case of those whose virtue is abundant, when they fulfill their spirituality, then knowledge is not important; when they come to know the subtlety of transformation, then righteousness is not worthy of mention. The transformation of Heaven follows *qi* (the vital force); the transformation of man fits in with *time*. If there is no *qi* or time, then where comes the name of transformation? Where does actuality of transformation bear upon! *The Doctrine of the Mean* says: "To be great and then be capable of transformation." Mencius says: "To

be great and then be capable of transforming." All these indicate that the virtue of man comprehends *yin-yang*, and thus forms one flow with Heaven and Earth and nowhere it cannot penetrate. The so-called *qi* does not depend on becoming condensed and coalesced in order to be seen by eyes and consequently known. If one can speak of qualities such as strength and smoothness, motion and rest, vastness and purity of *qi*, then one can call *qi* phenomena. *But if phenomena are not qi, then what does the term "phenomena" refer to? If time is not phenomena, then what does the term "time" refer to?* (Shenhua Zhengmeng by Zhang Zai)

Selected Bibliography

Adler, Joseph A. *Divination and Philosophy: Chu Hsi's Understanding of the I-Ching (China, Religion)*. Santa Barbara: University of California Press, 1984.

———. *Reconstructing The Confucian Dao: Zhu Xi's Appropriation of Zhou Dunyi*. Albany: State University of New York Press, 2014.

Alexander, S. *Space, Time, and Deity*. Vol. 2. London: Macmillan, 1920.

Allais, L., 2015, *Manifest Reality: Kant's Idealism and his Realism*. Oxford: Oxford University Press.

Allison, H. *Kant's Transcendental Idealism: An Interpretation and Defense*. New Haven: Yale University Press, 2004.

Angle, Stephen C. *Sagehood: The Contemporary Significance of Neo-Confucian Philosophy*. Oxford: Oxford University Press, 2009.

Armour, Lesley. "Looking for Whitehead." *British Journal for the History of Philosophy* 18, no. 5 (2010): 925–39.

Beyer, C. "Edmund Husserl." In *The Routledge Companion to Nineteenth Century Philosophy*, edited by Dean Moyar, 887–910. London: Routledge, 2010.

Broad, Charlie D. *Leibniz: An Introduction*. Cambridge: Cambridge University Press, 1975.

Chan, Wing-tsit, ed. and trans. "The Great Synthesis in Chu Hsi." In *A Source Book in Chinese Philosophy*, 605–63. Princeton, NJ: Princeton University Press, 1963.

———. trans. *Reflections on Things at Hand: The Neo-Confucian Anthology*. Compiled by Chu Hsi and Lu Tsu-ch'ien. New York: Columbia University Press, 1967.

———. *Life and Thought*. Hong Kong: The Chinese University Press, 1987.

———. *Confucian Moral Metaphysics and Heidegger's Fundamental Ontology*. Netherlands: Springer, 1984.

Chai, D. "Thinking Through Words: The Existential Hermeneutics of Zhuangzi and Heidegger." In *Relational Hermeneutics: Essays in Comparative Philosophy*, edited by Paul Fairfield and Saulius Geniusas, 205–19. New York: Bloomsbury, 2018.

Chen Lai. *Gudai zongjiao yu lunli (Ancient religion and ethics)* (in Chinese). Beijing: Shenghuo dushu xinzhi, 2017.
Chen, Ku-Ying. *Yizhuan Yu Daojia Sixiang* (in Chinese). Taipei: Taiwan Commercial Press, 1994.
Cheng, Chung-Ying. "Dialectic of Confucian Morality and Metaphysics of Man." *Philosophy East and West* 21, no. 2 (1971): 111–23.
———. "On Yi as a Universal Principle of Specific Application in Confucian Morality." *Philosophy East and West* 22, no. 3 (1972): 269–80.
———. "Religious Reality and Religious Understanding in Confucianism and Neo-Confucianism." *International Philosophical Quarterly* 22, no. 13 (1973): 33–61.
———. "Greek and Chinese Views on Time and the Timeless." *Philosophy East and West* 24, no. 2 (1974): 155–59.
———. "Chinese Philosophy and Symbolic Reference." *Philosophy East and West* 27, no. 3 (1977): 307–22.
———. "Toward Constructing a Dialectics of Harmonization: Harmony and Conflict in Chinese Philosophy." *Journal of Chinese Philosophy* 4, no. 3 (1977): 209–45.
———. "Categories of Creativity in Whitehead and Neo-Confucianism." *Journal of Chinese Philosophy* 6, no. 3 (1979): 251–74.
———. "On the Environmental Ethics of the Tao and the Ch'i." *Environmental Ethics* 8, no. 4 (1986): 351–70.
———. "Confucius, Heidegger, and the Philosophy of the I Ching: A Comparative Inquiry into the Truth of Human Being." *Philosophy East and West* 37, no. 1 (1987): 51–70.
———. "On Harmony as Transformation: Paradigms from the I Ching." *Journal of Chinese Philosophy* 16, no. 2 (1989): 125–58.
———. "Philosophical Significances of Guan (Contemplative Observation): On Guan as Onto-Hermeneutical Unity of Methodology and Ontology" (in Chinese), in *Guoji Yixue Yanjiu (International Journal In Yi Studies)*, edited by Zhu Bokun, 156–203. Beijing: Huaxia Shudian, 1995.
———. "On a Comprehensive Theory of Xing (Naturality) in Song-Ming Neo-Confucian Philosophy: A Critical and Integrative Development." *Philosophy East and West* (1997): 33–46.
———. "Confucian Onto-Hermeneutics: Morality and Ontology." *Journal of Chinese Philosophy* 27, no. 1 (2000): 33–68.
———. *Benti Yu Quanshi (Ontology and Interpretation)* (in Chinese). Beijing: Sanlian Publishing, 2000.
———. "Dao (Tao): The Way." *Encyclopedia of Chinese Philosophy*, edited by Antonio S. Cua (2003): 202–6.
———. "Qi (Ch'i): Vital Force." *Encyclopedia of Chinese Philosophy*, edited by Antonio S. Cua, 615–17. New York: Routledge, 2003.

———. "A Theory of Confucian Selfhood: Self-Cultivation and Free Will in Confucian Philosophy. In *Confucian Ethics: A Comparative Study of Self, Autonomy, and Community*, edited by K. Shun & D. Wong, 124–47. Cambridge: Cambridge University Press.

———. *Contemporary Chinese Philosophy*. New York: John Wiley & Sons, 2008.

———. "The Yijing as Creative Inception of Chinese Philosophy." *Journal of Chinese Philosophy* 35, no. 2 (2008): 201–18.

———. "The Yi-Jing and Yin-Yang Way of Thinking." In *the Routledge History of Chinese Philosophy*, edited by M. T. Bo, 83–118. London: Routledge, 2008.

———. *Tai Chên's Inquiry into Goodness: A Translation of the Yuan Shan, with an Introductory Essay*. Honolulu: University of Hawai'i Press, 2019.

———. *The Primary Way: Philosophy of Yijing*. New York: State University of New York Press, 2020.

Ch'in, A., and F. Mansfield. *Tai Chen on Mencius*. New Haven: Yale University Press, 1990.

Cobb, John B. *Beyond Dialogue: Toward a Mutual Transformation of Christianity and Buddhism*. Oregon: Wipf and Stock Publishers, 1998.

———. *Christ in a Pluralistic Age*. Oregon: Wipf and Stock Publishers, 1999.

———. *A Christian Natural Theology: Based on the Thought of Alfred North Whitehead*. 2nd ed. Louisville: Westminster John Knox Press, 2007.

Cobb, John B., and David Ray Griffin. *Process Theology: An Introductory Exposition*. Louisville: Westminster John Knox Press, 1976.

Cook, Daniel J., and Henry R. "The Pre-established Harmony Between Leibniz and Chinese Thought." *Journal of the History of Ideas* 42, no. 2 (1981): 253–67.

Chis Hsi. *Introduction to the Study of the Classic of Change*. Edited by Joseph A. Adler. Provo: Global Scholarly Publications, 2002.

Chis Hsi, Čchu Si, and Xi Zhu. *Learning to Be a Sage: Selections from the Conversations of Master Chu, Arranged Topically*. Berkeley: University of California Press, 1990.

Confucius. *The Original Analects: Sayings of Confucius and His Successors*. Translated and edited by E. Bruce Brooks and A. Taeko Brooks (Translations from the Asian Classics). New York: Columbia University Press, 1998.

Curley, Edwin M. *Descartes against the Skeptics*. Cambridge, MA: Harvard University Press, 2013.

Dallmayr, Fred. "Tradition, Modernity, and Confucianism." *Human Studies* 1½no. 1/2 (1993): 203–11.

Descartes, René. *The Philosophical Writings of Descartes*. Vol. 2. Cambridge: Cambridge University Press, 1984.

———. *Descartes: Selected Philosophical Writings*. Cambridge: Cambridge University Press, 1988.

———. *Descartes: Philosophical Essays and Correspondence*. London: Hackett Publishing, 2000.
Desmet, Ronny, and Bogdan Rusu. "Whitehead, Russell, and Moore: Three Analytic Philosophers." *Process Studies* 41, no. 2 (2012): 214–34.
Dostal, Robert, ed. *The Cambridge Companion to Gadamer*. Cambridge: Cambridge University Press, 2021.
Ebbs, Gary. *Rule-Following and Realism*. Cambridge, MA: Harvard University Press, 1997.
———. *Carnap, Quine, and Putnam on Methods of Inquiry*. Cambridge: Cambridge University Press, 2017.
Frankena, W. K. *Ethics and The Environment*. Notre Dame, IN: University of Notre Dame Press, 1979.
Frankfurt, H. G. *Leibniz: A Collection of Critical Essays*. New York: Anchor Press, 1972.
Fraser, Julius Thomas. *Of Time, Passion, and Knowledge*. Princeton, NJ: Princeton University Press, 2021.
Fung, Yu-lan. "Why China Has No Science—An Interpretation of the History and Consequences of Chinese Philosophy." *International Journal of Ethics* 32, no. 3 (1922): 237–63.
———. *A History of Chinese Philosophy*. Translated by Derk Bodde. Princeton, NJ: Princeton University Press.
Garber, D. "Leibniz: Physics and Philosophy." In *The Cambridge Companion to Leibniz*, edited by E. Jolley, 270–352. Cambridge: Cambridge University Press, 1995.
Gardner, Daniel K., and Xi Zhu. *Chu Hsi and the "Ta Hsueh": Neo-Confucian Reflection on the Confucian Canon*. Vol. 118. Harvard University Asia Center, 1986. https://doi.org/10.2307/j.ctt1tg5gzn.
Gedalecia, D. "Excursion into Substance and Function: The Development of the T'i-Yung Paradigm in Chu Hsi." *Philosophy East and West* 24, no. 4 (1974): 443–51.
Giorgi, A., and Barbro G. *Phenomenology*. Los Angeles: Sage Publications, 2003.
Goodpaster, Kenneth E., and Kenneth M. Sayre. "Ethics and Problems of the Twenty-First Century." *Mind* 90, no. 360 (1981): 624–627.
Graham, Angus C., trans. *Chuang-tzu: The Seven Inner Chapters and Other Writings from the Book Chuang-tzu*. Boston: Allen and Unwin, 1981.
———. *Chuang Tzu: The Inner Chapters*. London: Hackett Publishing, 1981.
Griffin, David R. "Parapsychology and Philosophy: A Whiteheadian Postmodern Perspective." *Journal of the American Society for Psychical Research* 87, no. 3 (1993): 218–88.
———. *God, Power, and Evil: A Process Theodicy*. Louisville: Westminster John Knox Press, 2004.
———. "John Cobb's Whiteheadian Complementary Pluralism." *Deep Religious Pluralism* (2005): 39–66.

———. *Unsnarling the World-Knot: Consciousness, Freedom, and the Mind-Body Problem*. Eugene, OR: Wipf and Stock Publishers, 2008.
Harman, G. *Heidegger Explained: From Phenomenon to Thing*. Chicago: Open Court, 2011.
Harris, Errol E. "Time and Eternity." *The Review of Metaphysics* (1976): 464–82.
Heidegger, Martin, et al. *The Cambridge Companion to Heidegger*. Cambridge: Cambridge University Press, 1993.
———. *The Heidegger Reader*. Bloomington: Indiana University Press, 2009.
Hodge, Joanna. *Heidegger and Ethics*. London: Routledge, 2012.
Hon, Tze-Ki. *The Yijing and Chinese Politics: Classical Commentary and Literati Activism in the Northern Song Period, 960–1127*. Albany: State University of New York Press, 2005.
Husserl, Edmund, et al. *The Cambridge Companion to Husserl*. Cambridge: Cambridge University Press, 1995.
Hsi, Chu, and Xi Zhu. *Further Reflections on Things at Hand: A Reader*. Washington, DC: University Press of America, 1991.
Hylton, Peter. *Quine*. London: Routledge, 2017.
Inwood, M. *A Heidegger Dictionary*. Oxford: Blackwell Publishing. 1999.
Institute of Archaeology, Chinese Academy of Social Sciences. *Archaeological Discoveries and Research in New China* (in Chinese). Beijing: Wen Wu Press, 1984.
Jolley, Nicholas, ed. *The Cambridge Companion to Leibniz*. Cambridge: Cambridge University Press, 1994.
Jung, Hwa Yol. "Confucianism and Existentialism: Intersubjectivity as the Way of Man." *Philosophy and Phenomenological Research* 30, no. 2 (1969): 186–202.
Jung, C. Foreword to *The I Ching or Book of Changes*. Translated by Cary F. Baynes. Princeton, NJ: Princeton University Press, 1967.
Kant, I., and Paul G. *The Cambridge Edition of the Works of Immanuel Kant*. Cambridge: Cambridge University Press, 1992.
Knoblock, J. *Xunzi: A Translation and Study of The Complete Works*. Vol. 1. Stanford: Stanford University Press, 1988.
Kraut, Richard. *Aristotle on The Human Good*. Princeton, NJ: Princeton University Press, 1991.
Kunst, Richard A. *The Original Yijing: A Text, Phonetic Transcription, Translation, and Indexes, With Sample Glosses (I Ching, China)*. Berkeley: University of California Press, 1985.
Lau, Dim Cheuk. *Mencius*. London: Penguin UK, 2004.
Leibniz, Gottfried Wilhelm. *Monadology and Other Philosophical Essays*. Translated by Paul Schrecker and Anne Martin Schrecker. New York: Prentice Hall, 1965.
———. *New Essays on Human Understanding*. Edited and translated by Peter Remnant and Jonathan Bennett. Cambridge: Cambridge University Press, 1996.

———. *Philosophical Essays*. Translated by Roger Ariew and Daniel Garber. Indianapolis: Hackett Publishing, 2015.

Li Guangdi, ed. *1714, Zhuzi quanshu [Collected Works of Zhu Xi]*. 2 vols. Reprint, Taipei: Guangxue, 1980.

Legge, J., ed. *The I Ching*. Vol. 16. Chicago: Courier Corporation, 1963.

Legge, Ja, and Max M. Friedrich. *The Sacred Books of China: The Texts of Confucianism*. Vol. 16. Oxford: Clarendon Press, 1882.

Lynn, Richard John, trans. *The Classic of Changes: A New Translation of the I Ching as Interpreted by Wang Bi* (translations from the Asian Classics). New York: Columbia University Press, 1984.

Marx, W. *Heidegger and the Tradition*. Evanston, IL: Northwestern University Press, 1982.

Machle, Edward J. "Leibniz and Confucianism: The Search for Accord, and: Discourse on the Natural Theology of the Chinese." *Journal of the History of Philosophy* 18, no. 4 (1980): 476–77.

Minford, J. *I Ching: The Essential Translation of the Ancient Chinese Oracle and Book of Wisdom*. New York: Penguin USA, 2014.

Moran D., and Joseph C. *Introduction to Phenomenology*. London: Routledge, 2002.

———. *The Husserl Dictionary*. London: Bloomsbury Publishing, 2012.

Mungello, David E. "Leibniz's Interpretation of Neo-Confucianism." *Philosophy East and West* 21, no. 1 (1971): 3–22.

———. *Curious Land: Jesuit Accommodation and the Origins of Sinology*. Honolulu: University of Hawai'i Press, 1988.

———. *Leibniz and Confucianism: The Search for Accord*. Honolulu: University of Hawai'i Press, 2019.

Mou Zongsan. *Zhide zhijue yu Zhongguo zhexue*. Taipei: Taiwan shangwu yinshu guan, 1971.

———. *Authority and Governance* (in Chinese). Taipei: Xuesheng Shuju, 1991.

Møllgaard, Eske J. "Zhuangzi's Word, Heidegger's Word, and the Confucian Word." *Journal of Chinese Philosophy* 41, no. 3 (2014): 454–69.

Ng, On-Cho. "Affinity and Aporia: A Confucian Engagement with Gadamer's Hermeneutics." In *Interpretation and Intellectual Change*, edited by Ching-I Tu, 297–310. London: Routledge, 2017.

Nielsen, B. *A Companion to Yi Jing Numerology and Cosmology*. London: Routledge, 2013.

Nelson, Eric S. "The Yijing and Philosophy: From Leibniz to Derrida." *Journal of Chinese Philosophy* 38, no. 3 (2011): 377–96.

Neville, Robert C. "Behind the Masks of God." *Theological Studies* 52, no. 3 (1991): 586.

———. *Normative Cultures*. Vol. 3. Albany: State University of New York Press, 1995.

———. "Value and Selfhood: Pragmatism, Confucianism, and Phenomenology." *Journal of Chinese Philosophy* 42, no. 1 (2015): 197–212.

Pu Pang. *One Is Divided into Three, Investigation and Interpretation of Chinese Traditional Thoughts* (in Chinese). Shenzhen: Haitian Publishing House, 1998.
———. *The Study of Confucian Dialectics* (in Chinese). Beijing: Zhong Hua Book Company, 2009.
Perkins, Franklin. *Leibniz and China: A Commerce of Light.* Cambridge: Cambridge University Press, 2004.
Petzet, Heinrich Wiegand, and Martin Heidegger. *Encounters and Dialogues with Martin Heidegger, 1929–1976.* Chicago: University of Chicago Press, 1993.
Quine, Willard V. *Word and Object.* Cambridge, MA: MIT Press, 1960.
———. *Theories and Things.* Cambridge, MA: Harvard University Press, 1981.
———. *From Stimulus to Science.* Cambridge, MA: Harvard University Press, 1995.
Raphals, Lisa. *Divination and Prediction in Early China and Ancient Greece.* Cambridge: Cambridge University Press, 2013.
Raschke, Carl A. "Reconstruction of Thinking. Robert Neville." *Journal of Religion* 64, no. 3 (1984): 398–99.
Redmond, Geoffrey, trans. *The I Ching (Book of Changes): A Critical Translation of the Ancient Text.* London: Bloomsbury, 2017.
Richardson, William J. *Heidegger: Through Phenomenology to Thought.* The Hague: Martinus Nijhoff Publishers, 1974.
Rorty, Richard. *Essays on Heidegger and Others: Philosophical Papers.* Vol. 2. Cambridge: Cambridge University Press, 1991.
Routley, Richard, and Val Routley. "Against the Inevitability of Human Chauvinism." In *Ethics and Problems of the 21st Century*, edited by R. E. Goodin, 36–59. Notre Dame, IN: University of Notre Dame Press, 1979.
Rowbotham, Arnold H. "The Impact of Confucianism on Seventeenth Century Europe." *The Journal of Asian Studies* 4, no. 3 (1945): 224–42.
Russell, B. *The Philosophy of Leibniz.* London: Routledge, 1992.
Rutherford, Donald. *Leibniz and the Rational Order of Nature.* Cambridge: Cambridge University Press, 1998.
Shaviro, Steven. *Without Criteria: Kant, Whitehead, Deleuze, and Aesthetics.* Cambridge, MA: MIT Press, 2009.
Shchutskii, Iulian K. *Research on the I Ching.* Vol. 213. Princeton, NJ: Princeton University Press, 2017.
Sheehan, T. Review of *The Heidegger Controversy: A Critical Reader. Ethics* 103, no. 1 (1992): 178–81.
Smith, Richard J. *The I Ching: A Biography.* Vol. 9. Princeton, NJ: Princeton University Press, 2012.
Smith, Kidder, et al. *Sung Dynasty Uses of The I Ching.* Princeton, NJ: Princeton University Press, 2014.
Swetz, Frank J. "Leibniz, the Yijing, and the Religious Conversion of the Chinese." *Mathematics Magazine* 76, no. 4 (2003): 276–91.
Tang Junyi, "Lun Zhongguo zhexue sixiang zhong 'li' zhi liu yi." *Xin Ya xuekan* 1, no. 1 (1955): 45–160.

Tang Yongtong. *Weijin xuanxue lungao (Preliminary Studies of the Learning of the Deep during the Wei-jin Period)*. Shanghai: Shanghai renmin chubanshe, 2015.

Tillman, Hoyt Cleveland. *Confucian Discourse and Chu Hsi's Ascendancy*. Honolulu: University of Hawai'i Press, 1992.

Tillman, Hoyt C., P. B. Embrey, and C. Hsi. "Chu Hsi's Family Rituals: A Twelfth-Century Chinese Manual for the Performance of Cappings, Weddings, Funerals, and Ancestral Rites; Confucianism and Family Rituals in Imperial China: A Social History of Writings about Rites." *Philosophy East and West* 43, no. 4 (1993): 754.

Tiwald, J. "Xunzi Among the Chinese Neo-Confucians." In *Dao Companion to the Philosophy of Xunzi*, edited by Eric L. Hutton, 435–73. Dordrecht: Springer, 2016.

———. "Confucianism and Neo-Confucianism." In *Oxford Handbook of Virtue*, edited by Nancy E. Snow, 171–89. New York: Oxford University Press, 2018.

Tiwald, Justin, and Bryan W. Van Norden. *Readings in Later Chinese Philosophy: Han to the Twentieth Century*. Indianapolis: Hackett Publishing, 2014.

Van Norde, Bryan, trans. *Mengzi: With Selections from Traditional Commentaries*. Cambridge, MA: Hackett Publishing, 2008.

Verhaegh, Sander. *The Nature and Development of Quine's Naturalism*. Oxford: Oxford University Press, 2018.

Waley, Arthur. "Leibniz and Fu-Hsi." *Bulletin of the School of Oriental and African Studies* 2, no. 1 (1921): 165–67.

Wang, Yang-ming. *Instructions for Practical Living*. Translated by Wing-tsit Chan. New York: Columbia University Press, 1963.

Warnke, G. *Gadamer: Hermeneutics, Tradition and Reason*. New York: John Wiley & Sons, 2013.

Watson, B., trans. *Chuang Tzu: Basic Writings*. New York: Columbia University Press, 1964.

———. *The Complete Works of Chuang Tzu*. New York: Columbia University Press, 1968.

———. *Han Feizi: Basic Writings*. New York: Columbia University Press, 2003.

———. *Zhuangzi: Basic Writings*. New York: Columbia University Press, 2003.

Whitehead, Alfred N. *An Introduction to Mathematics*. Oxford: Oxford University Press, 1958.

———. *Symbolism: Its Meaning and Effect*. 1927. Reprint, New York: Fordham University Press, 1985.

———. *Adventures of Ideas*. 1933. Reprint, New York: The Free Press, 1967.

Wilhelm, H. *Change: Eight Lectures on The I Ching*. Vol. 62. Princeton, NJ: Princeton University Press, 2019.

Wilhelm, R. *The Soul of China*. New Jersey: Lethe Press, 2007.

Williams, Bernard. *Descartes: The Project of Pure Enquiry*. London: Routledge, 2014.

Wright, Kathleen. "Hermeneutics and Confucianism." In *The Routledge Companion to Hermeneutics*, edited by Jeff Malpas and Hans-Helmuth Gander, 698–715. London: Routledge, 2014.

———. "Gadamer's Philosophical Hermeneutics and New Confucianism." In *Gadamer and Ricoeur: Critical Horizons for Contemporary Hermeneutics*, edited by Francis J. Mootz III and George H. Taylor, 249–51. London: A&C Black, 2011.

Woo, Kun-Yu. "A Comparative Study of Lao-Tzu and Husserl: A Methodological Approach." In *Phenomenology of Life in A Dialogue Between Chinese And Occidental Philosophy*, edited by A. T. Tymieniecka, 65–73. Berlin: Springer Science & Business Media, 2012.

Wyatt, Don J. *The Recluse of Loyang: Shao Yung and The Moral Evolution of Early Sung Thought*. Honolulu: University of Hawai'i Press, 1996.

Xunzi. *Xunzi: The Complete Text*. Translated by Eric L. Hutton. Princeton, NJ: Princeton University Press, 2014.

Yang Bojun. *Lunyu yizhu (An Interpretive Commentary to the Analects)* (in Chinese). Hong Kong: Zhonghua shuju, 2015.

Yushun, Huang. "Return to Life and Reconstruct Confucianism: An Outline of Comparative Study on Confucianism and Phenomenology." *Frontiers of Philosophy in China* 2, no. 3 (2007): 454–73.

Zhang, Zai. *Zhang Zai ji* (in Chinese). Beijing: Zhonghua shuju, 1978.

Zhou Dunyi, *Zhou Dunyi ji [Collected Works of Zhou Dunyi]*. Edited by Chen Keming. Beijing: Zhonghua shuju, 1990.

Zhu Gaozheng. "On Confucianism—Demonstrating the Original Meaning of Confucianism—from the Ancient Classics of the Book of Changes" (in Chinese). *Traditional Culture and Modernization* 1 (1997): 18–25.

Zhu Xi, (Qing). *Hui'an xiansheng Zhu Wengong wenji [Collected Writings of Hui'an Master, Zhu Wengong]*. Sibu congkan edition. Shanghai Hanfenlou Library Ming Dynasty edition.

———. *Zhuxi yulei [Classified Dialogues of Master Zhu]*. Edited by Li Jingde. Beijing: Zhonghua shuju, 1986.

Index

Actual Occasions, 119, 126, 180
Adam, 161
A hundred flowers, 39
A hundred schools, 39
Airen 爱人, 48
Analects 论语, 4, 78, 91, 158, 161, 183, 187, 192
Ancestral spirits, 2, 15, 158, 162
Anthropological egoism, 85
Appropriation (Ereignis), 181
A pragmatism of practical significance, 163
Aristotelian metaphysics of primal matter and pure form, 166
Augustine, 151
Axial age, 30, 42
Axial thinkers, 38, 42–44
Axiology of the Yi 义, 154

Bagua 八卦, 24, 62, 95, 114, 243, 244–245
Barth, Karl, 150
Bianhua 变化, 62
Bianyi 变易, 22, 62, 181, 198
Book of Change 易经, 218, 223, 263, 265
Book of divination, 27
Book of Filial Piety 孝经, 157
Bu 卜, 27
Buci 卜辞, 20

Buddhism, 105–106, 108
Buddhist co-origination, 117–118
Buddhist notion of kong 空, 117
Butong er he 不同而和, 137
Buyi 不易, 22, 148, 181, 198

Categorical imperative, 85
Ceaselessly creative (shengsheng buyi 生生不已), 148
Chan 禅 Buddhism, 138
Change theory of time, 180, 183
Characteristic symbols, 231
Cheng 诚, 62, 79, 82, 97, 186, 189
Cheng 诚 as Shen 神 and Sheng 圣, 79
Cheng 程 Brothers, 136
Cheng Hao 程颢, 223
Cheng Yi 程颐, 190, 229, 265
Chinese Christian families, 158
Chinese Philosophy, 2, 7, 11, 14, 25, 30–31, 58–59, 141–143, 157, 165
Christian religion, 75, 124, 128, 157
Christianity, 58, 105–106, 108–109, 115, 120, 132, 137–139, 151, 157, 160, 162, 166
Chunqiu 春秋, 3, 30–32, 35, 43
Cobb, John, 10, 119
Comparative Analysis of Time, 180
Comparative approach, 9
Comparative insights, 9

Complementarity, 23, 25, 30, 108, 113–115, 119, 121–122, 136, 139
Complementary opposites or polarities, 23
Complementary pluralism, 4, 108–109, 119, 122, 125, 129
Comprehensive love, 85
Comprehensive observation, 24–25, 36, 169–171, 227, 238–241, 244, 249, 258
Comprehensive observation (guan 观), 24–25, 36, 169–171, 238–239, 240–241 244, 249, 258, 277
Concrescence, 118–119
"Configurational theory" and "metaphysics of change and time," 170
Confucian-Christian, 156–157
Confucian-Daoist, 139, 222
Confucian heaven as a Divine Person, 132
Confucianism-Christianity, 138
Confucian personhood, 85, 104
Confucian proprieties, 159
Confucian trinity, 91, 97
Confucius's life, 70
Consequential Nature of God, 119
Cosmic Epoch, 119
Cosmo-Eco-Ethics, 100, 102–103
Cosmo-Ethics, 86, 90, 98
Cosmological-ecological-ethical, 100
Cosmological creativity, 103, 145–147, 154, 200
Cosmo-ontological creativity, 147–148
Creatio ex nihilo, 6, 111, 122–123
Creative Advance, 98–99, 118, 122, 124, 136, 221
Creativity and God, 109, 111, 119, 121, 152
Creator-God, 87, 130–132
Cultivational humanism, 89

Cultivation of Mind, 225, 228
Curley, E. M., 235

Dai Dongyuan 戴东原, 114
Daoism, 3, 8, 10, 30, 39–40, 44, 56–58, 62, 76, 109, 116, 122, 128, 133, 135–139 142, 144, 146, 152, 181–183, 186, 189, 206, 221, 264, 269, 275
Daoism-Buddhism, 138
Daoist theory of reality, 69, 71, 73
Daoist True Person (zhenren 真人), 132
Dao-metaphysics, 44–45
Daotong weiyi 道通为一, 71
Dark Ages, 87
Dasein, 168–169, 180
Daseinization of time in Heidegger, 169
Datong 大同, 159–160
Daxue 大学, 52, 92, 194, 229
De 德, 20
Deconstructive, 45, 56–58
Deistic God, 87
De qi huan zhong yi yin wu qiong 得其环中 以应无穷, 183
Desire-ridden, 44
Dewey, 151, 210
Di 帝, 18
Dialectical thinking, 24, 29
Didao 地道, 57, 185
Differential pluralism, 4, 108
Disintegration, 7, 30–32, 39, 41–42, 45, 209, 215
Divine, 28, 75, 79–82, 109, 132, 171, 237, 250
Divinity, 18, 60–65, 76–77, 80–83, 98, 135, 237
Divination, 171, 178, 241, 248–250, 267, 269, 279
Divinity without theology, 75, 77, 80
Doctrine of the Mean, 80–81, 186, 270

Dong Zhongshu 董仲舒, 35
Dui 兌, 24
Duhua 独化, 188
Dynamics of nature, 24

Eco-Cosmology, 86
Ecological cosmology, 90
Eden, 162
Emperors Yongzheng 雍正 and Qianlong 乾隆, 163
Environmental ethics, 10, 101
Ethical God, 130–131, 133
Ethics of timeliness, 201
Exclusive humanism, 4, 90, 269

Fan 反, 73
Fanming 反命, 73
Faustian tradeoff, 87
Fission (mitosis), 110–111
Five-power (wuxing 五行) theory of nature, 34
Foreknowledge (xianzhi 先知), 81
Forever-transcending, 182
Foucault's archaeological approach to knowledge, 12
Four Books 四书, 161
Fraser, J. T., 210
Fu 复, 73
Full naturalization and depersonalization of the tian 天, 76
Fu Xi 伏羲, 24

Ganying 感应, 223
Gen 艮, 24
God and World, 119
God in the Bible, 161
Great and transforming, 79
Greek value theory, 141
Griffin, David, 120, 124
Group selfishness, 85
Guan 观, 36, 112, 170, 237, 241, 244, 249, 258

Gui 鬼, 17
Guo Xiang 郭象, 187–190

Harmonization in Time, 117, 222
He 和, 19, 26
Heart-mind, 26–27, 151, 177
Heaven and Earth, 4, 38, 68, 71, 80–82, 94–97, 102, 113, 145, 157–158, 175, 186, 221–225, 228, 239–240, 248, 255–256, 264
He er butong 和而不同, 137
Heidegger, 7, 75, 103, 165–166, 168–169, 171, 180–181, 189
Henan 河南, 15
Hermitic, 45
Hierarchical Theory of Time, 210
Hierarchy of Generation, 222
Housheng 厚生, 36
Hua 化, 19
Huangdi Neijng 黄帝内经, 36
Huayan 华严 buddhism, 118
Hubei 湖北, 15
Hui Neng 慧能, 150
Human chauvinism, 85
Humanism, 2–4, 15, 20, 30–34, 37–39, 41, 46, 53, 70, 85–91
Humanism for cultivation, 89
Humanistic awakening, 33, 37

Immanent Confucian models, 164
Inclusive humanism, 4, 86–90
Inner core of the Confucian Trinity, 91
Integration of creativity, 109
Integrative pluralism, 4–5, 105, 108–109, 122, 127–129, 131–139
Intrinsic reverence, 2, 14
Islam, 105–106, 132

Jaspers, Karl, 42
Jia 家, 43
Jianyi 简易, 22, 181

Jide 积德, 57
Jieqi 节气, 202
Jiji 既济, 26
Jing 精, 77
Jing (敬) and piety, 16
Jinxin 尽心, 79, 96, 228
Jinxing 尽性, 96, 228
Jizhizhe shanye 继之者善也, 100
Junzi (君子), 32, 47, 80, 195, 250

Kan 坎, 24
Kant, 167–169, 171, 180, 195, 274
Kantian framework, 167
Keiji Nishitani, 147
King Wen of Zhou 周文王, 28
King Yu 禹王, 35
Kolb, David A., 261
Kun 坤, 95
Kun yuan 坤元, 153, 238

Late Chunqiu 春秋, 43
"Learning of metaphysical profundities" (xuanxue 玄学), 151, 186
Leibniz, 7–10, 231–238, 245–246, 250–253, 255–259
Li 礼, 47–48
Liang Shuming 梁漱溟, 191
Liangyi 两仪, 62
Liji 礼记, 29, 38, 52, 159
Lilun 礼论, 161
Li 理 Neo-Confucianism, 135
Liuqi (six vapors) 六气 35
Liu Shuxian 刘述先, 262
Lixue 理学, 151
Liyi fenshu 理一分殊, 152
Liyong 利用, 36
Longshan Culture 龙山文化, 15
Lord-on-high (shangdi 上帝), 149
Luli 履礼, 57
Lunar Calendar (huangli 黄历), 201
Lu Xiangshan 陆象山, 136, 191, 229

Mandate of Heaven (tianming 天命), 20–21, 36–37, 49
May Fourth, 156
Mencius 孟子, 4, 37–42, 49–52, 77, 79–80, 92, 96, 135, 148, 159, 162, 185, 194–195, 200, 228–229
Metaphysics, 1–3, 8–10, 21, 44–45, 55–56, 69, 75, 144, 148, 151, 166, 169, 152, 170, 186, 215, 218, 222, 233, 263, 273
Micro-observation, 25
Mind is qi 气, 228
Mind is the quintessence of qi 气, 228
Ming 命, 26
Mingjia 名家, 41
Mo 墨, 17
Mohism, 40, 52, 55, 58
Mohist belief in the tianzhi 天志, 40
Monad, 233, 248, 257
Mou Tsung-shan 牟宗三, 191
Multi-interactive harmony, 65
Mungello, D. E., 246
Myth of the Hou Yi 后羿, 17

Naturalism, 2–3, 15, 30–32, 34–35, 37–39, 41, 45
Naturalistic-pragmatic conceptualization, 34
Naturalistic understanding, 34–36
Natural spirits, 15–18, 27, 32, 77
Neng you wanwu 能有万物, 57
Neo-Confucians of the Song 宋 and Ming 明 periods, 91
Neo-Daoism, 181, 186, 189, 206
Neolithic time, 15
Neo-Neo-Confucian, 191
Neville, 5–6, 9–10, 141–149, 150–163, 272
Newtonian physics, 168
Newton-Smith, W. H., 183
Nietzsche, 87, 131, 210

Nirvana, 107, 117, 132
Nongjia 农家, 40
Non-linear, 183
North Whitehead, Alfred, 34, 90, 108, 271
Nowness, 207, 215–218, 225–229
Number-corresponding, 231

One and Many, 117
Onto-cosmological Theory of Time, 196
Onto-cosmology, 2–3, 5–9, 24–25, 27–28, 30, 35, 62–63, 65, 69, 75, 83, 90–92, 95, 98, 103, 112–119, 122, 130, 135–142, 147–148, 156, 160, 176, 196–197, 199, 200–202, 267, 269
Onto-hermeneutical, 5, 115, 119, 123, 130, 155, 256
Ontological creativity, 147, 151, 155, 160, 273
Ontological God, 130–131, 133–134
Ontological principle, 5, 126–127
Ontology, 1, 9, 37, 104, 114–115, 117, 127, 132–133, 135, 141–143, 146–147, 155–156, 160, 168, 178, 233, 251
Ontology of Wu 物, 141, 143
Organicism, 35
Origins, 2, 9, 11–15, 25, 31, 57–59, 107, 119–120, 129
Origins of a philosophy, 11–13
Origins of Chinese Philosophy, 11, 31, 58

Pei Yangfu 伯阳父, 35
Period of Jade, 15
Philosophical idea, 12–13, 43, 58
Philosophical Schools, 39, 41, 43
Plato, 141, 151, 165–166, 180–211, 216, 227, 262–263, 265
Platonic paradigms of time, 116

Polar-generative process, 69
Post-heaven (houtian 后天), 35
Post-medieval, 87
Practical, 12–13, 27, 29, 32, 40, 52, 56–57, 91–92, 101, 104, 108, 151, 155, 163–165, 170–171, 193, 203–204, 254
Praxis, 91–92
Primordial Nature, 99, 119, 211
Principle of Intensive Relevance, 126
Proto-typical, 39
Pu 卜, 202

Qian 乾, 95
Qian yuan 乾元, 153
Qi 气 Neo-Confucianism, 135
Qiwulun 齐物论, 183

Real Dao 道, 150
Real God, 150
Records of Rites, 159
Ren 仁, 46–47
Reverence (jing 敬), 17–19, 157
Roman Catholic Pope, 163
Ruler-people relationship, 113
Russell, 234

Sagacity (sheng 圣), 80
Sage-kings, 15, 33
Sage-ruler, 132
Salvific God, 134
Sandiyuanrong 三谛圆融, 118
Schubert M. Ogden, 124
Self-aggrandizement, 89
Self-assertion, 89
Self-glorification, 87, 89
Semi-Pluralism, 124–125
Serious-minded, 70
Shan 善, 174, 224
Shangshu 尚书, 33–35, 37, 267
Shang 商 people, 76

Shao Yong 邵雍, 190, 221–222, 224, 229, 241
Shangdi 上帝, 2, 18, 20, 149–150, 273
Shandong 山东, 15
Shen 神, 79
Shengren 圣人, 47
Shengsheng 生生, 5
Shengsheng buyi 生生不已, 73
Shengsheng zhi wei yi 生生之谓易, 218
Shi 筮, 27
Shijing 诗经, 76
Shishiwuai 事事无碍, 118
Shizhong 时中, 7
Shujing 书经, 76
Sixiang 四象, 62
Society-centered, 36
Stabilized by being unified (ding yu yi 定于一), 39
Sub-contraries, 64
Symbolic realism, 7–8, 231
Symbolization, 241, 243–245, 248, 258

Taiji (太极)-God, 122, 130, 133
Taiji Tu 太极图, 98
Taiji tushuo 太极图说, 8, 116, 233
Taixu 太虚, 190, 229
Tang Zhunyi 唐君毅, 191
Teilard de Chardin, 210
Temporal and eternal, 146
The dao 道 and the taiji 太极 as two sides of the yi 易, 172
The Great Chain of Being of Lovejoy and in the Greek Thinking of Heidegger, 166
The hidden and the subtle, 82
Theorizing of theories, 6, 155
The practice of li 礼, 15
The primary paradigm of Yi 易, 169
The Relativity Principle, 127
The rise of li 礼, 19
Tian 天, 18
Tiandao 天道, 76, 185
Tian ren bu xiang sheng 天人不相胜, 104, 182
Tiantai 天台 Buddhism, 118
"Time as growth," "time as change," and "time as happening," 165
Timeliness, 7, 165, 179, 184–186, 197, 200–202, 204, 225, 275
Time-onto-cosmology, 203
Tradition of li 礼, 30, 36–37
Tradition of zhi 智, 30, 36–37, 58
Transcendence-within-immanence, 3
Transcendent Christian models, 164
Transcendental, 7, 34, 45, 51, 91, 167–168, 179–180, 182, 216–218, 265
Trans-valuation, 42
Tuan Commentary 彖传, 186, 203

Ultimate Reality, 2, 26, 45, 49, 68, 94–95, 120–125, 128–129, 131–133, 135–138, 182, 185, 218–219, 227–228, 263
Unity of feeling, 34
Universe disjunctively, 110

Valuational thinking, 154
Virtues (de 德), 20, 33, 37, 48–50, 77, 95–97, 134, 184–185

Wang Bi 王弼, 186–187, 190
Wang Fuzhi 王夫之, 191
Wang Yangming 王阳明, 135–136, 152, 191
Wangzhi 王制, 161, 274
Wave-particular, 113
Weiji 未济, 26
Weijizhixue 为己之学, 151
Weishi 唯识 buddhism, 118
Western Paradigms of Time, 165

Wubutong 无不通, 187
Wubuwei 无不为, 56, 182, 199
Wuji 无极, 68, 73, 116–117, 119, 121, 135, 148, 189, 219
Wuji er taiji 无极而太极, 116
Wusi 无私, 101
Wuwei 无为, 40, 56, 72, 101, 182, 199, 224
Wuwu 无物, 72
Wuyu 无欲, 72

Xiangshu 象数, 190
Xiao 孝, 48
Xiaoren 小人, 47
Xici 系辞, 1, 24–25, 62–63, 65, 68, 75, 77, 95, 112, 114–115, 148, 154, 172, 174, 176–178, 186, 203, 239–241, 255
Xing 性, 26, 51, 92, 174, 185, 191, 224, 228, 230, 268
Xin 心 Neo-Confucianism, 135
Xinxue 心学, 151
Xiongqi 凶器, 103
Xiong Shili 熊十力, 191, 273
Xu 虚, 3, 71, 229
Xuanxue 玄学, 151, 186
Xun 巽, 24
Xunzi 荀子, 40, 43, 51–52, 92, 161–162, 171, 250, 274

Yangshao 仰韶 culture/Dawenkou 大汶口 culture/Liangzhu 良渚 culture/Hongshan 红山 culture/Hemudu 河姆渡 culture, 15
Yigusheng, liangzehua 一故生, 两则化, 135
Yi 易, 5, 16, 141
Yijing 易经, 1, 61
Yijiyiqie, Yiqieyiji 一即一切, 一切即一, 118
Yijing (易经)-Whitehead-Cobb, 130
Yijing (易经)-Whiteheadean Onto-Cosmology of Creativity, 122
Yijing (易经)-Whiteheadean, 122, 134
Yin qishi er ti 因其时而惕, 204
Yin-yang 阴阳 relationship, 23, 113
Yinyang Wuxing 阴阳五行, 40–41
Yizhuan 易传, 3, 4, 61
Yizhuan 易传 theory of reality, 62–63, 69–70
Youhuan 忧患, 154
You wei shi you fu wei shi you shi ye zhe 有未始有夫未始有始也者, 183
Youwu 有物, 72
Youwu xiangsheng 有无相生, 72, 182
Yuanchengshi 圆成实, 118
Yu qishi 于其时, 204
Yu shi juxing 与时俱行, 124

Zhanguo 战国, 31–32, 36
Zhang Zai 张载, 94, 135, 189–190, 222, 229
Zhen 震, 24
Zhengde 正德, 36
Zhenren 真人, 104, 132
Zhenglun 正论, 161
Zhenzhi 真知, 104
Zhi 智, 30, 36–37, 42, 49–51, 58, 97, 100
Zhicheng (至诚 utmost sincerity), 81
Zhou Dunyi 周敦颐, 68, 73, 112, 116–118, 135, 148, 188, 219, 224, 228, 233
Zhong 中, 26
Zhong 忠, 48
Zhou Rites 周礼, 157
Zhouyi 周易, 4, 6, 22
Zhuangzi 庄子, 43, 46, 63, 71, 73, 77, 83, 103–104, 135–136, 148–150, 183, 186, 188, 219, 222, 224, 263

Zhu Xi 朱熹, 116, 135–136, 148, 152, 190–191, 219, 222, 228–229, 259, 265
Zi Dashu 子大叔, 38
Zihua 自化, 224
Ziran 自然, 71, 101, 273
Zonghengjia 纵横家, 40
Zuozhuan 左传, 33, 36, 38, 268

Glossary Index

After explaining the rise of the meaning of litigation (song 讼), the Tuanzhuan 彖传 continues to say: "There is good faith in song; lacking caution but reaching middle is good fortune. For the firm comes in the central positions. In the end there is ill-fortune and litigation cannot be established." 253

Although Wang Bi 王弼 also refers to qi 气 (vital breath, vital force, and energy of all forms) in his annotation on Laozi 老子, he did not elaborate on the unifying and transformative nature of qi 气. 187

An important development of Zhang Zai 张载 also consists in his combining the position of Wang Bi 王弼 and the position of Guo Xiang 郭象 in terms of the unity of the notion of "great void" (taixu 太虚) and the notion of "great harmony" (taihe 太和). 190

Apart from the Xici 系辞, the present Tuan Commentary and other commentaries such as Wenyan 文言, Xiang 象, Shuogua 说卦, Xungua 巽卦, and Zagua 杂卦 can be also regarded as results of similar philosophical reflections. 203

Being similar to heaven and earth, there is no violation of the existing order (gubuwei 故不违) in our thinking. 239

Even in greater detail we may speak of desire-time, emotion-time, will-time within the domain of mental time, or earth-time, sun-time, metal-time, electron-time, quark-time, quantum-time within the domain of physical time, and so forth, 179

Following this basic idea, all the Daoist ideas in Laozi 老子, such as "All things hold the yin 阴 and embrace the yang 阳," and "Do nothing and everything will be done," will naturally fall into place and present an implicit theory of time as the dao 道 and the implicit theory of the dao 道 as the process and substance of time, 182

Given this framework, one can see that the symbolization of the yin-yang 阴阳 positions by the broken line—and the unbroken line—captures the basic modes and qualities of being, namely yin-yang 阴阳, dong-jing 动静, gang-rou 刚柔, and what is experienced along this line. 243

"Heaven generates all things by yang 阳, and accomplishes all things by yin 阴; generation is a virtue of benevolence (ren 仁) and accomplishment is a virtue of righteousness (yi 易)" (Tong Shu 通书 11). 189

Hence the first statement of the Daodejing 道德经 that "The dao that can be spoken is not the constant dao 道" betrays the understanding that underlying all changes there is the timeless, which is time as a whole and time as a creative power that motivates everything or enables everything to be moved by themselves. 182

Hence, the Tuanzhuan 彖传 of the song continues: "It is advantageous to see the great man, it is because it is a matter of holding to centrality and correctness. It is not advantageous to cross over the large rivers, because it would lead one to deep waters." 254

Hence, we can see the level of sixiang (四象, four figures) where there are 2x2 distinctions, the level of bagua (八卦, eight trigrams) where there are 2x2x2 distinctions, and the level of zhonggua 重卦 where there are 2 to the 6th power or 64 distinctions. 243

If one loses this sense of self-duty, one would lapse into a life of what Mencius calls "self-violation" (zibao 自暴) and "self-abandonment" (ziqi 自弃). 195

I have shown that Zhouyi 周易 contains such an "onto-cosmology of time" and "time theory of onto-cosmos (the whole of things with their ontological grounding)," which enables us to interpret onto-cosmos in terms of time, and interpret time in terms of onto-cosmos so that we may reach a dynamical identification between the two in a hermeneu-tical fusion of horizons. 197

It might be pointed out that although we could represent all situations in binary numbers, such as 111111 for qian 乾 and 000000 for kun 坤, it is clear that we would lose the original representational efficacy of the yin-yang 阴阳 symbols. 246

In point of fact, one can see that the idea of harmony is shared by both systems; the best possible world is a world of highly compatible and compossible essences or concepts, which is worth being implemented as actuality and is considered by Leibniz to be actually actualized by a benevolent God, whereas the "Principle of Harmonization" in the Yijing 易经 is the basis for the existence of the world, and it is interpretation as it is considered constitutive of the cosmolog-ical process based on comprehensive observation. As the essence of the transformation of the world, harmony is intrinsically present and urged to be extrinsically brought out by the man who is endowed with the creativity to participate and act. 258

Instead, he can only speak of a calculus of "estimation of degrees of probability," the "weight of proofs," suppositions, conjectures, and criteria. 232

Instead, the reason for their existence is to be seen in how they originate from a source of formation and transformation (shenghua 生化) and how they correlate with other things, which exist as reflection on our comprehensive observation. 238

I think that this paradox in Plato and other Greek philosophers anticipates the formulation of the modern paradox of time: the McTaggart paradox. 262

It is in this lack of awareness in seeing the taiji 太极 as the dao 道 that one may suggest that even in Heidegger there is a residue of Platonism in which the timeless is always separable from the time. 181

It is in light of the well-worked out philosophy of time that the character "yi" (易, transformation) acquires the meanings of change (bianyi 变易), non-change (buyi 不易), and simplicity (jianyi 简易) all at the same time. 181

It is in the Tuan 彖 and Wenyan 文言 Commentaries of the Yijing 易经 that we find many indications of explication of the time-philosophy in the Yijing 易经 and its applications to the individual gua 卦 as a representation of a situation. 204

Mencius has titled Confucius "a sage of time or timeliness," and this no doubt betrays Mencius's own profound understanding of time in the spirit of the Yijing 易经 tradition. 185

Morality in both duty-performance and virtue-comprehension is in line with and also derives from human existence. 185

Nevertheless, one could still take the Yijing 易经 symbolism seriously, for one could impose one's own definite and finite analysis on a situation relative to one's purpose and in this way achieve a finite analytical-hypothetical understanding of a contingent proposition. 247

Not only does the guaci 卦辞 represent a new level of meaning, but later levels also arise through a more systematic interpretation of the symbolism with regard to human action and human prospects in the forms of commentaries, such as, notably, the Tuanzhuan 彖传 and the Xiangzhuan 象传. 249

One can see that for a sagely person like Confucius, divination is not necessary, and the Yijing 易经 becomes a book of wisdom, showing where one's mandate of heaven (tianming 天命) lies. Xunzi 荀子, the latter-day Confucian rationalist, simply maintained that the superior man (junzi 君子) does not practice divination. 250

One may even see Mencius's distinction between "nature" (xing 性) and "destiny" (ming 命) as full of time-significance in this sense. 185

On the contrary, the yi (易)-symbolism is a creation of the sages who understand things via their comprehensive observation and who attempt to formulate the principles of change in the presence of things and changes. It requires a participatory and confrontational understanding of the things at hand so that we can see that things are to be viewed and understood in symbols and relations of symbols, and at the same time, how symbols and relations of symbols could be applied to things. 241

Ontologically, one must see that "nature" comes from activity of heaven—a principle of creativity of time (to be called tiandao 天道 or Qiandao 乾道), whereas "destiny" results from the passivity of earthly life—a principle of receptivity of time (to be called didao 地道 or Kundao 坤道). 185

Perhaps generation of forms from simpler unities (the One and the Indefinite Dyad) is simply a logical derivation presented to a timeless and yet perfect intelligence or mind, while this generation in the sense of logical derivation is even dispensable when viewed from the angle of a timeless perfect intelligence such as God. 261

Perhaps what Guo Xiang 郭象 has in mind is that the qi 气 provides a universal context for the arising of yin 阴 and yang 阳 opposites, which then give rise to diversity of things in terms of mutual generation of opposites (xiangyin 相引 and duisheng 对生) on different levels. 188

Philosophers such as Bergson, James, and Dewey have also embraced the evolutionary position, which traces the evolution from matter and brains to consciousness and intelligent minds. Philosophers such as Samuel Alexander argue from this view, in which god, mind, animal life, and inanimate matter together form an ordered structure. 210

That is why mind is called void (xu 虚), subtle in activity (ling 灵), illuminating (ming 明), and perceptive (jue 觉). 229

The application is not simply a matter of mechanical procedures, but involves complex considerations (weighing) for establishing understanding and appraisal of a situation. 192

The conclusion to be drawn from this observation is that Chinese philosophical schools are formed from the natural spreading of ideas that reflects both the social and cultural trends of the time and the appeal of the ideal and ideas of the "axial thinkers" as founders of the schools. 43

The key to the prime model of Confucian ethics is stated by Confucius in his saying "Do not do to others what you do not wish others do to you" (Analects 15). 192

There are many other guas 卦 that have tuan 彖 referring to the "having time" (youshi 有时), "moving together with time," "not losing time" (bushishi 不失时) or "losing time" (shishi 失时), "following time" (suishi 随时), or "rising and resting together with time" (yushixiaoxi 与时消息). 205

There is qian–yuan (乾元 the Creative Source), which creates or produces things, and kun-yuan (坤元 the Receptive Source), which nourishes and cherishes things. 238

The same difficulty of understanding holds for the Greek sense of self-coincident activity in Aristotle and Plotinus. Apparently one has to understand such activity in time and then conceive of it out of time. 261

"The Ultimateless; the Great Ultimate; Yin 阴 and Yang 阳; Movement and Rest; the Five Processes and Agencies of fire, water, metal, wood and earth; the Female way and the Male way; and the production and transformation of all things in the world." 219

The Xici shang 系辞上 says of this cosmos-forming as the way of interchange of the yin-yang 阴阳, "One yin 阴 and one yang 阳 in alternation is called the dao 道. To follow this is good (shan 善), to accomplish this is nature (xing 性). 174

This is a view that we may label the "onto-cosmological theory of time" or "time theory of onto-cosmology" as represented by the implicit and underlying philosophy of the Yijing 易经. 196

This is exemplified by the twelfth-century Japanese Zen master Dogen when he says, "Dogs and tigers are times." 197

This is the stage of the time-less: the stage of eternal objects and ideas—the stage of Aristotelian God where all things are completed, and creativity becomes fully realized and potentiality fully actualized. 213

This means that time can be considered as having two sides, the substance side of wu 无, which is the formless and infinite origin of things, and the function side of you, which is always a matter of producing diversification of things (inclusive of the so-called "biodiversity of nature"). 187

This trait and this disposition have been clearly notable in Plato, Aristotle, Newton, Kant, and later in Whitehead and Heidegger. 180

Thus the Xici Shang-11 系辞上 says, "Thus the yi 易 has the taiji 太极, which generates the two norms (i.e., yin 阴 and yang 阳), two norms generate the four forms and four forms generate eight gua (卦, trigrams)." 176

To put it in an abstract manner, we may see ren 仁 as giving one's time-potentiality for benefiting others, and as such transcending oneself and therefore one's lifetime in an effort for reaching values of timelessness. 184

Traditionally, this has been called the extension of an image (yanxiang 衍象) whereby its meaning would also be extended. Obviously, such an extension of images and meanings must always involve insight, interpretation, and relevant measures of empirical and logical justifications. 245

Unlike Plato, the Neo-Confucians in general recognize the necessity of embodying the universality of principles in the multitude of individual things. But nevertheless, such Neo-Confucians as Cheng Yi 程颐 and Zhu Xi 朱熹 are confronted with the problem of deciding whether or not principle (li 理) is prior in existence to qi 气. 265

Unlike the duty performed in the Kantian ethics, the Confucian ethics makes the duty performance a growth of the moral person and thus makes moral duty a matter of virtue, perhaps to be called "virtue of duty," to be contrasted with Kant's notion of "duty of virtue." 195

We may call this the "Principle of Sufficient Experience" in contrast to Leibniz's "Principle of Sufficient Reason." It is on the basis of comprehensive observation that we could even generalize on existing things as having sufficient reasons for their existence. 238

We might also mention that the Yijing 易经 philosophy of time and its paradigms of time have even influenced the formation and presentation of Chinese Buddhism in regard to its views on time, change, and transformation of life and world (from the Madhyamika school to the Tiantai 天台 school, and from the Huayan 华严 school to the Chan 禅 school). 181

Wenyan 文言 has used two important phrases to indicate very clearly the time-content and time-motif in the human action: "To move with time (yu shi xiexing 与时偕行," and "To reach the limit with time (yu shi xieji 与时偕极)." These two important principles are clearly applied in the explication of the sixth line (yao 爻) of the kun gua 坤卦. Terms like "arising from time (shifa 时发)" and "moving from time (shixing 时行)" are used to suggest that all kun 坤 actions, like the qian 乾 actions, are fundamentally based on time and considerations of time. 205

What is then ren 仁? Ren 仁 is to discipline oneself for consideration and respect toward others. 184

Whitehead has suggested, through his comprehensive philosophical system, the concept of "actual occasion" for naming concrete events and processes. 208

With similar analysis, we may also show how time-philosophy is essentially relevant for determining human action and conduct in other systems of philosophy such as Daoism, Neo-Daoism, Neo-Confucianism, and even contemporary Chinese philosophy based on the Chinese tradition. 206

Zhang Zai 张载 has applied these two notions to the notion of qi 气 and thus produced a philosophy of reality in terms of the unity of time-being (namely taixu 太虚) and being-time (namely taihe 太和). 190

www.ingramcontent.com/pod-product-compliance
Lightning Source LLC
Chambersburg PA
CBHW031706230426
43668CB00006B/132